"Excellent . . . a distinguished public service."
Peter F. Drucker

"The authenticity of PARACHUTE is what makes it stand out over what could be called the glut of job-hunting books coming out today."
Journal of College Placement

"Everyone agrees that the giant title in the field is Richard N. Bolles's WHAT COLOR IS YOUR PARACHUTE?, which first appeared in 1972 and has been updated annually ever since. [Four] million copies have been sold, and it has been on the *New York Times* best-seller list for four years."
The New York Times

"One of the most useful manuals for job-hunters and career changers. Written with humor and humanity . . ."
Washington Opportunities for Women

"In a domain positively viscous with lame books, this perennial best-seller has no serious competition. It is updated *annually* (that's impressive), it is cheery for a reader who probably could use some cheer, it has sound, detailed advice for an all-important task that is well-served with a bit of skill. (Suggested by everybody.)"
Stewart Brand
The Next Whole Earth Catalog,
Second Edition

"One of the finest contributions to the literature of life/work planning, this book is written in a light tone, which serves to hold the reader's interest while showing that job hunting, self-assessment, and career planning need not be dull, arduous, awesome tasks. Other literature suggests that successful life-style planning requires a large investment of time and effort, but Bolles shows the reader a way to do it that is enticing . . ."
Harvard Business Review

"*What Color Is Your Parachute?* is probably the finest contribution written to date on the joint theme of career planning/job hunting . . . Bolles must have read every other book on the subject—his footnotes are extensive and there is a lengthy bibliography. But the content is such that little further reading will be necessary . . . Bolles' prescription is a lot of work. But the rewards are worth the effort."
The Business Graduate
(Journal of the Business Graduates Association in Great Britain)

This is an annual. That is to say, it is substantially revised each year, the new edition appearing a month and a half before the New Year begins (e.g., the 1992 edition first appears in mid-November 1991). Those wishing to submit additions, corrections, or suggestions for the 1992 edition should submit them prior to March 31, 1991 using the form provided in the back of this book. (Letters reaching us after that date will, unfortunately, have to wait for the 1993 edition.)

What Color Is Your Parachute?

Other Books by Richard N. Bolles

The Three Boxes of Life,
And How To Get Out of Them

Where Do I Go From Here With My Life?
(co-authored with John C. Crystal)

1991 Edition

What Color Is Your Parachute?

A Practical Manual for Job-Hunters & Career Changers

by

Richard Nelson Bolles

Ten Speed Press

The art on the front cover is "The Millpond" by Maxfield Parrish (American: 1870–1966). Oil on masonite. 1945. Size 22½×18″. Private Collection. Photo courtesy of Alma Gilbert Galleries, Burlingame, CA.
Used by special permission.

•

The map drawing on pages 54–55 is by Steven M. Johnson, author of *What The World Needs Now*.

•

Library of Congress Catalog Card No. 84-649334
ISBN 0-89815-385-9, paper
ISBN 0-89815-386-7, cloth
Published by Ten Speed Press, P.O. Box 7123, Berkeley, California 94707

Type set by Wilsted & Taylor, Oakland, California
Consolidated Printers, Inc., Berkeley, California
Printed in the United States of America

This is dedicated to the one I love
(my wife, Carol)

Contents

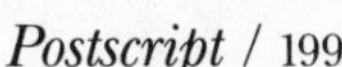

continued

288 *Appendix B:*

Special Problems in The Job-Hunt: Books and Additional Comments by the Author

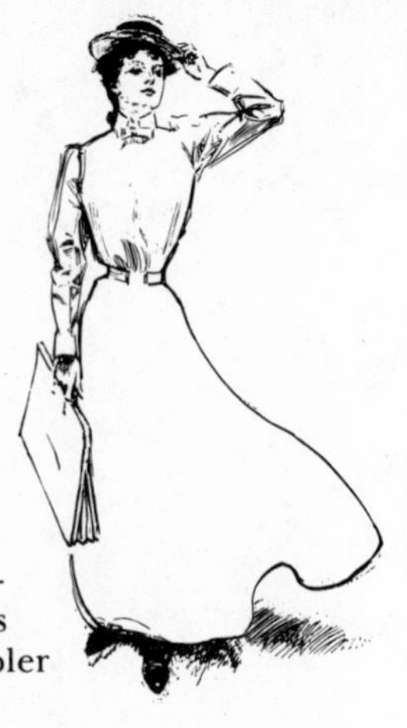

Preface

From the first year that this book was published, 1970, I have tried to stay very accessible to its readers, by including my address in several places throughout the book, each year, when it is revised. The result is, I receive one or two thousand letters a year from my readers. This contact with so many of you means a great deal to me, when you write to express gratitude for what the book has meant in your life, and how you have used it to find more fitting work. Needless to say, I appreciate these letters immensely.

A great number of people express to me each year their desire to hear some of these letters, so that -- in a sense -- reader might reach out to reader. I have generally resisted these appeals, since it seems to me that an author quoting letters from satisfied readers is painfully similar to a 'snake-oil salesman' sharing 'testimonials.' A book, I think, should instead rise or fall on its own intrinsic merits.

However, it would appear that what people want is not so much *proof* that *Parachute* works (that is long since settled) as some *illustrations* of how people have actually used it. So, twice before in the twenty years of *Parachute*'s life, I have *bent* a little, and shared some of these letters. This is now the third time. I have used initials instead of names, to protect the privacy of the writers:

A man from California writes:

"I'm a 31 year old mechanical engineer who had worked for 5 years, then chucked it all to go overseas for 1½ years. By the time I returned and was prepared to return to work, 2 years had gone by. Since I'd been originally recruited out of college, I knew nothing about conducting a full-blown job search, so I decided to read your book from A to Z. And I felt if this was to be the first of several job searches in my life, I'd better build a strong foundation and do it all. Enclosed is a rather blurry photograph of my 'flower diagram' (from Appendix A), entitled, 'Brian's Ideal Job,' which took me about 2 weeks to complete. The words I'd written I could actually visualize and this helped me during every interview. I did want that good job so much that (as you say) the thought of it would bring tears to my eyes.

And I now have it. I'm an application engineer for a small electronics firm in the mountains here. It's a beautiful area and the people are great. Thanks so much for helping me." (B.C.)

A man from New Hampshire writes:

"I'm writing to thank you for all the help and inspiration your writing has provided me. I only wish that Parachute *had been available when I was in college (1961–1965). I've learned more from your writing than my University ever thought of teaching. You taught me not to be afraid of my natural instincts and to cultivate my talents. Your writings helped me to see that what I really wanted to be all my life was an author, and an author I finally am -- with 100,000 copies in print of my first book. I hope someday we can meet."* (R.C.P)

A man from Oklahoma writes:

"Your book helped me develop a healthy attitude. Then it helped me figure out what I really wanted to do. Then it helped me interview honestly. Now I have a job doing exactly what I want to do, exactly where I want to do it for great money. Thanks for everything." (N.N.)

A woman from Pennsylvania writes:

"I am an English/Economics Management Double Major graduating from College here in Pennsylvania. I wanted to thank you for the help Parachute *has given me through all this mess of graduating and finding a job. You made me feel good about myself, and now I am smiling."* (J.L.B.)

A man from Canada writes:

"I have been meaning to write to you for sometime -- but have always postponed the short letter in favour of a long one with all the gory details. You have been spared. Anyway, I want to thank you very much for your work in Parachute. *I took it away with me for a year, and before I started on it, I thought it would solve my problem of being good at a number of diverse things and never having grown up, I thought I would finally nail down what I always wanted to be. Instead, having completed the book, I see a broader picture -- I now feel like a pilot who can lift the right wing skill flap, turn the tail fin skill and soar through all sorts of jobs that I can't yet imagine. Anyway, I settled on one to start with, and decided I wanted to edit a magazine -- so I sent my application in the form of a dummy issue. On my second attempt I got the sort of position I was after. I suppose this letter is a way of shaking your hand. Thank you sir."* (H.B.)

A woman from Atlanta writes:

"The other day I was invited into a prospective landlord's living room to fill out an apartment application. During our conversation he told me

that he was trying to figure out what to do with his life. We talked for a while and I never thought of telling him about Parachute -- *which I used in 1980 to help me with the same dilemma. It turned out that I didn't have to tell him. On my way out of his apartment I spied a blackboard with these words inscribed,* What Color Is Your Pair of Shoes? *You can only imagine my delight; he said a friend had mentioned this phonetic play upon your book's title to him over the phone. By the way, your book helped me find my way into selling IBM and Macintosh software for one of the top ten. I love this job: I get to train folks, do presentations, write promotions, and use my organizational skills."* (J.M.F)

A man from London writes:

"At the risk of boring you, I'd like to tell you a little bit of what's happened in my life. I qualified as a doctor of medicine -- albeit a very ambivalent one -- in 1977. From 1980 to 1983, when I finally fell out of the profession in a state of misery and confusion, I was training as a psychiatrist. The next few years continued the lostness. Many things improved,

largely through the presence of a very loving wife, but the confusion only began to clear when I was introduced to Parachute. *It was two and a half years before I finally got my new career started, but the road forward began then. I moved from Tokyo to London. I used one of the counselors listed in the back of your book, Walt Hopkins, who was an immense help to me. And the result of all this is that I have become the Commercial Manager of a small graphic design consultancy within a highly successful marketing services group, where I have found more of the ideal elements that I had identified from doing Appendix A, than I could have dreamed of -- and where I get to exercise enough of my favorite skills, while learning new ones daily.* Parachute*'s impact on my career is dramatic enough, but it doesn't stop there. The whole way of thinking; the experience of re-examining my life and finding it far better than I had thought; and then the experience of being able to take hold of my life and change it. These things so reshaped my view of things that I now operate very differently in my life. And all of these things began with and built on what I gained from my* Parachute-*based experience of changing careers. I am indebted and grateful to you -- and Walt -- more than I can say."* (G.L.)

A mother from Texas writes:

"I had had Parachute *less than 24 hours before your approach to career planning helped me deal with an immediate question that had nothing to do with job hunting or changing careers. Now, that's what I call a useful book, rather like buying a book on horse training that, sort of by-the-by, tells you a clever way to manage the mess in the tackroom. I'm beginning to see exactly what my skills are, and I see now why I drive my engineer mother up the wall sometimes. Best of all, your book is helping me analyze the skills of our handicapped child from a more useful angle than that of the school therapists, who are far more interested in what he* can't *do. Even though I'm not planning a career change just now, I'm going to go through all the exercises, to see what else I can learn. So thank you very much for writing such a useful, lively, intelligent and thoughtful book. It should help others avoid the years of floundering that I went through."* (E.N.M.)

A man from Louisiana writes:

"I have seen your books in bookstores for years now, but at age 40, having gone through a series of devastating crises (divorce, bankruptcy, and recovery), and trying to reconstruct my life (Phoenix-style), I bought one of them. After reviewing it, and becoming hooked on your spirituality section, I have been working seriously on all the exercises. I appreciate particularly the style and quality of your writing. You are helping me as much as any counseling I have ever gotten. Thank you zillions." (T.C.)

Well, there's a glimpse. I appreciate so much the kindness and care that is evidenced by your taking the time to sit down, and take pen or keyboard in hand, to tell me about your life-changes and the part that my books have played in those changes. I shed many tears as I read these letters, tears of great gratitude to God, and to you. I think no man (or woman) has ever had a more fulfilling life than I.

Though the thanks in the letters are directed to me, there is actually a small army of people involved, in one way or another, with getting the annual revision of this book out, each year. First of all, I have no large research staff to help me with this annual revision (*as some suppose*), but only one staff person, Erica Chambré, who has been my right hand since 1975. She makes my life and my work easier in a million ways; and of course after having worked with me for the better part of sixteen years, she knows my mind in all things. It's lovely to work with a mindreader. Besides which, she is always cheerful and fun to work with. *Mil gracias, Erica.*

For the layout of the book, I want to express for the umpteenth time my great debt of gratitude and affection for Bev Anderson, who has done the layout of this book (*and all my other written works*) year after year, since it first came out commercially -- in November of 1972 (*a Ten Speed/Bev Anderson anniversary, coming up next year*). I love working with her, as we labor over the layout of every page of this book, together; she is a delight.

My thanks to Alma Gilbert of the Alma Gilbert galleries in San Mateo, California, for granting us permission to use the Maxfield Parrish painting that appears (with overlay) on our front cover this year.

And my deep gratitude as always to Phil Wood, my publisher. Ever since we first met in 1972, when he proposed putting out *Parachute* commercially, he has become not only my publisher but my friend. I would give my books to no other. I also appreciate all the help that his associate, George Young, and Jackie Wan give each year in helping this book get done and get done right. "Get done right" doesn't, of course, include the elimination of all typos. These manifestly are introduced into the book by *gremlins*, after the book is sitting on the presses. (*Gremlins are the subject of the first chapter in a projected work of mine, entitled, How to Avoid Taking Responsibility for Your Own Actions.*)

Going beyond the form of the book to its substance, I want to thank all those leaders in this field of career development or job-hunting, who have shared with me their wisdom, their ideas and most of all their friendship over the years: Daniel Porot, Sidney Fine, John Holland, Dick Lathrop, Tom and Ellie Jackson, Arthur Miller, Bob Wegmann, Carol Christen, Howard Figler, Peter Drucker, Bernard Haldane, Nathan Azrin, and *above all*, the late John Crystal, whose *In Memoriam* graced these pages two years ago. Plus, of course, *thousands* of job-hunters and career-changers, who over the years have taken the time and trouble to write and share *their* wisdom and experiences, for which I am ever grateful.

I would also like to acknowledge the Lord God, our Great Creator, as the One who has given me the talents and the inspiration to write this book -- and the will to revise it each year. Indeed, He has given me whatever modest gifts of wisdom and compassion I may possess. My thanks to my dear aunt, Sister Esther Mary, of the Community of the Transfiguration (Episcopal) in Glendale, Ohio, now in her vivacious eighty-eighth year, who has taught me so much about all of this -- from my youth up. And finally, I want to thank -- above all others -- my dear wife, Carol, for all her wit, wisdom, encouragement and love over the years. As my four grown children and all who know her will attest, she is a wonderful woman. I am most blessed to be her husband, and the lucky thing is, I know it.

R.N.B.
P. O. Box 379
Walnut Creek, California 94597
June 1, 1990

A Grammar Footnote

I want to explain why singular antecedents are used throughout this book with the apparently plural pronouns "they" or "them" or "their." Casey Miller and Kate Swift, authors of the classic *The Handbook of Nonsexist Writing* suggested this approach. In their book, and in their correspondence with me, they contended that the pronoun "they" once was treated as both plural and singular in the English language, just as "you" was and is; but with respect to "them" this usage changed at a time in English history when agreement **in number** became more important than agreement **in gender**. Faced today with such common artifices as s/he, or he/she, they argue that it is time now to bring back the earlier usage of "they," because given the sexist consciousness of most writers and readers these days, agreement in gender is now more important than agreement in number. They further argue that this return to an earlier usage has already become quite common out on the street -- witness a sign by the ocean which reads "Anyone using this beach after 5 p.m. does so at their own risk." So, this is what I have done. I offer this explanation because I have gotten my share of letters from grammarians who, when they see "they" used with a singular antecedent, dash off scolding letters to authors -- that say, "If you want to be a writer, start by cleaning up your grammar!"

As for my commas, which invariably offend unemployed English teachers **so much** that they write me to apply for a job as my editor, -- in order to save unnecessary correspondence I guess I'd better also explain these. The commas are all deliberately used according to my own rules -- rather than according to the rules of historic grammar (which I do know; I add this to reassure my old English teachers back at Harvard in 'the fifties'). My own rules are: write conversationally, and put in a comma **wherever I would normally stop for a breath, were I speaking the same line.**

Fairy Godmother,
where were you
when I needed you?

Cinderella

CHAPTER ONE

A Job-Hunting We Will Go

Okay, this is it.
You've been idly thinking about it, off and on,
For some time now, wondering what it would be like,
To be earning your bread in a different place,
Or in a different way; choosing another job--or career--
The old one having run out of gas, as they say.
Anyhow, the moment of truth has arrived.
For one reason or another, you've got to . . . have to . . . must
Go out, and look for a job out there, for the first or twentieth time.
You've heard of course, all the horror stories.
Of people who sent out 800 resumes, and
Nothing!
Of housewives forced to start as secretaries, at the age of 45,
Of former college profs with two degrees
Working as counterpeople at the local deli.
Of union workers striking as they always have,
Except, *this time,* they strike *out*
Permanently.
Ah yes, you've heard. And you wonder, of course,
Just what lies in store for *you.*

Well, maybe it's no big deal, for you.
The problem may all be solved, this time,
Before you even start. Some friend
Or relative has cleared the way; has said
"Hey, what are friends for? You come
And work for me." Oh, sweetest words
That ever fell, upon a human's ear.
Your job-hunt has ended, your career-change accomplished,
Before it has even begun. Praise God,
Praise your friend, and never look back.
This time you are saved by the bell. Or, well,
Maybe that isn't your story.
Maybe you've been in your glory, for years,
Doing some job really well.
But you left, to try out that dream that you had,
And it hasn't been going so well; what the heck!
You know that you're welcome back at the old job,
"Anytime," they said; and--assuming they meant it--

You've got it made in the shade, my man--or woman.
If you can go back without hating yourself
Every morning.

Well, anyway, for the vast majority of us,
That isn't at all how it goes. Not nice and easy, at all.
We have to find a job, we do,
Or maybe it's change our career, we fear.
And no one's making it easy, at all.
We're Don Quixote, with lance in our hand;
Our windmill, the job-hunt. Out there, a great land,
The wind blows, we tremble, we feel a great fright--
There's not an employer, at all, in our sight.

We look, of course, for advice,
From others; but they
All tell us the very same thing:
That when our job-hunting time comes, this is what
We *all do:*
We procrastinate,
That's what we do.
We're busy winding things up, we say.
Or, just waiting until we feel a little less
'Burnt-out,' and more 'up' for the task
Ahead, we say; though actually, if the truth were known,
We're hoping for a little miracle,
You know the one:
That if we just sit tight long enough,
We won't have to go job-hunting at all,
The job will come hunting for us.
(How clever!)
Right in our front door, it will come.
To prove we are destiny's favorite,
Or to show that God loves us so.

But, this doesn't happen, of course, of course,
And eventually, we realize, with more than a touch of panic,
That time and money are beginning

To run out.
It's time to run out and begin our job-hunt
In real deadly earnest, we say. To ourselves.
And immediately all our familiar friends
Are at our elbow, just giving advice--
More advice, solicited or unsolicited, as to what we should do.
"Jean or Joe, I've always thought you would make a great teacher."
So we ask who they know
In the academic world,
And, armed with that name,
It's a-calling, we go. Yes, calling, and
Sitting, and cooling our heels
In the ante-room of the office la Dean,
Until, at the last, we are ushered right in,
"And what can I do for you, Mr. or Ms.?"
We tell them, of course, that we're job-hunting now,
"And one of my friends thought that you..." O wow!
Look at that face change, are we in the soup!
As we wait for the heave-ho, the ol' Alley-oop!
"You feel I'm 'over-qualified'? I see.
Two hundred applications, you say, already in hand
For five vacancies? I see.
No, of course I understand."

We extricate ourselves from there, and determine to try
Again; more advice from our friends: "Jean or Joe,
Have you tried the employment agencies yet?
No? Well they seem a very good bet."
"Good thinking. Which ones do you think I should try?
The ones that deal with professionals? Downtown?
Okay. Good. Down I will go."
And down we do go.
Down, down, down, in and to those agencies.
The ante-room again. And all those hopeful, haunted faces.
A new twist, however: our first bout
With The Dreaded Application Form.
"Previous jobs held.
List in reverse chronological order."
Filling all the questions out. Followed by
That interminable sitting, and waiting. For naught.

The interviewer, at last. Again.
She of the over-cheerful countenance, and mien--
She talks to us. "Let's see, Mr. or Ms.,
What kind of a job are you looking for?"
"Well," we say,
"What do you think I could do?"
She studies, again, the application form;
"It seems to me," she says, "that with your background
--It is a *bit* unusual--
You might do very well in sales."
"Oh sales," say we. "Yes, sales," says she, "in fact
I think I could place you immediately.
We'll be in touch. Is this your phone?
I'll call you tomorrow night, at home."
We nod, and shake her hand, and that is the
Last time
We ever hear from her.
Words, ah, words! Sometimes are not what they say.
Sometimes they are used just to soften rejection.
We have to start, again.

Now, our original ballooning hopes that we would quickly land a job
Are running into some frigid air,

So we decide to confess at last
Our need of help--to some of our truly successful friends
in the business world (if we have such)
Who *surely* will know what we should do,
What Don (or Donna) Quixote should do.
The windmill is tiring us.
Maybe we need a newer career.
"Well," say our friends (beaming, warmly),
"What kind of a job are you looking for?"
Ah, *that,* again! "Well, you know me well,
What kind of a job do you think
I could do? I'll try almost anything,"
We say, now that it's two minutes to midnight, as it were.
"You know, with all the *kinds* of things I've done--"
We say; "I mean, I've done this and that, here and there,
Right or wrong. What it adds up to, sort of puzzles me.
But I was thinking--you're so much wiser than I--
That you would know, what eludes me."
"Have you tried the want-ads?" asks our friend.
"Or have you gone to see Bill, and Ed, and John, and Frances and Marty?
Ah, no? Well tell them I sent you."
And we are prostrate, with thanks; ah, this will do it,
For sure. Our friend has solved it all.
Want-ads, he said. We study them all. Gad,
What misery is hidden in
Those little boxes. Misery in jobs which are built
As little boxes, for the large spirits of men and women.
Well, we dutifully send our resume, such as it is,
To every box that looks as though
It might not be a box.
And wait for the avalanche of replies, from bright-eyed people
Who, seeing our resume will surely know
Our worth; even if, at this point, our worth seems increasingly
Questionable in our own eyes.
Avalanche? Not even a rolling stone. (Sorry, Bob.) Not a pebble.

Oh, well, time to go see those people our friend said we
Ought to go see.
You know: Bill, and Ed, and John, and Frances and Marty.
They seem quite perplexed, as to why we've come out,

And in the dark just exactly about
What they're supposed to do; no, they haven't a clue.
We take them, try to take them off the hook;
We say, "Look, friend of my friend,
Your company might need--of course, my experience *has*
Been limited, but I am willing to learn, and I thought
That you..."

The interview drags on, downhill now, all the way
As our host finishes out the courtesy debt,
Not to us but to the friend that sent us; and
Then it is time for us to go.
Boy, do we go! over hill and valley and dale,
Talking to everyone who will listen,
Listening to everyone who will talk
With us; and thinking that surely there must be
Someone who knows how to crack this terribly
Frustrating job-market.

A job-hunt seems the loneliest task in the world.
And we idly wonder: is it this difficult for other people?

Well, friend, the answer is *YES.*

Are other people *this* discouraged, and desperate
And frustrated, and so low in self-esteem after
A spell of job-hunting?

The answer, again--unhappily--is
YES.

YES.

YES.

Well, yes, you do have great big teeth; but, never mind that. You were great to at least grant me this interview.

Little Red Riding Hood

CHAPTER TWO

Rejection Shock

Chapter 2

From our youth up, we are taught to hate rejection. At least **most** of us are. I know rejection rolls off some people like water off a duck's back. It doesn't bother them at all. Or at least so it appears. And I know that others actually crave rejection and thrive on it, as ancient warriors went out to meet the dragon. Not so with me. Faced with rejection, I usually go into a corner and whimper a lot. Or jump into bed, curl into the fetal position, and turn the electric blanket up to nine. And so apparently it is with the majority of us. We hate rejection. We'll do anything to avoid it, and I mean **anything**.

But then, along comes the job-hunt. Eight times in our lifetime we have to go through this painful process. And, except at its very end, it is **nothing but** a process of rejection, even as I described in the previous chapter. My friend Tom Jackson (in his *Guerrilla Tactics in the Job Market*) has aptly captured this, in his depressingly accurate description of a typical job-hunt as:

NO NO NO NO NO NO NO NO NO NO NO NO NO NO
NO NO NO NO NO NO NO NO NO NO NO NO NO NO
NO NO NO NO NO NO NO NO NO NO NO NO NO NO
NO NO NO NO NO NO NO NO NO NO NO NO YES.

And why does the job-hunting system in this country put us through all this? Because, **the job-hunting system in this country is no system at all**. It is in fact Neanderthal. (Say it again, Sam.)

Year after year, that 'system' condemns each of us to go down the same path, face the same obstacles, make the same mistakes, and face the same rejection.

Moreover, the 'system' is such that often we are given absolutely no warning that we are about to become unemployed. All of a sudden, it is upon us.

And gradually, but only gradually, do we begin to learn what the rules are of this 'system.' And what the rules are, concerning the whole world of work. Slowly and painstakingly we piece them together, and discover finally that there are twelve of them:

1. You will get hired sometimes, for reasons which may have nothing to do with how qualified you are, or aren't. On some unconscious level, you just strike a spark.

2. You will not get hired sometimes, for reasons which may have nothing to do with how qualified you are, or aren't. On some unconscious level, you just don't strike a spark.

3. You will get promoted sometimes, for reasons which may have nothing to do with how well you are doing there.

4. You will not get promoted sometimes, for reasons which may have nothing to do with how well you are doing there.

5. Your employer may treat you well, in accordance with their stated values.

6. Your employer may treat you very badly, in total contradiction of their stated values.

7. Your employer may go on forever, and you may have a job for life, if you want it.

8. Your employer may go out of business, without warning and at a moment's notice, dumping you out on the street.

Reprinted by permission; Tribune Media Services. Not to be reproduced without permission of Tribune Media Services.

9. Your employer may stay in business, but you may be abandoned, terminated, fired, or otherwise put out on the street, without warning, and at a moment's notice.

10. If you are terminated suddenly, your employer may do everything in the world to help you find other employment.

11. If you are terminated suddenly, your employer may feel that they do not owe you anything. You will feel as though you had been unceremoniously deposited on the rubbage heap.

12. Other employees may promise they will fight to save your job, but you need to be prepared for the fact that when the chips are down, they may actually do nothing to help you.

THE REACTION

Our instinctive first reaction to the fact that "this is how things are" is usually anger. Sometimes fierce anger. Sometimes just a kind of cold soul-chilling disillusionment about the workplace and how it treats its people. If we are wise, we learn to let go of that anger and get on with our lives. But many ex-workers, we know, stay locked in to that anger for the remainder of their lives. They can never forgive the world of work for being so different from what they thought it was going to be. Their anger is a burning fire within them, gradually consuming them.

This would not be so, if it were relatively easy to find another job. The anger is perpetuated by the fact that the job-hunting system slowly and systematically strips men and women of their self-esteem, and leaves them feeling devalued and discarded by our society. When it happens to **You**, you go into personal psychological Shock, characterized by a slow or rapid erosion of your self-image, and the conviction that there is something wrong with you. This assumes, consequently, all the proportions of a major crisis in your life, where irritability, withdrawal, broken relationships, divorce, and loneliness may become your constant companions; and even suicide is not unthinkable. All because of the job-hunting system in this country, which is actually a 'non-system.'

This 'non-system' has been given a name by personnel experts. They call this non-system "The Numbers Game." That's right, the numbers game.

THE NUMBERS GAME AND HOW TO USE IT

You can guess where the term came from. It came from the world of gambling, where if you place sufficient bets on enough different numbers, one of them is bound to pay off, for you. Ah, I see you have grasped immediately what this has to do with job-hunting. Resumes, you say? Ah yes, resumes.

If you're going to use them, you have to play them just like a numbers game: send out just as many as you possibly can. Because, according to a study some time back, only one job offer is tendered and accepted in the whole world of work, for every 1,470 resumes that are floating around out there. Sending 1,469 gets you nowhere. The 1,470th gets a job. Hence, "the numbers game."

It's terrible. But you should try to understand it, in all its parts. The reason why you ought to understand it is that you may want to use some parts of it to **supplement** your main job-hunt, as outlined in chapters 4 through 6.

A study of *The Job Hunt* by Harold L. Sheppard and A. Harvey Belitsky[1] revealed that the greater the number of auxiliary avenues used by the job-hunter, the greater the job-finding success. It makes sense, therefore, to know all the avenues that are open to you, how they work and what their limitations are, so that you can choose which avenue or avenues you want to use, and how you want to use them. You will then be in the driver's seat about these matters, as you should be.

The parts of this game most commonly alluded to in books, articles, and elsewhere are:

- mailing out your resume
- answering newspaper ads
- placing newspaper ads
- going to private employment (or placement) agencies
- going to the federal/state employment agency
- contacting executive search firms
- contacting college placement firms
- using executive registers or other forms of clearinghouses
- making personal contacts through friends, personal referrals and so forth.

We will look at the virtues, and defects, of each of these now, in rapid succession; to see why they usually don't work -- and how you might *get around* their limitations. I will quote some statistics as I go along, in order to illustrate the aforementioned defects. So, on with our exciting story.

---

1. In their book, *The Job Hunt: Job-Seeking Behavior of Unemployed Workers in a Local Economy.*

ANSWERING NEWSPAPER ADS

Experts will advise you, for the sake of thoroughness, to study the job advertisements in your newspaper **daily** and to study all of them, from A to Z -- because ads are alphabetized by job title -- and there are some very strange and unpredictable job titles floating around. Then you are advised that if you see an ad for which you might qualify, even three-quarters, send off:

a) your resume, OR
b) your resume and a covering letter, OR
c) just a covering letter

NEWSPAPER ADS

Where found:
1. In the business section of the Sunday *New York Times* and the education section; also in Sunday editions of the *Chicago Tribune* and the *Los Angeles Times.*
2. In the business section (often found in the sports section) of your daily paper; also daily *Wall Street Journal* (especially Tuesday's and Wednesday's editions).
3. In the classified section of your daily paper (and Sunday's, too).

Jobs advertised: Usually those which have a clear-cut title, well-defined specifications, and for which either many job-hunters can qualify, or very few.

Number of resumes received by employer as a result of the ad: 20 to 1,000, commonly.

Time it takes resumes to come in: 48 to 96 hours. Third day is usually the peak day, after ad is placed.

Number of resumes **not** screened out: Only 2 to 5 out of every 100 (normally) survive. In other words, 95 to 98 out of every 100 answers *are* screened out.

Things to beware of in newspaper ads

FAKE ADS (*positions advertised which don't exist*) -- usually run by placement firms or others, in order to fatten their "resume bank" for future clout with employers. Often with just a box number, so they'll *sound* like an employer.

BLIND ADS (*no company name, just a box number*). These, according to most insiders, are *particularly* unrewarding to the job-hunter's time. But many job-hunters are skilled at answering them with just the information asked for, and they do get a job as a result. *However*, if by chance you are presently working, there is always the danger that this ad was placed by *your* company unbeknownst to you. If that is the case, you can get fired on the spot -- just for answering it. *It has happened, believe me.*

PHONE NUMBERS in ads: most experts say, "don't use them except to set up an appointment." Period. (*"I can't talk right now. I'm calling from the office."*) They counsel that you should beware of saying more, lest you get screened out prematurely over the telephone. *Other experts, however*, think it is useful to use the phone number *if* you can talk to the actual person you would be working for (*not* the personnel department).

THOSE PHRASES which need lots of translating, like:
"Energetic self-starter wanted" (= You'll be working on commission)
"Good organizational skills" (= You'll be handling the filing)
"Make an investment in your future" (= This is a franchise or pyramid scheme)
"Much client contact" (= You handle the phone, or make 'cold calls' on clients)
"Planning and coordinating" (= You book the boss's travel arrangements)
"Opportunity of a lifetime" (= Nowhere else will you find such a low salary and so much work)
"Management training position" (= You'll be a salesperson with a wide territory)
"Varied, interesting travel" (= You'll be a salesperson with a wide territory)

In short, what they're telling you is that you're playing the Numbers Game, when you answer ads. And the odds are stacked against you just about as badly as when you send out your resume scatter-gun fashion. How badly? (Better sit down.) A study conducted in two sample cities revealed, and I quote, that "85% of the employers in San Francisco, and 75% in Salt Lake City, did not hire any employees through want ads" in a typical year. Yes, that said *any* employees, *during the whole year.*[1] Well, then why are ads run? That explanation is rather long, and beyond the scope of this book. But if you're dying to know the answer, I refer you to the chapter called "Blind Ad Man's Bluff" in David Noer's book, *How to Beat the Employment Game.*[2]

Of course, you may be one who still likes to cover all bets, and if so, you will want to know how your resume can be the one that gets through the Screening Process. (Let's be realistic: in spite of the overwhelming odds, answering ads does pay off for *some* job-hunters.)

Most of the experts say, *if* you're going to play this game:

Pointers for Answering by Letter

• Keep your answer *brief*. All you're trying to do, in answering the ad, is to be invited in for an interview. Period. Whether you get hired or not is *the task of that interview*, not the task of this answer to their ad. Just quote *all* of the ad's specifications, and *only* the ad's specifications; then list what experience or qualifications you have *that exactly match* ***each*** *of those specifications*, and *leave it at that.* List them as a series of points, with perhaps "bullets," as they are called (•), in front of each point (as here). If there's some specification you don't meet, *we'll call it X*, you may wish at least to say, "interested in *X*" (*if it's true*) as one of your points. Once you're done with this, you're done. Send it in. If there is anything else you want to tell them, save it for the interview, *if you get invited in.*

• In your written answer, omit all else. Volunteer nothing else. Period. (So there is no further excuse for *screening you out.*)

• If the ad requested that you state your salary requirements, some

---

1. Olympus Research Corporation, *A Study to Test the Feasibility of Determining Whether Classified Ads in Daily Newspapers Are an Accurate Reflection of Local Labor Markets and of Significance to Employers and Job Seekers.* 1973. From: Olympus Research Corporation, 1670 East 1300 South, Salt Lake City, UT 84105.
2. Ten Speed Press, Box 7123, Berkeley, CA 94707. Or at your local library.

experts say *ignore the request*; others say, *state a salary range* (of as much as three to ten thousand dollars variation) adding the words "*depending on the nature and scope of duties and responsibilities*," or words to that effect. The overall iron-clad rule is: if the ad *doesn't* mention salary requirements, don't you either. Why give another excuse for getting your response *screened out*?

• Your final sentence in your letter ought to be something positive about the next step. Not "I *hope* to hear from you," but "I look forward to hearing from you." You should be sure to include your phone number, in case that's the way the employer prefers to contact you.

• You must *make certain* the spelling in the letter (and resume) is *absolutely errorless*. Show it to at least two of your family, friends or workmates whom you know to be *excellent spellers*. Don't skip over this step! Spelling errors will normally cause your letter and resume to be put at the bottom of the pile of prospects (if they're *desperate*) or immediately dismissed, if they're not. If a spelling error *is* found, rewrite the entire letter (using *white-out* is a no-no).

• Consider sending your answer by Federal Express; until *everyone* is doing this (and they're not *yet*), your response will stand out in the mind of the employer, *believe me*.

• Some experts counsel other strategies -- *such as*, putting "Personal and Confidential" on your envelope; *and/or* mailing your letters so as to *arrive* in mid-week (that's Tuesday, Wednesday or Thursday); *and/or* following up with a phone call seven days later -- at either the beginning of the employer's workday, or near the end of it. Trouble is: some employers are *irritated* by these strategies. *On the other hand, some aren't.* You decide.

• Some job-hunters read their local newspaper every day, and make note of ads which *they would like to respond to*, but they don't have all the credentials, qualifications or experience that the ad calls for. They may send their resume and a covering letter in, anyway. Then they watch to see if that ad stops running, *then starts running again* some days or weeks later. That's usually a sign that the employer couldn't find a person with the qualifications he or she was looking for. Now you have a chance to bargain. Here's how one job-hunter reported her success with this strategy: "*The particular ad I answered the first time it ran required at least an associate degree, which I did not have. What I did have was almost ten years' experience in that particular field. When the ad reappeared a month later I sent a letter saying they obviously had not found what they were looking for in the way of a degree, so why not give me a chance; they already had my resume. Well, it worked. I got the interview, I made them an offer that was $6,000 less than they were going to pay a degreed person, but still a $6,000 increase for me, over my prior position. I got the job. Needless to say, everyone was happy. I have recommended this same procedure to three of my friends, and it worked for two out of three of them also.*"

Pointers If You're Answering By Phone

Experts say that generally speaking you should not use the phone to respond to ads. But if you do, use the call merely to inquire for more information about the job (without talking about yourself or your own qualifications). When the employer starts to ask about *you*, it is appropriate to respond simply with, "Can I send you my resume?" If the employer ignores this, or says, "*Yes, but. . . .*" and proceeds to *grill* you over the phone about your qualifications, you can be pretty sure the purpose of the phone number in the ad was indeed to allow them *to screen you out.* In such a case, politely resist the probing, thank them for their time, and gently hang up. Then send your resume in (it can't hurt), without ever mentioning that you were the one who talked to them on the phone. *On the other hand, if the employer says yes, send your resume,* and doesn't try to probe further, be sure and thank them for their time, and then ask to be turned over to their secretary, so that from the latter you can get *the exact spelling* of this employer's name, title, and address. Then send a covering letter plus resume. In the covering letter you can say something like, "Thank you for our phone conversation, and thank you for encouraging me to send you my resume." In the remainder of the covering letter, then, highlight the parts of the interview you want them to recall.

PLACING ADS YOURSELF

Sometimes job-hunters try to make their availability known, by placing ads themselves in newspapers or journals.

PLACING ADS

Name of ads (commonly): *"Positions Wanted"* (by the job-hunter, that is).

Found in: *Wall Street Journal,* professional journals, and in trade association publications.

Effectiveness: Very effective in getting responses from employment agencies, peddlers, salespeople, and vultures who prey on job-hunters. Practically worthless in getting responses from prospective employers, who rarely read these ads. But it *has* worked for some.

Recommendation: If you take odds seriously, you'd better forget it. Unless, just to cover all bets, you want to place some ads in professional journals appropriate to your field. Study other people's formats first, though.

Cost: Varies.

ASKING PRIVATE EMPLOYMENT AGENCIES FOR HELP

The two places that every job-hunter knows instinctively to turn to when looking for a job is want ads and employment agencies. We just dealt with the first of these. Now let us look at the second. Employment agencies seem very attractive when one is "up against it." We all like to think that somewhere out there is someone who

PRIVATE EMPLOYMENT AGENCIES

Number: There are at least 8,000 private employment or placement agencies in the U.S. Maybe a lot more. Nobody knows, since new ones are born, and old ones die, every week.

Specialization: Many specialize in executives, financial, data processing, or other specialties.

Fees: Employer or job-hunter may pay. Be sure to ask which is the case. Fees vary from state to state. Tax deductible. In New York, for example, a fee cannot exceed 60% of one month's salary, i.e., a $15,000-a-year job will cost you $750. The fee may be paid in weekly installments of 10% (e.g., $75 on a $750 total). In 80% of executives' cases, it is the employer who pays the fee.

Contract: The application form filled out by the job-hunter at the agency **is** the contract.

Exclusive handling: Don't give it, even if they ask for it. If you find a job independently of them, you may still have to pay *them* a fee.

Nature of business: Primarily a volume business, requiring rapid turnover of clientele, with genuine attention given only to the most-marketable job-hunters, in what one insider has called "a short-term matching game."

knows just exactly where all jobs are to be found. Unhappily **no one** in this country knows where all the jobs are. The best that anyone can offer to us is some clues about where it is that **some** jobs are to be found. Those places which know where some jobs are to be found are called private employment agencies. The Yellow Pages of your phone book will give you their names.

PRIVATE EMPLOYMENT AGENCIES continued

Effectiveness: Some time back, a spokesman for the Federal Trade Commission announced that the average placement rate for employment agencies was only 5% of those who walked in the door. That means a 95% failure rate, right?

Loyalty: Agency's loyalty in the very nature of things must lie with those who pay the bills (which in most cases is the employer), and those who represent repeat business (again, employers).

Evaluation: An agency, with its dependency on rapid-turnover volume business, usually has no time to deal with **any** problems (like, career-changers). Possible exception for you to investigate: a new, or suddenly expanding agency, which needs job-hunters badly if it is ever to get employers' business.

ASKING THE FEDERAL-STATE EMPLOYMENT SERVICE FOR HELP

UNITED STATES EMPLOYMENT SERVICE

Number: This is the Federal/State employment system; indeed, many job-hunters suppose that the local office in their town or city is merely the State employment system (for their particular state). But it is actually part of a nationwide network.

About one-third of the 2,000 USES offices in the country call themselves "Job Service." In other states, they use other names: Employment Development Department, the State Unemployment Office, and so on. USES has seen its staff and budget, nationwide, greatly reduced over the past twenty years.

Services: Most state offices of USES not only serve entry level workers, but also have services for professionals. About one-tenth of these offices offer job-search workshops, from time to time -- depending on the demand, and whether or not a counselor is available who knows how to teach it.

Middle management and professionals still tend to avoid USES. One attempt to change this is the Job Service Resume System, a cooperative effort by six Midwest States (Illinois, Indiana, Michigan, Minnesota, Ohio, and Wisconsin) which currently have about 11,000 resumes in their system, mostly on computer, updated every three months (ideally). It is open only to "professionals" in those States (*"professionals" are defined as such people as managers, supervisors, accountants, writers, physicians, clergy, and even actors and actresses*) and they are encouraged to register, either in person at their local Job Service Office in those states, or by writing that office for an application.

UNITED STATES EMPLOYMENT SERVICE continued

Caution: over the past 20 years, most computerized operations, governmental or private, which have tried to link up job-hunter with would-be employer have been infinitely more successful at helping the employer, than at helping the job-hunter. In computerized 'job-matching' systems, typically less than one resume in a hundred has actually received a job-offer; and this Job Service Resume System is no exception to this rule. Don't for heaven's sake put all your eggs in this basket. But it is a relatively new system, and the folks who run it are trying hard to increase its effectiveness rate, so if you are a professional of one kind or another it's certainly worth trying as an auxiliary to your main job-hunting strategy.

Nationwide network: In any city, your local USES or Job Service office will have access to the Interstate Job Bank listings. This will tell you about job opportunities in other states or cities. The normal number of listings runs around 6,000 at any one time; 98% of the USES offices have these listings on microfiche, and 20% of the offices *also* have a computer hookup. The listings are typically two weeks old before you see them, but many of them are for 'constant hires,' so that doesn't matter.

Openings: The most recent study revealed that about 7 million non-agricultural job vacancies were listed with USES during the year. *Some* states maintain a list of those jobs which are most in demand. Ask if yours does. In California, for example, at this writing, jobs on their *Demand List* included: Assembler; Attendant/companion; Auto mechanic; Baker; Carpenter; Cashier; Clerk, general office; Cook; Electronics assembler; Electronics technician;

UNITED STATES EMPLOYMENT SERVICE

Heating/air-conditioning mechanic; Housekeeper; Janitor; Kitchen helper; Landscape laborer; Machinist; Nurse aide; Receptionist; Roofer; Salesclerk; Secretary; Security guard; Teller; Truck driver; Waiter/waitress.

Placements: One study revealed that approximately 30% of those who search the job listings at USES find a job thereby. Another survey, however, revealed that 57% of **those** were not working at that job just 30 days later. This reduces the *net* placement rate to 17%. Another study found USES placed only 13.7% of those who sought a job there, hence failed to find a job for 86.3% of those who went there to find a job. **The point of all this?** *If* you go there, *be realistic* about your chances of finding a job thereby. Your chances are 13 out of a 100. *Don't* put all your eggs in this basket.

ASKING HEADHUNTERS, OTHERWISE KNOWN AS RECRUITERS OR EXECUTIVE SEARCH FIRMS FOR HELP

If you play the numbers game, and especially if you pay someone to guide you through it, you will be told to send your resume to Executive Search firms. And what, pray tell, are they? Well, they are recruiting firms that are retained by employers. The very existence of this thriving industry testifies to the fact that employers are as baffled by our country's Neanderthal job-hunting 'system' as we are. **Employers don't know how to find decent employees, any more than job-hunters know how to find decent employers.** So, what do employers want executive recruiting firms to do? They want these firms to *hire away from other firms or employers*, executives, salespeople, technicians, or whatever, who are already employed, and rising. (In the old days, these firms searched only for executives, hence their now-outdated title.)

EXECUTIVE RECRUITERS

Name: Executive search firms, executive recruiters, executive recruitment consultants, executive development specialists, management consultants, recruiters.

Nicknames: Headhunters, body snatchers, flesh peddlers, talent scouts.

Number: More than 2000 firms, with over 12,000 employees.

Volume of business: They have combined billings of more than two and a half billion dollars a year.

Number of vacancies handled by a firm: As a rule, each staff member can only handle 6 to 8 searches at a time; so, multiply number of staff that a firm has (if known) times 6. Majority of firms have 1 to 2 staff (hence, are handling 6 to 12 current openings); a few have 4 to 5 staff (24 to 30 openings are being searched for); and the largest have staffs handling 80 to 100 openings.

You will realize these head-hunting firms are aware of, and trying to fill, known vacancies. That's why, in any decent scatter-gun sending out of your resume, you are advised -- by any number of experts -- to be sure and include Recruiters. Not surprisingly, there is more than one place that will sell you lists of such firms, for example:

1. *Directory of Executive Recruiters*, published by Consultant News, Templeton Rd., Fitzwilliam, NH 03447. Published yearly. Lists several hundred firms and the industries served.

2. *Directory of Personnel Consultants by Specialization (Industry Grouping)*. Published by the National Association of Personnel Consultants, Round House Square, 3133 Mt. Vernon Ave., Alexandria, VA 22305, 703-684-0180.

The question is: do you **want** these lists, i.e., are they going to do you any good?

Well, let's say you decide to send recruiters your resume (unsolicited -- they didn't ask you to send it, you just sent it uninvited). The average Executive Search firm will get as many as 1,000 such unsolicited resumes, or "broadcast letters," a week. Your chances of surviving? Well, *if* you currently make $75,000 or more per year, and *if* your resume and cover letter look *thoroughly* professional and well thought out, and *if* you send your resume to one of the larger executive search firms in this country, experts say you have a one in ten chance that they will contact you. On the other hand, the *first* to be eliminated will be those who a) are not presently on the level being looked for, or b) are not presently employed -- even if they *are* on that level, or c) are not presently rising in their firm. That's why many experts say to the unemployed, in general: *Forget it!*

I do think it is necessary, however, to point out that things are changing in the Recruiting field. For one thing, onetime employment agencies now prefer to call themselves Recruiters or Executive Search firms. (Employment agencies typically have to operate under more stringent state or federal regulations, hence the appeal of a different, less supervised, genre such as Executive Search.) Whatever they call themselves, these new Recruiters now represent employers; but they are hungry for the names of job-hunters, and in many cases will interview a job-hunter who comes into the office unannounced or mails them a resume. I have known so-called Recruiters in some of the smaller firms who truly extended themselves on behalf of very inexperienced job-hunters. So, were I job-hunting this year, I think I would get one of the aforementioned Directories, look up the firms that specialize in my particular kind of job or field, and go take a crack at them. As long as you don't put all your eggs or hopes in this one basket, you really have nothing to lose -- except some stationery and stamps.

ASKING COLLEGE PLACEMENT CENTERS FOR HELP

COLLEGE PLACEMENT OFFICES

Where located: Most of the 3,280 institutions of higher education in this country have some kind of placement function, however informal.

Helpfulness: Some are very good, because they understand that job-hunting will be a repetitive activity throughout the lives of their students; hence they try to teach an empowering process of self-directed job-hunting. Other offices, however, still think they have done their job if they have helped "each student find a job upon graduation," through the use of recruiters, bulletin board listings, and the like; i.e., if they help their students with this one job-hunt *this one time.*

Directory: A directory listing many of these offices is published, and is available for perusal in most Placement Offices. It is called the *Directory of Career Planning and Placement Offices*, and is published by the College Placement Council, Inc., 62 Highland Ave., Bethlehem, PA 18017, 215-868-1421.

If you are not only a college graduate but also a hopeless romantic, you will have a vision of blissful cooperation existing between all of these placement offices across the country. So that if you are a graduate of an East Coast college, let us say, and subsequently you move to California, and want help with career planning, you should in theory be able to walk into the placement office on any California campus, and be helped by that office (a non-altruistic service based on the likelihood that a graduate of that

"CATHY" by Cathy Guisewite

California campus is, at the same moment, walking into the placement office of your East Coast college; and thus, to coin a phrase, "one hand is washing another"). Some places do do this.

But, alas and alack, dear graduate, in *most* cases it doesn't work like that. You will be told, sometimes with genuine regret, that by official policy, this particular placement office on this particular campus is only allowed to aid its own students and alumni. And sometimes not even its own alumni. One Slight Ray of Hope: on a number of campuses, there are career counselors who think this policy is absolutely asinine, so if you walk into the Career Planning office on that campus, **are lucky enough to get one of Those Counselors**, and you don't mention whether or not you went to that college -- the counselor will never ask, and will proceed to help you just as though you were a real person.

This restriction (to their own students and graduates) is less likely to be found at Community Colleges than it is at four-year institutions. So if you run into a dead end, do try a Community College near you.

ASKING REGISTERS OR CLEARINGHOUSES TO HELP YOU

These are attempts to set up "job exchanges" or a kind of bulletin board where employer and job-hunter can meet. The private clearinghouses commonly handle both employer and job-hunter listings, charging each.

REGISTERS OR CLEARING-HOUSE OPERATIONS

Types: Federal and private; general and specialized fields; listing either future projected openings, or present ones; listing employers' vacancies, or job-hunters' resumes (in brief), or both.

Cost to job-hunter: Ranges from free to $75 or more.

Effectiveness: A register may have as many as 13,000 clients registered with it (if it is a private operation), and let us say 500 openings at one time, from employer clients. You must figure out what the odds are for you as job-hunter. Some registers will let employers know of every client who is eligible; others will pick out the few best ones. A newer register may do more for you than an older one.

The idea of registers or clearinghouses is a very popular idea, and new entrants in the field are appearing constantly. On the following cards, we list some examples:

REGISTERS ETC.
continued

General Clearinghouse Listing Present Vacancies: The State Employment Offices in 48 states, covering more than 300 separate labor market areas, have set up a computerized (in most cities) job bank to provide daily listings of job openings in that city. If every employer cooperated and listed every opening they had, each day, it would be a great concept. Unhappily, employers prefer to fill many jobs above $11,000 in more personal, informal ways. So the Job Bank remains a rather limited resource for such jobs. Can be a helpful research instrument, however. A summary of the job orders placed by employers at Job Banks during the previous month used to be published

REGISTERS ETC.
continued

under the title of "Occupations in Demand at Job Service Offices." It is no longer available.

A Clearinghouse of Newspaper Ads: The idea of someone reading on your behalf the classified sections of a lot of newspapers in this country, and publishing a summary thereof on a weekly basis (or so), is not a new idea -- but it is apparently growing increasingly popular. Problem: how old the ads may be by the time you the subscriber read them. You'll recall from page 14 that most classified ads receive more than enough responses within 96 hours of the ad's first appearing; how likely an employer is to wait for you to send in your response many days, or even weeks, later, is something you must evaluate for yourself -- and weigh that against the cost of the service. If you

REGISTERS ETC. continued

want it, there are several places offering this service. Among the most reliable: the *Wall Street Journal* publishes a weekly compilation of "career-advancement positions" from its four regional editions. Available on some newsstands, or order from: National Business Employment Weekly, 420 Lexington Ave., New York, NY 10170, 212-808-6792.

Register for Teachers: *The NESC Jobs Newsletters* are published by the National Education Service Center, 221A E. Main St., Riverton, WY 82501, 307-856-0170. Between April and August, this weekly series of newsletters lists about 58,000 job openings annually. Each week's edition contains only new listings, none repeated. The newsletters are published year 'round, with fewer listings in the months August to April. You select one or more of fourteen different job categories, and receive listings of jobs in those categories only.

Register for Government Jobs: *Federal Career Opportunities*, published biweekly by Federal Research Service, Inc., 370 Maple Ave. W., Box 1059, Vienna, VA 22180, 703-281-0200. Each issue is 64 pages, and lists 3,200+ currently available federal jobs, in both the U.S. and overseas.

Register for Nonprofit Organizations: ACCESS, Networking in the Public Interest, 50 Beacon St., 4th Floor, Boston, MA 02108, 617-720-5627. ACCESS is the first national clearinghouse of job opportunities for the country's 1.2 million nonprofit organizations. Jobs range from entry level to Executive Director positions. This information is

REGISTERS ETC.
continued

disseminated through the publication *Opportunities in Nonprofit Organizations (ONPO)* to hundreds of colleges/universities, libraries and other referral centers in over 40 states. This information is updated monthly with over 200 new jobs and internships. The jobs are divided by organizational focus (environment, education, etc.) and it is best to look through the listing yourself. Please call your school or local library and ask for this job-register by name. If they do not yet have this information, ACCESS will perform a Public Service Job Search for you, for a nominal processing fee, based on a resume and cover letter describing your job interests, desired geographical locations, and salary.

Registers in The Church: Intercristo is a national Christian organization that lists over 30,000 jobs, covering hundreds of vocational categories within over 1,000 Christian organizations in the U.S. or overseas. Their service is called Christian Placement Network. In 1987, 13,000 people used the Christian Placement Network; one out of every twenty-five job-hunters who used this service found a job thereby. (That, of course, means twenty-four out of twenty-five didn't.) Their address is 19303 Fremont Ave. N., Seattle, WA 98133, and their toll-free phone number is 800-426-1342. Jeff Trautman, Executive Director.

Register for The Blind: Job Opportunities for the Blind, 1800 Johnson St., Baltimore, MD 21230, 301-659-9314, or 1-800-638-7518. Exists to inform blind applicants about positions that are open with public and private employers throughout the country. Maintains a computerized listing. Also, they have cassette instructions on everything for the blind job-seeker. Operated by the National Federation of the Blind in partnership with the U.S. Department of Labor.

OTHER REGISTERS OR CLEARINGHOUSES

Is a thing a register or not? If job listings exist all by themselves, they tend to be legitimately called "registers." If they exist within the framework of a journal or magazine which also contains other material, they tend to be called "ads." There is a list of such journals: see Feingold, S. Norman, and Hansard-Winkler, Glenda Ann, *Where the Jobs Are: A Comprehensive Directory of 1200 Journals Listing Career Opportunities*. Garrett Park Press, Garrett Park, MD 20896. 1989. As you can tell by the title, this book lists more than 1200 journals, which all together describe (allegedly) over one million available jobs each year. The following list is only a sampling of some of these journals:

REGISTERS ETC.
continued

For Internships and Jobs with Nonprofit Organizations: *Community Jobs*, published by the Community Careers Resource Center, 1516 P St. NW, Washington, DC 20005, 202-667-0661.

For Jobs Overseas: *International Employment Hotline*. Monthly issues profile international employment opportunities. International Employment Hotline, Box 6170, McLean, VA 22106.

For Jobs in Criminal Justice: The *NELS Monthly Bulletin*, National Employment Listing Service, Criminal Justice Center, Sam Houston State Univ., Huntsville, TX 77341, 409-294-1692. A nonprofit service providing information on current job opportunities in the criminal justice and social services fields.

REGISTERS ETC.
continued

For Jobs Outdoors: Environmental Opportunities, Box 670, Walpole, NH 03608, publishes a monthly listing of environmental jobs, internships, and positions-wanted notices under the same name. Each issue contains twenty-four to forty full-time positions in a variety of disciplines. The Association for Experiential Education, CU Box 249, Boulder, CO 80309, 303-492-1547, publishes a nationwide jobs clearinghouse list.

One final word about registers: the very term "register" can be misleading. The vision: one central place where you can go, and find listed every vacancy in a particular field of endeavor. **But, sorry, Virginia; there ain't no such animal.** All you'll find by going to any of these places is A Selected List of some of the vacancies. A smorgasbord, if you will.

So far as finding **jobs for people** is concerned, these clearinghouses and agencies, like employment agencies, really end up finding **people for jobs**. (Think about it!) Heart of gold though they may have, these agencies serve employers better than they serve the job-hunter.

And yet there are always ways of using such registers to gain valuable information for the job-hunter and to suggest places where you may wish to start researching your ideal job (more in chapter 5). So at the least, you *may* want to consult the 'job bank' at your local Federal/State Job Service unemployment office, if they have one, and perhaps a relatively inexpensive Register (if there is one in your particular field), as *auxiliaries* to the main thrust of your job-search.

OTHER IDEAS THAT MAY HELP YOU

OTHER IDEAS

Your resume in a book: Some organizations circulate small booklets to employers, containing mini-resumes of a number of job-hunters. Forty-Plus Clubs do this, through their *Executive Manpower Directory*. So do some of the State Job Service/Employment Development Departments (California, for example, has such a system, called PRO-MATCH, with 23 offices, which does this for experienced professionals). So do some of the executive registry places. Evaluation of its worth to you as job-hunter: well, it's a gamble, just like everything else in this Numbers Game system. A real gamble, if you are trying to start a new career. You're in that booklet with a *lot* of other people. You have to boil your resume down to a very few words, and then decide *if you stand out*. If not, forget it. If yes, well . . . *take a shot at it*. But don't put all your eggs in this one basket, *puh-leeze*!

Offbeat methods: Mailing strange boxes to company presidents, with strange messages (or your resume) inside; using sandwich board signs and parading up and down in front of a company; sit-ins at a president's office, when you are simply determined to work for that company, association, or whatever. You name it, and if it's kooky, it's been tried. Sometimes it has paid off. Kookiness is generally ill-advised, however. The $64,000 question every employer must weigh: if you're like this *before* you're hired, what will they have to live with *afterward*?

To summarize the effectiveness of all the preceding methods in a table (you do like tables, don't you?), we may look at the results of a survey the Bureau of the Census made. The survey, made in 1972 and published in the *Occupational Outlook Quarterly* in the winter of 1976, was of 10 million job-seekers. The conclusions reached in this study are still totally consistent with the experience of today's job-hunters:

USE AND EFFECTIVENESS OF JOB-SEARCH METHODS

Percent of Total Job-seekers Using the Method	Method	Effectiveness Rate*
66.0%	Applied directly to employer	47.7%
50.8	Asked friends about jobs where they work	22.1
41.8	Asked friends about jobs elsewhere	11.9
28.4	Asked relatives about jobs where they work	19.3
27.3	Asked relatives about jobs elsewhere	7.4
45.9	Answered local newspaper ads	23.9
11.7	Answered nonlocal newspaper ads	10.0
21.0	Private employment agency	24.2
33.5	State employment service	13.7
12.5	School placement service	21.4
15.3	Civil Service test	12.5
10.4	Asked teacher or professor	12.1
1.6	Placed ad in local newspaper	12.9
.5	Placed ad in nonlocal newspaper	**
4.9	Answered ads in professional/trade journals	7.3
6.0	Union hiring hall	22.2
5.6	Contacted local organization	12.7
.6	Placed ads in professional or trade journals	**
1.4	Went to place where employers come to pick up people	8.2
11.8	Other	39.7

*A percentage obtained by dividing the number of job-seekers who actually found work using the method, by the total number of job-seekers who tried to use that method, whether successfully or not.

**Base less than 75,000.

More recently, the outplacement firm of Drake Beam Morin Inc. surveyed its candidates for the period 1981–1987, and reported the following very similar findings:

68% found their job through personal contacts
15% through a search firm's activities
9% by answering classified ads
8% by doing a mass mailing of their resumes and/or letter

So, Mr. or Ms. Job-Hunter, that just about covers the favorite job-hunting system of this country at its best, *except for personal contacts, which we give special treatment in chapter 5:*

The Numbers Game.

If it works for you, right off, great! But if it doesn't, you may be interested in the other plan -- you know, the one they had saved up for you, in case all of this didn't work? Small problem: with most of the personnel experts in our country, there is no other plan.

And that is that.

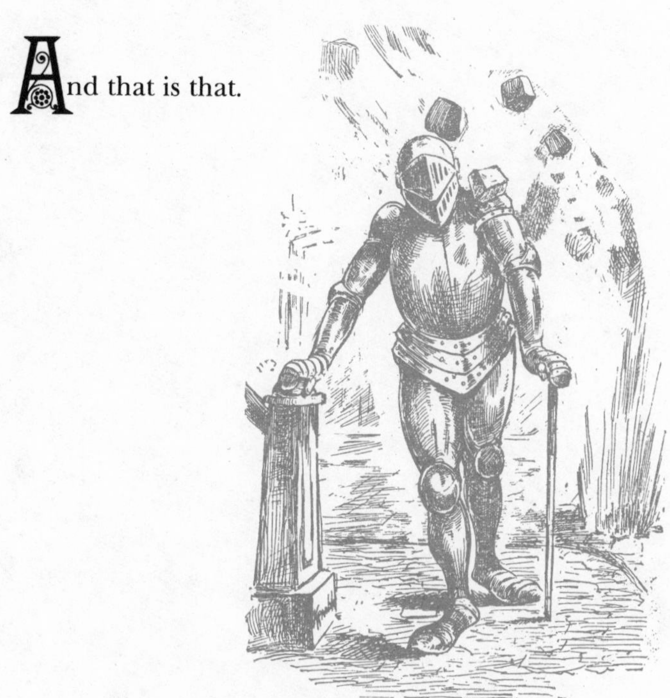

PRAY, as though everything
depended on God;
then work, as though everything
depended on You.

CHAPTER THREE

You Can Do It!

Chapter 3

Reprinted with special permission of King Features Syndicate, Inc.

The upshot of the previous chapters is: we all start out in life thinking that if we are ever tragically thrown out of work, or quit, someone out there will come to our rescue, steer us in the right direction, and hook us up with a proper job. Voila! Our troubles will be short-lived. We are, of course, unclear about **who** that someone will be: a union, or the government, or private agencies, or newspapers -- but we believe it will be **someone**. Alas, when our time comes, and we are completely out of work, instead of someone coming to save us, there is only the sound of silence.

Many unemployed people have sat at home, waiting for God to prove that He loves them, by causing a job to just walk in the door. It does happen. But not often enough for you to ever count on it. The previous chapter surely drove home to you these common sense facts:

No one else on earth cares as much about what happens to you as you do. Therefore **it is You who must take over the management of your own job-hunt or career-change, if it is to be successful**. No one else is going to be willing to lavish so much time on it, as you will. No one else will be so persistent, as you will. No one else has so exact a picture of what kind of job you are looking for, as you do.

If your job-hunt were a movie script, and we were casting the lead, we would have to choose You, as the best qualified for the part. By a long shot.

So let us assume you are currently looking for work. You may not be. Lots of people use this book and do the exercises in Appendix A simply in order to raise their self-esteem. They write and tell me so. "Don't let your readers think these exercises are only useful if you're job-hunting or changing careers! I found a whole new sense of well-being from doing the exercises, even though I'm in a job I love."

But, let's assume you're reading this book because you *are* currently looking for work. If you are, this may be due to either of two forces in your life: external or internal.

The **external forces** you are already familiar with, I'm sure: mergers, takeovers, "downsizing," restructuring, places going out of business, age discrimination, racial discrimination, sex discrimination, and heaven knows what else. Between 1983 and 1988, for example, 10 million workers lost their jobs through such causes. When it happens to you, the grand overall picture, however, doesn't mean much: all you know is that *you* are summarily dismissed, fired, canned, terminated, 'made redundant,' or whatever other euphemism our society can come up with. Any way you slice it, you are out of a job -- and in many cases, totally without warning. It may be that you gave that organization the best years of your life, and you are of course livid, angry, and depressed.

On the other hand, perhaps you are now looking for work due to **internal forces**. No one has taken your job away; you could probably still have it for the next twenty years. But the pressure to leave that job is inside of you. The internal time clock has struck midnight. You're ready to chuck this job. You're tired of it, bored, fed up, and hungry for something new, exciting, and challenging. Or, if your work has given you that in spades, you're stressed, burnt out, exhausted, and hungry for something peaceful, calm, and secure. You're ready -- in a word -- to change careers.

Either way, whether due to external or internal forces, you're looking for work. The time is now. And you want some guidance and help. Now, what can we tell you to do?

Well, we don't know what to tell you until you say how much time you're willing to put to it, and how systematic you want to be. **Many job-hunters do not want a system.** They do not want to

forge through all the chapters of this book. They do not want to spend hour after hour on self-searching exercises. They do not want to put blood, sweat, and tears into their job-hunt. Rather they want essentially to throw themselves on the river of job-hunting, and see where it carries them.

They want, well, just a few hints. And maybe a little Hope, thrown in. That's all. They figure if someone will tell them just a few things they should be aware of, or a few things they could do differently, that should be enough to get them through.

I have to say that **if it's a full-fledged career-change you're thinking about, a few hints won't be enough. You will need all of the systematic process discussed in Chapters 4, 5, and 6.** But if you're just going out looking for the kind of work you've always done, and you're not in the mood to put in a lot of time and effort on your job-hunt, maybe one of the following thirty-five hints will give you a brainstorm, and be just enough to make your job-hunt work. You never know.

Okay, here they are:

THIRTY-FIVE HINTS FOR TODAY'S JOB-HUNTER

(Can be read in the time it takes to eat a burger at a fast-food outlet.)

1

You must be ready to go job-hunting *anytime*, for no matter how good a job you have been doing at your present workplace, that job may vanish -- Poof! -- tomorrow without any warning whatsoever, due to circumstances entirely beyond your control.

2

If you have been unjustly let go, your first great need is to let go of your righteous anger at how different the world of work is from what you thought it would be; otherwise, that anger will cripple your job-hunting efforts. You will reek of it to every employer you go see, even as a drunk reeks of strong drink.

3

No one owes you a job; you have to fight to win a job.

4

By and large, the major difference between successful and unsuccessful job-hunters is **the way that they go about their job-hunt** -- and **not** some factor "out there," such as a tight labor market.

5

If you want your job-hunt to succeed, make a list of what you would do if you had to make your job-hunt fail. Yes, I said fail. Put the factor that would most surely make your job-hunt fail, at the top of your list, then the next one, and so forth. (One man's surest factor was "Sit at home.") In a second column, state the opposite of each factor (for example, "Get out of the house every single day") and you will then have a list of what you must do in your job-hunt, **and** the order in which you must do it, in order to make it succeed.

6

Do not expect that you will necessarily be able to find exactly the same kind of work that you used to be doing. Be prepared to define some other lines of work that you can do, and would enjoy doing, using your same skills and experiences. Always have a Plan B.

Take the job-label (e.g., "I am a steelworker") off yourself. You are a person who . . . .

The more time you spend on figuring out what makes you stand out from nineteen other people who can do what you do, the better your chances.

9

Forget "what's available out there." Go after the job you really want the most.

10

If a thing turns you on, you'll be good at it; if it doesn't, you won't. *(This hint courtesy of David Maister.)*

11

Figure out whether you're best with People, or with Things, or with Information. It makes a difference.

12

In trying to change careers or go into a new field (for you), don't look for the **rules** or generalizations. Look for the **exceptions** to the rules. The rule is: "In order to do this work you have to have a master's degree and ten years' experience at it." You search for the exception: "Yes, but do you know of anyone in the field who hasn't got all those credentials? And where might I find him or her?"

13

Go after organizations with twenty or less employees. That's where two-thirds of all new jobs are. You will want to see the boss, not "the personnel department." (Only 15% of all organizations, mostly large organizations, even have personnel departments anyway.)

14

Two-thirds of all job-hunters spend five hours or less a week, on their job-hunt; determine to spend six times that much. I said "six times."

15

Job-hunters visit an average of six employers a month; determine to see at least two a day.

16

The greater the number of job-hunting avenues you use, the greater the likelihood that you will find a job. That's what studies of job-hunting have revealed. As we saw in the previous chapter, page 36, there are at least nineteen different job-hunting avenues out there. The average job-hunter uses less than two of these nineteen methods. The greater the number **you** use, the greater the likelihood of your finding a job.

17

Expect that your job-hunt is going to be quite long, before you conclude it successfully. *Experienced outplacement people claim your job-hunt will probably take one month for every $10,000 of salary that you are seeking. But like most oft-repeated formulas, this one doesn't hold up well under examination: sometimes the job-hunt is shorter than that, and sometimes longer*. The job-hunt in the U.S. typically lasts somewhere between eight and twenty-three weeks, depending on the state of the economy, how old you are, and how high you are aiming. In any event, don't count on the "eight weeks" minimum. Be mentally prepared for the twenty-three. (Male college graduates, for example, average nineteen weeks to find new jobs.) Currently, one unemployed person in three abandons their job-search before finding a job. *(These figures courtesy of Bob Wegmann.)*

18

Look as sharp as you can **at all times** while you are out of work. Be neat, clean, well-dressed whenever you are outside your home; you never know who will see you -- and possibly recommend you to someone who is hiring.

19

Go after many different organizations in the field that interests you, instead of just one or two.

20

Go face-to-face with employers, whenever possible, rather than sending paper, such as a resume.

21

The major issue you face with employers is not what skills you have, but **how** you use them: whether you just try to "keep busy" or try to actually solve problems, thus increasing your effectiveness and the organization's effectiveness, too.

22

Whatever you produce, be sure it is something you are proud of. A University of Michigan study found that one out of four American workers felt so ashamed of the quality of the products they were producing, that they would not buy them themselves.

23

The manner in which you do your job-hunt and the manner in which you would do the job you are seeking -- are **not** assumed by most employers to be two unrelated subjects, but one and the same. A slipshod, half-hearted job-hunt is taken as a warning that you might do a slipshod, half-hearted job, were they foolish enough to ever hire you.

TRAVELS WITH FARLEY by Phil Frank © 1982 Field Enterprises, Inc. Courtesy of Field Newspaper Syndicate

24

There are not merely two things which will get you a job -- Training or Experience -- but three: Training, Experience, **or** a Demonstration of your Skills right before the employer's eyes. If there is any way that you can show an employer what you are capable of doing -- through pictures, samples of things you have made or produced, or whatever -- do it, during the interview.

25

If you and the employer really hit it off, but they cannot at that time afford to hire you, you might consider offering to do volunteer work there for a week or two, so they see firsthand how good you are at what you do. Or if you feel you're worth, say, $25,000 a year, but they can only pay $15,000 you might consider offering them three days a week of your time (15/25 = 3/5 of your week), and you can go look for other work to fill the remaining two days. *(This hint courtesy of Daniel Porot.)*

26

Don't be wearied by rejection. We saw Tom Jackson's model (from *Guerrilla Tactics in the Job Market*) of the typical job-hunt as NO NO NO NO NO NO etc. But remember, you only need two YESES. Two, so that you'll have at least two things to choose between. And the more NOs you get out of the way, the closer you are to those YESES.

27

If you are handicapped, don't feel that you're different from other job-hunters. Every job-hunter is handicapped. The only question is: What is the handicap, and how much does it show? If you are a job-hunter, and you think you're *not* handicapped, think again. There are probably 13,000 truly different skills that human beings possess. The average job-hunter can only do 700 of those. Believe me, you're handicapped. Sit down and put Mozart on your stereo or CD player, when you're searching for some humility.

28

Treat every employer with courtesy, even if it seems certain they can offer you no job there; they may be able to refer you to someone else next week, *if* you made a good impression.

29

Don't assume **anything**. ("But I just assumed that . . . .")

30

Send short handwritten thank-you notes that very night, to everyone you talked to that day in your job-hunting activities -- secretaries, receptionists, etc. -- thanking them for seeing or helping you.

31

Be gently persistent, and be willing to go back to places that interested you, at least a couple of times, to see if their "no vacancy" situation has changed.

32

Once you know what kind of work you are looking for, tell **everyone** what it is; have as many other eyes and ears out there looking on your behalf, as possible. If you happen to own a telephone answering machine, you might even consider putting it on that machine, in your opening message.

33

When calling on an employer, ask for twenty minutes only, and don't stay one minute longer unless the employer *begs* you to. Tell them you like to honor commitments. This will almost always make a big impression.

34

Whenever you are speaking to an employer, don't "hold forth" all by yourself for longer than two minutes, at any one time. During the entire interview, talk one-half the time, listen one-half the time.

35

Organizations only hire winners; go to that organization and to the interview as "a resource person," not as "a job-beggar." *(This hint courtesy of Daniel Porot.)*

WHEN HINTS AREN'T ENOUGH

Now, these hints may be **all** that you need. One or two of them may strike just the right chord in you, give you just the idea that you need, in order to go out and do a smashing job on your job-hunt. But, what if you still can't find a job? Well, then **you need a**

more systematic way of getting at your job-hunt. As I said earlier, this is *particularly* true if you're thinking of changing careers.

Why might you be thinking of changing careers? Well, because that's an inevitable part of the job-market in this country. According to a survey published in the *Occupational Outlook Quarterly,* Summer 1989, and in the *Monthly Labor Review,* September 1989, between 8.9% and 12% of the total labor force change careers each year. In the most recent year surveyed, 1986, 9.9% of the total labor force or about 10 million people changed careers. 5.3 million did it *voluntarily* -- for better pay or better working conditions. 1.3 million did it *involuntarily*, because of what was happening in the labor market -- i.e., their plant closed, or their position was abolished, etc. The other 3.4 million who changed careers did it *semi-involuntarily* because of changed personal circumstances, such as moving, going from part-time to full-time work, or vice versa, etc.

Well, ten million people changing careers in a year, is a lot of people. That's why this book is called 'A Practical Manual for Job-Hunters *and Career-Changers*.'

But ever since this book was first published twenty years ago, we have held a peculiar point of view about career change. We do not believe that you *necessarily* have to go back to college and get re-trained, in order to change careers. **We do believe you have to sit down and do the most thoroughgoing homework on yourself, as well as thorough interviewing of people already doing what you are contemplating changing to.** Chapters 4, 5 and 6, plus the very crucial Appendix A, tell you *exactly* how to do this, step by step.

Fortunately, this homework on yourself can be done in one good solid weekend. The interviewing can be done in the weeks that follow. You *have* got those weeks at your disposal. Remember, a job-hunt in this country typically averages a little over three months.

And do remember, this is a repetitive activity throughout the rest of your life. Jobs in this country last an average of 5.2 years. In actual fact, a particular job that you have may last longer than 5.2 years -- especially as you grow older. Nonetheless, surveys reveal that the number of times you will have to go job-hunting during your lifetime will likely be around eight. The time you expend on mastering your job-hunt *now* will stand you in good stead the next time you go job-hunting. Do it well *this time* and you make life easier for yourself next time.

If *now* is the time that you face the job-hunt or career-change, these are the choices you have to make:

1 *Should I make a career change?*
OR
Should I stay in the same field/career?

2 *If I choose to stay in the same field/career:*
Should I move to a different organization, though staying in the same type of job?
OR
Should I stay in the same organization where I am now?

3 *If the same organization:*
Should I stay in the very same job as I am now in?
OR
Should I move to a different department or a different job there?

4 *If I make a career change:*
Should I change careers by going back to school and retraining?
OR
Should I change careers without going back to school?

5 *If I change careers without further schooling:*
Should I look for a new career in which I work for someone else?
OR
Should I look for a new career in which I work for myself?

6 *If I look for a new career in which I work for someone else:*
Should I seek a job at decent or even high pay?
OR
Should I seek for a volunteer job at first, or even an internship?

THE MANY PATHS
THROUGH JOB-LAND
SAME CAREER
BUT IN A NEW
PLACE
STAYING AT
YOUR PRESENT
ORGANIZATION
CONTINUING
IN YOUR
PRESENT
CAREER
STARTING
A NEW
CAREER
JOB-LAND
HUNTING FOR A
JOB WHILE STILL
EMPLOYED
HUNTING FOR
A JOB WHILE
UNEMPLOYED

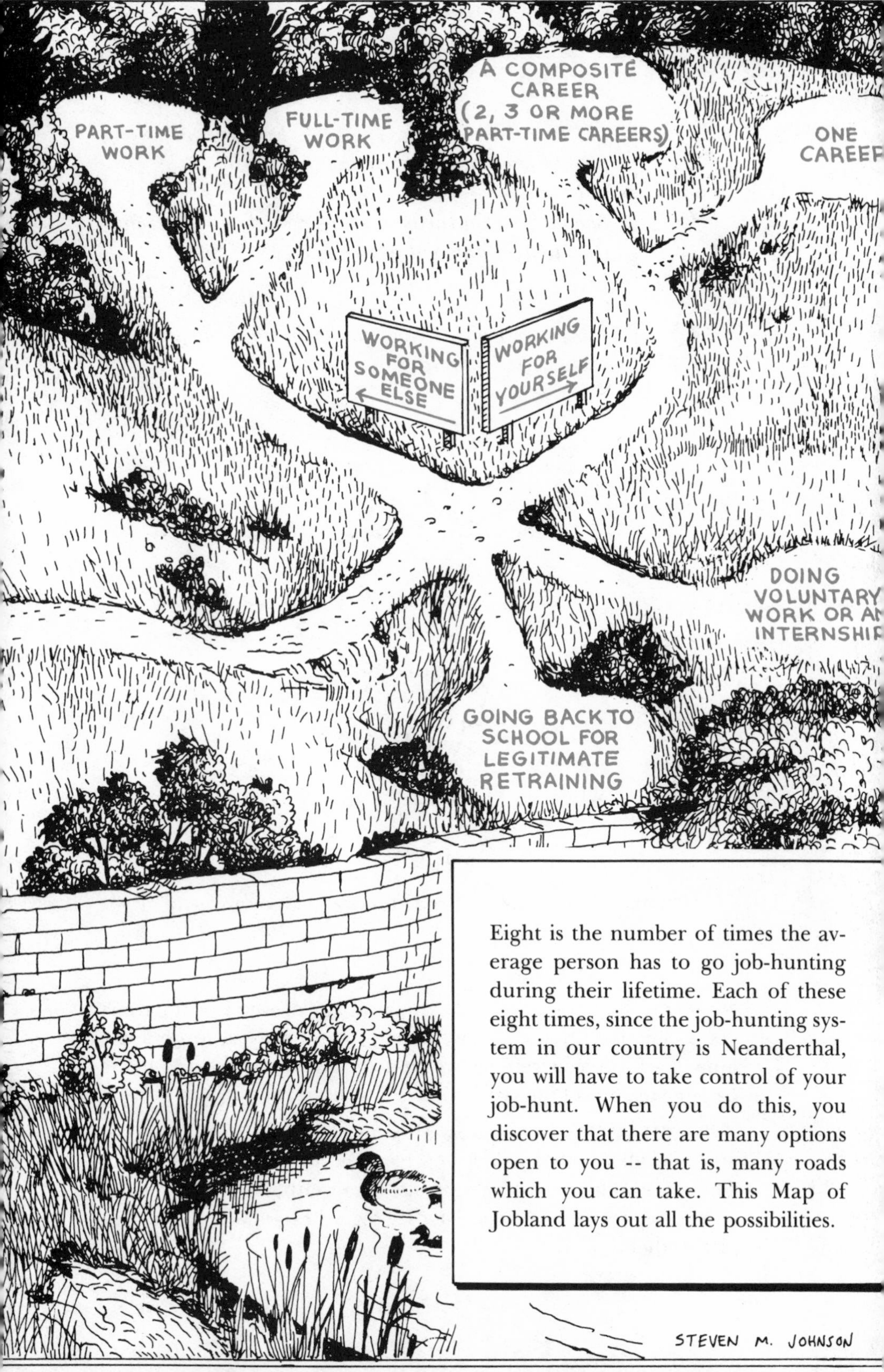

Eight is the number of times the average person has to go job-hunting during their lifetime. Each of these eight times, since the job-hunting system in our country is Neanderthal, you will have to take control of your job-hunt. When you do this, you discover that there are many options open to you -- that is, many roads which you can take. This Map of Jobland lays out all the possibilities.

7 *If I look for a new career in which I work for myself: Should I seek a career made up of just one job?*
OR
Should I seek a composite career, made up of several (two to five) different jobs/careers?

8 *And, once I have answered all the above questions,* **what *is it I should do?***

"Same career, change of career, same career... change of..."

No matter how you answer these questions (or even if you haven't got a clue as to how to answer them), **you have got to do some homework on yourself before you go out there pounding the pavements**. This homework always has three parts to it:

1. **WHAT.** This has to do with your skills. You need to inventory and identify what skills you have that you most enjoy using. These are called transferable skills, because they are transferable to any field/career that you choose, regardless of where you first picked them up.

2. **WHERE.** This has to do with job environments. Think of yourself as a flower. You know that a flower which blooms in the desert will not do well at 10,000 feet up -- and vice versa. Every flower has an environment where it does best. So with you. You are like a flower. You need to decide where you want to use your skills, where you would thrive, and do your most effective work.

3. **HOW.** You need to decide how to get where you want to go. This has to do with finding out the names of the jobs you would be most interested in, **and** the names of organizations (in your preferred geographical area) which have such jobs to offer, **and** the names of the people or person there who actually has the power to hire you. **And**, how you can best approach that person to show him or her how your skills can help them with their problems. How, if you were hired there, you would not be part of the problem, but part of the solution.

Now, to be sure, these three basic questions will be approached by you in a slightly different way, depending on your goals and choices, above. If you ultimately become sure that you want to go into business for yourself, then the HOW will consist in identifying all the people who have already done something like the thing you are thinking of doing, so that you can go interview them and profit from their learnings and mistakes before you set out on your own. And the HOW may consist in identifying the potential customers or clients who would use your services or buy your product.

Or again, if you plan on staying at the same job and in the same organization where you presently are, you may find that the HOW section applies to how you move (get promoted, etc.) **within your organization**, rather than out in the job-market. And even if you plan to stay in the same job exactly, the WHAT and the WHERE questions will help you to function much better there because you will know more surely what your skills or strengths are, and where you can best use them.

(As one satisfied worker recently wrote me, "The skills inventory you have people do in Appendix A of your book is something I do every two or three years. Each time I do it, I find out more specific things about what I do well. This information tells me what to watch for in the world -- what kind of tasks I can volunteer for and do very well at. I know more about the **kind** of thing I want to be, do, be surrounded by. I am now sensitized and ready to recognize them when they swim by.")

The Process of Career Change

Plan A

1. Start only with the options you are already aware of.

2. Reject any which do not please you.

3. Do interviewing or research in the library and reject any others which do not please you.

4. Settle on one of those which are left; if none of these pleases you very much,

5. Settle on the one that you dislike the least.

Plan A
above, is the normal process of career change in our culture, as practiced by job-hunters left to their own devices, or by some counselors -- who are overly-dependent on computer programs.

Plan B
The next page, is The Prescription of The Creative Minority.

Plan B

1. Start with the few options that you are already aware of.

2. Expand your options by taking inventory of your basic building blocks of transferable skills and special knowledges.

3. Use these building blocks to increase your awareness of the many other jobs or careers that you might do and truly enjoy.

4. Then narrow this down to a definite picture of what it is that you would like to do (in your flower), by prioritizing each building block.

5. Now talk to people and use printed resources to expand your ideas of all the different job-titles and all the different places that would fit your picture above.

6. Then start talking to people and using printed resources in order to eliminate those jobs which do not interest you, or fit in with your skills.

7. Of those which remain, identify the one you love most, the next most, etc.

Find the places which have such jobs, and go after them, in that order.

Narrow down your choices to two.

THE RULE: TAKE NO SHORTCUTS

You *will* need to systematically deal with all three questions of WHAT, WHERE, and HOW. You will not want to skip over any of the three.

If you only do the homework on the WHAT, you will be like a cart without any horse to pull it. It just stands helplessly beside the road.

"WHAT" furnishes you with the cart; "WHERE" furnishes the horse to pull it; and "HOW" furnishes the road along which your cart and horse travel, to your chosen destination.

HANDICAPS AND YOUR JOB-HUNT

Most of us think that when we go job-hunting, we have some special handicap, that requires special handling. We need a book written just for job-hunters who have our handicap. Or so we think. Here is a list of some of these handicaps -- an expansion of a list originally put together by Daniel Porot.

If you check off one or more items on this list, you are a handicapped job-hunter (though that **doesn't** mean you need a special book for job-hunters with your handicap):

POSSIBLE JOB-HUNTING HANDICAPS

- ☐ I am Hispanic
- ☐ I am Black
- ☐ I am Vietnamese
- ☐ I have a physical handicap
- ☐ I have a mental handicap
- ☐ I never graduated from high school
- ☐ I never graduated from college
- ☐ I am just graduating
- ☐ I just graduated a year ago
- ☐ I graduated too long ago
- ☐ I am a self-made man
- ☐ I am a self-made woman
- ☐ I am too handsome
- ☐ I am too beautiful
- ☐ I am too ugly
- ☐ I am too thin
- ☐ I am too fat
- ☐ I am too young
- ☐ I am too old
- ☐ I am too new to the job-market
- ☐ I am too near retirement
- ☐ I have a prison record
- ☐ I have a psychiatric history
- ☐ I am disabled
- ☐ I have never held a job before
- ☐ I have held too many jobs before
- ☐ I have only had one employer
- ☐ I am a foreigner
- ☐ I have not had enough education
- ☐ I have had too much education
- ☐ I am too much of a generalist
- ☐ I am too much of a specialist
- ☐ I am a clergyperson
- ☐ I am just coming out of the military
- ☐ I've only worked for volunteer organizations
- ☐ I have only worked for large employers
- ☐ I have only worked for small employers
- ☐ I am too shy
- ☐ I am too assertive
- ☐ I come from a very different kind of background
- ☐ I come from another industry
- ☐ I come from another planet

The true meaning of the above comprehensive list is that there are about three weeks in your entire life when you are employable. That is, if your handicaps could not be overcome. But of course they can be overcome. I will say this at greater length in Chapter 6, but for now let me emphasize this lifesaving truth: **there are two kinds of employers (or clients or customers) out there:**

- those who *will* be put off by your handicap, and therefore *won't* hire you;
  AND
- those who will *not* be put off by your handicap, and therefore *will* hire you, if you are qualified for the job.

You are *not* interested in the former kind of employer, client, or customer, no matter how many of them there are. You are only looking for those employers who are *not* put off by your handicap, and therefore will hire you if you can do the job.

The most important thing for you to know is that **your best chance of bridging whatever handicap you have or think you have is careful preparation on your part**.

As Daniel Porot says, the employers, clients, customers who will not care about your handicap will be most impressed if you approach them, not as a job-beggar, but as a resource person. The secret of coming to them as A Resource Person is that you tackle Chapters 4, 5, and 6 systematically and methodically.

In this sense, these three questions -- WHAT, WHERE, and HOW -- when thoughtfully and diligently answered through your own persistent homework, give you a bridge over any handicap you may have.

BEWARE OF THE DESIRE FOR MAGIC

How do you go about answering the WHAT, WHERE, and HOW most effectively?

You want, of course, to hear that we are about to reveal a bunch of techniques which will inexorably guarantee you a job, if only you follow them faithfully. This desire for magic, the thirst to see unicorns, and to restore pretty maidens once sawed in half, lives on in us all. But alas! No such luck.

Any successful job-hunter or career-changer will tell you there is rarely magic. And that's because it takes three things to find a job:

a. **Techniques and Effort.** There are things others can teach you, and they **will** increase your effectiveness and improve your chances. You need to take these very seriously and really keep at them (that's the Effort). But, by themselves, these are not enough. Hence the need for Art, and Luck.

b. **Art.** As in the phrase: "There's a real art to the way she does that." We refer here to the special stamp that each person's individuality puts on what they do. A certain amount of the job-hunt others cannot teach you. You bring your own unique art to the job-hunt, as you do to everything else you do. It's that extra pizzazz, enthusiasm, and energy that is uniquely yours, which must be present, before you can be successful at the job-hunt. We cannot clone you. Genuine individuality always marks every successful job hunt.

c. **Luck.** Following certain techniques faithfully, and combining them with your own individual art in the way you do it, will not in and of themselves get you the job. There is always a certain amount of luck involved in any successful job-hunt. You have to be the right person in the right place at the right time. If you are the right person in the wrong place at the wrong time, you won't find that job -- no matter how much technique, effort, and art you have put into it.

These factors have varying importance, depending on which part of the job-hunt you are dealing with.

Your own individual way of doing things, your "art," is most important during the WHAT. This is because skill identification is more of an art, than a science. We can give you the basic rules, but a lot of it you have to do in your own individual way.

Techniques become most important during the WHERE and the HOW: those parts of the job-hunt can more easily be defined.

And Luck becomes most important during the HOW part of your job-hunt.

What Can a Systematic Approach Give You? Obviously, it cannot give you good luck, or give you individuality. You must already possess that individuality, and you must have Lady Luck smile on you at least a little, for your job-hunt to succeed. But, by using the Systematic Approach in the next three chapters, the **amount** of luck you will need is greatly reduced. "Luck favors the prepared mind," as someone has observed. This Systematic Approach, if followed faithfully by you, **will** give you a thoroughly prepared mind.

The remainder of this book is therefore devoted to describing those techniques in detail, along with instructions on how you are to go about them. Chapter 4 is devoted to WHAT. Chapter 5 to WHERE. Chapter 6 to HOW. Appendix A has a workbook which every reader of this book ought to work through, as it brings together the WHAT, WHERE and HOW.

RESOURCES FOR YOU TO DRAW ON

As you go through the following chapters, you will naturally want to know *what* or *who* there is to help you, as you go through your job-hunt or career-change. Here are the types of resources you can draw on:

I *Yourself*. Doing homework, by tackling the exercises in Appendix A, and reading and rereading Chapters 4, 5, and 6, is to be preferred above all other resources, for any number of reasons. First of all, knowledge which you gain for yourself is more ingrained than knowledge that is simply handed to you by others. Secondly, the job-hunt process rightly understood is itself a preparation for, and training in, skills you will need to exercise once you get the job; to deprive yourself of the opportunity to get valuable practice in these skills during the job-hunting process, is to make it just that much more difficult for yourself on the job. Thirdly, even if you pay money (and a whole lot of it) to one kind of professional agency or another, there is no guarantee that they will do the process any better than, or even as well as, you would do it yourself.

> MORAL
>
> Every investment of your money is a gamble unless you have first tried to do it on your own, know what you did find out, what you did not find out, and therefore what kind of help you now need from others.

II *Books and other visual or audio materials.* If there's a particular place where you get bogged down, a particular technique that confuses you, a particular obstacle you want help in getting around, then check out Appendix B -- where such things are listed, by subject. I would urge you, however, to read all the way through chapters 4, 5, and 6 **first**, to get an overview. I get letters from readers which say, "I've only read part of your book so far, but I want to know what you have to say about . . ." And, of course, they refer to a subject that is covered in the chapters they haven't yet read. (Usually a second, embarrassed letter follows: "Please disregard my first letter . . . . .") So, do look before you leap, do read before you write. And if, after you read this book, there's something that's perplexing you, do check out the different subjects, books, and comments of mine that are to be found in Appendix B. That's why they're there.

III *Free professional help.* When people get bogged down in their job-hunt, they often rush off to pay some career counselor to help them. Well, that's okay; counselors need to make a living too, and they are often **very** helpful. But sometimes, if you'll just stop to analyze exactly what you need at that particular moment, you might discover there is professional help for you that is available **at no cost**. Examples of where such free help is to be found:

- the reference librarian, at your local library or college library;
- career counseling offices at your nearby community college;

- job-clinics at your local chamber of commerce, federal/state employment agency, advertising council, and the like;
- local federally funded "job clubs," for specific populations, such as WIN recipients, etc. Your local federal/state employment office often knows their locations and times of meeting; funding comes, in most cases, from the Job Training Partnership Act of the Federal Government;
- self-directed job-support groups that meet in local churches or synagogues, in many communities.

There is a section in Appendix C at the back of this book that lists **a few of these,** only, and tells you how to find others. In some cases, the help listed there isn't totally free. But the charges are so small, that for all intents and purposes one may classify them as free.

The likelihood that such help is available in your community increases if you are from certain disadvantaged groups, such as low income, or welfare recipients, or youth, or displaced workers, or those laid off permanently. Ask around.

IV *Professional help for a fee.* Now here, a lot depends on what kind of help you need or want. Is it aptitude/skills testing? The granddaddy of all such firms (I myself went to them, back in 1946) is Johnson O'Connor Research Foundation, Inc., which began true aptitude testing in 1922, and currently is located in the following cities in the U.S.: Atlanta, Boston, Chicago, Dallas/Ft. Worth, Denver, Houston, Los Angeles, New Orleans, New York, San Francisco, Seattle, Tampa, and Washington, D.C. There are other such firms around the country, which do aptitude testing and not merely *interest* testing. Also, many colleges and universities will give you vocational testing, for somewhat more modest fees. Do remember to ask if it is **aptitude** testing or merely **interests** testing. The distinction is important.

If you want *help* with the overall process of job-hunting, Appendix C in the back of this book has a **Sampler** that lists some of the career counseling places to be found around the country. Unfortunately, it only lists some of these, because it is just a Sampler. Your Yellow Pages will help you find a more comprehensive list of these in your area, under the headings of "Aptitude and Employment Testing," "Career Counseling," "Executive Consultants," "Management Consultants," "Personnel Consultants," and "Vocational Consultants." You will have to pick your way with great care

"Let's put it this way—if you can find a village without an idiot, you've got yourself a job."

through those woods. Just when you think you've gotten safely to grandmother's house, you may find there is a wolf there. Appendix C is a section **which I would urge you to read no less than three times** before you ever venture forth to press your money and your job-hunt or career-change into somebody else's hands.

Some professional groups have their own counseling centers. For example, if you are a clergyperson, you will want to look at the church career development centers which have sprung up all over the country. A list of them is to be found on page 326.

V *Your family or friends.* I believe as a general rule -- there are exceptions -- you ought to try never to go through the job-hunt all by yourself alone. Co-opt **somebody** -- your partner or mate, a grown-up son or daughter who lives nearby, your best friend, someone you know well from your church or synagogue to be your weekly support person.

PRACTICAL EXERCISE (SO YOU DON'T GO IT ALONE)

Choose a helper for your job-hunt -- friend rather than family, if possible. A **tough** friend. You know, taskmaster. Ask them if they're willing to help you. Assuming they say yes, put down in both your appointment books a regular weekly date when they will guarantee to meet with you, check you out on what you've done already, and be very stern with you if you've done little or nothing since your previous week's meeting. Tell them that it is at least a 20,000-hour, $500,000 project. Or whatever. It's also responsible, concerned, committed Stewardship.

Where did we get 20,000 hours? Well, a forty-hour-a-week job, done for fifty weeks a year, adds up to 2,000 hours annually. So, how long are you going to be doing this new job or new career that you are looking for? How many years do you plan to stay in the world of work? Ten years? That means 20,000 hours. Longer than that? Even more hours. So, it's at least a 20,000-hour project.

Why $500,000? Well, figure it out for yourself. Say you hope to start this new job or new career of yours at $20,000 a year. Even if you are forty years old, you still have thirty good years of work left in you. So, let us say that over that period of thirty years you get enough raises to make your annual salary somewhere between $25,000 and $30,000. Multiply this by thirty years, and you get a total earnings of something in the neighborhood of more than half a million dollars. If you've got more years ahead of you, or a higher potential salarywise, you're talking about even more money.

So, it's at least a 20,000 hour, $500,000 project that you're working on, with this job-hunt or career-change of yours. That should get you going!

P.S. *Be sure and check with your local IRS office or a reputable accountant to find out if you can deduct the expenses of your job-hunt on your Federal (and State) income tax returns. At this writing,* some *job-hunters can,* if -- big IF -- *this is not your first job that you're looking for, if you haven't been unemployed too long, and if you aren't making a career-change. If IRS tells you you* are *eligible, keep careful receipts of* everything *related to your job-hunt, as you go along.*

You can judge your age
by the amount of pain
you feel when you come in
contact with a new idea.

—John Nuveen

CHAPTER FOUR

The Systematic Approach To The Job-Hunt and Career-Change:

PART I

What Skills Do You Most Enjoy Using?

Chapter 4

INTRODUCTION TO THESE NEXT THREE CHAPTERS

Let us begin by getting motivated.

There is a vast world of work out there in this country, where at least 118 million people are employed -- *many of them* bored out of their minds. All day long. Not for nothing is their motto TGIF -- "Thank God It's Friday." They **live** for the weekends, when they can go do what they really want to do.

There are already more than enough of such poor souls. The world does not need you or me to add ourselves to their number. What the world does need is more people who feel true enthusiasm for their work. People who have taken the time to *think* -- that is, to think out what they uniquely can do, and what they uniquely have to offer to the world.

This is what you are doing when you are going about the job-hunt in the careful, thoughtful manner described in these next three chapters and Appendix A. You may think all of this is a kind of selfish activity -- figuring out what ***you*** want -- but it is not. It is giving the world what it most needs: your uniqueness. The world needs you to be doing work that you love to do; moreover that is your birthright, and your destiny.

Life is a community, and your work is a part of that community. Career-planning, such as you are doing here, can never be just a case of *'I'm gonna do what I want, and never mind what others do.'* All of us who are involved in the world of work are like members of a symphony orchestra. The flute players there -- for example -- cannot reproduce Beethoven's Sixth all by themselves. But, on the other hand, neither can the rest of the orchestra reproduce Beethoven's Sixth without the flute players. They need *each other*. The flute players must always perform with this consciousness -- must learn their part; and learn it well, by spending hours rehearsing their part, practicing it, getting it just right. But at the same time, they must never forget that it takes all the others before there can be a symphony performed. In *the orchestra of work*, you are the flute player. Your work is a *part* of what is necessary for the whole world to function. You must learn your own part; and learn it well. That is what you are doing in these next three chapters, and Appendix A. But you must remain ever conscious of, and ever grateful for, the fact that many other players are helping you to do what you do so well.

However, none of this defining your part just falls into your lap. **You have to put in time and effort to make it happen.** You need to do this process *carefully* and *systematically*, as described in these

three chapters and Appendix A. I do not think I need to argue this point with those who are contemplating a career-change, and trying to pull it off without having necessarily to go back to school for extensive retraining. It is obvious, upon even the slightest thought, that such career-change requires careful and systematic inventorying.

It may not be so obvious that you need to read these next three chapters and do all the exercises in Appendix A, if you already know what kind of work you want to do, and it is generally along the lines of work you have been doing before. If it is just the job-hunt you are facing (and not a full-blown career-change) you may wonder if you really need to read these next three chapters and do all the exercises in Appendix A. Well the answer is that even in an ordinary job-hunt if you are facing *any kind of difficulty*, as for example a tough job-market, or you have some kind of disability or handicap, then you are going to **need** every weapon you can possibly muster in that battle. For, **anytime** you face a job-hunt where you feel you are having a tough time competing with the other job applicants, **reading these next three chapters and doing all the exercises in Appendix A is a must**.

OK, so how do you begin? You begin by inventorying your skills. Is this inventorying just hard work and drudgery? Well, it can be. Or is it fun? Well, it can be. It all depends on your attitude. I remind you of some words of the famed Victor Frankl:

> "We who lived in concentration camps can remember the men who walked through the huts comforting others, giving away their last piece of bread. They may have been few in number, but they offer sufficient proof that everything can be taken from a man but one thing: the last of the human freedoms -- to choose one's attitude in any given set of circumstances, to choose one's own way."

And so it is, that in tackling this systematic preparation for your career-change or job-hunt you can *choose* to see it as a lot of drudgery and hard work, which you would never do were it not for the difficult labor market that you face. Or, you can choose to see it as **fun** -- an exploration of the inner world of yourself, where you unwrap your skills with the joy that children have when they unwrap their gifts at Christmastime.

You can also choose to see this process as a means of gaining the weapons to protect yourself from being manipulated by others. For, at job-hunting time you are very vulnerable, and therefore very much at risk of being thus manipulated by others, be they those who might make money off your plight, or future employers, or even well-meaning friends.

Not long ago, I overheard two college students talking, in Central Park in New York City. We'll call them Jim and Fred. In half a minute of conversation they perfectly illustrated how well-meaning friends can "do you in":

Jim: Hey, what are you majoring in?
Fred: Physics.
Jim: Physics? Man, you shouldn't major in physics. Computer science is the thing these days.
Fred: Naw, I like physics.
Jim: Man, physics doesn't pay much.
Fred: Really?
Jim: Switch to computer science.
Fred: Okay, I'll look into it tomorrow.

Well, you see my point. Upon such little conversations do huge life-decisions depend. This is why it is so important for you to do your homework, identifying your favorite and strongest skills. Settle it in your mind right now:

> Before you go out to pound the pavement, **you have got to know what it is you want**, or else someone is going to sell you a bill of goods somewhere along the line that can do irreparable damage to your self-esteem, your sense of worth, and your stewardship of the talents that God gave you.

WHY DO YOU BEGIN WITH YOUR SKILLS?

"... and give me good abstract-reasoning ability, interpersonal skills, cultural perspective, linguistic comprehension, and a high sociodynamic potential."

You begin the systematic approach -- whether you're just doing a normal job-hunt or you want this to be a full-fledged career-change -- in exactly the same way: by first of all identifying your skills. Now, many people just "freeze" when they hear the word "skills." It begins with high school job-hunters: "I haven't really got any skills," they say. It continues with college students: "I've spent four years in college. I haven't had time to pick up any skills." And it lasts through the middle years, especially when a person is thinking of changing his or her career: "I'll have to go back to college, and get retrained, because otherwise I won't have any skills in my new field." Or: "Well, if I claim any skills, I'll start at a very entry kind of level." All of this fright about the word "skills" is very common, and stems from a total misunderstanding of what the word means. A misunderstanding that is shared, we might add, by altogether too many employers, personnel departments, and other so-called "vocational experts."

By understanding the word, you will automatically put yourself way ahead of most job-hunters. And, especially if you are weighing a change of career, you can save yourself much waste of time on the folly called "I can only change careers by going back to school for extensive retraining." *Maybe* you need some retraining, but very often it is possible to make a dramatic career-change without *any* retraining. It all depends. And you won't *really* know if you need further schooling, until you have finished all the exercises in Appendix A. So let's get on with:

OUR CRASH COURSE ON SKILLS

Skills are the most basic unit -- the atoms -- of your life in the world of work. You can see this from this diagram:

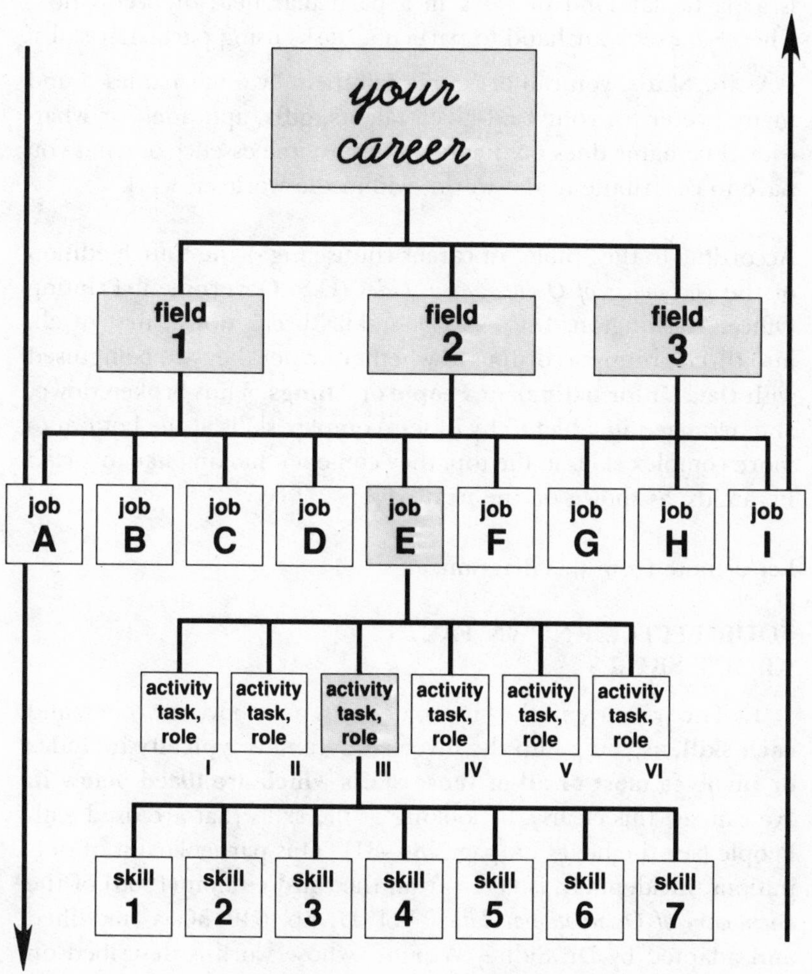

If you prefer definitions to diagrams, here they are.

• A **career** is *technically* your total life in the world of work. Careers are often, in everyday conversation, spoken of as though they were synonymous with "**Fields** of knowledge" or "majors" -- so that when it is technically precise to say "field change" we often use instead the less precise phrase "career-change." This has become such common jargon in the everyday world, now, that we could never turn the clock back. *Career-change* today means leaving one occupation and going to another.

• A **job** is defined by what is above it and below it. Above it is "Field," and below it are "**Tasks**" and "Skills." Thus it is that a job is a particular kind of work in a particular field or occupation, where you set your hand to particular tasks using particular skills.

• As for **Skills**, you can of course call them by other names -- and many prefer to: your God-given talents, gifts, aptitudes, or whatever. The name does not matter. They are the essence of what you have to contribute to the world, within the world of work.

According to the "Bible" of career counseling -- the fourth edition of the *Dictionary of Occupational Titles* (U.S. Government Printing Office, Washington, D.C., 1977) -- skills break down, first of all, into three groups according to whether or not they are being used with **Data (Information)**, or **People** or **Things**. Thus broken down, and arranged in a hierarchy of less complex skills at the bottom to more complex skills at the top, they come out looking like inverted Pyramids, as shown on the next page:

Let us note from this diagram:

FOUR LITTLE KNOWN FACTS ABOUT SKILLS

1. The skills are ranked in a hierarchy, one above the other, and **each skill,** as you go up the inverted pyramids **typically includes or involves most or all of those skills which are listed below it.** We can see this clearly, by looking at the skills that are used with People (see the boxes on pages 80–81). This particular list of definitions, incidentally, is taken from the third edition (1965) of the *Dictionary of Occupational Titles*, Vol. II, pp. 649–50, as modified and adapted by Dr. Sidney A. Fine, whose work is described on

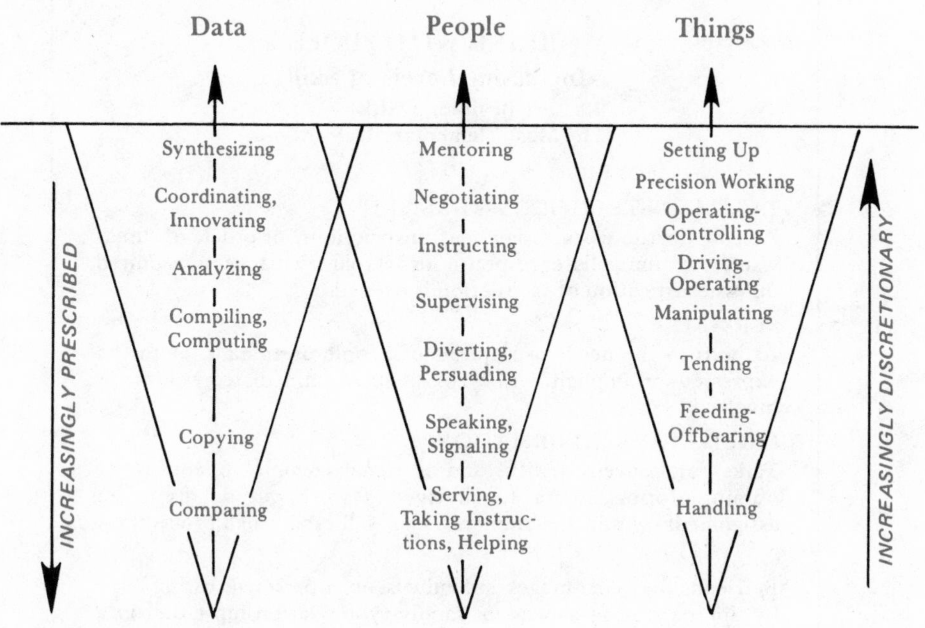

page 292. If you are a great person for detail, you will note that this list differs slightly from the previous pictorial, as well as from the skills list found in Appendix A.

At your public library, in the 1977 edition of the D.O.T., as the *Dictionary of Occupational Titles* is called, you can find similar lists for Data and Things (on pp. 1369–71).

2. As you note the increasing complexity of the higher skills on these Pyramids, you will of course -- in keeping with the modest nature for which you are doubtless known far and wide -- be *tempted* to check off your skills as being down near the bottom of the inverted pyramids -- "just to be on the safe side." No, no, no, my friend. It is in your own best interest to claim the *highest* skills that you **legitimately** can. Because, the higher the skill that you in fact **have**, the more you will be given room to be creative. You will be freer to carve out the job so that it truly fits you. But the lower the skill you claim, the more you will have to "fit in" -- following the instructions of your supervisor and doing exactly what you are told. No one likes to just "fit in," if they can possibly avoid it.

WORKING WITH PEOPLE

Increasing Levels of Skill

Beginning With
The Most Elementary Definition

TAKING INSTRUCTIONS – HELPING

Attends to the work assignment, instructions, or orders of supervisor. No immediate response or verbal exchange is required unless clarification of instruction is needed.

SERVING

Attends to the needs or requests of people or animals, or to the expressed or implicit wishes of people. Immediate response is involved.

EXCHANGING INFORMATION

Talks to, converses with, and/or signals people to convey or obtain information, or to clarify and work out details of an assignment, within the framework of well-established procedures.

COACHING

Befriends and encourages individuals on a personal, caring basis by approximating a peer- or family-type relationship either in a one-to-one or small group situation, and gives instruction, advice, and personal assistance concerning activities of daily living, the use of various institutional services, and participation in groups.

PERSUADING

Influences others in favor of a product, service, or point of view by talks or demonstrations.

DIVERTING Amuses others.

CONSULTING

Serves as a source of technical information and gives such information or provides ideas to define, clarify, enlarge upon, or sharpen procedures, capabilities, or product specifications.

INSTRUCTING

Teaches subject matter to others, or trains others, including animals, through explanation, demonstration, practice, and test.

TREATING

Acts on or interacts with individuals or small groups of people or animals who need help (as in sickness) to carry out specialized therapeutic or adjustment procedures. Systematically observes results of treatment within the framework of total personal behavior because unique individual reactions to prescriptions (chemical, behavioral, physician's) may not fall within the range of prediction. Motivates, supports, and instructs individuals to accept or cooperate with therapeutic adjustment procedures, when necessary.

INCREASING LEVELS OF SKILL continued

SUPERVISING
Determines and/or interprets work procedure for a group of workers, assigns specific duties to them (particularly those which are prescribed), maintains harmonious relations among them, evaluates performance (both prescribed and discretionary), and promotes efficiency and other organizational values. Makes decisions on procedural and technical levels.

NEGOTIATING
Exchanges ideas, information, and opinions with others on a formal basis to formulate policies and programs on an initiating basis (e.g., contracts) and/or arrives at resolutions of problems growing out of administration of existing policies and programs, usually after a bargaining process.

MENTORING
Deals with individuals in terms of their overall life adjustment behavior in order to advise, counsel, and/or guide them with regard to problems that may be resolved by legal, scientific, clinical, spiritual and/or other professional principles. Advises clients on implications of diagnostic or similar categories, courses of action open to deal with a problem, and merits of one strategy over another.

3. The higher the level of skills that you can honestly and legitimately claim for yourself, on the basis of your past performance, the less likely it is that the jobs which use such skills will be advertised through normal channels. And because they are not advertised through normal channels, you will need to use the unorthodox methods described in Chapters 5 and 6 to find out about them.

4. However, the more unorthodox the methods you use to find such jobs, the less people there will be to compete with you for that job. And in fact, if you succeed in uncovering an unmet need within the organizations of your choice, there is an excellent chance that they will be willing to create for you a job that did not even exist before you walked in. (They may have been **thinking** about creating such a job, but they never got around to doing it until they saw you.) This means you will be competing with no one, since you will be the sole applicant for that newly created job.

> **THE PARADOXICAL MORAL OF ALL THIS**
> **The higher a skill level you legitimately claim, the more likely you are to find a job. Just the opposite of what the typical job-hunter or career-changer starts out believing.**

So, if you would do your job-hunt or career-change most effectively, you must identify your skills according to the methods outlined in Appendix A, so that you will then be able to fill out this diagram completely, as in the sample shown here:

A Completed Skills Petal
(Sample)

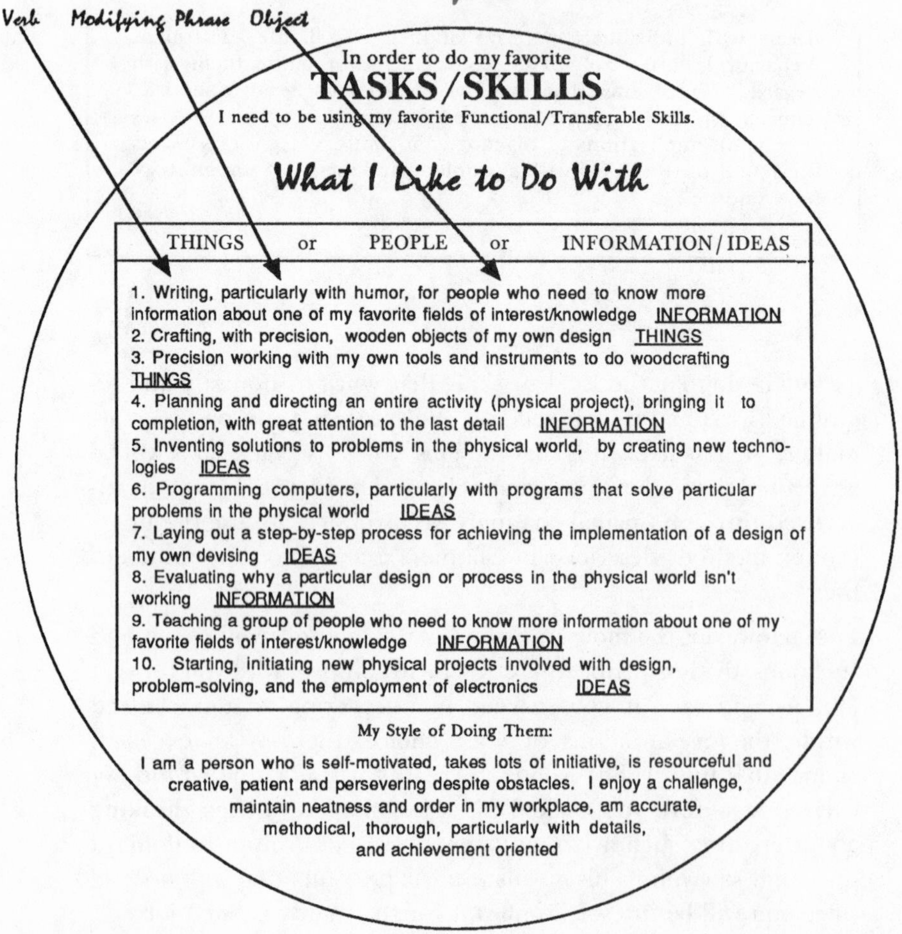

Verb Modifying Phrase Object

In order to do my favorite
TASKS/SKILLS
I need to be using my favorite Functional/Transferable Skills.

What I Like to Do With

THINGS or PEOPLE or INFORMATION/IDEAS

1. Writing, particularly with humor, for people who need to know more information about one of my favorite fields of interest/knowledge INFORMATION
2. Crafting, with precision, wooden objects of my own design THINGS
3. Precision working with my own tools and instruments to do woodcrafting THINGS
4. Planning and directing an entire activity (physical project), bringing it to completion, with great attention to the last detail INFORMATION
5. Inventing solutions to problems in the physical world, by creating new technologies IDEAS
6. Programming computers, particularly with programs that solve particular problems in the physical world IDEAS
7. Laying out a step-by-step process for achieving the implementation of a design of my own devising IDEAS
8. Evaluating why a particular design or process in the physical world isn't working INFORMATION
9. Teaching a group of people who need to know more information about one of my favorite fields of interest/knowledge INFORMATION
10. Starting, initiating new physical projects involved with design, problem-solving, and the employment of electronics IDEAS

My Style of Doing Them:

I am a person who is self-motivated, takes lots of initiative, is resourceful and creative, patient and persevering despite obstacles. I enjoy a challenge, maintain neatness and order in my workplace, am accurate, methodical, thorough, particularly with details, and achievement oriented

Now or later, but before you go out to pound the pavements, sit down and do Appendix A! You must, you must, you must know what you have to offer an employer (or, if you would be self-employed, what you have to offer your clients or customers).

WHAT USE IS THIS INFORMATION?

That's a question you should ask about **everything** in the job-hunt. And I'll tell you why. There is a school of thought out there in the world that thinks that as long as you are **busy** doing paper and pencil exercises on yourself, you are on your way to fame and fortune in the job-hunt. However, if you aren't clear as to where all this busyness is taking you, you will end up feeling like a hamster running on a treadmill. The first fifteen laps may be fun, but after that . . . phooey.

So, you *always* need to know **why** some particular information is important to your job-hunt or career-change. And here the answer boils down to this: every time you go into a job-interview, you must be able to tell an employer convincingly what you have to offer him or her. The answer is **your skills**, spelled out in detail. Therefore you must know them **by heart**, backwards and forwards. And this is even more true if it is a true career-change that you are contemplating.

WHY SHOULD THE LIST OF YOUR SKILLS BE PRIORITIZED?

Not only must you know your skills, you must know them in their order of importance, or priority. You must be able to say, "This is my greatest strength, this is my next greatest, etc." when you approach **any** employer, even if you are only applying for the kind of job you have held before.

Moreover, every time you decide to turn your job-hunt into a full-fledged career-change, you will likely be *rearranging* the "building blocks" of your skills, into a new order of priority. Hence the absolute importance, once you know what your skills are, of **putting your skills in order of importance or priority for you**, as in the building-block diagram on the next page: If you skip over this step, you are essentially committing job-hunting suicide.

If you don't know how to prioritize your skills (**and 83.7% of all job-hunters and career-changers don't**), then you will find detailed instructions for doing this in old Appendix A once again, on page 216. Before you go out pounding the pavements, or sending out your resume, go to Appendix A **and do it!**

SPECIAL PROBLEMS

In doing all the aforementioned homework in Appendix A, it will not be surprising if you run into some problems. Let us look at the more common ones that have arisen for our readers in the past:

1

> *"I don't see why I should look for skills I enjoy; it seems to me that employers will want to know what skills I do well, whether I enjoy using them or not."*

Well, to be more accurate, **bad** employers will not care whether you enjoy a particular task -- they will only want to know if you know how to do it. But **good** employers will care greatly. They know that unless a would-be employee has **enthusiasm** for his or her work, the quality of that work will *always* suffer.

It is **very** important for you to find the skills you do well, but generally speaking that is hard for you to evaluate about yourself. Even aptitude tests don't always make it clear. So it's better to take the simple equation which experience has shown to be true: if it is a skill we do well, we generally enjoy using that skill, and instead of hunting for the elusive "Do I do it well?" hunt for the much more easily-identifiable "Do I enjoy doing it?" I repeat: experience has shown that people *rarely* enjoy something they do very badly (there **are** occasional exceptions, usually in the area of athletics or leisure). But so far as the world of work is concerned, listing the skills you most enjoy is just another way of listing the skills you do best.

The reason why this idea (*of making enjoyment the key*) causes such feelings of uncomfortableness with so many job-hunters or career-changers is that we have an unwritten tradition that says you shouldn't really enjoy yourself in life. This tradition was established years and years ago in this country by a group of people who thought it actually a sin if you enjoyed life. They were called Puritans. It would be nice if by this time the Puritans had vanished from our culture; but, alas and alack, the Puritan mentality is still very much with us, as any careful perusal of the daily papers will quickly show.

It's hard to tell when you meet a Puritan, at first. Because, Puritans today come in all sizes, shapes, genders, ages, and colors. Puritans allegedly believe in God; but, what a god! A Puritan believes that God didn't intend us to enjoy anything. And that if you enjoy it, it's probably wrong for you. Let us illustrate:

Two girls do babysitting. One hates it. One enjoys it thoroughly. Which is more virtuous in God's sight? According to the Puritan, the one who hates it is more virtuous.

Two Puritans met on the street. "Isn't this a beautiful day?" said one. "Aye," said the other, "but we'll pay for it."

Puritans will talk about their failures, but hardly ever about their successes and even then, always with a feeling that "*God is going to get me, for this.*" They fear that the idea one has successes is boasting, and is manifestly sinful because it is manifestly too enjoyable!

Given the Puritan's belief in God, one may speak directly to the Puritan within the framework of that belief. "Look at the birds of the air," we say to him or her, "and look at the animals at play. You will notice one distinctive fact about all of God's creation: **joy follows right action.** When an animal does what it is meant to do, it manifests true joy.

"What you as Puritan fail to recognize is that in human life also, joy follows right action. It's a part of God's plan for all His creation. God wants us to eat; therefore God designs us so that eating is enjoyable. God wants us to sleep; therefore God designs us so that

sleeping is enjoyable. God wants us to procreate, love, and make love; therefore God designs us so that sex is enjoyable, and love even more so. And: God gives to each of us unique *combinations of* skills and talents which He wants us to contribute to His general plan; therefore He designs us so that when we use the talents **He most wants us to use, that is our time of greatest joy**. Furthermore, we gain a sense of achievement from them. Everywhere in God's plan for His creation, joy follows right action.

"So, Puritans arise; if you believe in God, believe in One who believes in you. Downgrading yourself is out -- for the duration of your job-hunt, and for the duration of your life here on earth."

"I believe in doing this skill identification; but I can't come up with enough good stories about any enjoyable accomplishments I've ever done in my life."

Well, first of all, let's be sure you're **not** trying to find some achievement which *you* have done that no one else in the world has ever done before you. Like, climbing some unknown mountain in the world that no one's ever scaled before. That's *not* what you're looking for. You're looking for *any* time in your life when you did something that was, **at that time of your life**, an accomplishment *for you*. It might have been "Learning to ride my bike." Who cares if a lot of other people have already done it? In *your* life, at *that* time, it was an accomplishment or achievement. Bernard Haldane's definition of an achievement is: "Something you yourself feel you have done well, that you also enjoyed doing and felt proud of." That's the kind of thing you are looking for. An accomplishment which gave you two pleasures: enjoyment while doing it, as well as satisfaction from the outcome. It doesn't mean you may not have sweated as you did it, but basically you enjoyed *the whole process*.

Typically, your story about some accomplishment or achievement of yours will have these parts to it:

a) **Some kind of goal** that you formulated in your own mind. You knew what you wanted to accomplish. *"I wanted to be able to take a summer trip with my marriage partner and children."*

b) **Some kind of hurdle, obstacle or constraint** (self-imposed or otherwise) that you had to work around. *"We had a very limited budget, and could not afford to stay in motels."*

c) **A description of how you went about doing your accomplishment, in spite of that hurdle or constraint -- step by step.** *"I decided to rig our station wagon as a camper. First I went to the library to get some books on campers. I read those books. Next I drew up a plan of what I had to build, to outfit the inside of the station wagon. Then I went and purchased the necessary wood. On weekends, over a period of six weeks, I . . . . . ." etc., etc.*

d) **A description of the outcome or result.** *"When we went on our summer trip, we were able to be on the road for four weeks, and we stayed within our budget, since we didn't have to stay at motels."*

e) **Any measurable/quantifiable statement of that outcome, that you can think of.** *"As a result of doing this, I saved $1200 on motel bills, on our summer vacation."*

If you are trying to think of such enjoyable accomplishments in your life, but inspiration still isn't coming, then fall back to the drastic Plan B here: discipline yourself to sit down and write a detailed *mini*-autobiography *of your whole life* and all your remembered activities or accomplishments, without for the time being stopping to look for "enjoyable" or "satisfying."

This autobiography method is fully described in a companion book to this one, entitled *Where Do I Go From Here With My Life?* -- by the late John C. Crystal and some friend of his.

Here is an outline of the method, as you will find it in that book:

A. Write a detailed mini-autobiography of your entire life. An informal summary for your eyes only (who cares about your spelling or grammar?) of where you've ever been, and what you've ever done, where you were ever working, and what you did there (not in terms of job titles -- *forget them* -- but in terms of what you feel you accomplished there).

B. Describe your spare time, in each place where you lived. What did you do? What did you most enjoy doing? Any hobbies? Avocations? Great. Were there any activities in your work that paralleled the kinds of things you enjoyed doing in your leisure?

C. Concentrate both on the things you have done, and also on the particular characteristics of your surroundings that were important to you, and that you really enjoyed: green grass, the theater, tennis, warm climate, skiing, or whatever.

D. Keep your eye constantly on that "divine radar": **enjoyable**. It's not *always* a guide to what you should be putting down, but it sure is more reliable than any other key that people have come up with. Sift later. For now, put down anything that helped you to enjoy a particular moment or period of your life.

E. Don't be afraid if at times it sounds to your modest ears as though you are almost boasting -- *and* doing too much of it! Who's going to see this document besides you, God, and any loved one that you choose to show it to? So, let it rip. Just be *sure* to back up your elation and sense of pride with concrete examples, and figures.

F. Don't try to make this mini-autobiography very structured. You can bounce back and forth in time, if that's more congruent with *your* way of doing things.

G. When your mini-autobiography is all done, you may have a small book -- it can run 30 pages or more. (*My, you've done a lot of living, haven't you?*) Now go back and find just one story in it that you consider to have been an enjoyable achievement for you. Analyze it in the manner explained on page 230ff. After you are done analyzing it, go back to the autobiography and pick out a second story, in a different time period and a different arena of your life. Do skill identification on that second story. And so on.

This is more work than just trying to write stories cold; but if the story approach isn't working for you, this is your lifeboat. Try it. As the commercials say: "You'll be so glad you did."

3

> *"I've never had any experience in the world of work. I've been a homemaker all my life. I can think of stories of enjoyable achievements* within *the home, but I'm not sure I could ever sell an employer on that."*

If this is proving to be a hurdle for you, then you will want to write to the Educational Testing Service, Publication Order Services, CN 6736, Princeton, NJ 08541-6736 and ask for their I CAN lists, which are contained in the following inexpensive books, all of which are authored by Ruth B. Ekstrom: *HAVE Skills Women's Workbook -- Finding Jobs Using Your Homemaking and Volunteer Work Experience*; *How to Get College Credit for What You Have Learned As a Home-maker and Volunteer*; *HAVE Skills Employer's Guide -- Matching Women and Jobs*; *HAVE Skills Counselor's Guide -- Helping Women Find Jobs Using Their Homemaking and Volunteer Work Experience*. The I CAN lists classify all the skills of the homemaker under various roles and job titles in business, such as: administrator/manager, financial manager, personnel manager, trainer, advocate/change agent, public relations/communicator, problem surveyor, researcher, fund raiser, counselor, youth group leader, group leader for a serving organization, museum staff assistant, nutritionist, child caretaker, designer, clothing and textile specialist, and so forth. *Very* helpful to *anyone* who has never had any work experience outside the home, *not just women or homemakers*. It's helpful to teenagers, persons who happen to have disabilities and have not yet worked out there in the world, and so forth.

> *"I have no difficulty finding stories to write up, from my life, that I consider to be enjoyable achievements; but once these are written, I have great difficulty in seeing what the skills are, that I used in doing them -- even with the skills list you have in Appendix A."*

You will want to consider getting two friends or two other members of your family to sit down with you, and do skill identification through the practice of "Trioing" which I invented some years back. This practice is fully described in the book mentioned earlier, *Where Do I Go From Here With My Life?* In general, here is how it goes:

a. Each of the three of you quietly writes up some story of an accomplishment in their life that was enjoyable.

b. Each of the three of you quietly analyzes just your own story to see what skills you see there; you jot these down.

c. One of you then volunteers to go first. You read your story aloud. The other two jot down on a piece of paper whatever skills they hear you using. They ask you to pause if they're having trouble keeping up. You finish your story. You read aloud the skills *you* picked out in that story.

d. Then the second person tells you what's on their list: what skills *they* heard you use in your story. You copy them down, below your own list, even if you don't agree with every one of them.

e. Then the third person tells you what's on their list; what skills *they* heard you use in your story. You copy them down, below your own list, even if you don't agree with every one of them.

f. When they're both done, you ask them any questions for further elaboration that you may have. *"What did you mean by this skill? Where did you think you heard me using it?"*

g. Now it is the next person's turn, and you repeat steps 'c' through 'f' with them. Then it is the third person's turn, and you repeat steps 'c' through 'f' with them.

h. Now it is time to move on to a second story for each of you, so you begin with steps 'a' through 'g' all over again, except that each of you writes a new story. And so on, through seven stories.

"How do I know if I've done this all correctly? What if I just think I understood what I was supposed to do, but I really didn't? I want to be sure the stuff I've identified is really going to help me in my job-hunt."

Well, that's a reasonable anxiety, it seems to me. So, here are a few questions, to help you check out how you did:

a. Since all transferable skills are used either with Data, or People, or Things, do you now know which you most prefer working with? Is it some kind of Data, or some kind of People, or some kind of Things? And: which kind?

b. What's your second preference? Your third?

c. Have you described your skills with more than one word? One word is good to start with, but it isn't where you want to end up. In the end, you want to be able to describe what you do in more than just one word. "I'm good at **organizing**" doesn't tell us **anything**. Organizing what? People, as at a party? Nuts and bolts, as on a workbench? Or lots of information, lying in a computer? Those are three entirely different skills. The one word "organizing" doesn't tell us which one, at all. Sooooo, why don't you try going back over the skills you identified as yours, and make sure that each one-word definition gets **fleshed out** with an **object** -- some kind of Data/Information, or some kind of People, or some kind of Thing -- and maybe also an **adverb** or adjective. "I'm good at analyzing people **painstakingly by asking them a lot of questions**," and "I'm good at analyzing people **in a flash, by intuition**," are two *entirely different* skills. The difference between them is spelled out not in the verb, but in the adjectival or adverbial phrase there at the end. So, try expanding each definition of your six favorite skills as much as you can, by an object at the least, and also with an adverb or adjective if you can.

d. Have you got all your skills arranged in order of importance, or priority, for you? **Anytime** you have a bunch of information about yourself, it is relatively useless to you, until you have put it in order of priority. "Here's what I most enjoy doing, this is next, this is next, and so on." This is especially true of your skills. Looking ahead to your next job or career, which skill do you **most** hope you will get to use "on the job," which next, which next? and so on.

e. If you're trying to move into another career, have you avoided stating your skills in the jargon or language of your past career? This is a point on which clergy, in particular, often stumble and fall. "I am good at preaching" is not at all a useful skill identification if you are going to go looking for work out there in what you call the secular world. Your skill identification is still cloaked in the jargon and language of *one career and one career only*. So, ask yourself, what is its larger form? *"Teaching?"* Perhaps. *"Motivating people?"* Perhaps. *"Inspiring people to the depths of their being?"* Perhaps. **Only you can say what is true, for you.** But in one way or another be sure to get your skills out of *any jargon that locks you into your past.*

f. Have you thus far steered clear of putting a job title on what you're aiming toward? Skills can point to many different jobs, which have a multitude of titles. Don't lock yourself into a box prematurely. "I'm looking for a job where I can **use** the following skills," is fine. But, "I'm looking for a job where I can **be** a (job title)" is a no-no, until you've done more homework and more research.

g. Are you hanging loose, willing to look at a number of alternatives, as you move through this homework on your skills? Or is your desire to finish this off *fast* leading you to push prematurely for just one way to go? **Stay loose.** Keep **all** your options open.

h. As you have been working on the question of your future career or future job, have you begun to get some insights into other aspects of your life and being? Keep yourself open and sensitive to these insights, as they pop up. Notice particularly as you go, what your values **are**. Truth, beauty, color, light, nature, justice, spirituality, righteousness, ambition, compassion, security, service, popularity, status, power, friends, achievement, love, authority, freedom, glamor, giving, integrity, honesty, loyalty, sensitivity, caring -- which holds the most meaning and importance for you? Stay alert and sensitive to these. You will get much clearer about who you are willing to work with and for, and who you are not. Those who share your values will be on your hit parade; those who don't, won't.

ARE THERE ANY SHORTCUTS FOR THE LAZY?

Almost all of you will be reading this chapter 4 before you've actually gone and done the work that you must do, in Appendix A. And rightly so, for it's important to have an overview of where you're going before you actually set out. But now that you've finished this part of the overview, doubtless you're debating whether to go to Appendix A and do all that work. You're hoping that *maybe, just maybe*, there's a shortcut.

Well, what can I tell you? **Anyone** could be forgiven for not wanting to do all the work in Appendix A. Hoping there are some "Alternatives for the Lazy." Well, of course there are. I'll tell you at least three ways that some job-hunters have gone about Avoiding All This Job-Hunting Homework:

1. FIRST SHORTCUT: You just ask yourself, "What do I want to be and what do I want to do?" My friend John L. Holland first proposed this simple shortcut. In his earliest book, now out of print, he wrote: "Despite several decades of research, the most efficient way to predict vocational choice is simply to ask the person what he wants to be; our best devices do not exceed the predictive value of that method."

So, if you don't want to do a lot of paper and pencil exercises, you might try thinking out the answer to this question: "What do I want to be and what do I want to do?" Sit in a quiet place, pen in hand, and write down whatever comes to mind.

2. SECOND SHORTCUT: Just ask yourself, "Whose job do I most covet or admire?" One of our readers declined to do any of the skill identification found in Appendix A. But she did pose this question to herself: "Among all the people that I know or have seen or read about, **whose** job would I most like to have?" She decided that the person she most admired, whose job she most coveted, was a woman who appeared as hostess on a television program for children. Accordingly, she went to her local TV station with a carefully written, well-thought-out proposal for a similar children's television program. They not only eventually *bought* the idea, they asked her to be the hostess of it. Thus did she find her ideal job. "Without," she added triumphantly, "doing a single exercise in your book." Good for her! And maybe also good for you.

3. THIRD SHORTCUT: Use John Holland's "Self-Directed Search" which is referred to, on page 354. Instructions on how to order it are there. When you get it, it will take you about an hour to fill out. Once you have filled it out, and have discovered your "Holland Code" of skills (for example, "S I A") buy, borrow, or go to your local library for the *Dictionary of Holland Occupational Codes: A Comprehensive Cross-Index of Holland's RIASEC Codes with 12,000 DOT Occupations* and look up all the occupations you could do, with that code (i.e., with those skills). It will not tell you all the things you could do; but it will at least give you a list of **some** places where you could start your personal Research or Informational Interviewing, as described in the next chapter.

To whet your appetite for John's "Self-Directed Search," you might want to try your hand at the Party Exercise. It gives you a "quick fix" on what your "Holland Code" **might** be. You may think of it as a shortcut to a shortcut.

THE PARTY EXERCISE

What Skills You Have and Most Enjoy Using

In John Holland's system, all skills are divided into six clusters or families. To see which families you are *attracted to*, try this exercise:

On the next page is an aerial view of a room in which a two-day (!) party is taking place. At this party, people with the same or similar interests have (for some reason) all gathered in the same corner of the room.

R for "Realistic"

People who have athletic or mechanical ability, prefer to work with objects, machines, tools, plants, or animals, or to be outdoors.

I for "Investigative"

People who like to observe, learn, investigate, analyze, evaluate, or solve problems.

The Party

C for "Conventional"

People who like to work with data, have clerical or numerical ability, carrying things out in detail or following through on others's instructions.

A for "Artistic"

People who have artistic, innovating or intuitional abilities, and like to work in unstructured situations, using their imagination or creativity.

E for "Enterprising"

People who like to work with people-- influencing, persuading or performing or leading or managing for organizational goals or for economic gain.

S for "Social"

People who like to work with people-- to inform, enlighten. help, train, develop, or cure them, or are skilled with words.

(1) Which corner of the room would you instinctively be drawn to, as the group of people you would most *enjoy* being with for the longest time? (Leave aside any question of shyness, or whether you would have to talk with them.) Write the *letter* for that corner here: ☐

(2) After fifteen minutes, everyone in the corner you have chosen leaves for another party crosstown, except you. Of the groups *that still remain* now, which corner or group would you be drawn to the most, as the people you would most *enjoy* being with for the longest time? Write the letter for that corner here: ☐

(3) After fifteen minutes, this group too leaves for another party, except you. Of the corners, and groups, which remain now, which one would you most enjoy being with for the longest time? Write the letter for that corner here: ☐

THE PERIL OF SHORTCUTS

Well, there are the shortcuts. Nice, eh? It's *always* nice to think that there are shortcuts. But remember the principle enunciated earlier: the job-hunt in this country is essentially a matter of sheer luck. The *more* time you are willing to spend on some proven job-hunting or career-changing techniques, the *more* you cut down how much of your job-hunt depends on luck.

Conversely -- and this is the point you especially want to remember here -- the *less* time you are willing to spend on your own homework, the *more* you are *willy-nilly* returning to a dependence on sheer luck. *Shortcuts don't take much time.* **Think about it.**

You can try any shortcuts you want to. If you succeed in finding a fabulous job as a result, then luck was *obviously* on your side.

But, on the other hand if you try these shortcuts and you *don't* find a job thereby, then **you know what you must do:** the skills identification exercises that are back in Appendix A, *in detail.*

PRACTICAL EXERCISE (COOLING DOWN?)

If two weeks after putting down this chapter, you pick it up again, and realize you still haven't even begun identifying your skills through the exercises in Appendix A, then let's face it: you're going to **have to** pay someone to aid you. Too bad, because chances are that if you'd just try this on your own, you could do as well or better by yourself. But better this than nothing: turn to Appendix C, **study** the introductory section there, then in your town choose three possible counselors or places, and go ask them questions. Weigh their answers. Choose one. Pay them, and **get at this.**

Students spend four or more years learning how to dig data out of the library and other sources, but it rarely occurs to them that they should also apply some of the same new-found research skill to their own benefit -- to looking up information on companies, types of professions, sections of the country that might interest them.

Professor Albert Shapero
The late William H. Davis Professor of The American Free Enterprise System at Ohio State University)

CHAPTER FIVE

The Systematic Approach To The Job-Hunt and Career-Change:

PART II

Where

Do You Want To Use Your Skills?

Chapter 5

Once you've figured out the "WHAT?", you turn to the "WHERE?" Once you've figured out what are your favorite and strongest skills, you turn to the question:

> **Where** do I want to use these skills? What occupation or occupations will use as many of my strongest skills, and on as high a level as possible -- so that I will be doing my most effective work, and also my most enjoyable work?

This "WHERE?" question can be stated in two different forms -- in terms of your **dreams,** or in terms of **principles that will help you cut down the territory you have to cover, in your job-hunt.**

"WHERE" IS THE KEY TO YOUR DREAM JOB

Suppose your strongest and most favorite skills involve welding. The "WHERE?" question is: Do you want to weld together a wheel, or do you want to weld the casing of a nuclear bomb? *You can see, the "WHERE?" is* ***terribly*** *important.* Again, suppose your strongest and most favorite skills are secretarial ones. The "WHERE?" question is: Do you want to be working in a legal office, or in an office of a gardening store? *Again, the "WHERE?" can make all the difference in the world.*

It is not sufficient, therefore, merely to know WHAT are your favorite skills. You must press on, to this next step in your systematic approach to career-change or job-hunting: WHERE do you want to use your favorite skills?

You are starting here at exactly the opposite place from where most job-hunters begin. They begin with Vacancies. They comb the newspapers, professional journals, agencies and other places to try to find out where there are Vacancies. They let the Vacancies call the shots, for their life. You are going about your job-hunt **intelligently** by *not* beginning there.

Instead, you are starting with the issue of where you would **like** to work. Later, you can inquire whether or not there are such jobs, and whether or not the places which have such jobs do in fact have a vacancy. **But you begin with the high energy and excitement generated (inevitably) by your dreams.** You ask yourself, What would be a dream job for me? So-called Realists scorn this idea of dreaming, of course. At least when it comes to their job. Elsewhere? That's another story.

Elsewhere, almost **everyone** has visions and dreams dreams. We dream of where we'd like to go next summer. We dream of what we're going to do for Christmas next year. We dream of what we'd do if we won the lottery. And so on, and on. It's only when we come to our job that we suddenly think our visions and dreams should be shelved. But the experts have discovered that, quite the contrary, with job-hunting in general and career-change in particular, the more you can tap into your dreams the more you **increase your chances** of being able at last to do what you always wanted to do with your life.

So, dream, dream, dream. Never mind "being realistic." According to the experts, 80% of the workers in this country are "under-employed." That's what comes of "being realistic." You don't want to end up in the same fix. But you will, if while you dream you corrupt your dream by keeping one eye fixed on what you **think** you know about the job-market. People who fall into this trap, are always saying something like: "I'm dying to be able to do this and that, but I **know** there is no job in the world like that."

You don't know any such thing. So, think out what would truly be your dream job! And just forget the "Yes, buts."

"*Yes, but* . . . dreams don't always come true in every detail." Well, it's possible that in the end you may not be able to find **all** that you want. But as John Crystal always used to say, why not aim for it, and then settle for less if and when you find out that you simply have to? Just **don't foreclose your future prematurely.** You'd be surprised at what you may be able to turn up.

"*Yes, but* . . . dreams don't always come true all at once." Well, sometimes they do have to be taken in stages. If you want to be president of a particular enterprise, for example, you may have to work your way toward it in two or three steps. But it is quite likely you will eventually succeed -- if *your whole heart* is in your dream.

So, take a look at what would be a dream job for you. You may want to do a warm-up exercise, to surface some of those forgotten dreams of yours:

ON THE LAST DAY OF MY LIFE

Spend as much time as necessary writing an article entitled "Before I die, I want to . . ." (And then you list things you would like

"Oh, darn, and just as I was beginning to take charge of my life."

to do, before you die.) Confess them to a piece of paper now, and maybe you can begin to make them happen in your life.

You may prefer to write an article on a similar topic: "On the last day of my life, what must I have done or been so that my life will have been satisfying to me?" Spend an hour or two on this. When finished, go back over it and make three lists: Things Already Accomplished, and: Things Yet To Be Accomplished, and: a third column, beside the second, listing the particular steps that you will have to take, in order to accomplish these things:

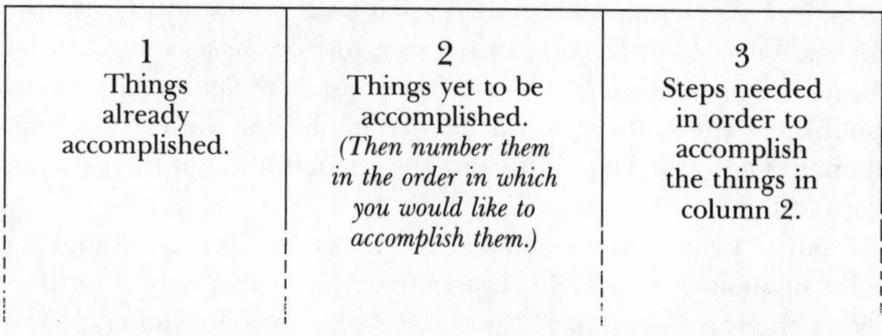

1 Things already accomplished.	2 Things yet to be accomplished. *(Then number them in the order in which you would like to accomplish them.)*	3 Steps needed in order to accomplish the things in column 2.

As you get involved with this exercise, you may notice that it is impossible to keep your focus only on your career. You will find some dreams creeping in concerning your leisure or your lifelong learning, of places you want to visit, and experiences you want to have that are not on-the-job. **Don't omit these.** Be just as specific as possible.

The above exercise is a general, intuitional way of approaching the matter of your dreams. It's like flying at 30,000 feet. When you want to come in for a landing, however, you need to get a little more specific (maybe a **lot** more specific).

THE ESSENTIAL PARTS OF A DREAM

Dreams, when they concern your future ideal job, should have certain *parts* to them, namely, five. *You need to be sure you have all those parts*, when you are setting your dreams down in detail, on paper. Your description of your dream is not complete, until you have answered *all* these questions:

(1) **COMPENSATION AND OTHER REWARDS.** What kind of salary or other types of compensation do you want to have, in your ideal life's work? What kinds of rewards do you hope your work will bring you?

For some job-hunters, the answer to this question seems simple. "*I want to become wealthy*," or, "*I want to become a millionaire*." Experts claim there are in fact 1.4 million people in this country who *have* become millionaires; which adds up to one out of every 86 workers in this country. (Oh, come *on!*) Anyway, because the dream seems so *possible* in the good ol' U.S. of A., many job-hunters make this their sole ambition. You have only to go into a local bookstore, and browse in the business section to see how true this is. Half the books there have the word **money** in their title. On a recent browse, for example, I saw: *Money and Class in America*; *Homemade Money*; *Money Is My Friend*; *Money Guide*; *Memory Makes Money*; *Money Minutes*; *Money Manual*; and -- well, I've made my point. Obviously, publishers think there are a lot of people out there for whom **money** is both the beginning and ending definition of their dream occupation.

You, of course, know better. Even if you do succeed in making a lot of money in your life, you know that it will help a lot if -- along the way -- you are also *enjoying* what you are doing. More-

over, just because there are a lot of books and seminars *out there*, telling you how to get wealthy in thirty days or so, doesn't mean you *will* become wealthy. What those books and seminars *neglect* to mention is that *many* people dream this dream, but never make it. (If you don't believe me, just think about the State lotteries, where millions of people line up to buy tickets, but only a precious one or two actually *make it*.) So, it is crucial you choose work that is, to you, fascinating. Then **it will be its own reward** if you *don't* become wealthy.

Besides, there is a paradox here, namely: if you set out *just to make money*, it is very likely you will fail; but if you set out to do *something you are dying to do*, your very enthusiasm may cause it to also be financially rewarding. Hence, the popularity of Marsha Sinetar's book entitled: *Do What You Love, The Money Will Follow.*

In any event, COMPENSATION *can't* be the total definition of your dream. There are four other issues, that you need to think through:

(2) TASKS. What kinds of tasks, using what kinds of skills, do you see yourself doing in your ideal life's work? And with what kind of style? (You define this by doing the exercises in Appendix A.)

(3) TOOLS OR MEANS. What do you need in order to be doing your ideal life's work, by way of information, or things or other people?

(4) OUTCOME. What do you see your work producing, as its result? Immediately? Long-range?

(5) SETTING. In what kind of setting do you see yourself working, in your ideal life's work? Setting means both physical setting and also the invisible stuff: values and the like.

The above five parts are the "WHERE?" questions stated in terms of your dream job: WHERE do you want to work, *in terms of tasks, tools, outcomes, setting, and compensation.* (If you don't know the answer to these questions as you are reading through this book for the first time, don't worry. That's the whole point of Appendix A; do the exercises there, once you're through reading the main body of this book, and you *will* know the answers.)

"WHERE" IS THE KEY TO MASTERING THE JOB-MARKET

Now, suppose you were made in such a way that "WHERE" was of no personal importance to you. You feel you could be happy anywhere just as long as you were using your favorite skills. Almost no organization in the country would be ruled out.

So, you're ready to go charging out there **and look at them all.** *Lots of luck! You'll need it.* There are 15,000,000 organizations, hence 15,000,000 job-markets, out there for you to go look at. We'll see you again in about 43 years.

No, no, no. You have to **cut the territory down.** You have to find some way to narrow down the list of organizations that you will need to weigh, consider, go visit, or research. Otherwise your job-hunting territory will be just too big. If you are to be successful, your job-hunt must look essentially like this:

Cutting The Territory Down

You start with the whole job-market in this country--
15 million job-markets

• You narrow this down by deciding just what area, city or county you want to work in. This leaves you with however many thousands of job markets there are in that area or city. • You narrow this down by identifying your Strongest Skills, on their highest level that you can legitimately claim, and then thru research deciding what field you *want* to work in, above all. This leaves you with all the hundreds of businesses/community organizations/agencies/schools/hospitals/projects/associations/foundations/institutions/firms or government agencies there are in that area and in the field you have chosen. • You narrow this down by getting acquainted with the economy in the area thru personal interviews with various contacts; and supplementing this with study of journals in your field, in order that you can pinpoint the places that interest you the most. This leaves a manageable number of markets for you to do some study on. • You now narrow this down by asking yourself: *Can I be happy in this place, and do they have the kind of problems which my strongest skills can help solve for them?* • This leaves you with the companies or organizations which you will now carefully plan how to approach for a job, in your case, *the* job.

•

You will see the sense of this, at once. **Obviously,** the territory **must** be cut down. So, the only question is: **how do you go about doing this?**

Experience has revealed that there are **seven basic questions** that are useful for cutting the territory down, besides your functional, transferable skills with Things, Information and/or People (which we saw in the last chapter). These seven *other* basic questions are:

1

Do you prefer to work for an organization that
- ***Produces information***
- ***Or invents/produces/sells a product***
- ***Or otherwise serves people?***

This cuts down the territory for you, because once you've said which you prefer, you only need to look at organizations that "fit your bill."

What kinds of information do you prefer to work with or help others to know?

By this, we mean two things: Form, and Content.

a) **FORM** means your preferences about the *form* you like your information to come to you in -- chosen from the lists that are to be found in Appendix A. E.g., do you generally prefer to work with books, or computer printouts, or magazines, or articles, or catalogs, etc.?

b) **CONTENT** means what is often referred to as Fields of Knowledge -- the subjects you know and enjoy best.

This cuts down the territory for you, because once you've said what these are, you only need to look at organizations that work with information in such forms as you have specified, in those fields that require or prize those fields of knowledge.

What kinds of people do you prefer to serve or to work with?

By this, we primarily mean what kinds of people do you want as clients or customers -- but we do not want to leave out your co-workers, bosses, etc. That means, therefore, what kinds of people do you want beside you, above you, below you, in the organization? *This cuts down the territory for you, because once you've said what these are, you only need to look at organizations that work with or employ such people.*

4 *What kinds of things do you prefer to work with or help produce?*

By this, we mean your preferences chosen from the lists which are to be found in Appendix A. There you will find such questions as: do you prefer to work with automobiles, or computers, or adding machines, or telephones, or other tools (which other?), etc.
This cuts down the territory for you, because once you've said what these are, you only need to look at organizations that work with such things.

5 *What physical setting do you want for your work?*

By this, we mean two things: *general* and *specific*.
a) *General* is the **GEOGRAPHICAL AREA** you would ideally like to have as the setting for your work.
b) *Specific* is the **WORKING CONDITIONS** you would like to have the organization furnish as the setting for your work.
This cuts down the territory for you, because once you've said what physical setting you want, you only need to look at organizations in that geographical area that provide such a setting.

6 *What spiritual or emotional setting do you want for your work?*

By this, we mean what are your:

a) Opinions or values concerning Truth
b) Opinions or values concerning Beauty
c) Opinions or values concerning Moral Issues
d) Opinions or values concerning Faith, Spirituality, or Religion

This cuts down the territory for you, because once you've said what spiritual setting you want for your work, you only need to look at organizations that will honor such values.

What salary and level do you want at a maximum; what salary and level do you need at a minimum?

This cuts down the territory for you, because once you've said what salary and level you want for your work, at a maximum and at a minimum, you only need to look at organizations that offer that salary and level.

Now to be sure, it makes your head swim the first time you look at this list. But if you are serious about your career-change or job-hunt, you will become **very familiar** with this list, believe me.

So let us get an overview of the seven by picturing them in a diagram, on the next page -- Here 'tis:

The Keys to Cutting Down the Territory

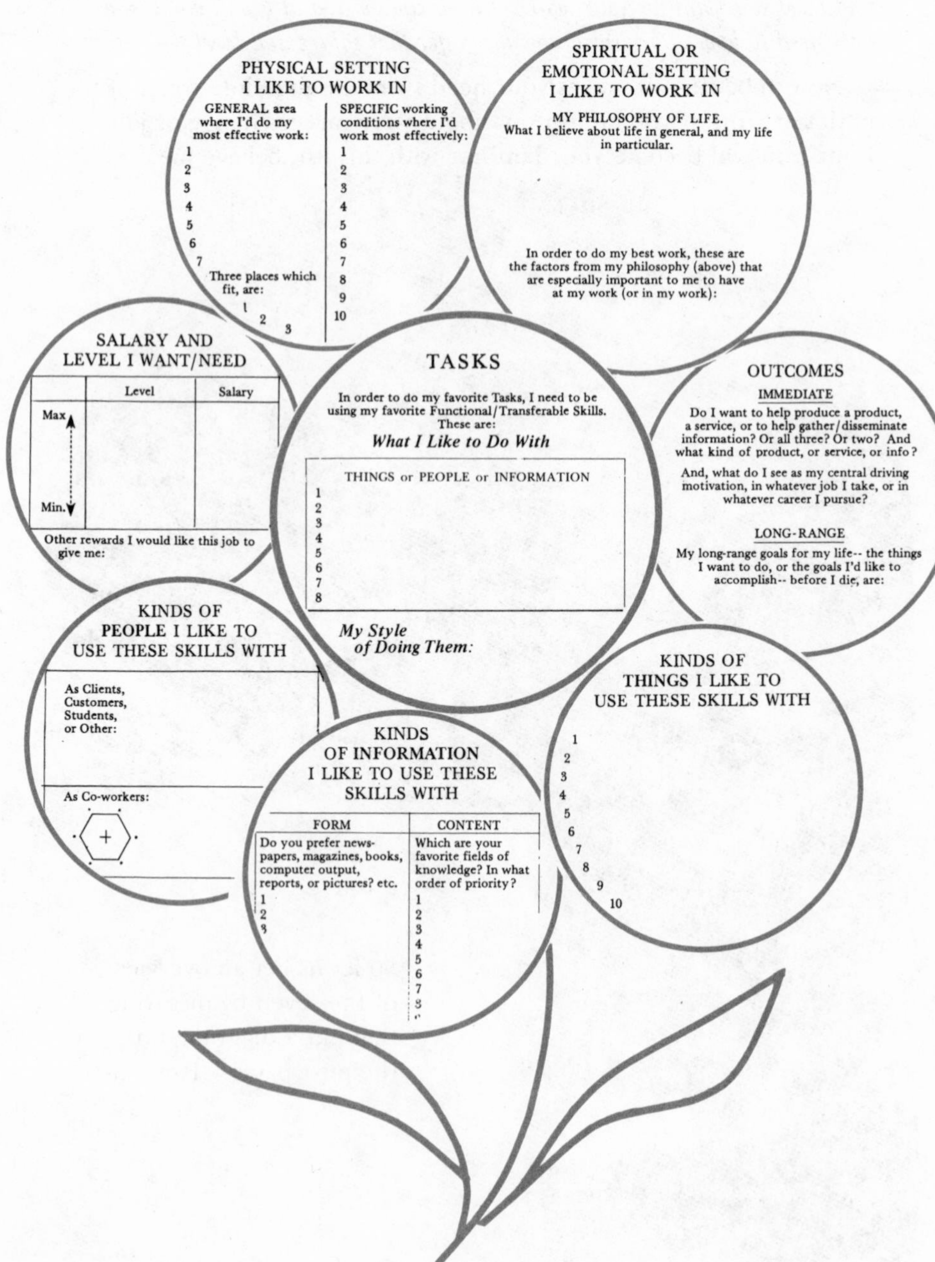

Incidentally, we call this The Flower Diagram for obvious reasons (add a stem at the bottom and some leaves, and it **looks** like a Flower -- if you stand forty feet back).

FILLING IN THE FLOWER

For a successful career-change, or even a successful job-hunt, you MUST know the answers to the questions above. You must fill out this Flower as you find it in Appendix A. You must, you must, you must cut the territory down.

Every hour you spend working on Appendix A and filling out the similar diagram there, is going to save you **days** of pounding the pavements. The tougher the job-market, the worse the state of the economy, the more people out of work, the bigger a switch you are thinking of making in your career, the **more important** it is that you take time to fill out this diagram in Appendix A. There you will find complete instructions on how to do that.

You may of course be A Lazy Job-Hunter. (There are at least ten of them in the world.) And you want to know what the alternative is, to doing all the work it takes to fill in the diagram above. Hey, that's easy: just plan on spending 43 years visiting all 15,000,000 employers in the U.S. OR: just take stabs at the job-market, hit or miss, and hope that God will prove He loves you by sending a job to your doorstep.

On the other hand, if these alternatives DON'T appeal to you a whole lot, then when you're done reading the body of this book, *get Thee to Appendix A, and start writing.*

Naturally, you will be curious to know -- at this point -- how the diagram above (**principles for cutting down the job-market** to manageable size) relates to the diagram of **the different parts of your dream job** that we talked about earlier on page 105ff. *You remember*: Tasks, Tools or Means, Outcome, Setting, Compensation.

Strangely enough, they are identical, as the following pictorial shows, wherein I have superimposed the "dream" titles on the Flower Diagram which we saw earlier.

The Keys to Your Dream Job

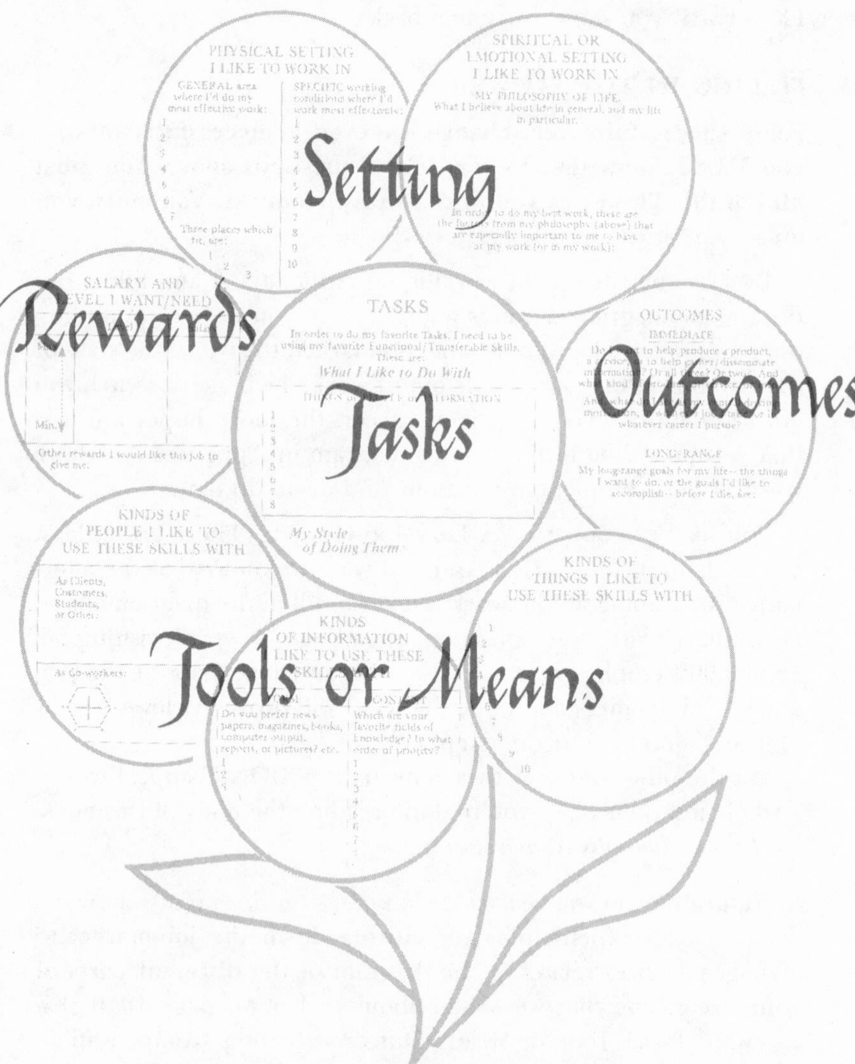

So, you can set about filling out this diagram from either viewpoint. **Think of filling out the Flower as filling out the details of your dream job, and you will automatically cut down the territory of your job-hunt. Or, think of filling out the Flower as trying to cut down the territory, and you will find that in the process of doing that, you are automatically defining your dream job.**

It's always nice when you can do two things at once; and this is one of those times.

ON TO THE RESEARCH PART OF THIS JOB-HUNT OR CAREER-CHANGE

Well, we must go on. Of course you haven't actually gone and filled out the Flower Diagram in Appendix A, yet. You're reading this book all the way through, first, to get the sense of it -- to see the overall plan. To make up your mind whether you want to follow this systematic approach, or just go back to the hints in chapter 3 and take your chances. I know, ah *how well I know*.

However, let's pretend that you **have** filled out the diagram in Appendix A, so we can legitimately ask: now what? What do you do next?

The answer is: **you have to go out and gather information** -- that activity which in high school or college we used to call "research for a term paper." *Oh no, not that!* Yes, that!

Don't let your stomach turn weak, or your knees turn to jelly. It's not difficult at all. It never is **IF you're researching something you love**. And that was the whole point of the Flower Diagram, wasn't it: to nail down what it is you **love**, in each of those eight arenas? You are going out to research that diagram: to find out **what** out there in the real world corresponds to the diagram you've drawn (and filled out) in Appendix A.

Courage, then. This research shouldn't be boring at all, in fact it usually turns into a lot of fun.

DON'T PAY SOMEONE TO DO THIS RESEARCH FOR YOU, WHATEVER YOU DO

Now, I know what you're thinking. *"Couldn't I pay someone to go do this for me? Aren't there organizations that already know the answers to the questions I need to research?"* I would love to be able to tell you, "Yes." Unfortunately, information which organizations gather is oftentimes **incredibly** outdated. But even if it were up-to-date, there are several reasons why *no one else* can do this job-hunting research for you -- not a career-counselor, not your best friend, not your children, not your parents, not your mate, **not anyone**. The reasons are three:

1. Only **you** really know what things you are looking for, and what things you want to avoid if possible, in your next job or career. If anyone else does it for you, *they'll cut corners*. This is **your** life; no one else has as much interest in making it work, as you do.

2. You need the self-confidence that comes to you as you practice this researching. You need it **before** you go after the organizations that interest you.

3. The skills you use to **find** a job are close to the skills you use **to do** the job, after you get it. Therefore, by doing all this research you are increasing your qualifications for the job itself. Thus, this conclusion: the more research you do, the more qualifications you will have for the job.

It is you yourself who **must** do it. **Can** you do it?

Surrrrrre you can.

SHYNESS VS. LOVE

Of course, just because I say that, doesn't necessarily mean you'll believe it. Many of us, when we go about job-hunting or changing careers, are sure that we have some handicap no one else in the world has. The favorite is -- you guessed it -- *shyness.* To be sure, some of us are willing to acknowledge that there are other shy people in the world; but we feel that our case is different. We have *Terminal Shyness.*

Well me too. Yet our records show that terminally-shy people have done **very** effective job-hunts, and very effective research during this "WHERE?" phase. Wanna know why?

It's simple. Shyness always yields in the face of Love. If you **love** gardens, you will forget all about your shyness when you're talking to someone else about gardens and flowers. If you **love** movies, you'll forget all about your shyness when you're talking to someone else about movies. If you **love** computers, then you will forget all about your shyness when you're talking to someone else about computers. (*Puh-leeze* don't drop me a line telling me that grammatically you can't **love** gardens, movies, computers, etc.; you can only love *people.* We both know what I mean.)

So, your shyness should be no obstacle **if** you have taken time to fill in the Flower Diagram in Appendix A FIRST. **For if you did, what you are now going out to explore is *something you just love.*** If this is your dream job, you will be **very** excited about finding it. If you **aren't** very excited about finding it, you need to rethink whether this is really your dream job that you've got on that Flower Diagram. Or did you try to "cut it down" to what you thought was really available out there? Get back to your true dream! Be *dying* to find it! And then as you go out, your shyness will not bother you.

Do remember this simple truth: your shyness is **your** servant. You are not its servant. Make it serve you. Put on your best clothes, stand tall and straight, shoulders back, and get out there. Conduct yourself as quietly confident that you would be an asset to any organization that you ultimately decide to serve. You will be, indeed. The thoroughness with which you're doing your job-hunting research, shows **that.**

THE PRACTICE JUST FOR PLEASURE

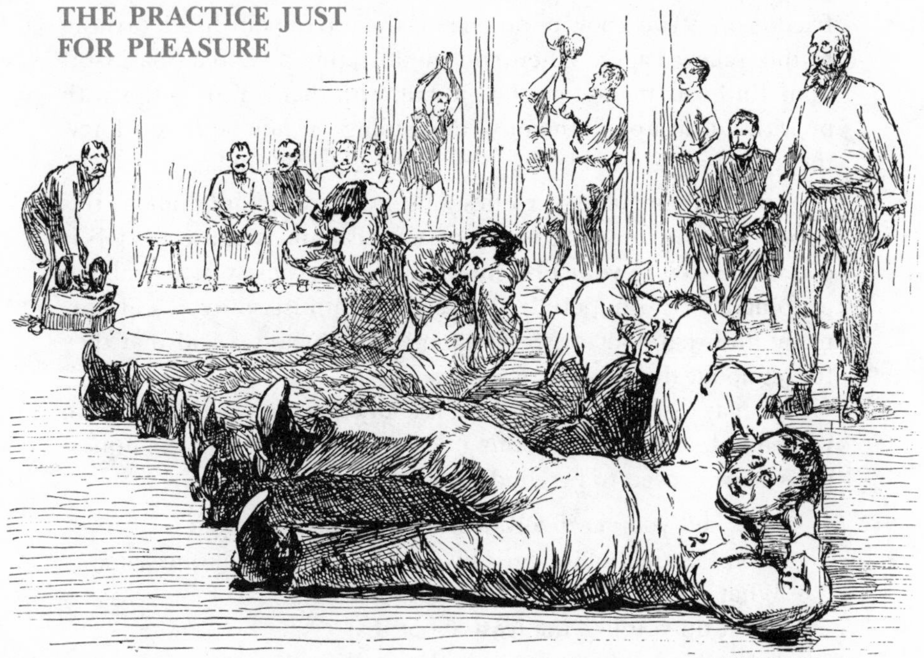

It will help you **a lot** if, before you start your research, you do some Practice first. John Crystal, back in 1972, invented an exercise which he called "The Practice Field Survey." **The purpose of this exercise is simply to get people comfortable about going out and talking to other people, by giving them something that is a pleasure to go out and talk with other people about.**

He suggested that if you are too shy to start doing research on your Flower Diagram (your ideal job/your Principles of Exclusion for cutting down the job-market), **you should practice first on a non-job-related enthusiasm of yours,** that you get great pleasure out of talking about. For example:

- a hobby, *such as skiing, bridge playing, exercise, computers, etc.*
- a curiosity, *such as how do they predict the weather*

- an aspect of the town or city you live in, *such as a new shopping mall that just opened*
- an issue you feel strongly about, *such as the homeless, AIDS sufferers, ecology, peace, health, etc.*
- or any other non-job-related enthusiasm of yours, *such as a movie you just saw, that you liked a lot*

Once you've identified this enthusiasm, you try to find Someone Else that you think *might* share your enthusiasm -- using your friends or, if you know of no one off the top of your head, turning to the Yellow Pages. When you identify this potential Sharer-of-Your-Enthusiasm, you go then to talk with them. You do this with or without an appointment -- depending on how well you know them, or how accessible they are to the general public.

You ask them whatever questions are on your mind about this hobby, curiosity, aspect, issue, or enthusiasm. Because no job is connected to it **in your present plans**, and because you are talking to someone who hopefully shares your enthusiasm, you will normally find that you forget all about your shyness. (And that they forget about **theirs**.)

You may discuss **anything** and ask **any questions** which come to your mind. However, if nothing occurs to you, the following questions have proved to be good conversation starters:

- How did you get involved with / become interested in this? ("*This*" is the hobby, curiosity, aspect, issue, or enthusiasm.)
- What do you like the most about it?
- What do you like the least about it?
- Who else would you suggest I go talk to that shares the same interest?
- Can I use your name?
- May I tell them you recommended that I talk to them?
- Then, choosing one person off the list of several names they may have given you, you say, Well, I think I will begin by going to talk to this person. Would you be willing to call ahead, so they will know who I am when I go over there?

Then go see that person. And then the next. If you need some support when you first go out to try this, **it's perfectly okay to take someone with you** -- at *this* stage of the job-hunt. Alone or with someone, **keep at this**, until you feel very much at ease in talking with people and asking them questions about things you are curious about. It may take your seeing four people. It may take ten. Or twenty. You'll know.

When you feel comfortable doing this, and it's easy to talk to people about topics in which you take great pleasure, then you are ready for:

THE REAL THING: RESEARCHING OR INFORMATIONAL INTERVIEWING

Here you are into full-blown research or information-gathering on your Flower Diagram in Appendix A. I'll give you an overview, and then we'll tackle the steps one by one. *First, the overview*: during this phase of your job-hunt or career-change, your research has Four Steps. You are trying to find the answers to four questions:

1. What are the names of jobs that would use my strongest and most enjoyable skills and fields of knowledge?

2. What kinds of organizations have such jobs?

3. What are the names of the organizations that I particularly like, among those uncovered in Question #2?

4. What needs do they have or what outcomes are they trying to produce, that my skills could help with?

Now to these Four Questions in detail, one by one. We'll start, of course, with the first.

The First Step In Your Research:

1	What are the names of jobs that would use my strongest and most enjoyable skills and fields of knowledge?

Remember what's going on here. **You are genuinely curious to find out what there is out there that matches your Flower/Ideal Job.** This is **not** just a clever ploy to get in to see employers. In fact, it is not employers you go to see *at all* during this stage of your job-hunt. You go to see **workers who are actually doing the work you think you might like to do**.

In effect, what you are doing here is **trying on jobs to see if they fit you**. It is exactly analogous to your going to a clothing store and trying on different suits (or dresses) that you see in their window. Except instead of suits, it is jobs you are trying on. And why? Well, the suits that look terrific in the window don't always look so terrific when you see them on you. They don't hang quite right, etc., etc. Likewise, the jobs that look so terrific in the books or in your imagination don't always look so terrific when you see them up close, in all their true reality.

To be sure you understand what you are doing here in these **Information or Research Interviews**, let me emphasize how these differ from the **Practice Interview** (which you just did purely for pleasure) and the **Employment Interview** (which you are not ready for, yet). To explain these differences, study the following two diagrams which were put together by the job-hunting expert in Europe, Daniel Porot. I use them with his kind permission.

After studying (and I do mean *studying*) these two diagrams, hopefully you are clear about what you're doing during *this* phase of your job-hunt or career-change:

- You are doing the "I" in the "PIE."
- You are doing Research or Informational Interviewing.
- You are primarily interviewing **workers** doing the work you think *you* might like to do -- and when you are not doing *that*, you are interviewing **sources of information**, such as librarians, or poring over **directories** in libraries, such as the *Dictionary of Occupational Titles*.
- You are "trying on" jobs to see if they fit.

Initial:	Pleasure **P**	Information **I**	Employment **E**
Kind of Interview	Practice Field Survey	Informational Interviewing or Researching	Employment Interview or Hiring Interview
Purpose	To Get Used to Talking with People to Enjoy It; To "Penetrate" Networks	To Find Out If You'd Like a Job, Before You Go Trying to Get It	To Get Hired for the Work You Have Decided You Would Most Like to Do
How You Go to the Interview	You Can Take Somebody with You	By Yourself or You Can Take Somebody with You	By Yourself
Who You Talk To	Anyone Who Shares Your Enthusiasm About a (for You) Non-Job-Related Subject	A Worker Who Is Doing the Actual Work You Are Thinking About Doing	An Employer Who Has the Power to Hire You for the Job You Have Decided You Would Most Like to Do
How Long a Time You Ask For	10 Minutes (and DON'T run over -- asking to see them at 11:50 may help keep you honest, since most employers have lunch appointments at noon)	Ditto	
What You Ask Them	Any Curiosity You Have About Your Shared Interest or Enthusiasm	Any Questions You Have About This Job or This Kind of Work	You Tell Them What It Is You Like About Their Organization and What Kind of Work You Are Looking For.

	Pleasure	Information	Employment
Initial:	P	I	E
What You Ask Them *(continued)*	If Nothing Occurs to You, Ask: 1. How did you start, with this hobby, interest, etc.? 2. What excites or interests you the most about it? 3. What do you find is the thing you like the least about it? 4. Who else do you know of who shares this interest, hobby or enthusiasm, or could tell me more about my curiosity? a. Can I go and see them? b. May I mention that it was you who suggested I see them? c. May I say that you recommended them? ***Get their name and address***	If Nothing Occurs to You, Ask: 1. How did you get interested in this work and how did you get hired? 2. What excites or interests you the most about it? 3. What do you find is the thing you like the least about it? 4. Who else do you know of who does this kind of work, or similar work but with this difference: ____________? 5. What kinds of challenges or problems do you have to deal with in this job? 6. What skills do you need in order to meet those challenges or problems? ***Get their name and address***	 You tell them the kinds of challenges you like to deal with. What skills you have to deal with those challenges. What experience you have had in dealing with those challenges in the past.
AFTERWARD: That Same Night	SEND A THANK YOU NOTE	SEND A THANK YOU NOTE	SEND A THANK YOU NOTE

WHY THIS RESEARCH MAKES SENSE EVEN IF YOU'RE LOOKING FOR THE SAME KIND OF WORK YOU'VE ALWAYS DONE

I am sure you will see the sense of all this research **if you are plotting a career-change.** You are by definition switching from a job you knew well to some other job or career that you don't know at all. Naturally, you want to find out all the attractive possibilities that lie before you -- which would fit your Flower Diagram in Appendix A. Naturally you want to find out what's good about each possibility, and what's bad about it. So, in the case of a contemplated career-change, this sort of research obviously makes a lot of sense. "Look before you leap."

You may not see the sense of all this, however, if all you're doing is going out looking for just the kind of job you always have done. *What's the point?* Well, the point is this:

(1) You don't know that you will be able to find the same kind of work you used to do; those sorts of jobs may all be taken. Or they may be slowly vanishing off the face of the earth, replaced by technology or whatever. So, **you've got to have a Plan B**.

(2) You don't know that the same kind of work you used to do would be the most fulfilling for you. Maybe you can find something more fulfilling, that even pays better, this time around. This job-hunt could be your ticket to freedom. It's worth taking the time and effort to find out if there is something better out there, for you.

"WE'RE OFF TO SEE THE WORKERS . . ."

How do you decide **who** to go see? That's easy. You will go back to the Flower Diagram once you have filled it out, in Appendix A.

On a separate sheet of paper, then, copy down your favorite Transferable Skills (the center of the Flower Diagram) and your favorite Fields of Knowledge (the bottom petal). Now, show this list to all your family and friends, and ask them what jobs come to mind, that they think would use such Skills and such Knowledges.

You can also ask them where they think you would find the people who do those kinds of jobs (**the workers**).

I repeat, only because countless job-hunters and career-changers have experienced some confusion here no matter how many times one repeats this: **at this stage of your research you are not interested in talking to employers, or people who have the power to hire. Rather, you are only interested in talking to people who are actually doing the work that you think you might enjoy doing.** You are trying to find out if this job fits you; you are trying to find out if this job fits the Ideal Job that you depicted on your Flower Diagram.

Toward this end, the questions you will find most useful to ask of the workers you interview are:

1. **How did you get into this work?**

"I used to ask myself,
'What can I do to help my fellow man?' but
I couldn't think of anything that wouldn't have put me
to considerable inconvenience."

2. **What do you like the most about it?**
3. **What do you like the least about it?**
4. **And, where else could I find people who do this kind of work?** (OR, if you have discovered from this interview that this kind of job definitely turns you off, then you ask them for ideas as to who you could go talk to about the other kinds

of work your friends/family suggested fit your Flower Diagram.) Then you go visit the people they suggest.

You should always ask them for more than one name, so that if you run into a dead end at any point, you can easily go back and visit the other people they suggested.

"SAVING TIME, SAVING MONEY, SCREENING OUT JOBS *BEFORE* WE'RE HIRED"

Please don't think you're doing something screwy, by undertaking this interviewing. **Everybody screens out jobs; it's just that most of them do it after they're hired.** In a survey done in the San Francisco Bay Area it was found that of those people placed in jobs by the U.S. Employment Service, 57% of them were not in that job just thirty days later. Granted that some of them probably only wanted work for a few days, it is still true that many *must* have tried out the job and found out that they didn't like it -- it just didn't fit them. *But, in order to find this out, they had to go through all the hassle of searching for that job, convincing the boss that they were right for that job, taking that job, starting work, telling all their friends that they had found a job, and then finding to their dismay that the job didn't fit them. So they had to quit, or manipulate management into firing them. What a lot of work, for nothing!*

How much more intelligent it is to go talk to people about their jobs **before** you get hired in that line of work. How much more intelligent to find out ahead of time if the job doesn't fit you. Or if it does! This is what you are doing with your interviewing of *workers who are doing work you think you might like to do, at places where you might like to work;* this is what you are doing with the "I" in the PIE phase.

"MY RESEARCH KEEPS GETTING BETTER ALL THE TIME"

As you go about this phase of your research, you will discover that the separate and distinct parts of your Flower Diagram/Ideal Job begin to fit together.

As you go about this phase of your research, you will also discover that you are becoming better and better at figuring out who can give you the information you need.

To illustrate these two points, let us suppose that you have discovered from your Flower Diagram that:

(a) you are skilled in counseling people, particularly in one-to-one situations;
(b) you are well versed in psychiatry; and
(c) you love carpentry and plants.

How do these three separate ideas start to come together as one unified career?

Well, **that** depends on your becoming better and better at figuring out who can give you the information that you need. To do that you begin by translating each of the skills, knowledges or interests you have, into a corresponding **person**. In this particular case, Counseling = a counselor, psychiatry = a psychiatrist, carpentry = a carpenter, plants = a gardener.

Next, ask yourself which of these persons is most likely **to have the largest overview?** This is often, but not always, the same as asking: who took the longest to get their training? The particular answer here: the psychiatrist.

In the place where you presently are, then, plan to go see a psychiatrist (pay them for fifteen minutes of their time, if there is no other way) or go see the head of the psychiatry department at the nearest college or university, and ask them: Do you have any idea how to put all the above together in a job? And if you don't, who might?

In this particular case, you will eventually be told: "Yes, it can all be put together. There is a branch of psychiatry that uses plants to help heal people. You can use all your skills and interests. You can even use your carpentry to build planters for those plants."

You keep at this sort of interviewing until you find some jobs out there that closely resemble or are identical to the Dream Job you described on your Flower Diagram. Once you have begun to get a pretty good idea of what jobs interest you the most, because they use your favorite Skills and your favorite Fields of Knowledge, you are ready for:

The Second Step in Your Research:

2 What kinds of organizations have such jobs?

You will of course have already stumbled upon some of this information, while you were going about interviewing workers whose jobs you thought you might like to have. When you talked with them, usually at their place of business, you got to know that type of business, **and** they may have told you of other types of businesses where such jobs exist.

But now it is time to focus your research solely on this issue. You want to find out all **the different kinds** of organizations you might consider, in looking for the jobs that most closely matched your Ideal Job/Flower Diagram, during Step One of your research here.

To give you an example of what I mean, suppose you found out during Step One that the job of teacher comes closest to your Ideal Job. Now, to our question: what **kinds** of organizations have such jobs? The answer is not what you might first suppose: "*just schools.*" No, no, my friend, not just schools. There are countless other kinds of organizations and agencies out there which have a teaching arm, and therefore employ teachers. For example, corporate training and educational departments, workshop sponsors, foundations, private research firms, educational consultants, teachers' associations, professional and trade societies, military bases, state and local councils on higher education, fire and police training academies, and so on, and so forth. You want to discover **all** such places. Your local town or city librarian can be a great help.

If during Step One of this research you found there were four different jobs that seemed close to your Ideal Job/Flower Diagram, you will now need to discover all the kinds of places that have such jobs, **in each of the four cases.**

"Kinds of places" means many things, such as:

- places that would employ you full-time;
- places that would employ you part-time (maybe you'll end up deciding to hold down two or even three part-time jobs, which altogether would add up to one full-time job, in order to give yourself more variety);

- places which you yourself would start up, **if** you want to be your own boss;
- places that are for profit;
- places that are nonprofit;
- places that take temporary workers, on assignment for one project at a time;
- places that take consultants, one project at a time;
- places that operate with volunteers, etc.

Needless to say, you should plan on devoting a number of days to this Step of your research. **Since, above entry-level, the average job-hunt typically may last five or six months, you've got the time, believe me.** Stay with the research as long as it is really fun. You want to find everything that is in the deck of cards called the job-market. Remember, Confucius says: "Never choose a card, except from a full deck."

WRITTEN STUFF AND PEOPLE

If you are a normal job-hunter or career-changer, you will find that during this Step (and the next two Steps, as well) of your research or Informational interviewing, you will be dealing *alternately* with:

written materials -- such as books, journals, magazines, or other materials which librarians can direct you to -- and with

people, who can tell you what you need to know.

In general, the pattern is: you **read**, until you need some information that no book seems to have. Then you go **talk** to people until you have found out what you needed to know. Back then to do some more reading.

I caution you to do as much reading as you possibly can before you go and visit people. As a general rule, **people who have jobs are busy people and usually do not appreciate answering questions that you could just as easily have looked up in some directory, book, or annual report.** On the other hand, they are usually *glad* to answer questions whose answers cannot be found in any printed materials.

HOW TO RECEIVE A CORDIAL WELCOME

You will normally be accorded a cordial welcome by most people you go to see for information. That is obviously true in a small organization with easy public access (like a Mom-and-Pop grocery store). If you run into a real grumpy person, seek elsewhere for your information. If your information hunt takes you to larger organizations, here are some things to keep in mind. You will be given a **cordial** welcome in most large organizations:

a. **provided** that you know what questions you are trying to find answers to, and the answers can't easily be found in printed materials, microfiche, or on disk.

b. **provided** that you approach no organization until you've first gotten your hands on everything they've got in print, about who they are and what they do -- and provided that you've thoroughly digested this stuff before you go in to see them.

c. **provided** that when it is time for you to approach people, you approach first of all those people whose business it is to give out information to the public, and find out everything they know about the questions or curiosities that are plaguing you. I am thinking of such people as the front desk in personnel offices, receptionists, public relations officers, librarians, and the like.

d. **provided** that when you approach an organization, you talk to those in lesser authority first, to find out everything that they

know, before you approach someone higher up in the same organization. The principle here is that you only approach people for the information they alone know. Incidentally, visiting a senior person in that organization unannounced ("I just happened to be in the neighborhood") is universally perceived as the conduct of an amateur. If you would like to be seen as a professional, make an appointment; and state at that time that you only need a brief amount of their time (twenty minutes, max), plus **what it is that you are trying to find out.** Someone else may have the information you are looking for, and they will tell you so over the phone, thus saving you from a fruitless errand.

WHEN IT COMES TO BOOKS, WHAT KINDS OF BOOKS WILL LIKELY PROVE USEFUL?

The kinds of books that you will likely find useful to you at this stage of your research, as well as subsequently, are in the following list. Note that many of these resources are much too expensive for the average job-hunter to purchase, but fortunately most of them are to be found down at your local public library, or business library.

Some of you will look at the list below, and toss up your hands. *Too much!* Well, you don't need to use *all* of the directories listed below. Just those that will help you with what you are trying to find out. Suppose you're trying to find out what are all the kinds of organizations that use teachers. There are three ways to go about this:

1. Go to your helpful local librarian and tell him or her what you're looking for, and ask what directories they think would help. See what they suggest.

2. If there's no librarian, or no *helpful* librarian, then look over the list below and take a stab at what directories you think might have the information you're looking for.

3. If you are absolutely baffled as to which directory to consult, there are *(mercifully)* indexes to all these directories. See:

- *Klein's Guide to American Directories*

  or
- *Directories in Print, 1990*, 7th ed. Gale Research Inc., which contains over 10,000 current listings of directories, indexed by title or key word or subject (over 3,500 subject headings).

A SAMPLER OF INFORMATION SOURCES for You, the Job-Hunter or Career-Changer, To Use

(Before you consult these, write out on a piece of paper, for your own use, "This is the information I am trying to find out: ____________.")

American Men and Women of Science.

American Society of Training and Development Directory.
Who's Who in Training and Development, Suite 305, 600 Maryland Ave. SW, Washington, DC 20024.

Better Business Bureau report on a particular organization that you may be interested in (call the BBB in the city where the organization is located).

Business Information Sources, by Lorna M. Daniels.
University of California Press, Berkeley, CA 94720.
Annotated guide to business books and reference sources.

Career Guide to Professional Associations. Garrett Park Press, Garrett Park, MD 20896.

Chamber of Commerce data on an organization or field that interests you (visit the Chamber in the appropriate city or town).

College library (especially business school library), if there is one in your chosen area.

Company/college/association/agency/foundation *Annual Reports.* Get these directly from the personnel department or publicity person at the company, etc., or from the Chamber or your local library.

Consultants and Consulting Organizations Directory 1988, 8th ed. Gale Research Inc. Lists over 12,000 firms, individuals and organizations engaged in consulting work. Consultants are usually experts in their particular field, and hence may be useful to you in your information search about that job or career-change that you are contemplating.

Contacts Influential: Commerce and Industry Directory.
Businesses in particular market area listed by name, type of business, key personnel, etc. Contacts Influential, Market

Research and Development Services, 321 Bush St., Suite 203, San Francisco, CA 94104, if your library doesn't have it.

Corporate and Industry Research Reports. Published by J. A. Micropublishing Inc., in Eastchester, N.Y. Can be very helpful.

Dictionary of Holland Occupational Codes.

Dictionary of Occupational Titles.

Directory of American Research and Technology: Organizations Active in Product Development for Business. R. R. Bowker Co., 205 E. 42nd St., New York, NY 10017.

Directory of Corporate Affiliations. National Register Publishing Co., Inc.

Directory of Information Resources in the United States. (Physical Sciences, Engineering, Biological Sciences) Washington, DC. Library of Congress.

Directory of Special Libraries and Information Centers 1988, 11th ed. Gale Research Inc. Lists 18,600 research facilities, on various subjects, maintained by libraries, research libraries, businesses, nonprofit organizations, governmental agencies, etc. Detailed subject index, using over 3,500 key words.

Dun & Bradstreet's Million Dollar Directory. Very helpful.

Dun & Bradstreet's Reference Book of Corporate Managements.

Encyclopedia of Associations 1989. Vol. 1, National Organizations of the U.S.; Vol. 2, Geographic and Executive Indexes; Vol. 3, New Associations and Projects. Gale Research Inc., Book Tower, Dept. 77748, Detroit, MI 48277-0748. Lists 22,000 organizations, associations, clubs and other nonprofit membership groups that are in the business of giving out information. This is complemented by their book: *Regional, State and Local Organizations 1988–1989*, which lists over 50,000 similar organizations on a regional, state or local level.

Encyclopedia of Business Information Sources, 6th ed. Gale Research Inc. Identifies electronic, print and live resources dealing with 1,100 business subjects. Their companion volume is entitled *Business Organizations, Agencies and Publications Directory*, listing over 24,000 entries, such as federal government advisory organizations, newsletters, research services, etc.

Encyclopedia of Information Systems and Services 1988. 8th ed. Gale Research Inc. Lists 30,000 computer-based information systems and services, here and abroad. Their companion volume, *Computers and Computing Information Resources Directory*,

1st ed., lists trade shows, conventions, users' groups, associations, consultants, etc., worldwide.

F & S Indexes (recent articles on firms).

F & S Index of Corporations and Industries.
Lists "published articles" by industry and by company name. Updated weekly.

Fitch Corporation Manuals.

Fortune Magazine's 500.

The Foundation Directory.

How to Reach Anyone Who's Anyone, by Michael Levine. Price/Stern/Sloan, 360 N. La Cienega Blvd., Los Angeles, CA 90048.

How To Read A Financial Report: Wringing Cash Flow and Other Vital Signs Out of the Numbers. 3rd ed., by John A. Tracy, CPA. John Wiley & Sons, Business Law/General Books Division, 605 Third Avenue, New York, NY 10158-0012. Also Chichester, Brisbane, Toronto and Singapore.

International Business Travel and Relocation Directory, 5th ed. Gale Research Inc. It presents all the relevant details for every country in the world. There is a companion volume, *International Organizations 1988*. This lists 4,000 international organizations, concerned with various subjects.

Investor, Banker, Broker Almanac.

Macmillan's Directory of Leading Private Companies.

MacRae's Blue Book.

Moody's Industrial Manual (and other Moody manuals).

National Business Telephone Directory. Gale Research Inc. In one single alphabetical listing, contains phone numbers, address and city for over 350,000 business and industrial establishments that have more than 20 employees. Particularly useful when you know the name of an organization, but not what city or state it is located in.

National Directory of Addresses and Telephone Numbers. Concord Reference Books, 240 Fenel Lane, Hillside, IL 60162.

National Recreational Sporting and Hobby Organizations of the U.S. Columbia Books, Inc., 777 14th St. NW, Washington, DC 20005.

National Trade and Professional Associations of the United States and Canada and Labor Unions. Garrett Park Press, Garrett Park, MD 20896.

Newsletters Directory, 4th ed. Gale Research, Inc. Detailed entry on 10,000 newsletters in various subject fields, or categories. It includes newsletters that are available only on-line, through a computer and modem. There is a companion volume, *Association Periodicals*, 1st ed., which lists 12,000 newsletters, periodicals and journals put out by national associations in particular.

Occupational Outlook Handbook.

Occupational Outlook Handbook for College Graduates.

Register of manufacturers for your state or area (e.g., *California Manufacturers Register*).

Research Centers Directory 1988, 12th ed. Gale Research Inc. Also: *Research Services Directory*, 3rd ed. The two volumes together cover some 13,000 services, facilities, and companies that do research into various subjects, such as feasibility studies, private and public policy, social studies and studies of various cultures, etc.

Standard and Poor's Corporation Records.

Standard and Poor's Industrial Index.

Standard and Poor's Industry Surveys. Good basic introduction, history, and overview of any industry you may be interested in.

Standard and Poor's Listed Stock Reports (at some brokers' offices).

Standard and Poor's Register of Corporations, Directors and Executives. Key executives in 32,000 leading companies, plus 75,000 directors.

Standard Industrial Classification Manual, 1985. Published by the U.S. Government Printing Office. Gives the Standard Industrial Classification code number for any field or industry -- which is the number used by most business references in their indices.

Statistics Sources 1988, 11th ed. Gale Research Inc. Tells you where to find statistics on more than 20,000 specific topics. Key live sources are also featured.

Telecommunications Systems and Services Directory, 3rd ed. Gale Research Inc. Lists over 2,000 national and international firms dealing with communications systems, teleconferencing, videotext, electronic mail, fax services, etc.

Telephone Contacts for Data Users. Customer Services Branch, Bureau of the Census, 301-449-1600, for statistical information on any subject.

Thomas' Register of American Manufacturers. Thomas Publishing Co.

Trade association periodicals.

Trade journals.

Training and Development Organizations Directory, 4th ed. Gale Research Inc. For those of you interested in teaching or training, it lists over 2,500 firms and their areas of interest and expertise.

United States Government Manual.

U.S. Industrial Outlook. Published by the U.S. Department of Commerce. Covers 350 manufacturing and service industries. Gives the trends and outlooks for each industry that you may be interested in.

Value Line Investment Survey, from Arnold Bernhard and Co., 5 E. 44th St., New York, NY 10017. (Most libraries have a set.)

Walker's Manual of Far Western Corporations and Securities.

Ward's Business Directory, 3 vols. (Vol. 1, Largest U.S. Companies; Vol. 2, Major U.S. Private Companies; Vol. 3, Major International Companies). Information Access Company, 1201 Davis Dr., Belmont, CA 94002. Updated yearly. Despite the titles, helpful in identifying smaller companies.

Who's Who in Finance and Industry, and all the other Who's Who books. Useful once you have the name of someone-who-has-the-power-to-hire, and you want to know more about them.

Besides these directories, some periodicals are worth perusing: *Business Week, Dun's Review, Forbes, Fortune,* and the *Wall Street Journal.*

For help on a question no one seems to know the answer to, try the National Referral Center at the Library of Congress, 202-287-5670. Also, you can call the Federal Information Center of the General Services Administration at 202-755-8660 to find the names of experts in any field.

Some of you will find this research tedious but necessary. Others of you will find it great fun. You will enjoy discovering how much you can find out in this "Information Society" of ours, if you just set your mind to it. If you really get into this and want to find out more about how one finds **any** information about **anything,** here are some books for you to browse at your leisure:

Todd, Alden, *Finding Facts Fast: How to Find Out What You Want and Need to Know.* Ten Speed Press, Box 7123, Berkeley, CA 94707. 1979.

Horowitz, Lois, *Knowing Where to Look: The Ultimate Guide to Research.* Writer's Digest Books, 1507 Dana Ave., Cincinnati, OH 45207. 1988.

Ferraro, Eugene, *You Can Find Anyone!* Marathon Press, 407 W. Santa Clara Ave., Santa Ana, CA 92706. 1988.

Mann, Thomas, *A Guide to Library Research Methods.* Oxford University Press, Inc., 200 Madison Ave., New York, NY 10016. 1987.

Pryor, Bill, *Secret Agent, Vol. 1.* Eden Press, Inc., P.O. Box 8410, Fountain Valley, CA 92728. 1986.

Harry, M., *The Muckraker's Manual: How to Do Your Own Investigative Reporting.* Revised and expanded. Loompanics Unlimited, Box 1197, Port Townsend, WA 98368. 1984.

Ullmann, John, with Honeyman, Steve, Ed., *The Reporter's Handbook.* St. Martin's Press, Inc., 175 Fifth Ave., New York, NY 10010. 1983.

I have gone into all of this at some length in order to show you that finding out what **kinds** of organizations have the jobs you are interested in is *not* a very difficult job. It just takes determination and persistence. Anyhow, one way or another, through people or books, once you have identified the kinds of organizations that have the kinds of jobs you are ready for:

The Third Step in Your Research:

3	What are the names of such organizations that I particularly like?

CUTTING DOWN THE NUMBER OF ORGANIZATIONS

Your problem here is that you must first of all cut down the territory. The kinds of organizations may total some twenty-five or thirty, and the list of the names of organizations which are of those thirty kinds may total 2,000. You can't go visit 2,000 organizations. So your task will be much more manageable if before you start collecting names, you first look over your list of organizations that have your Ideal Dream Job, and cross out **the kinds of organizations you don't like.** Here are some questions that may help you do this:

• 1. "Do I want to do the same kind of work I've always done, or do I want to start a new career now?"

• 2. "Do I want to work for somebody else, or would I rather start my own business at this time of my life?"

• 3. "If I want to start my own business, who among the people I visited would be the best models, as to how my own business should be set up?" You will need to go back and talk to them, to pick their brains for everything they're worth.

• 4. "Do I want to hold down just one job, or have several part-time jobs?" If you are interested in several part-time jobs, you might want to look at temporary agencies; they exist for many different fields now, not just for secretaries (as in days of old).

• 5. "If I choose to work for somebody else, do I want to work for a large organization or a small one?"

• 6. "Do I want to work for an older and larger organization, or get in on the ground floor of a new and smaller one, with growth possibilities?" If you're in an area where hiring is "tight," look long and hard at the new and smaller organizations. It's true that their failure rate is high; but it's also true that that's where two-thirds of all new jobs get created -- in businesses with twenty or less employees.

• 7. "Do I want to work for a profit-making company, a nonprofit firm, agency, college, association, foundation, small business, the government, or what?"

• 8. "Do I want to work for a 'going concern' or for 'a problem child' type of operation?" As the experts say, a company in trouble is a company in search of leadership. The same goes for foundations, agencies, etc. If that is your cup of tea (well, is it?), you can probably find such places without too much investigation. Some experts say if you go for such a challenge, give yourself a time limit, say three to five years, and then if you can't solve it, get out. The average job in this country only lasts 5.2 years, anyway. If your goal is to advance rapidly, you'll probably need to look at an organization with solid plans for expansion -- overseas or at home.

• 9. *Other questions*: "What do I want to accomplish with my skills? what working circumstances do I want? what opportunities? what responsibilities? what kinds of job pressures am I willing to exist under, and do I feel capable of handling? what kinds of people do I want to work with? starting salary? salary five years from now? promotion opportunities?"

DON'T TRY TO STAY VAGUE AND 'WIDE-OPEN' TO 'ANYTHING THAT COMES ALONG'

As you undoubtedly realize by now, **the more you can cut the territory down, the easier it will be to conduct your job-hunt. And the more detailed you are, the easier it will be for you to cut the territory down, and find the names of organizations that truly interest you.** Conversely, the less specific you are willing to be, the harder it will be for you to find the names of specific organizations which might hire you for the job you most want.

For example, let us see how two of the exercises you will be doing for your Flower Diagram/Ideal Job, in Appendix A, can be of particular relevance and helpfulness, at this point: General Physical Setting (i.e., Geography), and Specific Physical Setting (i.e., Working Conditions).

Geography, for one, can save you from saying, "I'm looking for the names of organizations which hire welders," which is much too broad. Suppose the San Jose area of California is your preferred physical setting for your future Ideal Job. You will be helped by your Geography statements then to a statement which cuts your job-hunting area down to a more manageable size, such as: "I'm looking for the names of organizations in the San Jose area which hire welders."

Your preferred **Working Conditions** will further aid you in cutting down the territory. If you stated that you preferred to work for an organization with fifty or less employees, then you add this to your statement, so that it now reads: "I'm looking for the names of organizations having fifty or less employees which hire welders, in the San Jose area."

If, on top of this, you throw in other statements from your Flower Diagram or your earlier research, your task will get easier still. Suppose you decided you want to work for an organization which produces wheels. Then your statement gets further modified, to: "I'm looking for the names of organizations in the San Jose area, which produce wheels, hire welders, and have fifty or less employees." Now, you're talking! That's a manageable area in which to do your job-search!

CONTACTS, CONTACTS, CONTACTS USE THOSE CONTACTS!

Once you're able to say just exactly and most specifically what **kinds** of organizations you want to find, how do you go about discovering their **names**?

Well, you know: the same kind of research that you've been doing. You use books, and people, people and books.

In this quest for names, you use every **contact** that you have. That means members of your family. Every friend. Your relatives. Your doctor, dentist, gas station attendant (a vanishing race), and the check-out clerk at your supermarket. **Everyone** you meet, anywhere, during the week.

They can not only tell you names of organizations, they often know what's going on at those places.

You see, to do your job-hunt well, you need to be in twenty places at once, with your eyes and ears wide open. And you just can't be. But your contacts can -- **if** they know what you are looking for, and **if** you have enlisted them to keep their eyes and ears open on your behalf.

Whenever a job-hunter writes me and tells me they've run into a brick wall, as far as finding out the names of organizations is concerned, I know what the problem will usually turn out to be. They aren't making sufficient use of their contacts. **The more people you know, the more people you meet, the more people you talk to, the more people you enlist as part of your own personal job-hunting network, the better your job-finding success is likely to be.**

Now, to be sure, your memory is going to be overloaded during your job-hunt or career-change, so do keep the names of your contacts on 3×5 file cards with addresses, phone numbers, and anything about where they work or who they know that may be of use at a later date. Go back over those cards **frequently.**

Some job-hunters have written to tell me they cultivate new contacts wherever they go. For example, if they go to hear a speaker on some subject that interests them, they make it a point to join the crowd that gathers 'round the speaker at the end of the talk, and -- with notepad poised -- ask such questions as: "Is there anything special that people with my technical expertise can do?" And here they mention their specialty: computer scientist, health professional, chemist, writer, or whatever. Very useful information has thus been turned up. You can also ask if you can contact the speaker for further information -- "and at what address?" Conventions, likewise, afford rich opportunities to make contacts. Says one college graduate: "I snuck into the Cable Advertisers Convention at the Waldorf in N.Y.C. That's how I got my job."

Another way people have gathered contacts, is -- if they have a phone answering machine -- to leave a message on that machine which tells everyone who calls that they are looking for work. One job-hunter used the following message: "This is the recently laid off John Smith. I'm not home right now because I'm out looking for a good job in the telecommunications field; if you have any leads or just want to leave a message, please leave it after the tone."

You may also find contacts by studying the *things* that you like to work with, and then writing to the manufacturer of that *thing* to ask them for a list of organizations in your geographical area which use that *thing*. For example, if you like to work on a particular machine, you would write to the manufacturer of that machine, and ask for names of organizations in your geographical area which use that machine. Some manufacturers will not be at all responsive to such an inquiry; but others will, and may give you some very helpful leads or contacts.

A CAUTIONARY WORD: CHECK AND CROSS-CHECK

In gathering information from people, one person's word should rarely be taken as gospel. There are people who will tell you something that absolutely isn't so, but they will tell it to you with every conviction in their being because **they think** it's true. Sincerity they have, one hundred percent. Accuracy is something else again. You will need to check and cross-check any information that people tell you or that you read in books (even this one).

For example, if someone tells you that the only way you can get into a certain kind of job is to have had fourteen years of post-high-school education, make a quiet mental note to check it out. "*It ain't necessarily so. . . .*" Your response, while you're still talking to that person, should be, "Yes, but do you know of **anyone** who got into this kind of job **without** having had all that education?"

Anyway, be careful. Be thorough. Be persistent. This is your life you're working on, and your future. Make it glorious. Whatever it takes, find out the names of those organizations. That will bring you, then, to:

The Fourth and Last Step in Your Research:

4	What needs do they have or what outcomes are they trying to produce, that my skills could help with?

"Needs" is a polite word. So is **"challenges."** You know what we're **really** talking about here. We're talking about:

AN ORGANIZATION'S PROBLEMS

All organizations have some success. What you want to do is increase their success. What you are looking for are their problems -- specifically, problems that your skills can help solve. What problems are bugging this organization? Ask; look. But you should probably avoid direct use of the word 'problems' since few organizations like to admit to outsiders that they have any problems.

ANALYZING AN ORGANIZATION'S PROBLEMS

☐ If it's a decent-sized company, send for (or go pick up) their annual report to stockholders; granted it's a public relations piece, it still may help quite a bit. If the organization is too small to have an annual report, get whatever pamphlets they have, describing their work. Also, use your contacts to try to find people who know a lot about them. Then, after studying what you find out, you will want to weigh the following questions:

IF IT IS A LARGE COMPANY:

☐ How does this organization rank within its field, or industry? Is this organization family owned? If so, what effect has that on promotions? Where are its plants, offices or branches? What are all its projects or services? In what ways have they grown in recent years? New lines, new products, new processes, new facilities, etc.? Existing political situations: imminent proxy fights, upcoming mergers, etc.? What is the general image of the organization in people's minds? If the organization sells stock, what has been happening to it (see an investment broker and ask).

QUESTIONS TO BE ASKING YOURSELF REGARDLESS OF THE COMPANY'S SIZE:

☐ What kind of *turnover of staff* have they had? What is the attitude of employees toward the organization? If you've been there, are their faces happy, strained, or what? Is promotion generally from within, or from outside? How long has the chief executive been with the organization?

☐ Do they encourage their employees to further their educational training? Do they help them pay for it?

☐ How do *communications* work within the organization? How is information collected, and by what paths does it flow? What methods are used to see that information gets results – to what authority do people respond there? Who reports to whom?

☐ Is there a "time-bomb" – a problem that will kill the organization, or drastically reduce its effectiveness and efficiency if they don't solve it real fast?

So, if you know some people within a company or organization that looks interesting to you, ask them ever so gently: What is the biggest **challenge** you are facing there?

The problem, or challenge, does not have to be one that is bothering only **that** organization. You want to ask if there is a problem common to the whole industry or field -- low profit, obsolescence, inadequate planning, or what? Or it may be there is a problem that is common to the geographic region: labor problems, minority employment, etc. All you really need is to put your finger on one major problem that you would truly delight to help solve.

If you feel you have no skills at analyzing an organization's problems or needs, think again. Visualize five stores you have been in, where you debated whether you would ever go back. Why was that? Well, of course, because of some problem they had. And don't tell me you didn't know what the problem was. You know very well that you did, and do. You weren't waited on, when it was your proper turn. You weren't told all the information you needed to know, in order to make an intelligent purchase. The person with whom you were dealing insisted on going by the rule book, no matter what common sense and compassion would otherwise dictate. The person with whom you were dealing had some small amount of power but was misusing that power for all it was worth. The organization had installed a computer where a person used to be, and the person between you and the computer seemed to be taking orders from it, rather than vice versa. The organization had, in a word, lost the human touch. You could tick off every one of those problems. It doesn't take a genius. You saw it all. You're not blind.

All you're doing at this stage of your job-hunt is putting this old skill to a new use. You will quickly realize that you are more skilled at analyzing an organization's problems than you thought you were. All you have to do now is polish this awareness of yours.

Anyway, assuming you did the work outlined on the previous pages, you have a manageable list of specific places now that interest you, and their names. What you want to do before you go there (or back there) is to identify -- within the area, department, or tasks that interest you -- what kinds of problems you could help solve, if they hired you.

Some of this you can figure out, just by thinking, and using logical analysis. You may, for example, want to think how an unsatisfactory employee would behave in the job you are going to go after, and what problems such behavior would create. You of course intend to be just the opposite: a very competent, and enthusiastic employee, if you get that job. Therefore, you will automatically eliminate the problems that an unsatisfactory employee would cause. Just know what they are, before you ever go for an employment interview.

Beyond 'just thinking about it,' there is research. You want to go talk to every contact you have to learn as much as you can about the workings of the companies or organizations that interest you: what they are trying to accomplish, how they go about it, and -- like that.

As you go through all this intensive research concerning the places where you might like to work, two things will happen:

1. **Your list will get smaller,** as you discover some of the places that interested you **did not upon inspection turn out to have the kind of problems or difficulties that your strongest skills would enjoy solving.** Eliminate these places from your list. You would be unhappy there, even if they hired you. Know that now, and cross them off.

2. You will get to know **a great deal** about the remaining organizations which still interest you, including -- most specifically -- their problems, and what you could do to help solve them.

SELF-EMPLOYMENT, TEMPORARY WORK, VOLUNTEER WORK, INTERNSHIPS

I have, throughout this chapter, assumed that you are looking to be employed by someone else in a permanent, full-time job. That is what the vast majority of job-hunters and career-changers in this country are looking for. But *you* may be an exception. And you will then want to know how all of this chapter can be translated, so that it still is helpful to *you*.

It's not hard to make the translation. For example, if you are thinking of starting your own business, you need to go out and interview everyone you can who is running that kind of business in your broad geographical area. I say 'broad' geographical area, because it is best not to go see someone in your same town; they will only see you as potential competition, and may be very reluctant to tell you what you want to know. (There are exceptions: generous souls who cheerfully tell you all they know, because they believe that that is the only way to live. May their tribe increase!)

But if you are thinking of starting your own business in, say, Passaic, New Jersey, you would do well to conduct your informational interviewing in New York City. What you of course want to find out is: what skills and knowledges does it take to run such a business successfully? (We will call this **List A**.) Then, when you have checked and cross-checked this information, you take from the Flower Diagram the inventory of the skills and knowledges *you* already have. (We will call this **List B**.) You subtract B from A, which results in a list we shall call **List C**. List C is a list of the skills and knowledges you **don't** have; that is therefore a list of the skills and knowledges you will **have** to go out and hire, if your business is to be a success. In summary, the key to success is "A – B = C; then hire C."

When you find people running the same kind of business or organization or service that you would like to start up, you ask them (of course) the four questions that are on page 124. Later, when it comes time to think about problems, you try to think of what problems your potential clients or customers have, and then how your product/service/information would help them. Or sometimes it is a matter of researching to see **who** has the kinds of problems you are trying to solve with your product/service/information. This helps to target your marketing.

Applying the steps in this chapter to any other path that you want to follow will likewise help you immensely. That includes volunteer work, internships, temporary work (which agency should you sign up with), etc. It's just a detailed common sense application of the old refrain, "Look before you leap."

Many job-hunters **and career-changers** have found that a useful way to explore organizations is to sign up with some temporary agency. Temporary agencies, in the old days, were solely for clerical workers and secretarial help. But the field has seen an explosion of services in recent years -- according to the Bureau of Labor Statistics, temporary or part-time workers now number over 35 million in number, and represent 29% of the total civilian labor force -- and now there are temporary agencies (at least in the larger cities) for many different occupations. See your local phone book, under 'Temporary Agencies.' The advantage to you of temporary work is that if there is an agency which loans out people with your particular skills and expertise, you get a chance to visit a number of different organizations over a period of several weeks, and see each one **from the inside.** Not so coincidentally, a number of employers now use temporary agencies as a way for **them** to shop for permanent employees. Both of you get a chance to look at each other, without any long-range commitment.

YOU'LL LIKE THIS JOB, EXCEPT EVERY NOW AND THEN, WHEN THEY DUMP A LOT OF PAPER WORK ON YOU.

Another useful way to explore a field, particularly if you're new to the job-market, or contemplating a career-change to a new field, is volunteer work. Again, because you're a volunteer, it's relatively easy to get them to let you work there for a while at the target of your choice; and thus you get a chance to know them from the inside. Not so coincidentally, if you decide you would really like to work there permanently, they've had a chance to see you in action, and when you are about to end your volunteer time there, may want to hire you permanently. It has happened, very often; though you cannot absolutely count on this.

THE END OF THE 'I' IN THE 'PIE'

Well, that's it. Once you've found the answers to the four questions we've been discussing since page 119, namely,

1. WHAT ARE THE NAMES OF JOBS THAT WOULD USE MY STRONGEST AND MOST ENJOYABLE SKILLS AND FIELDS OF KNOWLEDGE?
2. WHAT KINDS OF ORGANIZATIONS HAVE SUCH JOBS?

3. WHAT ARE THE NAMES OF THE ORGANIZATIONS THAT I PARTICULARLY LIKE, AMONG THOSE UNCOVERED IN QUESTION #2? and
4. WHAT NEEDS DO THEY HAVE OR WHAT OUTCOMES ARE THEY TRYING TO PRODUCE THAT MY SKILLS COULD HELP WITH?

you're done with this phase of your job-hunt or career-change. You're done with the "WHERE?" You've defined your Ideal Job, you've discovered what out there most closely corresponds to that Ideal Job. Now you're ready for the "HOW." "How do I get that job?" But before we turn to that, in our next chapter, we have one final problem to consider here.

WHAT IF I GET OFFERED A JOB ALONG THE WAY, WHILE I'M STILL ONLY GATHERING INFORMATION

You probably won't. During this information gathering, you're not talking primarily to employers. You're talking to workers. *Do remember this, please.* Of course, an occasional employer **may** stray across your path during all this research. And that employer **may** be so impressed with the carefulness you're showing, in going about your career-change or your job-hunt, that they want to get their hands on you **immediately.** So, it's possible that you might get offered a job while you're still doing your information gathering. Not "likely" but "possible." And if that happens, what should you say?

Why, of course, you simply tell them what you're doing. You tell them that the average job-hunter tries to screen a job **after** they take it. But you are doing what you are sure this employer would do if they were in your situation: you are examining careers, fields, industries, jobs, organizations **before** you decide where you can do your best and most effective work.

You tell them that during this part of your job-hunt, it is premature for you to be thinking about accepting a job offer; you don't know where you can be most effective, until you've concluded this part of your research.

And then you add something along these lines: "Of course, I'm tickled pink that you would want me to be working here. I'm sure you understand, however, that until I've finished my survey and am clearer about where my skills could best be used, I just can't say Yes or No to your kind invitation. But, when I've finished my personal survey, I'd sure be glad to get back to you about this, as this seems to me to be the **kind** of place I'd like to work in, and the kind of people I'd like to work with."

You don't walk through any opened doors yet; but neither do you slam them shut.

A SUMMARY FOR THOSE WHO LIKE SUMMARIES

This has been a chapter filled with many ideas. Your head is swimming. You want a simple digest of the whole chapter, so you can remember it. Voila!

Job-hunting is a two-way street. For the time being, whether the places you visit during your research happen to have a vacancy, or happen to *want* you, is premature and irrelevant. In this dance of life, you get first choice: you get to decide first of all whether or not **you** want **them**. Only after you have decided that you **do** want them, is it appropriate to ask if they also want you.

You're a bunch of jackasses. You work your rear ends off in a trivial course that no one will ever care about again. You're not willing to spend time researching a company that you're interested in working for. Why don't you decide who you do want to work for and go after them?

Professor Albert Shapero (again) to his students

CHAPTER SIX

The Systematic Approach To The Job-Hunt and Career-Change:

PART III

How

Do You Find The Person Who Has The Power To Hire You For The Job That You Want?

Chapter 6

OVERVIEW OF THIS CHAPTER

How do you find the person who has the power to hire you for the job that you want? The answer, in a nutshell, is:

- through **your contacts**, and then
- through **your final research.**

But before we get into how you do that, let's look back and see where we've come, so far. As we saw back in Chapter 3, in a syste-

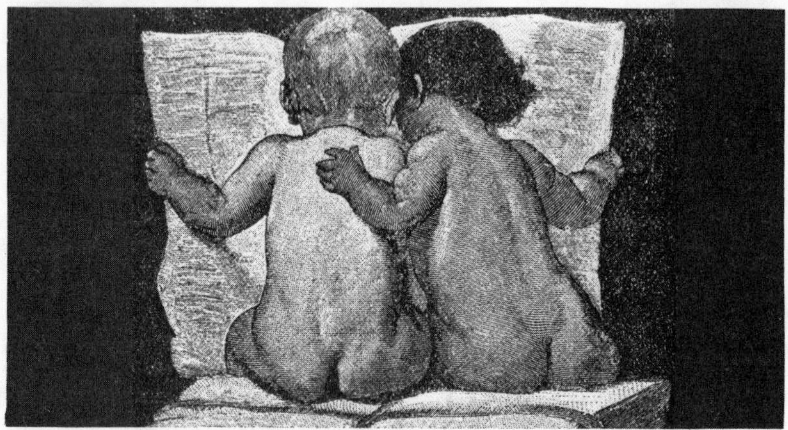

matic job-hunt or career-change there are three parts: **What**, **Where**, and **How**. You've been reading in the previous two chapters instructions for figuring out the **What**, and the **Where** -- *though you haven't actually done this yet.* And you won't do this, until you get to Appendix A.

Whatever you do, don't try to leap over Appendix A. You *must* do the paper and pencil exercises found there and have the answer firmly in your grasp *before* you can actually do the **Where** steps described in Chapter 5, or the **How** steps that I am about to describe in this chapter.

So, why read this chapter (and Chapter 5) before you do Appendix A? *Well, you know.* You want to have an overview of the whole process, so you can see what use you will make of Appendix A, once it is completed. After doing Appendix A, you will come back to Chapter 5 and then this chapter, and actually follow their directions step by step.

So let's assume that by the time you come back to this chapter, you have done Appendix A, *and* carefully followed the step-by-step instructions in Chapter 5. If so, when you turn to this chapter to follow *its* instructions, you will have already:

- found the career field you like best,
- found what kind of organization within that field appeals to you the most,
- found the names of specific organizations of that kind, that truly interest you,
- found what kinds of needs these organizations have and what sorts of problems or challenges they are facing,
- narrowed down the possible organizational targets to four or five places that stand out above all the rest, in terms of what you're looking for.

And now what will you be doing, in this chapter? Well, you will be going out and talking to ***the*** **person in each organizational target of yours who has the power to hire you**. And as Daniel Porot, the job-hunting expert in Europe puts it, you will be going not as a **"job-beggar"** but as a **"resource person."** That is to say, you will not be going there because there is something you want to beg from them; you will be going there because there is something you have to offer them, in return for a salary: your time, your brains, your hands, your skills. Here endeth our overview. Now let's get to the heart of the matter.

THE THREE 'HOW' QUESTIONS

We call this the **HOW** phase of the job-hunt, because the questions facing you here are three **HOW** questions:

1. HOW do I find out who has the power to hire me, there?
2. HOW do I get in for a job interview with that person?
3. HOW do I **convince** them that they should hire me?

The answer to the first question, as I said above, is: **"Through the research you already did, and through your contacts."** Contacts, you recall, means every single person that you meet, talk to, blunder into, stumble across, can write letters to, phone up, or whatever. It does **not** mean "just business people." It means **everyone you know.**

Let us say it is a mythical Capachin Corporation that interests you, but you can't find out who has the power to hire you there. What do you do? Well, you use your library, and search the directories there that we saw listed in the previous chapter. Hopefully that will yield the information you want. If it doesn't, which will particularly be the case with smaller organizations, **then you use your contacts.** You approach as many people as necessary among all those you know, and the question you ask them all is, "Do you know anyone who works at Capachin Corporation?" Once you find someone who does, you then ask them:

- What is the name of the person at Capachin?
- May I tell them it was you who recommended that I talk with them?
- Would you be willing to call ahead, to set up an appointment for me, and tell them who I am?

Then you keep that appointment (**always** arriving promptly or slightly ahead of time) and talk to that person. Because they are inside the organization that interests you, they are usually able to give you the exact answer to your HOW Question #1: "Who would have the power to hire me here, for this kind of position (*which you then describe*)?"

Discovering this information is not as difficult as job-hunters and career-changers presume. It simply takes time and persistence to uncover it. Either the library or your contacts should yield up the answer. People assume this is difficult information to discover, because when they think of going out looking for a job they are always picturing themselves approaching some large organization, where they can't figure out whether it's somebody on the twenty-first floor or the fourteenth that they should be approaching. However, since as we have said **two-thirds of all new jobs are in fact to be found in organizations of twenty employees or less,** in most cases this is not a difficult information search at all. If the place that interests you is basically a "mom-and-pop" operation, then the issue of identifying "who has the power to hire" is pretty simple: it's either mom or pop.

THE DREADED 'PERSONNEL DEPARTMENT'

In all cases, you will likely discover that the individual (or committee) who has the power to hire you is **not** within the Personnel Department. There are two reasons why this is so.

First, as we saw in Chapter 3, **only 15% of all organizations even have personnel departments**. Ergo, 85% of the organizations you may approach are too small or too understaffed or whatever, to have such departments.

Secondly, even in those organizations which do, it is not *normally* the function of the personnel department to do the hiring (except for entry-level or lower-level positions). The function of the personnel department is to *screen out* applicants and then send the ones who survive that screening on 'upstairs' to be interviewed by the person who actually has the power to hire. You will see immediately that **from the point of view of the organization,** the personnel department is a great idea. It saves busy executives from being bothered by too many applicants, when the time for hiring has come. But, from the point of view of the job-hunter or career-changer (*namely, you or me*) this passage through the hands of the personnel department can result in disaster.

There are actually two kinds of personnel departments in those organizations which do have them. **Some** personnel departments harbor the kindest and warmest souls in the entire building, who will move heaven and earth to help you find a job there. But other personnel departments harbor souls who either a) are overzealous about protecting the people "upstairs," or b) get some perverse delight out of screening people out, or c) are frightened about losing their own job. If you fall into **their** hands, you can get screened out -- and thus never get to see the person who actually has the power to hire you -- even though in fact you might be exactly the person he or she is looking for.

THE MOST LIKELY SCENARIO

Of these two scenarios, getting help or getting screened out, **the more likely one** is that by going to personnel you will get screened out. Because no personnel executive wants to hear some "upstairs" executive say, "You're sending me too many people to see," personnel tends to live by the motto: "*When in doubt, screen them out*" -- which means that **you can get screened out by the personnel**

department even if you were absolutely right for the job. This is to *your* disadvantage, obviously; but do not forget it is also to the disadvantage of the person "upstairs" who would like to have seen you and would have hired you -- but now will never know. Furthermore, because personnel is not always clear about exactly what is wanted "upstairs," they may in fact be sending up people who are not what the job requires. Hence, the hiring executive **may** end up having to hire someone with less qualifications than yours.

To repeat the point of earlier chapters, the whole job-hunting process in this country is Neanderthal. And, this "Neanderthalness" **hurts the employer** as much as it does the job-hunter.

In any event, all this that I have said concerning the personnel department dictates that the intelligent job-hunter (generally speaking) **avoid that department.** It is better to identify the person who has the power to hire you, through research and use of your contacts as described previously, and then to get in to see him or her directly, without first going through this unnecessary extra step where you risk getting screened out.

This leads us, then, directly into our second HOW question: how do I get in for a job interview with that person? The traditional answer, as you know, is "By sending a resume." Unfortunately, this isn't the best or most effective way, by a long shot. So let's see why.

Résumés
A CRASH COURSE

My conversations with job-hunters, over the years, have convinced me that there is a passionate belief in resumes that is out of all proportion to how often they in fact ever get anyone an interview for a job. I think the faith placed in resumes is a very misplaced faith. For every person *you* know who did get a job-interview by sending out resumes, I know ninety-nine who didn't.

I said this once to a group of college placement people, many of whom were devoting large blocks of time to teaching students how to write a resume. When I sat down afterward, I found myself next to the personnel director for a huge public utility company, which employed thousands of people. He leaned across to me. "I listened to what you said about resumes," he began. I waited for the axe to fall. However he went on: "I've been trying to tell these counselors for years to get off this obsession they have with resumes. I'll interview anyone. But I don't read resumes. Haven't read one in five years. I can't tell a thing about a candidate from a resume. I was so glad you said what you did. Maybe they'll listen if they hear it from you."

Okay, so much by way of introduction to this crash course. Perhaps now I ought to briefly summarize what we know about resumes.

> **RÉ-SU-MÉ rez-ə-mā** n [F. *résumé* fr. pp. of *résumer* to resume, summarize] SUMMARY *specif:* a short account of one's career and qualifications prepared typically by an applicant for a position. -- Webster's

Resumes serve four different functions:

(1) they can serve as a **self-inventory,** preparing you before the job-hunt to recall all that you've accomplished thus far in your life;

(2) they can be an **extended calling card,** whose purpose is to get you invited in for an interview, by the employer(s) to whom you send that "calling card";

(3) they can be an **agenda for an interview,** affording the interviewer a springboard from which to launch his or her inquiry about you, after you have been invited in;

(4) and, finally, resumes can be a **memory jogger** for the employer after the interview, or for a whole committee -- if a group is involved in the hiring decision.

FRANK AND ERNEST ® by Bob Thaves

SENDING A RESUME TO GET AN INTERVIEW

It is as **extended calling card** that the resume is most often used. Indeed, as calling card it may be sent out to hundreds of prospective employers. Its lack of effectiveness in this role I cited in Chapter 2. But let me remind you again: in this country, only one job offer is tendered for every 1,470 resumes that the average company receives.

Well, okay, so maybe they don't always work. But what's the harm in trying out a resume, just in case? Well, unhappily, it can do you quite a bit of harm.

If you are presently employed at a particular place, and you use that company's stationery or envelopes for your resume, or if your resume is sent from that company's fax machine, that company's name appears at the top of every page when transmitted. The question this raises in the mind of the employer who *receives* your resume: "If I were to hire this person, what materials or services would they take from *my* place, without asking?" Ethics *are* becoming more important in business and politics (or hadn't you noticed?). You can't afford to get turned down just because your ethics look sloppy. And certainly not because your *resume ethics* look sloppy.

On that note, let's not forget that if a would-be employer decides to check out your resume, before calling you in, and you have fudged the truth about this thing or that -- particularly your educational degrees, and experience, the discovery that you have fudged (*that's spelled "l-i-e-d"*) will cost you the job.

Also, you can get fired for sending out a resume. We know someone this actually happened to. Let's call him Jim. He sent out one copy of his resume in answer to an ad, 'just to test the waters.' The employer to whom Jim sent that resume was (unbeknownst to him) a friend of his current employer, so he asked him, "Did you know one of your managers is looking for a new job?" Jim was called in and fired on the spot, despite his explanation. "You don't have the right attitude for working here," he was told. (They meant *loyalty*.)

Other damage your resume can do to you? Well, we have discovered in the past that **job-hunters who invest a lot of time on sending out their resume, often suffer tremendous damage to their self-esteem when their resumes are rejected or ignored.** This damage is created by the fact that *mythology* claims resumes usually work. That mythology is based on the following facts:

a) With at least 6.5 million job-hunters out there hunting for a job these days, the odds are that **some** job-hunters will actually get an interview, and subsequently a job, because they sent out resumes.

b) But **many, many more** job-hunters do **not** get a job by means of a resume. In fact, an incredible number do not even get **one** invitation to an interview, in spite of sending out 800 or 900 resumes.

c) The ones who do get a job thereby, talk a lot about it; the ones who find that resumes don't work for them, rarely say much *about that.* Consequently, the widespread **mythology** that 'this is a method which works for almost everyone.'

Needless to say, when resumes don't work at all for a particular job-hunter, he or she is usually devastated, and assumes something is drastically **wrong with them.** The result: plummeting self-esteem. It is not that a method has been tried, and failed. It is that a method *which you think works for almost everyone else*, has failed for you. Hence, depression, emotional paralysis, and even worse symptoms often come in the wake of the rejection shock mentioned in Chapter 2. *This has happened to tens of thousands of job-hunters. It has even happened to me. Don't let it happen to you.*

The moral of all these tales? Don't let anyone tell you: "it can't do any harm to just send out a lot of resumes." It can, it has, it does.

Well, then, if resumes have such a lousy track record as **extended calling cards,** how *do* you get in to see the person who has the power to hire? Good question. Now to the answer:

The alternative to resumes *that we know is effective most of the time* has three parts to it:

a) **Commitment.** Devoting six to eight hours a day, five days a week, to the job-hunt.

b) **Going Face-to-Face.** Knocking on the door, personally, at every organization that looks the least bit interesting to you, whether you think they have a vacancy or not.

c) **Using Contacts.** When you find a place you like, or are curious about, but you can't get an interview there, asking every person you know if they know someone who works there. And when someone says they do, asking them to set up an appointment for you to see them. Then go ask the person on the inside for the name of the person who has the power to hire there, for the kind of job you want to do.

An electrical engineer friend of mine used to sum up this whole matter thusly: "Paper is an insulating material. Never insert it between you and another person."

THE OTHER THREE USES OF RESUMES

Given the fact that the resume as **extended calling card** is tremendously ineffective, what can we say about its other three roles? Well, generally speaking the exercises in both our previous two chapters really supplant any need for the resume as **self-inventory.** So the only time you might need a resume for that purpose would be if you're too lazy to do the exercises. And your own research about organizations that interest you, as described in the previous chapter, really supplants any need for the resume as **agenda for an interview.** But, after talking with countless numbers of successful job-hunters, I am bound to say that there is one place where a resume may be *very useful*, and that is if you send it to the employer *after* the interview. The resume as **memory-jogger for the employer** has a very high effectiveness rate.

This explains the ancient saying in career-counseling: **"A resume is something you should never send ahead of you, but al-**

ways leave behind you." Based on the experience of successful job-hunters, I think there is great wisdom in that saying.

Further, I believe it is often -- if not always -- wise *not* to carry a resume on your person when you go into an interview, so that if you are asked for your resume you can say *absolutely truthfully*, "I don't have one with me, but I can mail it to you tonight." This saves you from having to hand the employer your "general-purpose one-size-fits-all" resume which mentions all your possible skills and every sterling attribute you possess; and instead, you have time to go home, edit your resume so that it mentions only the skills and experience needed in the job you both just discussed, *while leaving out all information that is not relevant to that job*, type it neatly (or have it typed up at a professional place if you wish), and then mail it that same night, along with a thank-you note as your cover letter.

In today's job-market, I think there is a genuine need for this use of the resume **as memory-jogger.** Many hiring decisions these days, even in small organizations, are made by a committee; and

you do not always have a chance to meet them all, at least in the first round or two. Furthermore, even where it is an individual who is making the hiring decision, you will oftentimes be called back for one or more additional interviews, before they decide who they want. Your resume, mailed to them after the first interview, will remind them of who you are, and keep them from confusing you with one or more among the nineteen other candidates they are looking at.

FOR THAT FARAWAY CITY, YOU MAY NEED TO SEND A RESUME

If you're interested in leaping across the country (or even part of the country) for your next job, it may be impractical for you to go there, at least in the beginning. You may want to research it first. But suppose *that* research is completed. You have discovered some organizations that, at this distance, look like "possibles." But you still aren't ready to invest the time or money to go there, just yet. So, what should you do?

Well of course you will begin by using every contact that you have developed *there* by mail or phone. If they know any of the organizations that interest you, and -- better yet, the name of the person who has the power to hire you -- a letter which mentions the name of a mutual friend in that faraway city, will always receive more favorable attention than would be the case if you were a total stranger. (Unless -- the job-hunter's nightmare -- your mutual "friend"/contact has *misrepresented* how close he or she is to your target employer, and as a matter of fact said employer can't stand the sight of this "mutual friend." *It has happened.* It is to die.)

In any event, *generally speaking* your letter to employers in that faraway city will be *much* stronger if you mention some *true* mutual friend. Should you also enclose a resume? Professional opinions vary widely. *Everything* depends on the nature of the resume, and the nature of the person you are sending it to.

RESUMES AND DATING

Resumes, after all, are a lot like dating. There is virtually no man who is liked by all the women he dates. There is virtually no woman who is liked by all the men she dates. And so with resumes: some employers like resumes, others hate them. Some will like *your* resume; others won't.

The only question that should concern you is: never mind if not all employers would like my resume -- will the employers **I care about** like it? And that is the $64,000 question.

I used to have a hobby of collecting resumes that had actually gotten someone an interview and, ultimately, a job. I delighted in showing them to employers whom I knew. Many of them didn't like the winning resume at all. "That resume will never get anyone a job," they would say. Then, being basically a mischievous man, I would tell them, "Sorry, you're wrong. It already has. What you are saying is that it wouldn't get them a job **with you.**"

The resume reproduced on the next page is an example of what I mean. (*You did want an example of a good resume, didn't you?*) Jim Dyer, who had been in the Marines for twenty years, wanted a job as a salesman for heavy construction and mining equipment thousands of miles from where he was then living. He devised the resume you see, and had fifteen copies made. "I used," he said, "a grand total of seven before I got the job in the place I wanted!"

Like the employer who hired him, I loved this resume. Yet, when I've shown it to other employers, they criticized it for using a picture, for being too long (or too short), etc., etc. In other words, had Jim sent his resume to *them,* they wouldn't have been impressed enough to invite him in for an interview.

So, don't believe anyone who tells you there's one right format for a resume, or one style that's guaranteed to win. It's still a gamble, where you're hoping that the employer(s) you like will also like your resume. Generally speaking, the most endearing quality needed in it, besides neatness and clarity, is that *you* shine through it all. One job-hunter, for example, found this unique *truthful* way of describing her period of job-hunting:

"Job-Hunter (Self-Employed) January 1990 – January 1991:

- Developed and executed all phases of marketing and advertising for product
- Targeted markets and identified the needs of diverse consumers
- Developed sales brochure
- Designed packaging, and upgraded visual appeal of product
- Scheduled and conducted oral presentations"

Thus, *she* shone through it all.

Okay. Here endeth our crash course on resumes. If you decide you do want a resume, preferably to leave behind you **after** the

E.J. DYER Street, City, Zip Telephone No.

I SPEAK
THE LANGUAGE
OF
MEN
MACHINERY
AND
MANAGEMENT
...

OBJECTIVE: Sales of Heavy Equipment

QUALIFICATIONS

* Knowledge of heavy equipment, its use and maintenance.
* Ability to communicate with management and with men in the field.
* Ability to favorably introduce change in the form of new equipment or new ideas... the ability to sell.

EXPERIENCE

Men and Machinery

* Maintained, shipped, budgeted and set allocation priorities for 85 pieces of heavy equipment as head of a 500-man organization (1975-1977).
* Constructed twelve field operation support complexes, employing a 100-man crew and 19 pieces of heavy equipment (1965-1967).
* Jack-hammer operator, heavy construction (summers 1956-1957-1958).

Management

* Planned, negotiated and executed large scale equipment purchases on a nation to nation level (1972-1974).

Sales

* Achieved field customer acceptance of two major new computer-based systems:
  - Equipment inventory control and repair parts expedite system (1968-1971)
  - Decision makers' training system (1977-1979).
* Proven leader ... repeatedly elected or appointed to senior posts.

EDUCATION

* B.A. Benedictine College, 1959. (Class President; Editor Yearbook; "Who's Who in American Colleges").
* Naval War College, 1975. (Class President; Graduated "With Highest Distinction").
* University of Maryland, 1973-1974. (Chinese Language).
* Middle Level Management Training Course, 1967-1968 (Class Standing: 1 of 97).

PERSONAL

* Family: Sharon and our sons Jim (11), Andy (8) and Matt (5) desire to locate in a Mountain State by 1982, however, in the interim will consider a position elsewhere in or outside the United States ... Health: Excellent ... Birthdate: December 9, 1937 ... Completing Military Service with the rank of Lieutenant Colonel, U.S. Marine Corps.

SUMMARY

A seeker of challenge ... experienced, proven and confident of closing the sales for profit.

interview, and the guidance I have given you here is not enough, I refer you to the books listed on page 296. The best of these, by a long shot, is Richard Lathrop's *Who's Hiring Who* (newly revised), wherein he describes and recommends "a qualifications brief" -- an idea akin to that which John Crystal used to propose: that in approaching an employer you should think of offering him or her **a written proposal** rather than "a resume." Of course there are those who say, "No matter what you try to call it, it's still a resume in the end." The other most helpful resume book (according to our mail) is *The Damn Good Resume Guide*, by Yana Parker.

THE ALTERNATIVE TO RESUMES

Now, back to our second HOW question. If resumes are not the preferred route to a job-interview, then how *do* you get in to see the person who has the power to hire?

The answer is: Through your contacts.

If you have found out that X is the name of the person who has the power to hire you for the kind of position you are interested in, then you ask *everyone* you meet and everyone you know, "Do you personally know X, over at Capachin Corporation, or do you know someone who does?"

If you persist with **every** person you know, in the family, among your friends, in your former places of employment, in the congregation of your church / synagogue / mosque the odds are 20 to 1:

a) that you are going to come across someone who knows X, and therefore

b) that you are going to get in to see him or her.

To the first person who says, "Yes, I know X," you of course are going to respond with the familiar litany:

- May I use your name?
- May I say you recommended that I talk with them?
- Would you be willing to call ahead, to set up an appointment for me, and tell them who I am?

And if you do this part successfully, you will then (and only then) need the answer to the third HOW question, namely,

How do I convince them that they should hire me?

Interviews
A CRASH COURSE

INFORMATION IS THE KEY TO A SUCCESSFUL INTERVIEW

Briefly stated, the answer is that you sell yourself by finding out as much about that organization as you possibly can **before you ever go in there for an interview.** You lay your hands on **everything** you can that is in print about them. If this is a large organization, you read all their brochures, annual reports, addresses of the chairman or boss -- whatever. If they have a personnel department or a public relations department, that's where you'll find the stuff. Also, you go to the library and ask the librarian or reference librarian (if they have one) to see every clipping they have about that organization.

If it is a small organization, you still find out if there is anything in print about their work or what they do. (Even places that only have two employees often have **something** in print about what the organization is trying to achieve. The small local paper may have run an article about them.) Also, you talk to **everybody** you know, to find out everything you can about the organization in question: their work, their history, who used to work there, etc.

If this strikes you as sort of prying into their private life, then recall to your mind the purpose of all this research. There are actually two purposes, both honorable:

1. As we saw in the last chapter, the tradition in our country is to find a job, take it, and then try to find out after you're in it whether it was a good job or not. You're trying to go against that tradition, as any sensible job-hunter or career-changer should, by finding out whether or not you'd like to work there **before** you ever accept a job there. You're saving **them** grief as well as saving yourself grief.

2. Organizations, be they large or small, profit or nonprofit, love to be loved. If you have gone to the trouble to learn a great deal about them before you ever walk in their doors, **you make**

that organization feel important. Most job-hunters don't ever go to this trouble. They walk in knowing little or nothing about the organization. According to the chairman of the National Association of Corporate and Professional Recruiters, a survey of theirs revealed "Candidates too often are so unknowledgeable about the company, industry, the situation of the culture that they cannot ask the right questions." Taking the trouble to learn something about the place before you have a job-interview there, makes you stand out from the other job-hunters, and greatly increases your chances of getting a job there. How much information should you gather? If possible, **more than you are ever going to have to use,** at least during the hiring interview. But the depth of your research will pay off in the quiet sense of confidence you exude.

WELL, YOU WANT TO SEE THEM, BUT DO THEY WANT TO SEE YOU?

This is the question which bothers almost everyone new to the job-hunt or new to career-change. We sort of just assume the answer is "No." This mental attitude is what Daniel Porot calls "our job-beggar mentality." We feel the employer would be doing us a tremendous favor by offering us a job; and particularly so, if we have some real or imagined handicap or some bad history working against us, such as age, or a psychiatric history, or a prison record, or whatever.

You need to remember, no matter what your real or imagined handicap may be, this simple but profound truth (post it on your bathroom mirror):

ALL EMPLOYERS DIVIDE INTO TWO GROUPS:

1. THOSE WOULD BE PUT OFF BY YOUR 'HANDICAP'

   and

2. THOSE WOULD NOT BE AT ALL PUT OFF BY YOUR 'HANDICAP'

No matter how numerous the first group may be, and how small the second, your job as a job-hunter or career-changer is to find the *second* kind of employer, and pay no never mind to the *first*, except as they may give you leads to the second.

To take the 'worst case' scenario, if out of 100 employers, 90 would be bothered by your handicap or your history, but 10 wouldn't care about it in the slightest so long as you can do the work well that needs to get done, **your job is to make your way as quickly as you can through the 90, and find those other 10. They are the only ones you want to work for, anyway.** You wouldn't **really** want to work for those who are prejudiced against your history or your handicap, now would you? We all want to work for an employer who's rootin' for us, not one who's waiting for us to fall on our face.

I can hear your objections, right now. You think **you've** got a handicap that's the exception to this rule. For example, that you're over 60 years old, and employers wouldn't want someone that old.

Okay, let's repeat it together: "All employers divide into two groups: 1) those who would be put off by your age, and 2) those who would not be put off by your age, so long as you are a good worker. Your job is to find the second kind of employer, and not pay any attention to the first."

Please! Make no generalizations about "employers." There isn't any such animal. In any and all circumstances that you can possibly come up with, **there are always two kinds of employers.** Your job is to find the second kind, and to try not to be bothered by the rejections you receive from the first kind.

'JOB-BEGGAR' VS. 'RESOURCE PERSON'

Having said that, remember this. You're not visiting an employer in order to get him or her to do **you** a big favor. If you've done your homework, you know you can be part of the solution there, and not part of the problem. Therefore you're going in to see this employer in order that you may do a favor **for each other.** That's not an arrogant posture for you to take. It **is** the truth, and it can be stated very quietly but confidently. You are coming to see this employer, in order to make an oral proposal, followed hopefully by a written proposal, of what **you** can do for **them.**

You will perceive immediately what a switch this is from the way **most** job-hunters approach an employer! And will he or she, in such a case, be glad to see you, when you're coming in to offer them skills and knowledges which will help them, with what they're trying to accomplish there? **In most cases,** you bet they will.

WHAT DO YOU SAY, ONCE YOU 'GET IN'?

Once you get in to see her or him, the interview has begun. The term "interview" shouldn't frighten you by this time. You will have had rich experience in interviewing people for information all along the way, up 'til now. From an objective standpoint, this is just another such interview. *So much for what your mind tells you!*

We all know in our gut that the Employment Interview **does** feel different from all previous interviews -- so let's see what its special characteristics are. For, if you understand what an interview is, you will be ahead of 98% of all other job-hunters who go into the Interview as a lamb goes to the slaughter. Moreover, you will then automatically know the kinds of things you ought to talk about.

So, what's to understand about the Employment Interview? There are two fundamental truths about it:

THE FIRST FUNDAMENTAL TRUTH ABOUT THE INTERVIEW:

Each of you has questions in the interview -- both you **and** the employer. The essence of the interview is that each of you is trying to find out the answers to those questions.

● YOUR QUESTIONS ARE:

First you report to them just exactly how you've been conducting your job-hunt, and what impressed you so much about their organization during your research, that you decided you wanted to come in and talk to them about a job. Then you get to your questions (or bow to theirs, first, if the employer is anxious to talk).

If this is a job that already exists, your questions are:

1. What does this job involve?
2. Do my skills truly match this job?
3. Are you the kind of people I would like to work with?
4. If we do match, can I persuade you to hire me?

You will rarely, if ever, say these questions out loud during the interview; but you will keep them in the front of your mind (or written on a pad) because these are the questions you came there to find the answers to, one way or another.

If the job in question is a job that you want them to create for you, then your four questions get changed into four statements:

1. What you like about this organization.
2. What sorts of **needs** you find intriguing in this field and in this organization (don't **ever** use the word "problems," as most employers resent it -- unless you hear the word coming out of their mouth, first).
3. What skills seem to you to be needed in order to meet such needs.
4. Your presentation of your claim, backed by evidence, that you have the very skills in question.

THEIR QUESTIONS ARE:

Well, **many.** In fact, some books publish a list of eighty-nine questions (or so) that an employer may ask you. They list things like:

- Tell me about yourself.
- Why are you applying for this job?
- What do you know about this job or company?
- How would you describe yourself?
- What are your major strengths?
- What is your greatest weakness?
- What type of work do you like to do best?
- What are your interests outside of work?
- What accomplishment gave you the greatest satisfaction?
- What was your worst mistake?
- Why did you leave your last job?
- Why were you fired (if you were)?
- How does your education or experience relate to this job?
- Where do you see yourself five years from now?
- What are your goals in life?
- How much did you make at your last job?

And so on. Fortunately, however, as John Crystal once taught us all, beneath these dozens of Possible Questions there are really only four. These four are:

1. **Why are you here?** *They mean by that,* why did you pick out our organization?
2. **What can you do for us?** *They mean by that,* what are your skills and your special knowledges?
3. **What kind of person are you?** *They mean by that,* do you have a personality that they will enjoy working with, or not? What are your values and how do you get along with people?
4. **Can they afford you?** *They mean by that,* what are your minimum salary needs, and what are your maximum salary hopes?

Now that you see the kinds of questions you each are bound to have, remember the object of the interview is:

1) to find out the information that **you** need to know, in order to decide whether **you** want to work there or not; and,

2) to help the employer find out the information that **he or she** needs to know, in order to decide whether **they** want to hire you or not.

And this is the case, even if the interview begins and ends without either of you ever putting these questions precisely into words, during the entire time.

HOW DO YOU ANSWER THEIR QUESTIONS?

1. **"Why are you here?"** If you did all your research, as described in the previous chapter, you'll know the answer. If you didn't, you won't. End of story. One job-hunter we know got an interview with IBM, through his college placement office. Before the interview he told many of his friends about his great luck, and speculated on how much the company would have to offer him before he would consider accepting the job. On the big day, he was shown into the interviewer's office, they shook hands, and then the interviewer said: "Can you tell me what the letters 'IBM' stand for?" He hadn't done any research on the company, so he didn't know the answer; the interview was over in forty-five seconds. There's no reward for laziness in the job-hunt. There *is* a reward for hard work, and *this* is where it pays off.

Incidentally, the essence of a good answer to the question, "Why are you here?" is some variation on: "I have become interested in organizations which are _______, and yours particularly attracted me because ______."

2. **"What can you do for me?"** What the employer is essentially wanting to know here, is: "Will you help this organization to do its work better, and achieve its goals more completely -- and if so, in what way?" Again, **if** you did your research, you will know what that company's work and goals are, what their problems and challenges are, **and** in what ways you would be an asset toward the accomplishing of that work, the achieving of those goals, and the

overcoming of those problems and challenges. You will usually be an asset in one of the following ways: with regard to **their money** (you will make it, save it, or cause it to go further); with regard to **their time** (you will save it because you ________); with regard to **their ability to compete with others in the same field** (you will help them to excel the others, because you ________); with regard to **helping them be more efficient;** and with regard to **making their work more stimulating, appealing, varied, and/or enjoyable.** Of course, you will remember won't you that it may look like an asset *to you*, on paper, but it isn't an asset in actual fact unless it's something *they* want. So, if you didn't do your research, you're in *big* trouble. Usually, in that case, *guessing* that they might want this particular benefit or asset won't save you. *'Bye, 'bye.*

3. **"What kind of person are you?"** This is a crucial question, but unhappily there's no right answer for you to memorize. You will answer this question by **everything** you say during the interview, and everything you do during the interview. It is likely that **nothing** will escape the scrutiny of the person across the desk from you. And I mean: your haircut or hairdo; your manner of dress; your posture; your use of your hands; your body odor or perfume; your breath (good or bad); your fingernails (dirty or clean, clipped or not); the sound of your voice; the way in which you do or don't interrupt; the hesitant or assured manner in which you ask your questions or give your answers; your values as evidenced by the things which impress you or don't impress you in the office, in your history, and so on; the carefulness with which you did or didn't research this company before you came in; the thoroughness with which you know your skills and strengths; your awareness of what you are willing to sell in order to get this job **and** what you aren't willing to sell in order to get this job; your enthusiasm for your work; and that's just for openers. We can also throw in whether or not you smoke (in a race between two equally qualified people, the nonsmoker will win out over the smoker 94% of the time, according to a study done by a professor of business at Seattle University); whether, if at lunch, you order a drink or not; whether you show courtesy to the receptionist, secretary, waiter or waitress, or not; and -- like that. *Everything* is grist for the mill, as the employer tries to divine "what kind of person is this?" What the employer will typically use to screen you out, are:

- any signs of dishonesty or lying;
- any signs of irresponsibility or tendency to goof off;

- any sign of arrogance or excessive aggressiveness;
- any sign of tardiness or failure to keep appointments and commitments on time;
- any sign of not following instructions or obeying rules;
- any sign of constant complaining or blaming things on others;
- any sign of laziness or lack of motivation;
- any sign of a lack of enthusiasm for this organization and what it is trying to do;
- any sign of instability, inappropriate response, and the like.

Since the employer will probably end up having to fire anyone with these personality traits, the employer would like to find these things out **now** rather than later.

Beyond these tangibles, there are the intangibles of **making a good impression.** Study after study has confirmed that if you are a male, you will make a better impression if:

- your hair or beard are neatly trimmed;
- you have obviously freshly bathed, used a deodorant and mouthwash, and have clean fingernails;
- you have freshly laundered clothes on, and a suit rather than a sports outfit, and sit without slouching;
- your breath does not dispense gallons of garlic, onion, stale tobacco, or strong drink, into the enclosed office air;
- your shoes are neatly polished, and your pants have a sharp crease;
- you are not wafting tons of after-shave cologne fifteen feet ahead of you.

And, if you are a female, you will make a better impression if:

- your hair is newly 'permed' or 'coiffed';
- you have obviously freshly bathed, used a deodorant and mouthwash, and have clean or nicely manicured fingernails;
- you wear a bra, freshly cleaned clothes, a suit or sophisticated-looking dress, and sit without slouching;
- your breath does not dispense gallons of garlic, onion, stale tobacco, or strong drink, into the enclosed office air;
- you wear shoes rather than sandals;
- you are not wafting tons of perfume fifteen feet ahead of you.

Now please, dear reader, do not send me mail telling me how asinine you think some of these 'rules' are. I **know** that. I'm only reporting that study after study reveals these things **do** affect whether or not you get hired. There are of course employers who care about none of these things, and will hire you if you can do the job. Period. Do remember, however, that where you have to work with other people, these things are given a lot of importance. This employer already has other employees; he or she wants to know that you will not alienate them, or cause friction. You must somehow 'fit in.'

If you don't want to 'fit in,' then you might want to consider forming your own (one-person) business, and -- particularly if it is a mail-order business -- you can dress or conduct yourself any way you like, and no one will be the wiser. If, however, you want to work for someone else, you are in a sense *on trial* during this interview. All of the above factors are a part of that trial.

Of course, what makes the job interview tolerable or sometimes even **fun,** is that **you** are studying **everything** about this employer, at the same time that they are studying everything about you. You are just as much in need of making up your mind about what kind of person **they** are, and whether or not you would like to work with them, as they are doing with you.

Two people, both sizing each other up. Well, that's what the employment interview is; and you know what it reminds you of. Dating. The job interview is indeed every bit like 'the dating game.' **Both** of you have to like the other, before you can get on to the question of 'going steady.' Thus the employer is just as much 'on trial' during the job interview as you are. Realizing **that,** can take some of the stress away.

4. **"How much are you going to cost me?"** Until they have said "We **want** you," **and** you have decided, "I want them," all discussion of salary is highly inappropriate. And that's true, *even if it is the employer who brings up the subject* early on in the interview.

IN SALARY NEGOTIATION, TIMING IS EVERYTHING

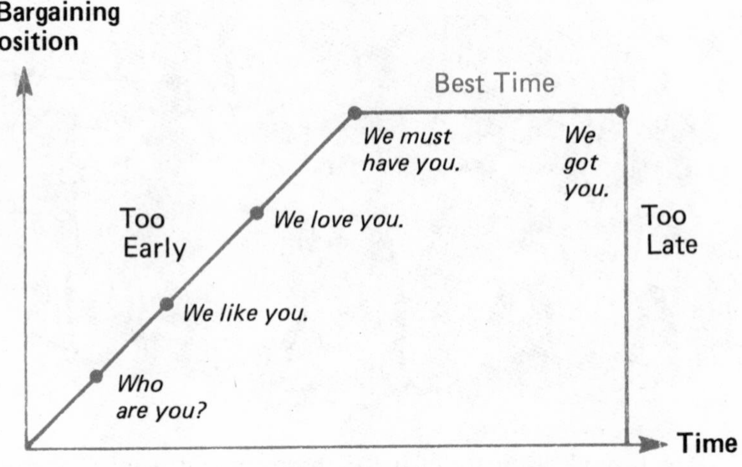

When To Negotiate Salary

Reprinted, by permission of the publisher, from *Ready, Aim, You're Hired*, by Paul Hellman, © 1986 Paul Hellman. Published by AMACOM, a division of American Management Association, New York. All rights reserved.

You may of course think to yourself, "Yes, but what if they have a fixed salary figure in mind, and it is way below what I could accept -- shouldn't I find that out as early as possible, so that I can graciously excuse myself, and go elsewhere?" That's logical, except for one minor little point: if you're the first person they've interviewed, and they haven't yet had a chance to get to know you very well, they may assume you are 'average material' and consequently mention merely an average kind of salary. But if they have seen a lot of people, **and** have had a chance to get to know you over two or three interviews, say. And **if** they are very impressed with you by this time, **obviously** they are going to be willing to do whatever they can to get a hold of you. And **if** that takes more money than they were originally prepared to offer, they may push themselves to find it. **This happens very often.**

If you allow discussion of salary to take place prematurely, you will be told **the lowest** figure they had in mind, but it will be presented as though it were **the highest.** They haven't yet seen you in all your splendor. They don't know what they would be getting if they got you. Or, what they would be losing, if they let you go. Therefore, until a firm offer has been made, try to **postpone** all discussion of salary.

There is more to be said about salary negotiation, but since such negotiation should **always** take place at the end of the interview, this discussion is at the end of this chapter.

TWENTY SECONDS TO TWO MINUTES

Well, we have now seen the first fundamental truth about the employment interview: it's two people trying to get answers to natural questions. If you understand that, then you're ahead of most other job-hunters.

Beyond the issue of **what** to say, is the issue of **how** to say it. *Studies have revealed that generally speaking the people who get hired are those who mix speaking and listening fifty-fifty in the interview.* That is, half the time in the interview the job-hunter **listens** and lets the employer do the talking, half the time in the interview the job-hunter does the **talking**.

When it is your turn to speak, studies conducted by Daniel Porot have revealed that to make the most favorable impression **you should not speak any longer than two minutes at a time**. In fact, a good answer to an employer's question sometimes only takes twenty seconds to give. This is useful information for you to know, in conducting a successful interview -- as you certainly want to do.

Okay, now let's turn to:

THE SECOND FUNDAMENTAL TRUTH ABOUT THE EMPLOYMENT INTERVIEW

If the employment interview were simply two people, job-hunter and employer, trying to get answers to natural questions, the interview would be a snap. Unfortunately, this simple exchange is corrupted by the fact that **both** individuals sitting there are filled with a number of fears and anxieties, **which they don't feel free**

to discuss openly. So they try to allay their fears by asking clever questions.

Hence, you must examine **every** question the employer asks, to see what fear lies beneath it, **so that you can answer the fear, and not just the surface question.** Because, in the employment interview questions don't always mean what they seem to mean at first sight.

Now, I emphasize this fundamental truth about the employment interview, because it is hardly ever mentioned in any discussion of job interviews that I have seen. Everyone assumes that **the job-hunter** is filled with fears in the interview, but that the employer is sitting there like some cool cat, wonderfully at ease. Not true. That employer, sitting across the desk from you, in the employment interview, usually has as many fears as you do. Maybe more.

For openers, the employer has the following ten major fears when you, the job-hunter, are face-to-face with him or her:

1. That You Won't Be Able to Do the Job: That You Lack the Necessary Skills or Experience

2. That If Hired, You Won't Put In a Full Working Day

3. That If Hired, You'll Be Frequently "Out Sick," or Otherwise Absent Whole Days

4. That If Hired, You'll Only Stay Around for a Few Weeks or At Most a Few Months

5. That It Will Take You Too Long to Master the Job, and Thus Too Long Before You're Profitable to That Organization

6. That You Won't Get Along with the Other Workers There, or That You Will Develop a Personality Conflict with the Boss Himself (or Herself)

7. That You Will Do Only the Minimum That You Can Get Away With, Rather Than the Maximum That You Are Capable Of

8. That You Will Always Have to Be Told What to Do Next, Rather Than Displaying Initiative; That You Will Always Be in a Responding Rather Than an Initiating Mode (and Mood)

9. That You Will Have a Work-Disrupting Character Flaw, and Turn Out to Be: Dishonest, a Spreader of Dissention at Work, Lazy, an Embezzler, a Gossip, Totally Irresponsible, a Liar, Incompetent -- In a Word: No Fun to Have Around

10. *(If This Is a Large Organization, and Your Would-Be Boss Is Not the Top Person)* That You Will Bring Discredit upon Them, and upon His or Her Department/Section/Division, etc., for Ever Hiring You in the First Place -- Possibly Costing Your Would-Be Boss a Raise or Promotion

Moreover, employers don't usually talk with each other about this sort of thing. So, oftentimes an employer is facing the job-interview thinking that he or she is the only employer in the world going into job-interviews with so many fears. They've never had a chance to check it out, and discover that other employers feel exactly the same way.

This makes the employer feel extremely isolated and alone. That's why, in larger organizations, the person who has the power to hire often begs to share the hiring decision with a committee or a veritable army of his or her peers in that organization. The cost of all this company time, plus the cost of relocation, moving, etc., added up (as recently as 1988) to an average cost of $6,076 for each new professional or managerial employee hired, *according to the Employment Management Association.* Therefore, that is also the *minimum* cost of a mistake. No wonder the employer is sweating bullets.

Everything depends on the interview. In the old days, an employer might get additional useful information from references to former employers. No more. In the past decade, as job-hunters have started filing lawsuits right and left alleging 'unlawful discharge,' or 'being deprived of an ability to make a living,' so now about half of all Previous Employers refuse to volunteer any information *except name, rank, and serial number* -- i.e., the person's job-title and dates of employment. The interviewer is therefore completely on his own -- or her own -- in trying to figure out whether or not to hire you. Hence the importance, *the supreme importance* to interviewers, of the questions they ask during the interview.

THE FEAR BENEATH THE QUESTIONS

The most important thing to keep in mind during the interview is that no employer cares about your past. The only thing any employer can possibly care about is your future. Therefore, the more a question **appears** to be about your past, the more certain you may be that some Fear is behind it. And that Fear is about your future -- i.e., what will you be like, **after** the employer decides to hire you, **if** they decide to hire you.

So, let's run down nine typical employer questions to see

a) what they are, and
b) what fear typically lies behind those questions, and
c) some key phrases that you can use to answer the questions, so as to allay the employer's Fear.

I

THE EMPLOYER'S QUESTION:

"Tell me about yourself."

"I'll tell you why I want this job. I thrive on challenges. I like being stretched to my full capacity. I like solving problems. Also, my car is about to be repossessed."

The Fear Behind the Question: The employer is afraid they won't ask the right questions during the interview. **Or:** The employer is afraid there's something in your background or in your attitude toward your work that will make you a Bad Employee.

The Point You Try to Get Across, to Answer Their Fear: You would make a good employee, and you have proved that by your past.

Ideas or Phrases You Might Use: The briefest history in the world, of where you were born and raised, hobbies, interests, etc. The briefest description of where you have worked or the kind of work you have done.

Any sentence or phrase which describes your past attitude toward your work in a positive way:

"Hard worker"

"Came in early, left late"

"Always did more than was expected of me," etc.

THE EMPLOYER'S QUESTION:

"What kind of work are you looking for?"

The Fear Behind the Question: That it isn't the same kind of job the employer needs to fill -- e.g., they are looking for a secretary, you are looking to be office manager; they are looking for somebody who can work alone, you are looking for a job where you would be rubbing shoulders with other people.

The Point You Try to Get Across to Answer Their Fear: You have picked up many skills, which are transferable from one field to another.

Ideas or Phrases You Might Use: You are looking for work where you can use your skills with People (specify what those skills are -- that you most enjoy).

and/or

You are looking for work where you can use your skills with Data or Information (specify what those skills are -- that you most enjoy).

and/or

You are looking for work where you can use your skills with Things/Machines/Tools/Plants, etc. (specify what those skills are -- that you most enjoy).

If you are applying for a known vacancy, you can **first** respond to this question by saying, "I'd be happy to answer that, but first it seems to me it's more important for you to tell me what kind of work this job involves."

Once the employer has told you, **don't forget** to then answer their question. But now you can couch your answer in terms of the skills you have, which are **relevant** to the work the employer has described.

THE EMPLOYER'S QUESTION:
"Have you ever done this kind of work before?"

The Fear Behind the Question: The employer is afraid you can't do the work, that you don't possess the necessary experience or skills.

The Point You Try to Get Across, to Answer This Fear: You have transferable skills.

Ideas or Phrases You Might Use: The same ones as in the last question, plus:

"I pick up stuff very quickly."

"I have quickly mastered any job I have ever done."

"Every job is a whole new universe, but I make myself at home in that universe very quickly."

THE EMPLOYER'S QUESTION:
"Why did you leave your last job?"

OR

"Why did your last job end?"

OR

"How did you get along with your former boss and co-workers?"

The Fear Behind the Question: The employer is afraid that you don't get along with people, especially bosses.

The Point You Try to Get Across, to Answer This Fear: That you do get along well with people, and your attitude toward your former boss(es) and co-workers proves it.

Ideas or Phrases You Might Use:

"My **job** was terminated" (if you were fired).

"My boss **and I** both felt I would be **happier** and **more effective** in a job where (here describe your strong points: e.g., I would be under less supervision and have more room to use my initiative and creativity)."

Say as many positive things as you can about your former boss and co-workers (without telling lies).

THE EMPLOYER'S QUESTION:
"How is your health?"

The Fear Behind the Question: The employer is afraid that you will miss work because of sickness.

The Point You Try to Get Across, to Answer This Fear: You are a hard worker, and you have no health problem **that keeps you from being at work daily.**

If you do have a health problem: You stress your attendance average in terms of how many days per month you have been absent at previous jobs, and you stress how hard you work on the days that you are there.

Ideas or Phrases You Might Use: Your productivity, compared to other workers, at your previous jobs.

VI

THE EMPLOYER'S QUESTION:

"How much were you absent from work during your last job?"

The Fear Behind the Question: The employer is afraid that you will be absent from work a lot, if they hire you.

The Point You Try to Get Across, to Answer This Fear: You Will Not Be Absent from Work.

Ideas or Phrases You Might Use: If you **were** absent quite a bit on a previous job, say why, and stress that it is a **past** difficulty (if it is).

If you were not absent on your previous job, stress your good attendance record, and **the attitude** you have toward the importance of always being at work.

THE EMPLOYER'S QUESTION:

"Can you explain why you've been out of work so long?"

OR

"Can you tell me why there are these gaps in your work record or work history?" *(Usually asked, after studying your resume)*

OR

"How long have you been out of work?"

The Fear Behind the Question: The employer is afraid that you don't really like to work, and will quit the minute things aren't going "your way."

The Point You Try to Get Across, to Answer This Fear: You like to work, and you regard times when things aren't going well as Challenges.

Ideas or Phrases You Might Use: You were working hard during the times when you weren't employed. Either: studying, doing volunteer work, sitting down to do lots of hard thinking about how you could most effectively use the talents you have been given, trying to get beyond merely "keeping busy" to finding some sense of mission for your life.

THE EMPLOYER'S QUESTION:

"Doesn't this work (or this job) represent a step down for you?"

OR

"Don't you think you would be underemployed if you took this job?"

OR

"I think this job is way beneath your talents and experience."

The Fear Behind the Question: The employer is afraid that you could command more salary and more responsibility, that you are only taking this job as a stopgap measure, and that you will leave him (or her) as soon as something better turns up.

The Point You Try to Get Across, to Answer This Fear: You will stick with this job just as long as you possibly can, so long as you **and the employer** agree this is where you should be.

Ideas or Phrases You Might Use: "This job isn't a step down for me. It's a step up -- from being on welfare."

"I like to work, and I've given my best to every job I've ever done."

"Every employer is afraid the employee will leave too soon, and every employee is afraid the employer might fire him (or her). We have mutual fears. I'll do the finest job I know how, and I'll stay as long as we both agree this is where I should be."

THE EMPLOYER'S QUESTION:

"Tell me, what is your greatest weakness?"

The Fear Behind the Question: The employer is afraid you have some work-flaw or character-flaw, and is hopeful you will confess to it, **now**.

The Point You Try to Get Across, to Answer This Fear: You have limitations just like any other person but you work constantly to improve them and make yourself into a more effective worker.

Ideas or Phrases You Might Use: Mention some weakness of yours that has a positive aspect to it. Stress that positive aspect, e.g., "I don't respond well to being over-supervised, because I have a great deal of initiative, and I like to use it, anticipating problems before they even arise."

There are many other interview questions we could look at; but the above nine should give you the principles which you can now apply to all.

From the foregoing you will see: in order for it to be a successful interview, the fears of each of you must get allayed, and you must both feel pretty good about each other. If that is the case, further interviews will hopefully be in store for you there, either with the same person, or with a committee. But for now, the first interview is over, and you are free to go home.

A CRASH COURSE

THE ABSOLUTELY CRUCIAL THANK-YOU NOTE

That evening, you put your feet up, turn on the TV, and have a pleasant evening to yourself or with your loved one, right? Wrong. That evening **you work.**

Each evening, you **MUST** take time to sit down and write (pen or typewriter) a brief thank-you note to **each person that you saw that day.** That includes employers, **secretaries, receptionists,** or anyone else who gave you a helping hand that day. It should be regarded as basic to the simplest rules of common courtesy and kindness, that you write such notes. After all, you are presenting yourself as one who has skills at treating people as people. Prove it. Your actions must be consistent with your words. This thank-you note serves several purposes, in addition to common courtesy:

First of all, it helps them to remember you. Even if the interview did not go well, and you lost all interest in working **there,** they may still hear of **other** openings, elsewhere, that might be of interest to you. In the thank-you note, you can mention this, and ask them to keep you in mind. Thus the thank-you note may gain you additional leads.

Secondly, if the interview went rather well, and you are hopeful of being invited back, then the thank-you letter can reiterate your interest in further talks.

Thirdly, the thank-you note gives you an opportunity to **correct** any wrong impression you left behind you. You can **add** anything you forgot to tell them. You can **underline** anything that you want to stand out in their minds, from among all those things you two discussed.

The importance of sending a thank-you letter to everyone is one of the most essential steps in the entire job-hunt. It is talked about *endlessly* in job-hunting books and job-hunting seminars. Yet it is the most overlooked step in the entire job-hunting process. We know of one woman who was told she was hired because she was **the only** interviewee, out of thirty-nine, who sent a thank-you letter after the interview.

That's right, the thank-you letter may actually get you the job. **You cannot afford to think of this as simply an optional exercise. It is critical to your getting hired.**

You may want to include with the thank-you note two other documents. The first, and preferred piece of paper, would be a written **proposal** from you as to what it is you would like to be able to do for that organization, what it is you hope you could accomplish for them. As evidence, you will want to cite **relevant** past accomplishments of yours, taking care **in each case** to cite:

a) what the problem was
b) what you did to solve it
c) what means you used
d) what the results were, of your actions, stated as concretely as possible in terms of things accomplished, money saved, money earned, etc.

The virtue of such a written proposal is that it looks forward rather than (as the resume does) backward. And it puts into writing the essence of the hiring interview: you are not asking them merely to do something for you. More importantly, you are offering to do something for them.

The second piece of paper you may wonder if you should include with your thank-you letter is a resume as **memory-jogger.**

If you have included a proposal, the resume is really unnecessary. If you haven't included a written proposal, then your resume or some kind of summary of your background and history should be included, to remind them of who you were in that parade of people that they interviewed.

MEANWHILE, BACK AT THE RANCH

While **you** are sitting there, writing out your thank-you letter, the employer you saw that day is also sitting at home, very likely reflecting on the day's interview. What's going on in his or her head, do you suppose? Well, you know. They are mentally sifting through all the candidates they saw, trying to decide **who stands out,** so far.

Usually, they've seen a number of candidates who -- in terms of skills and experience -- are basically equal. We will assume you are among those. Sooooooo, the problem the employer faces is trying to decide who stands out, **on other grounds.** And just how do you think they are going to decide that? On what grounds will they give the nod to one person over the other seventeen who are equally qualified? The answer will vary from employer to employer, but according to a survey we did, this is how the employer **typically** chooses one candidate over all the others. **They ask themselves:**

1) Does this prospective employee **fit in** with the people who are already here? Does this person share compatible perspectives, exhibit integrity, manifest a desire to work as part of a team, and have similar values and sense of humor?

2) Does this prospective employee give the feeling of great **enthusiasm for this particular job?** How much does he or she seem to **want** it?

3) Does this prospective employee have an **appearance** that I like? This is an intangible thing, and one can't define it, but it has

to do with the employer's intuition about the person, their face, the way they dress, and how reliable or stable the employer feels them to be, beneath all the externals. One looks for a quiet self-confidence.

4) Does this prospective employee give me the feeling that he or she would give that **extra boost of energy** to their work that I like to see, rather than just trying "to get by." This seems to be dependent on how much the prospective employee truly has their own individual goals, toward which they are striving.

5) Finally, does this prospective employee seem to have a genuine **enthusiasm for our organization** and what it is trying to do? Does he or she seem to like its goals, appreciate its style, and want to work for its success?

If you get chosen, it will probably be because you **stood out** from the other applicants, in these five areas. Therefore, in your thank-you note, and in your written proposal, **anything** you can point to that demonstrates you stand out in these areas, will be very much in your favor: particularly, your enthusiasm for that place and for that job.

WHEN YOU GET INVITED BACK

Well, first of all, what if you don't? What if you have no trouble getting interviews at various places that are of interest to you, but after every interview, you *never* get invited back? Well, it *may be* just a string of bad luck. But, let's face it, it also *may be* that something is dreadfully wrong with the way you come across in interviews. Unhappily, employers will hardly ever tell you this. You will *never* hear them say something like, "You're too cocky and arrogant during the interview." You will always be left completely in the dark as to what you're doing wrong in the interviews.

One way around their deadly silence, of course, is to *ask* for helpful feedback. This sometimes works, *so long as* you make the inquiry *real general* -- applying to *all* your interviews, and not just to the one with them. For example, after you've gotten turned down at a place, you *might* say, "You know, I've been on thirteen interviews at thirteen different places now, where I've gotten turned down. Is there something about me that comes across in an interview, that in your view is causing me not to get hired? If so, I'd really appreciate your giving me some pointers."

Most of the time you *still* won't get a frank answer. You'll just get blithering generalities or else a killing silence. But occasionally you will run into a loving soul, an employer who is willing to risk giving you the truth. No matter how painful it is to hear it, thank her or him, from the bottom of your heart. Their advice, seriously heeded, can bring about just the changes in your interviewing strategy that you most need.

In the absence of any help from employers, you might want to get a good friend of yours to role-play a mock interview with you, in case they see something glaringly obvious, that you're doing wrong.

But, all of this is only necessary *if* you're never getting invited back for a second interview at the same place. Assuming things *are* going favorably, you *will* be invited back for another interview, or interviews at a place that you liked. If you still like them, and they increasingly like you, a job offer will eventually be made. **That's** the time to deal with the fourth question that we saw earlier has got to be on the employer's mind:

"How much are you going to cost me?" As I said earlier, **if** this matter gets raised before you have each decided you want to work together, **turn the question gently aside.** If early on in the game the employer says, "How much salary are you looking for?", you can respond with gentleness and grace: "I think that's a fair question once we have **both** decided that this is where I should be working. First, however, there are other areas we need to explore."

But if you have explored those areas, and are agreeing 'to go steady,' **then** the subject of "how much are you going to cost me?" is not only legitimately raised, it is crucial that it be raised. "The laborer is worthy of his (or her) hire," says the Scriptures. Which, roughly translated, means: "You are entitled to get what you are worth, and not a penny less." So, **you** are interested **in getting as much as possible.**

There are times when the employer is in total sync with you, and offers you exactly what you were hoping for, or more, so that your jaw drops open in amazement. This does happen, but my advice would be not to count on it. Halley's comet happens too, but only once in every 76 years. Usually, your would-be **employer** is interested in saving as much money as possible -- therefore, in **getting you for as little as possible.** So, you two are (for the moment) at odds. Hence you need to negotiate. That's why this part of the job-interview is called "salary *negotiation*." And few of us are born knowing how to go about this. We need some instruction. So, here 'tis:

Salary Negotiation
A CRASH COURSE

"Let's talk salary. How does 'astronomical' sound to you?"

A woman was once describing her very first job to me. It was at a soda fountain. I asked her what her biggest surprise at that job was. "My first paycheck," she said. "I know it sounds incredible, but I was so green at all this, that during the whole interview for the job it never occurred to me to ask what my salary would be. I just took it for granted that it would be a fair and just salary, for the work that I would be doing. Did I ever get a shock, when my first paycheck came! It was so small, I could hardly believe it. What a lesson I learned from that!" Yes, and so may we all.

AT ITS SIMPLEST LEVEL

To speak of salary negotiation is to speak of a matter which can be conducted on several levels. The simplest kind -- as the above story reminds us -- involves remembering to ask during the job-hiring interview what the salary will be. And then stating whether, for you, that amount is satisfactory or not. **That** much negotiation, everyone who is hunting for a job must be prepared to do.

It is well to recognize that you are at a disadvantage if salary negotiation is approached on this simplest level, however. A figure may be named, and if you have not done any research, you may be totally unprepared to say whether or not this is a fair salary for that particular job. You just don't know.

AT ITS NEXT HIGHEST LEVEL

If you're really serious about finding out ahead of time what the job should pay, you will have to do a little research.

• If it's a non-supervisory job you are interested in, you can find out a "ballpark figure" for that industry, by having your library unearth for you the latest monthly issue of the U.S. Department of Labor's *Employment and Earnings*.

• If it's a manager's or supervisory job you are interested in, you will find many of the directories listed in our previous chapter will unearth the information you want. For those graduating from college, some of this information is to be found in the "Salary Surveys" put out by the College Placement Council, from Bethlehem, Pennsylvania. See your library, or the career counseling/placement office of a nearby college.

• *The Occupational Outlook Handbook* will also give you ballpark figures for a selected list of jobs. The job you are interested in **may** be included.

• The other books that you will find most helpful are listed on page 131ff, and page 297. See if your local library has them.

If your librarian simply cannot find or help you find the salary information that you want, do remember that almost every occupation has its own association or professional group, whose business it is to keep tabs on what is happening salary-wise within that occupation or field. To learn the association or professional group for the field or occupation you are interested in, consult the *Encyclopedia of Associations, Vol. 1*, at your library.

In all dealings with this kind of information, you must keep in mind that there are often *dramatic* variations in salary from region to region. Such regional differences in salary reflect, of course, a variety of factors, such as differences in cost of living, differences in supply and demand, etc.

MORE SOPHISTICATED YET

Some job-hunters want to get beyond these "ballpark figures" into more detailed salary negotiation. You may want to walk into an interview knowing **exactly** what That Place pays for a job. Why? Well, for one thing, the pay may be too low for you -- and thus you are saved the necessity of wasting your precious time on that particular place. Secondly, and more importantly, many places have -- as John Crystal insistently pointed out -- a **range** in mind. And if you know what that range is, you can negotiate for a salary that is nearer the **top** of the range, than the **bottom.**

By way of example, let's assume you have done all the homework outlined in the previous two chapters. You have done your research, gone out and knocked on doors, as well as visited libraries. And you have gotten your search down to three or five places that really interest you. You know in general what sort of position you are aiming at, in those particular places -- and you are ready to go for a job interview **as soon as you know what the salary range is for the position that interests you** (it matters not whether that position already exists, or is one you are going to ask them to create). How do you find out what the salary is, or should be, by way of range?

It's relatively easy to define. The rule of thumb is that you will, generally speaking, be paid **more** than the person who is **below** you on the organizational chart, and **less** than the person who is **above** you. There are, needless to say, exceptions to this rule: people who don't quite fit in the organizational chart, such as consultants or researchers who are financed by a grant. But in general, the rule of thumb holds true.

This makes the matter of salary research which precedes salary negotiation relatively (I said "relatively") simple. If through your own information search you can discover who is or would be **above** you on the organizational chart, and who is or would be **below** you, and what they are paid, you would then automatically know what your salary range is, or would be.

a) If the person who would be below you makes $22,000, and the person who would be above you makes $27,000, your range will be something like $23,000 to $26,000.

b) If the person below you makes $10,000, and the person who would be above you makes $13,500, then your range will be something like $10,500 to $12,500.

c) If the person below you makes $6,240, and the person who

would be above you makes $7,800, your range would be $6,400 to $7,600.

That's not so hard to figure out, is it? *Not as hard as you thought it was going to be, at any rate!*

Only one minor problem in the above equation: how do you find out what those who would be above and below you, make? Well, first -- to emphasize the obvious -- you have to find out the **names** of those who would be above and below you, or at least the names of their **positions.** If it is a small organization you are going after -- one with twenty or less employees -- finding this information out should be duck soup. Any employee will likely know the answer. And, since two-thirds of all new jobs are created by companies of that size, you would be **wise beyond your years** to be looking at such sized organizations, **anyway.**

But if you still like "the Big Guys," the large corporations with row upon row of cubicles, and floor after floor of offices, laboratories, or classrooms, then you need to fall back with mercy and pleading on our two familiar life preservers:

- your local reference **librarian** (at the library, you will be surprised at how much of this information is in the organization's annual report, or in other books available there)
- every **contact** you have (family, friend, relative, business, or church acquaintance) who might know the company, and therefore, the information you seek.

Try the library first, but when it has produced all it can for you, and you are still short of what you want to know, go to your contacts. You are looking for Someone Who Knows Someone who either is working, or has worked, at that particular place or organization that interests you, and therefore has or can get this information for you.

If you absolutely run into a blank wall on a particular organization (everyone who works there is pledged to secrecy, and they have shipped all their ex-employees to Siberia), then seek out information on their nearest **competitor** in the same geographic area, e.g., if Citibank were inscrutable, you would then try Chase Manhattan as your research base; or vice versa.

Perseverance and legwork pay off, in this. And if your enthusiasm flags along the way, just picture yourself sitting in the interview for hiring, and now you're at the end of the interview. The prospective employer likes you, you like them, and they say: "How much salary were you expecting?" And because you have done your homework, you know the range, and you name a figure near or at the **top** of their range -- justified by what you anticipate will be your superior performance in that job.

But suppose you **didn't** do your research. Then you're Shadowboxing in the Dark -- as they say. If you just take a stab at it and end

up naming a figure way too high, you're out of the running -- and you can't backtrack. ("Sorry, *we'd like to hire you, but we just can't afford you.*") If you take a stab at it and end up naming a figure way too low, you're also out of the running. ("Sorry, *but we were hoping for someone a little, ah, more professional.*") And if you're in the right range, but at the bottom of it, you've just gotten the job -- **but you have needlessly lost as much as $2,000 a year or more that could have been yours.**

So, salary research/salary negotiation, no matter how much time it takes, pays off *handsomely*. Let's say it takes you a week to ten days to run down this sort of information on the three or four organizations that interest you. And let us say that because you've done this research, when you finally go in for the hiring interview you are able to ask for and obtain a salary that is $2,000 higher in range, than you would otherwise have known enough to ask for.

In just three years, you'll have earned $6,000 extra, because of that research. Not bad pay, for ten days' work! And it could be much more. As we have said earlier, **information is the key to a successful job-hunt.** And there is no reward for those too lazy to go gather that information.

AT ITS MOST SOPHISTICATED LEVEL

Job-hunters with incredibly developed bargaining needs, always ask how salary negotiation is conducted at its most sophisticated level. By way of answering, let me say first of all that it is my personal conviction most job-hunters will **never** operate at this level, and therefore do **not** need this sort of information.

But in case you do, or in case you are simply dying of curiosity to know how it's done, it is completely described in *Where Do I Go From Here With My Life?* pages 140–42, as honed to a fine point by John Crystal. Briefly summarized, it goes like this:

You do all the steps described previously, so that you discover what the employer's range would likely be. Let us say it turns out that the range is one that varies two thousand dollars. You then "invent" in your mind a new range, for yourself, that "hooks" on the old one, in the following fashion:

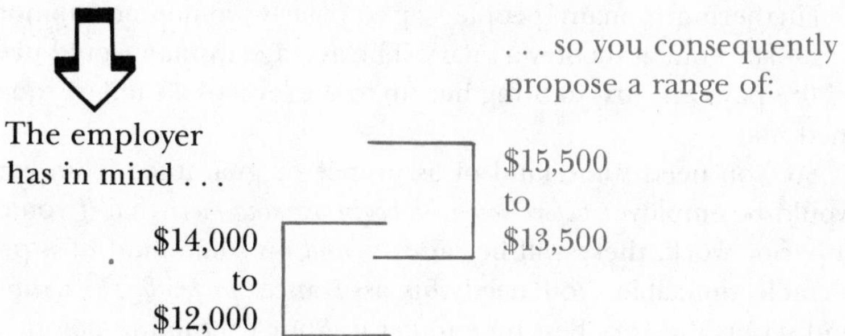

During the job-interview, then, when the employer says, "What kind of a salary did you have in mind?" you can respond, "I believe my productivity is such that it would **justify** a salary in the range of $13,500 to $15,500." This keeps you, at a minimum, near *the top* of their range; and, at a maximum, challenges them to go **beyond the top** that they had in mind, either immediately, or in the future, by means of promised raises. (Don't be afraid to ask "When?")

FRINGES

During your salary negotiation, do not forget to pay attention to so-called fringe benefits. 'Fringes' such as life insurance, health benefits or health plans, vacation or holiday plans, and retirement programs add another 25% to many workers' salaries. That is to say, if an employee receives $800 salary per month, the fringe benefits are worth another $200 per month. So, if the employee who is beneath you on the organizational chart gets $700 plus benefits, and the employee who is above you gets $1,100 plus benefits, while you are offered this new job at $800 and no benefits, you are being acquired rather cheaply. You should therefore remember to ask for similar benefits to those above and below you. If no benefits are possible, then you are justified in asking for a higher salary, which in this case ought to be $1,000.

FINALLY, THE MATTER OF A RAISE AND/OR PROMOTION

In 75 out of the last 100 years, the cost of living increased. That means that your initial salary will annually **decline** in value, as inflation takes its toll. You will need a regular series of raises, just to protect your starting salary against erosion.

Furthermore, many people -- particularly women and minorities -- start out at too low a salary. The average woman would need a 70% pay raise just to bring her up to the level of a similarly qualified man.

So, you need some kind of assurance or guarantee from your would-be employer *before you even begin working there* that *if* you do superior work, there will be raises -- *and* on some kind of a predictable timetable. You need this assurance, *preferably in writing*, and *now* is the very best time to get it. Your bargaining power diminishes to near zero once they've 'got you.'

Therefore, this question should be a part of your salary negotiation, without fail: *"If I accomplish this job to your satisfaction, as I fully expect to -- and more -- when could I expect to have my salary raised, and by how much? Would there be promotions in this job, and if so, on what kind of timetable?"* If you have certain needs or wishes in this area, you may have the right to say what they are.

Once this part of the salary negotiation is concluded to your satisfaction do ask to have it included in any letter of agreement or employment contract that they may be sending you. It may be you cannot get it in writing, but **do try!** The Road to Hell is paved with oral promises that went unwritten, and -- later -- unfulfilled. Many executives conveniently "forget" what they told you, or later deny they ever said it. Many executives leave the company for another position and place, and their successor or the one over you all may disown any **unwritten** promises: *"I don't know what caused them to say that to you, but they clearly exceeded their authority, and of course we can't be held to that."*

But even if you do get the promise in writing, raises and promotions are still something *you* have to justify, and on an annual basis. You will be amazed at how little attention your superiors will probably pay to your noteworthy accomplishments, and how little they are aware at the end of the year that you really are *entitled* to a raise. Noteworthy your accomplishments may be, but no one is taking notes . . . unless **you** do. Accordingly, career experts such as Bernard Haldane have suggested that you keep a weekly diary of your accomplishments, once you are on the job. I know employees who do just that. They take time each Friday afternoon or early evening to jot down reminders to themselves of just what it is that they accomplished that past week (or helped others to accomplish, if they were part of a team effort). *Do take this seriously.* Then, when the yearly anniversary of your hiring comes around, you can read through the diary, make up a *one-page summary* of its contents for that past year -- and take that summary in with you to support your request for a raise and/or promotion.

CONCLUSION

We have covered now the techniques of successful job-hunters. We discussed in Chapter 3 some brief hints that should help you in your job-hunt, if all you are looking for is hints. We discussed in Chapters 4 and 5 as well as in this chapter, the three secrets of **successful career-change** or truly **systematic job-hunting:** WHAT, WHERE and HOW.

If you have not only *read* (I did not say "skimmed") those chapters, but have actually *done the exercises* in those chapters *and in Appendix A,* you will have mastered the systematic techniques that successful job-hunters and career-changers use. With a little bit of luck, these techniques should work for you as they have worked for them.

Assuming they do, when you are in that next job (hopefully that Dream Job), you will know the truth of something Dick Lathrop first said many many years ago, in his book *Who's Hiring Who:*

> There may be others who applied there who could have done the job better than you. But it is true today, and it will ever be true: the person who gets hired is not necessarily the one who can do that job best; but, the one **who knows the most about how to get hired**.

POSTSCRIPT

Twenty-three years ago, during one of the times that I was myself job-hunting, I devoured everything in print about job-hunting, hoping someone had the magic key. I noticed one thing that all these books and articles had in common. They described what you should do, and then the very next line said, "Now, that you've gotten a job . . . " And I thought, "Oops. But what if you do everything they tell you to do, and it **doesn't** lead to a job? What then?" There was a leap the size of the Grand Canyon there.

I have a built-in suspicion of anyone who implies that they have some magic job-hunting formula that never fails. I hope you do, too. Certainly I want to make no such claim in these pages. We have tried to **improve your chances -- I would even say *greatly* improve your chances --** at conducting an effective and successful job-hunt or career-change. And we have tried to do this by describing what we have learned from talking to thousands of successful job-hunters. This is akin to what you would instinctively do if you wanted to learn how to run well, or how to play tennis, or master a craft. You would talk to *successful* runners, tennis players, or craftspeople, and pick their brains for everything they were worth.

In these pages I've carefully described all the techniques which successful job-hunters use. But I know the next question out of your mouth will be:

DOES THIS CREATIVE METHOD OF THE JOB-HUNT ALWAYS WORK?

Ah, dear reader, how I wish I could assure you that it does. There are two things that *are* absolutely true:

(1) It works **most of the time for most people** who diligently and persistently give the time and effort to their job-hunt that is required. And:

(2) **It works better than any other job-hunting technique in the world.**

But does it **always** work, and for everyone? Ah, now we're talking about a perfect world and perfect techniques. There is no such animal, at least not on this earth.

Follow every instruction in this book *precisely*, do every exercise *slavishly*, follow every prescription *religiously*, you still are not absolutely 100% guaranteed that you will find the job you are looking for. Or at least not right away.

There are two reasons why this is so: people don't follow the techniques in this book as thoroughly as they think they do; and, some part of job-hunting still depends on **luck,** no matter what you do to try to change that.

NOT BEING THOROUGH WHEN YOU THINK YOU ARE BEING THOROUGH

Each year, over 300,000 people purchase, read, and use this book. Each year, as many as 5,000 of them write to us. Most people write to tell the story of how the book helped them, or to make helpful suggestions for next year's update. But each year, about two of those letter-writers write to say that they tried all the ideas in this book, and they just didn't work.

I am prepared even before I read such a letter, to believe them. I can always picture exceptions to anything. It does not matter if these techniques work for **most** people; I can still picture someone in a small village where every job is not only taken, but numbered. I can picture someone with a handicap so formidable that no one is sympathetic enough to hire them. So, I have been ever ready with a sympathetic ear and heart. We have followed up these letters very carefully.

Sometimes it is just as I pictured. The writer deserves A+ for following all the steps outlined here in this book to a 'T.' But over the years of such follow-up I have learned something I had *not* anticipated. Namely, it has been astounding to me how often people *claimed* they had followed every prescription in this book, but unintentionally revealed they had skipped over some step that I had said was crucial. Like what? Well, for example, like sending thank-you notes.

Just to be sure we were talking on the same wavelength, I would go down a little checklist with the person who said they'd tried everything I'd suggested, and it just hadn't worked. In due time I'd come to "Send thank-you notes." "How many thank-you notes did you send out during your job-hunt?" I'd ask. "Thank-you notes? Was I supposed to send thank-you notes?" would come the reply. It is to tear out one's hair. "My dear fellow, it says thank-you notes have actually gotten people the job." "Oh. I don't recall ever reading that."

THE OTHER PROBLEM: THE NEED FOR JUST A LITTLE BIT OF LUCK

Even if you **have** done everything right, and left no stone unturned, there is still always the chance that the job-hunt won't go well. That's because, over and above everything else, over and above all the hard work and thinking that you expend on your job-hunt, you must have on your side at least a little bit of **luck**. By luck, I mean that accidental meeting with **just** the right person, or being in **just** the right place at **just** the right time, so that a door opens for you that leads to that job.

That seems to leave a lot to chance. So why not just start with chance, and chuck all the homework and other stuff we've talked about on these pages? Well wait just a minute.

HOW TO GET LUCKY

Based on interviews with countless numbers of successful job-hunters, we now know that "getting lucky" is not the random accident that it would seem to be. Articles and books have been written about who "gets lucky" and who does not. If you would "get lucky," there are things you can do. Here's what we now know:

(1) **Luck favors the prepared mind.** The reason for this is not difficult to understand. If you've done all the homework on yourself, diligently identified your favorite skills, *put them in order*, and if you've gotten a pretty complete picture of the kind of job you are looking for, **you will be more sensitive and alert to luck, when it crosses your path.**

(2) **Luck favors the person who is working the hardest at the job-hunt.** In a word, the person who is devoting the most hours to getting out there and pounding the pavement, doing their research, making contacts. Luck favors the person who is putting in thirty-four hours a week on their job-hunt much more than it favors the person who is putting in five hours a week. The more you are 'out there' the more you're going to run across that fortunate coincidence that others call 'luck.'

(3) **Luck favors the person who has told the most people clearly and precisely what he or she is looking for.** The more ears and eyes you have out there, looking on your behalf for the kind of job you want, the more likely that you will 'get lucky.' Forty eyes

and ears are 'luckier' than two. Eighty, a hundred and twenty, are 'luckier' still. But before you get 'this lucky,' you must have done your homework so carefully that you can tell those other eyes and ears just exactly what it is you want. Luck does not favor the vague.

(4) **Luck favors the person who has alternatives up his or her sleeve,** and doesn't just **bullheadedly** persist in following just one method, or going after just one place, or one kind of job.

(5) **Luck favors the person who WANTS WITH ALL THEIR HEART to find that job.** The ambivalent job-hunter, who is looking half-heartedly, for a job that inspires no enthusiasm in them, is rarely so 'lucky.'

(6) **Luck favors the person who is going after their dream -- the thing they really want to do the most in this world.** When you want something so much that it brings tears to your eyes at the thought of getting it, you will always be 'luckier' than the person who is settling for 'what's realistic.'

(7) **Luck favors the person who is trying hard to be 'a special kind of person' in this world, treating others with grace and dignity and courtesy and kindness.** The person who runs roughshod over others in their race to 'get ahead,' usually is not so 'lucky.' During the job-hunt you need 'favors' from others. If you treated them cavalierly in another day and age, now is their time to say, "Sure, I'll help you out," and then do nothing. **Getting even** is more popular than being helpful, if there is a score to be settled.

So, if you would have 'luck' on your side during this phase of the job-hunt, **do** take seriously the above **ways of improving your luck.**

My friend, I wish you **good luck.** I wish you **persistence.** I wish you **success,** not only with your job-hunt or career-change, but -- even more -- with your life.

WHAT IS SUCCESS?

To laugh often and much;

To win the respect of intelligent people
and the affection of children;

To earn the appreciation of honest critics
and endure the betrayal of false friends;

To appreciate beauty;

To find the best in others;

To leave the world a bit better, whether by
a healthy child, a garden
patch or a redeemed social condition;

To know even one life has breathed
easier because you have lived;

This is to have succeeded.

—*Ralph Waldo Emerson*

The Appendices

We make a living by what we get,
but we make a life
by what we give.

—Winston Churchill

Appendix A

The Quick Job-Hunting (And Career-Changing) Map

How to Create A Picture of Your Ideal Job or Next Career

A Booklet

Introduction

IN ORDER TO HUNT FOR YOUR IDEAL JOB, or even something close to your ideal job, you must have a picture of it, in your head. The clearer the picture, the easier it will be to hunt for it. The purpose of this booklet is to guide you as you draw that picture.

We have chosen a "Flower" as the model for that picture. While such expressions as "plugging in," "turning on," and other common phrases portray you (implicitly) as a machine, you are actually much more like a Flower than a machine. That is to say, you flourish in some job-environments, but wither in others. Therefore, the purpose of putting together this Flower Picture of yourself is to help you identify what kind of a work climate you will flourish in, and thus do your very best work. Your twin goals should be to be as happy as you can be at your job, while at the same time you do your most effective work.

The small picture of our Flower model on the next page gives you an overview. That picture of the Flower, however, isn't large enough, nor does each petal have enough detail, to be really useful as a worksheet.

The actual worksheets, dealing with one petal at a time, are scattered throughout the remainder of this booklet. You will deal with the petals in a *logical* order of learning, beginning with the ones that are easiest to fill out, and working on through to the harder ones.

The order in which you will work on the eight petals is:

1. Physical Setting
2. Spiritual or Emotional Setting
3. My Favorite Skills -- what I like to do with *Things*, *People* and/or *Information*
4. My Favorite Kinds of People I Like to Use These Skills with
5. My Favorite Kinds of Information I Like to Use These Skills with
6. My Favorite Kinds of Things I Like to Use These Skills with
7. Outcomes: Immediate and Long-range
8. Rewards: Salary, Level and Other

And when you are done, you will put all the petals together, so that they form one complete Flower picture of your Ideal Job. Okay? Then, get out your pen or pencil and *let's get started*.

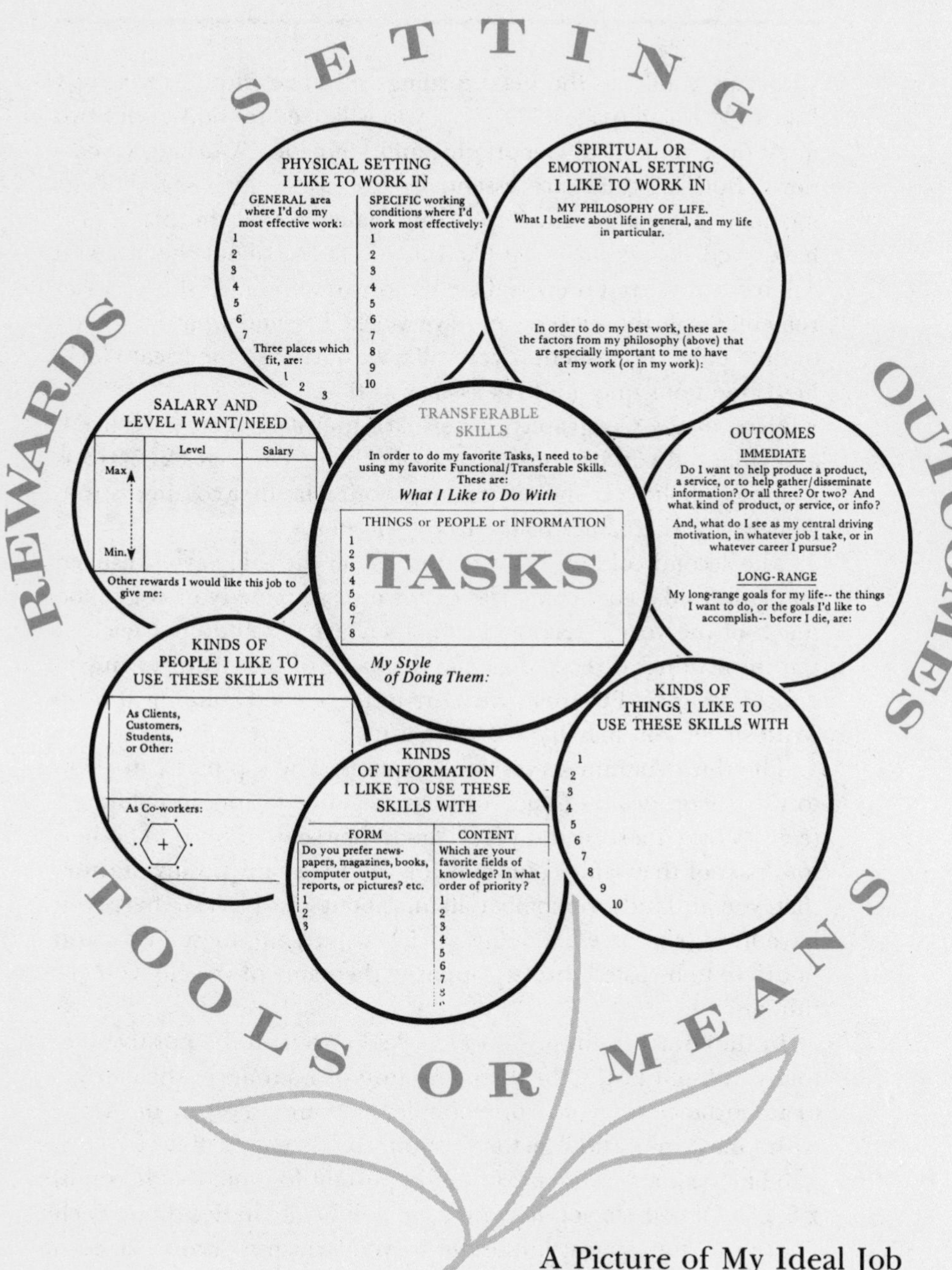

A Picture of My Ideal Job

Step One: Physical Setting

In order to fill out the petal dealing with The Physical Setting I Like to Work In (pages 214–215), you will need to think about two questions: your ideal Geography, and your ideal Working Conditions. Both of these are essentially exercises which search your memory. That is to say, if you can remember all the places you have lived -- and what you liked or didn't like about them -- you will have answered the Ideal Geography question. And if you can remember all the places you have worked -- and what you liked or didn't like about them -- you will have answered the Ideal Working Conditions question. It's as easy as that.

First, to the Geography. Where are the places you have lived, and what did you like or dislike about them? On pages 212-213 is a chart to help you answer this question. The first column is (obviously) for the names of the towns or cities.

The second column is for you to list all the things you disliked and still dislike about that city or town (e.g., "cloudy or foggy too much of the year," "terrible newspaper," etc.). You do not need to put these things directly opposite the name of the city or town you are thinking of. Put them *anywhere* in the second column. But do write small! You may have a lot to list.

The third column serves two purposes. The top part is for you to list the **opposite** of each of your negative factors in column 2 (e.g., "sunny most of the year," "good newspaper," etc.). The bottom part of that same column is for you to list any positive factors that you instantly remember liking about the places where you have lived (e.g., "we had a big yard," etc.). Again, these factors do not have to be listed directly opposite the name of the city you are thinking of.

In the fourth column, you are asked to put all the positive factors you listed in the third column (top or bottom) in their order of importance for you. For example, if "sunny most of the year" is the most important factor for you, that becomes #1. If "has a good newspaper" is the next most important for you, that becomes #2, etc. Of course, you may find some difficulty in deciding which Positive factor is most important to you, which is second, and so on; if that is the case, we urge you to use the Prioritizing Grids which you will find on pages 217 and 218, complete with instructions.

The fifth column requires your friends to help you. You read to them the list of Positive factors that you have arranged, in order, in the fourth column, and see what cities or towns they can think of, that have these characteristics. Don't stumble over two factors that seem to be contradictory, like "sunny all year round" and "skiing nearby." There's usually an answer (like, "Palm Springs with the tram up Mt. San Jacinto to the snow"). When your friends are through suggesting places, pick the one you like best, next best, and third best, and put them on the bottom left side of the petal on page 214f. If you don't know enough about them, put your three favorites in any order, and write away to their chambers of commerce, to find out more about them. The library also can help!

The last three columns are only to be used if you have a wife, husband, or partner, and you are doing joint decision-making about where you eventually want to move to. In that case, your partner will need to photocopy the Geography chart (before you fill it out, obviously) and do their own first five columns. If your preferred geographical areas turn out to be identical, then you are done with the chart. But if they don't, then go on to column #6 and copy your partner's positive factors from his or her column #4.

Now, on to column #7. Merge together, there, your "Ranking of My Positives" and your partner's ranking. Your factors, obviously, are numbered 1, 2, 3, 4, 5, etc. while your partner's are numbered, a, b, c, d, e, etc. You will notice that column #7 asks you first to list your partner's top priority, then your top one, then your partner's second priority, then your second one, etc.

When done, move on to column #8. It involves exactly the same procedure as column #5. Show column #7 to all your friends and ask them what cities or towns they think of, when they read this (combined) list of factors. Again, don't be put off by apparently contradictory factors. There's usually some place, somewhere, that can give you both factors.

Incidentally, you may have looked at this chart and sort of shrugged your shoulders, because you already know your geographical destination, and by name. It's either where you already are, or some place you both *have to* move to, or some place you both would love to move to. Nonetheless, try filling out columns #1 through #4, anyway. It helps a lot if you know, in that city or town, which characteristics you like best (or you each like best) -- and in what order.

My/Our Geographical

Decision Making for Just You			
Column 1 Names of Places I Have Lived	*Column 2* From the Past: Negatives	*Column 3* Translating the Negatives into Positives	*Column 4* Ranking of My Positives
	Factors I Disliked and Still Dislike about That Place		1.
			2.
			3.
			4.
			5.
			6.
			7.
			8.
			9.
			10.
		Factors I Liked and Still Like about That Place	11.
			12.
			13.
			14.
			15.

ʾreferences

	Decision Making for You and a Partner		
Column 5 Places Which Fit These Criteria	*Column 6* Ranking of His/Her Preferences	*Column 7* Combining Our Two Lists (Columns 4 & 6)	*Column 8* Places Which Fit These Criteria
	a.	a.	
		1.	
	b.	b.	
		2.	
	c.	c.	
		3.	
	d.	d.	
		4.	
	e.	e.	
		5.	
	f.	f.	
		6.	
	g.	g.	
		7.	
	h.	h.	
		8.	
	i.	i.	
		9.	
	j.	j.	
		10.	
	k.	k.	
		11.	
	l.	l.	
		12.	
	m.	m.	
		13.	
	n.	n.	
		14.	
	o.	o.	
		15.	

The First Petal

The Physical Setting I Like to Work In

GENERAL
Geographical Factors

The geographical area which would please me most, and therefore help me to do my most effective work, would have the following characteristics (e.g., warm dry summers, skiing in the winter, a good newspaper, etc.):

1.

2.

3.

SPECIFIC
Working Conditions

At my place of work I could be happiest and do my most effective work, if I had the following working conditions (e.g., working indoors or out, not punching a timeclock, a boss who gave me free rein to do my work, having my own office, etc.):

1.

2.

3.

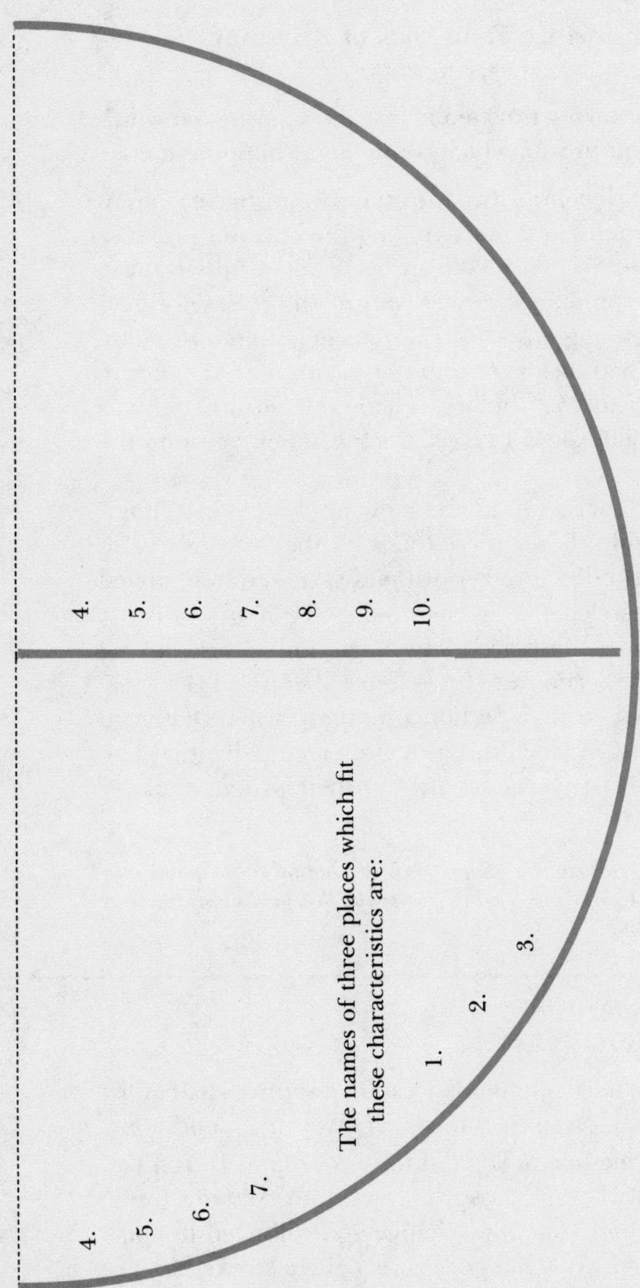

4.
5.
6.
7.
The names of three places which fit
these characteristics are:
1.
2.
3.
4.
5.
6.
7.
8.
9.
10.

How to Prioritize Your Lists of Anything

(A Digression)

Here is a method for taking (say) ten items, and figuring out which one is most important to you, which is next most important, etc.

• Insert the items to be prioritized, in any order, in Section A. Then compare two items at a time, circling the one you prefer -- between the two -- in Section B. Which one is more important to you? State the question any way you want to: In the case of geographical factors, you might ask, "If I were being offered two jobs, one in an area that had factor #1, but not factor #2; the other in an area that had factor #2, but not factor #1, all other things being equal, which job would I take?" *Circle it.* Then go on to the next pair, etc.

• When you are all done, count up the number of times each number got circled, all told. Enter these totals on the TIMES line in Section C. Then notice the number of times each item was circled ("Times" = "Times Circled"). This determines the item's ranking. Most circled = #1, next most circled = #2, etc. Enter this ranking on the RANK line in Section C. If two items are circled the same number of times, look back in Section B to see -- when those two were compared there -- which one you preferred. Give that one an extra half point. List the items, now in their proper rank, in Section D.

Each time you use this grid, make a photocopy of it, and fill in the photocopy rather than the original. (You will need to photocopy this grid many times as you go through this map.)

Working Conditions

Now that you have filled out the General Geographical half of the Physical Settings petal, on to the other half: Working Conditions.

You use the same method as you did for Geography. In fact you can make up a chart where you copy the first four columns (only) of the Geography Chart. The only change you will need to make is to relabel column #1 as "Names of Places I Have Worked." Here name all the companies, or all the jobs you have ever held.

Column #2, now, is "Factors I Disliked and Still Dislike About That Job." Examples would be "no windows," "a boss that oversupervised me," "had to come in too early," etc.

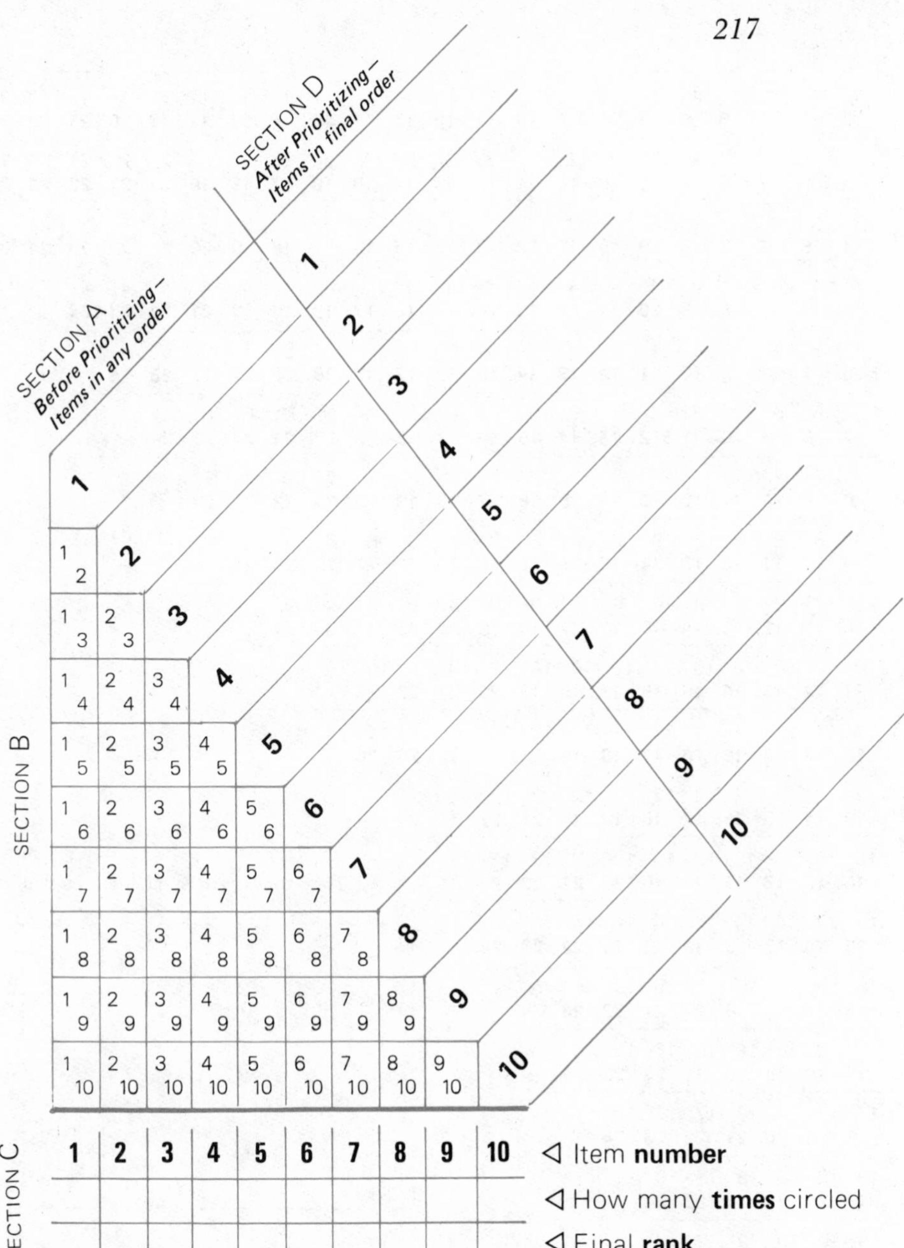

Prioritizing Grid for 10 Items

1 1 1 1 1 1 1 1 1 1 1 1 1 1 1 1 1 1 1 1 1 1 1
2 3 4 5 6 7 8 9 10 11 12 13 14 15 16 17 18 19 20 21 22 23 24

2 2 2 2 2 2 2 2 2 2 2 2 2 2 2 2 2 2 2 2 2 2
3 4 5 6 7 8 9 10 11 12 13 14 15 16 17 18 19 20 21 22 23 24

3 3 3 3 3 3 3 3 3 3 3 3 3 3 3 3 3 3 3 3 3
4 5 6 7 8 9 10 11 12 13 14 15 16 17 18 19 20 21 22 23 24

4 4 4 4 4 4 4 4 4 4 4 4 4 4 4 4 4 4 4 4
5 6 7 8 9 10 11 12 13 14 15 16 17 18 19 20 21 22 23 24

5 5 5 5 5 5 5 5 5 5 5 5 5 5 5 5 5 5 5
6 7 8 9 10 11 12 13 14 15 16 17 18 19 20 21 22 23 24

6 6 6 6 6 6 6 6 6 6 6 6 6 6 6 6 6 6
7 8 9 10 11 12 13 14 15 16 17 18 19 20 21 22 23 24

7 7 7 7 7 7 7 7 7 7 7 7 7 7 7 7 7
8 9 10 11 12 13 14 15 16 17 18 19 20 21 22 23 24

8 8 8 8 8 8 8 8 8 8 8 8 8 8 8 8
9 10 11 12 13 14 15 16 17 18 19 20 21 22 23 24

9 9 9 9 9 9 9 9 9 9 9 9 9 9 9
10 11 12 13 14 15 16 17 18 19 20 21 22 23 24

10 10 10 10 10 10 10 10 10 10 10 10 10 10
11 12 13 14 15 16 17 18 19 20 21 22 23 24

11 11 11 11 11 11 11 11 11 11 11 11 11
12 13 14 15 16 17 18 19 20 21 22 23 24

12 12 12 12 12 12 12 12 12 12 12 12
13 14 15 16 17 18 19 20 21 22 23 24

13 13 13 13 13 13 13 13 13 13 13
14 15 16 17 18 19 20 21 22 23 24

14 14 14 14 14 14 14 14 14 14
15 16 17 18 19 20 21 22 23 24

15 15 15 15 15 15 15 15 15
16 17 18 19 20 21 22 23 24

16 16 16 16 16 16 16 16
17 18 19 20 21 22 23 24

17 17 17 17 17 17 17
18 19 20 21 22 23 24

18 18 18 18 18 18
19 20 21 22 23 24

19 19 19 19 19
20 21 22 23 24

20 20 20 20
21 22 23 24

21 21 21
22 23 24

22 22
23 24

23
24

Total times each number got circled

1	2	3	4	5	6
7	8	9	10	11	12
13	14	15	16	17	18
19	20	21	22	23	24

Prioritizing Grid for 24 Items

Each time you use this grid, make a photocopy of it, and fill in the photocopy rather than the original. (You will need to photocopy this grid many times as you go through this map.)

Columns #3 and #4 remain the same. List, and then prioritize, the positive factors about the working conditions you like best. Remember, these are also the working conditions under which you can do your best and most effective work. When you're done, list them on the right hand side of the petal on page 214f.

And voila! The first petal is all finished.

Step Two: Spiritual or Emotional Setting

Every job or career has not merely a physical setting, but a spiritual or emotional one also: the realm of things we cannot see. For example, a man once phoned me to ask what he should do about a crooked contract his firm had just executed. I asked him who drew it up. He said, "I did." I asked him why. He said, "My boss told me it was that, or I'd lose my job."

You need to think out, as part of your picture of your Ideal Job, what is important to you in life -- in the area of things we cannot see: values, principles, what you are willing to stand up for, and what you are not willing to stand up for, what you care about.

The most useful way to do this is to take a piece of blank paper (or two) and write out on it your *philosophy about life*: which typically might include some statement of why you think we are here on earth, what it is that you believe we are supposed to do while we are here, what you think is important in life and what is not important, and which values of our society you agree with, and which ones you disagree with. As a suggested framework only, you might want to choose from among these elements (you don't have to use them all):

- Behavior: how do you think we should behave in this world
- Beliefs: what are your strongest beliefs
- Choice: what do you think about its nature and importance
- Community: what ways do we belong to each other, and what do you think our responsibility is to each other
- Compassion: what do you think is its importance, and how should it be manifested in our daily life

The Second Petal

Spiritual or Emotional Setting I Like to Work In

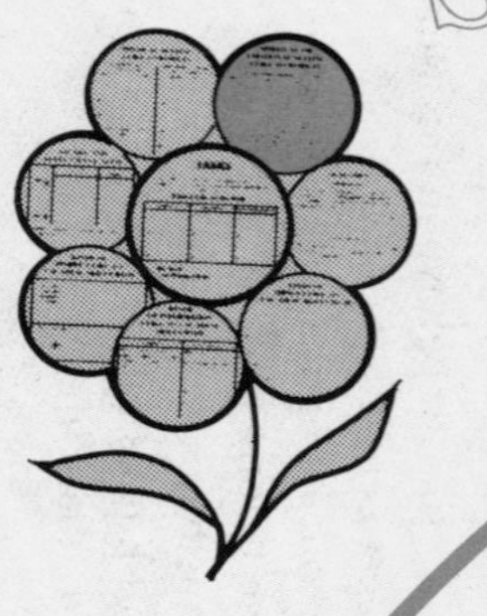

MY PHILOSOPHY OF LIFE.

What I believe about life in general,
and my life in particular:
(key ideas here)

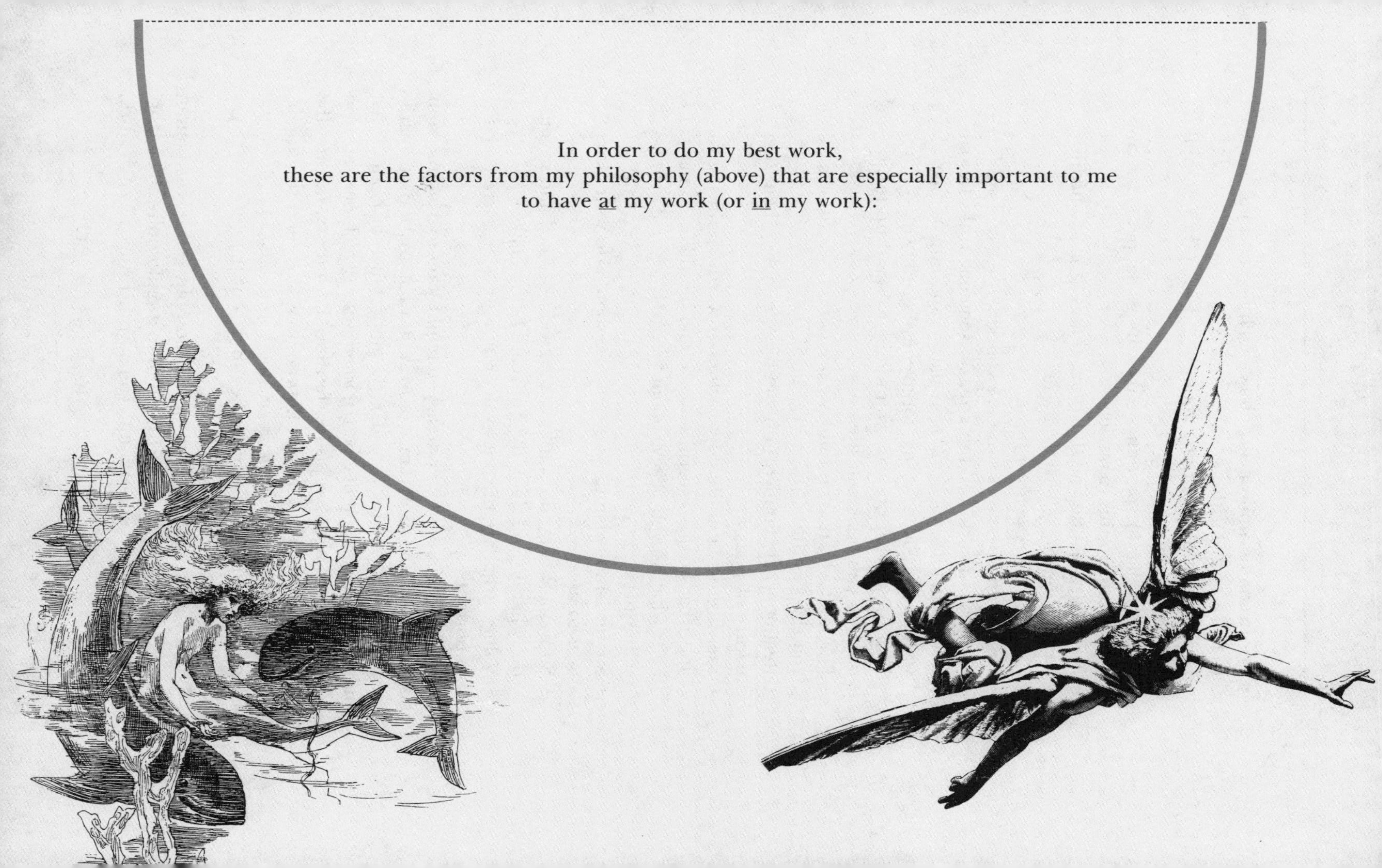

In order to do my best work,
these are the factors from my philosophy (above) that are especially important to me
to have at my work (or in my work):

- Confusion or ambivalence: how much do you think we need to learn to live with
- Death: what do you think about it and what do you think happens after it
- Events: what do you think makes things happen, and how do we explain this to ourselves
- Free will: what do you think: are things 'preordained to happen' or do we have free will
- God: see *Supreme Being*
- Heroes and heroines: who are yours
- Human: what do you think makes someone truly 'human'
- Love: what do you think is its nature and importance, along with all its related words: forgiveness, grace, etc.
- Principles: what ones are you willing to stand up for, which ones do you base your life on
- Purpose: why do you think we are here on earth, what do you think is the purpose of your life
- Reality: what comments do you have to make, about the nature of reality
- Sacrifice: what in life do you think is worth sacrificing for, and what kinds of sacrifice would you be willing to make
- Self: what do you believe about your self, ego, selfishness, selflessness
- Stewardship: what do you think we should do with God's gifts to us
- Supreme Being: do you have a concept of One, and if you do, what do you think the Supreme Being is like
- Values: what are the ones you hold most dear, sacred, and important

To help you in this latter area, you might want to examine your thoughts about the importance of *truth* (in what areas, particularly, does truth most matter to you?), the importance of *beauty* (what kinds of beauty do you like best?), *moral issues* (which ones are you most concerned about -- justice, feeding the hungry, helping the homeless, comforting AIDS sufferers, or what?), and the importance of *love*. Don't just *write*; take time also to *think!* Jot down the key ideas of your philosophy in the top part of the petal, on pages 220–221.

When you are done writing your philosophy of life, the bottom part of this petal asks you to lift out of that philosophy any factors which are especially important to you at your future place of work, or in your future work. For example, your philosophy of life might have reminded you: "I have to work in a place where I am never asked to do anything dishonest." Or: "I want to be among loving, supportive co-workers, and not among people who are always backbiting or gossiping about everyone." Whatever occurs to you, after studying your philosophy, put this stuff down, in the bottom part of that petal.

And, voila! The second petal is all finished.

Step Three: My Favorite Transferable Skills

Now, you know what it is you're going to do here. You are going to figure out what skills you use when you are enjoying yourself the most -- either in your work, or in your home, or when you are doing some hobby or recreation. These skills, no matter where you used them in the past, are transferable now to other jobs or careers.

There are two ways to identify your transferable skills: "Quick, but Superficial" and "Slow, but Absolutely Thorough." Let's look at "Quick, but Superficial" first.

The Party Exercise: What Skills You Have and Most Enjoy Using

As John L. Holland has taught us all, skills may be thought of as dividing into six clusters or families. To see which ones you are *attracted to*, try this exercise:

On the next page is an aerial view of a room in which a two-day (!) party is taking place. At this party, people with the same or similar interests have (for some reason) all gathered in the same corner of the room.

(1) Which corner of the room would you instinctively be drawn to, as the group of people you would most *enjoy* being with for the longest time? (Leave aside any question of shyness, or whether you would have to talk with them.) Write the *letter* for that corner here: ☐

(2) After fifteen minutes, everyone in the corner you have chosen leaves for another party crosstown, except you. Of the groups *that still remain* now, which corner or group would you be drawn to the most, as the people you would most *enjoy* being with for the longest time? Write the letter for that corner here: ☐

(3) After fifteen minutes, this group too leaves for another party, except you. Of the corners, and groups, which remain now, which one would you most enjoy being with for the longest time? Write the letter for that corner here: ☐

(If you want to explore this further, see Holland, John L., "Self-Directed Search, 1985 Revision." This is a self-marking test which you can use to discover your "Holland code" and what occupations you might ***start*** *your research with. You can order an SDS Specimen Set for less than $5, which includes the SDS, a brief* Occupations Finder, *and a booklet, "You and Your Career," from the publisher, Psychological Assessment Resources, Inc., Box 998, Odessa, FL 33556.)*

Now, on to "Slow, but Absolutely Thorough."

In order to find out this information, it will be necessary for you to write out seven (7) stories of some enjoyable and satisfying experiences or accomplishments which you have done in your life. Which stories should you choose? Ah, that's a good question. Not necessarily the ones which occur to you right off the top of your head. Sometimes you have to dig deeper.

To guard yourself against impulsively choosing stories which may not tell you much about your skills, it is helpful to construct a basic outline of your life, for yourself, first. One way to do this is through a Memory Net.

The Memory Net

That Net is on the next page. You should take at least three hours (with some hard thinking, as well as writing) to fill it in.

In the first column of the Memory Net are the years of your life, divided into five-year periods (cross out the years before your birth, of course). Some of you will be able to remember what activities you were doing during each of these five-year periods, just from seeing the dates. Use this column, then, to jog your memory, and fill in the rest of the Net.

The second column is for those of you who don't remember things by Dates, but by what job you were holding down (or what school you were attending). Use this column, then, to jog your memory -- fill it in, and then fill in the rest of the Net.

The third column is for those of you who don't remember things by either Years or Jobs, but by where you were living at the time. Use this column, then, to jog your memory -- fill it in, and then fill in the rest of the Net.

Once you've tackled the first three columns, as you go across the rest of the Memory Net you will generally find it pays to fill in the three Activities columns first (columns 4, 6, and 8), and then go back to the Accomplishments columns (5, 7, and 9). That is to say, once you remember what you were doing (activities) in the way of

Jogging Your Memory

Leisure

Column 1 In Terms of Five-Year Periods	Column 2 In Terms of Jobs You Have Held	Column 3 In Terms of Places You Have Lived	Column 4 Activities	Column 5 Accomplishments
e.g. 1986–1990				
1981–1985				
1976–1980				
1971–1975				
1966–1970				
1961–1965				
1956–1960				
1951–1955				
1946–1950				
1941–1945				
1936–1940				
1931–1935				
1926–1930				
1921–1925				
1916–1920				

Column 6	*Column 7*	*Column 8*	*Column 9*
Learning		Labor	
Activities	Accomplishments	Activities	Accomplishments

Leisure, Learning, or Labor (Work), you will then find it easier to think of specific accomplishments in your Leisure or your Learning or your Labor. Put down titles only, or a few words to jog your memory, rather than attempting any more detailed description of your accomplishments, at this time.

Once you have the Net all filled in, you are ready to choose and write your stories. You will need at least seven blank sheets of paper. On each of these sheets you are (eventually) going to write one of your stories -- picked from the Memory Net. Then you will analyze each story, one by one, to see what skills you were using, in that story.

For the time being, you start by writing **just one** of those stories. Look over your Memory Net, and most particularly at columns 5, 7, and 9. Look at your accomplishments. Whether they were early in your life, or more recently, whether they were in your leisure life, or your learning life, or your labor/work life, does not matter.

Just be sure also that it deals in turn with TASK, TOOLS, AND MEANS, and OUTCOME OR RESULT. See the example that follows here.

1. A TASK. Something you wanted to do, just because it was fun or would give you a sense of adventure or a sense of accomplishment. Normally there was a problem that you were trying to solve, or a challenge you were trying to overcome, or something you were trying to master or produce or create.

2. TOOLS OR MEANS. You used something to help you do the task, solve the problem, overcome the challenge. Either you had certain *Things* to help you -- objects, materials, tools or equipment, or you had other *People* to help you, or you got a hold of some vital *Information*. Tell us what tools or means you used, and how you used them.

3. AN OUTCOME OR RESULT. You were able to finish the task or solve the problem, overcome the challenge, master a process, or produce or create something. You had a sense of pride, even if no one else knew what it was you had accomplished.[1]

1. © Copyright 1988 by D. Porot. Adapted and used by his permission.

Once you have selected your first story, write it out in detail -- but keep it comparatively brief -- two or three paragraphs at most. Be sure that it is *a story* you tell -- that is, that it moves step by step. It may help if you pretend that you are telling it to a small whining child who keeps saying, "An' then whadja do?" "An' then whadja do?"

When you are done, label that sheet "#1".

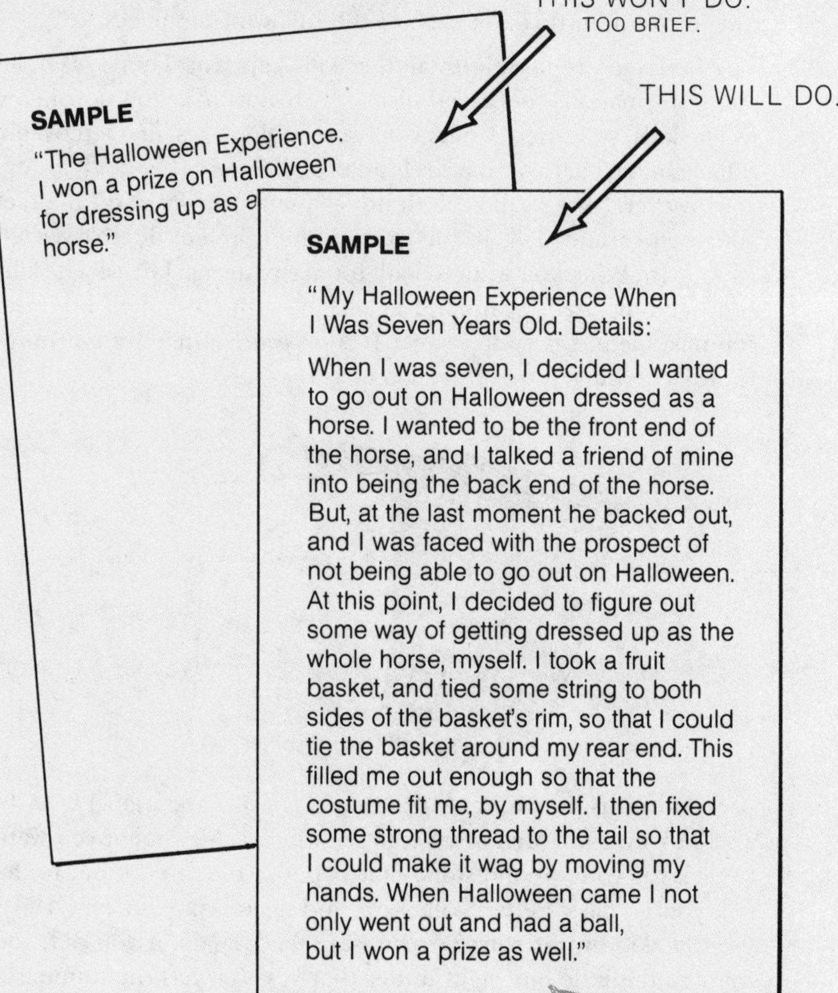

Identifying Your Skills

Once this first story is written, you are ready to identify what skills you used, in that story. The list of skills you are to use is found on pages 232–237. The skills resemble a series of typewriter keys. You go down each column vertically. As you look at each key, you ask yourself, "Did I use this skill **in this story**? (story #1)." If you did, you color in the little box *right under* that key which has the number 1 in it (color right *over* the "1"). We suggest you use a **red** pen, pencil, or crayon, to do this coloring in. Keep going down each column, in turn, on each of the following six pages.

When you are done with all the skills keys, for Things, People, and Information, you have finished with story #1. You now know what skills you used while you were doing this first enjoyable achievement, that you have selected to analyze.

However, "one swallow doth not a summer make," and the fact you used certain skills in this one accomplishment doesn't yet tell you much. What you want to look for are patterns: i.e., which skills keep getting used, again and again, in accomplishment after accomplishment, story after story. It is *the patterns* that are meaningful for choosing your future job or career.

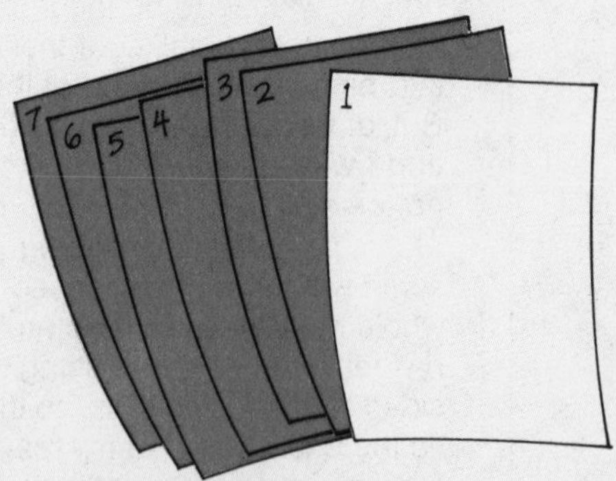

So now it is time to take a second sheet of paper, label it "#2", and look over the Memory Net to see which achievement you want to pick for your second story. Once you have written it out in detail, you go back to the Skills Keys and again ask yourself, "Did I use this skill **in this story?** (story #2)." And, again, if you did, you color in the little box right under that key that has the number 2 in it (color right over the "2"). Again, use the red pen, pencil, or crayon. Continue through the six Skill pages.

Take a third sheet and repeat the process, and so, continue on through sheet (and story) #7. When you are done, look over the Skills pages to see which skills stand out (i.e., which ones have the little boxes under them colored in the most).

Choosing Your Favorite Transferable Skills

You must now choose your favorites, from the Skills pages you just filled out. How you make that choice is entirely up to you. Here are two different methods for doing this:

a) **The Top Ten**. Look at all the Skills pages you just filled out, and put a big check mark by your ten favorite skills -- never mind whether they are with Things, People, or Information. It could turn out, for example, that eight of your favorite skills are with Things, and one with People and one with Information. On a sheet of scratch paper, list all ten and then rearrange them so that they end up being listed *in their order of importance for you*. You can do this prioritizing either by guess and by gosh, **or** by using the Prioritizing Grid on page 218. What you want to end up with is a *prioritized list* -- on which the skill that is most important to you is listed first, the skill that is next most important to you is listed second, next most important is third, next most important is fourth, and so on. Copy these onto page 239.

b) Alternative Method: **Eight, Eight, and Eight**. Look at the Skills pages and pick your eight favorites off *each diagram*: your eight favorite Skills with Things, your eight favorite Skills with People, and your eight favorite Skills with Information. Put *each* eight in order, again either by guessing, or by using the Prioritizing Grid three times. You will end up with three lists: your eight favorite Skills with Things, *in order of priority for you*; and your eight favorite Skills with People, *in order of priority for you*; and your eight favorite Skills with Information, *in order of priority for you*. Copy these onto page 240.

Optional: Restating Skills in Your Own Language

Now (and only now) that you have a list of your favorite skills -- either The Top Ten or the Eight, Eight, and Eight -- you *may* want to restate them in other language than was on the Skills diagrams, language that is more uniquely and personally yours. *If so,*

(continued on page 238)

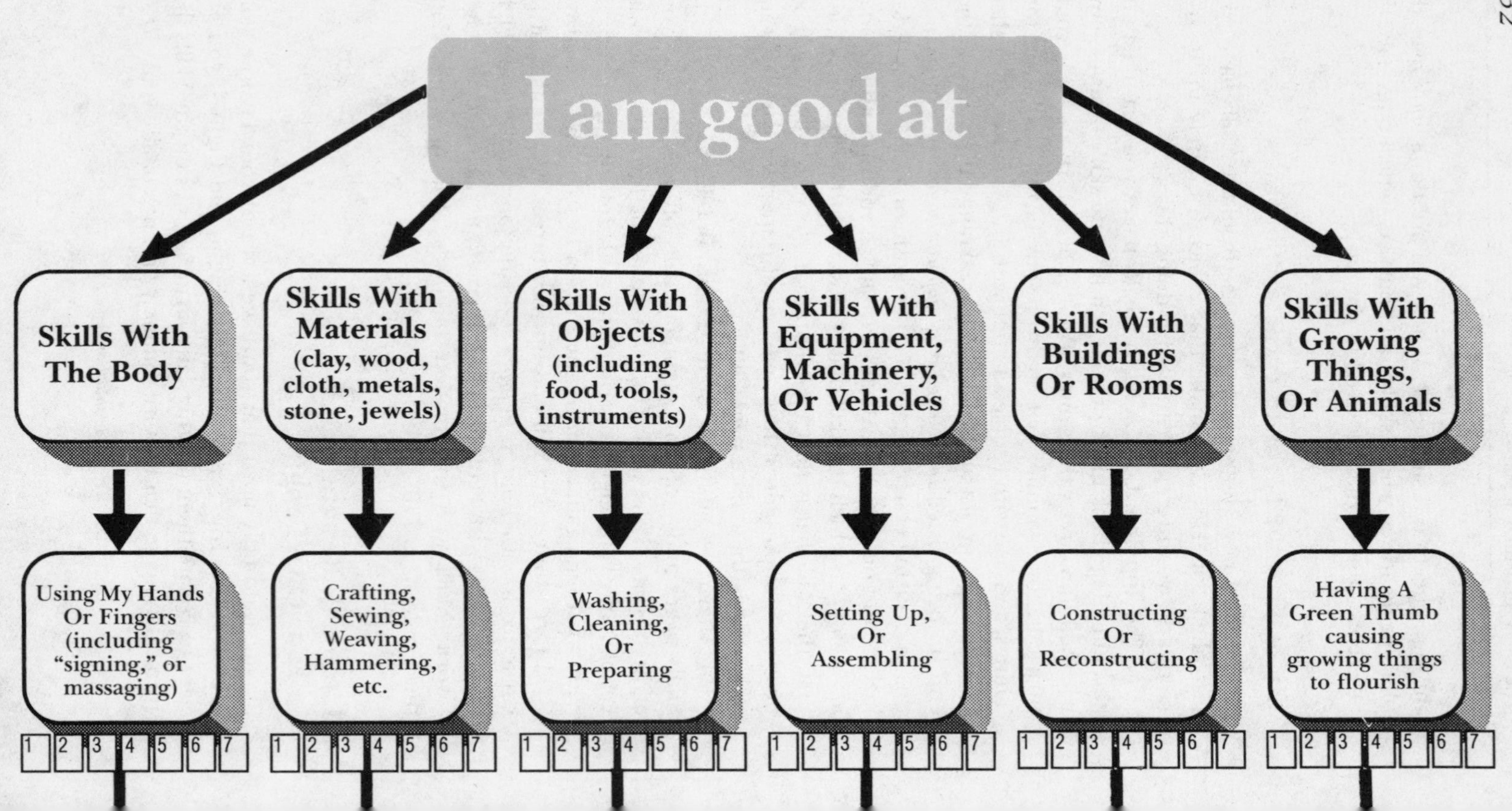
My transferable skills dealing with
THINGS
I am good at
Skills With The Body
Skills With Materials (clay, wood, cloth, metals, stone, jewels)
Skills With Objects (including food, tools, instruments)
Skills With Equipment, Machinery, Or Vehicles
Skills With Buildings Or Rooms
Skills With Growing Things, Or Animals
Using My Hands Or Fingers (including "signing," or massaging)
Crafting, Sewing, Weaving, Hammering, etc.
Washing, Cleaning, Or Preparing
Setting Up, Or Assembling
Constructing Or Reconstructing
Having A Green Thumb causing growing things to flourish
1 2 3 4 5 6 7

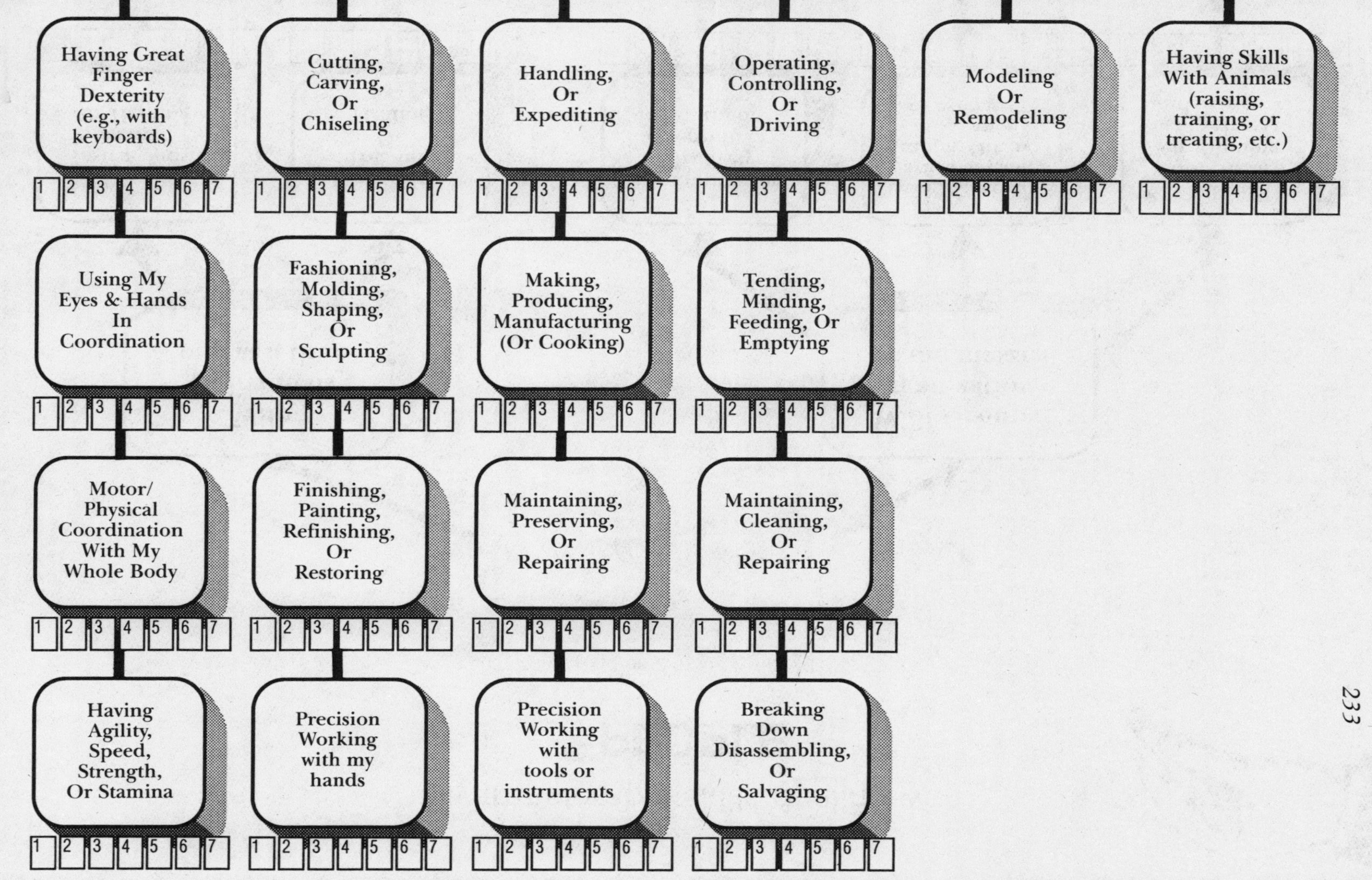
Having Great Finger Dexterity (e.g., with keyboards)
1 2 3 4 5 6 7
Cutting, Carving, Or Chiseling
1 2 3 4 5 6 7
Handling, Or Expediting
1 2 3 4 5 6 7
Operating, Controlling, Or Driving
1 2 3 4 5 6 7
Modeling Or Remodeling
1 2 3 4 5 6 7
Having Skills With Animals (raising, training, or treating, etc.)
1 2 3 4 5 6 7
Using My Eyes & Hands In Coordination
1 2 3 4 5 6 7
Fashioning, Molding, Shaping, Or Sculpting
1 2 3 4 5 6 7
Making, Producing, Manufacturing (Or Cooking)
1 2 3 4 5 6 7
Tending, Minding, Feeding, Or Emptying
1 2 3 4 5 6 7
Motor/ Physical Coordination With My Whole Body
1 2 3 4 5 6 7
Finishing, Painting, Refinishing, Or Restoring
1 2 3 4 5 6 7
Maintaining, Preserving, Or Repairing
1 2 3 4 5 6 7
Maintaining, Cleaning, Or Repairing
1 2 3 4 5 6 7
Having Agility, Speed, Strength, Or Stamina
1 2 3 4 5 6 7
Precision Working with my hands
1 2 3 4 5 6 7
Precision Working with tools or instruments
1 2 3 4 5 6 7
Breaking Down Disassembling, Or Salvaging
1 2 3 4 5 6 7

My transferable skills dealing with

PEOPLE

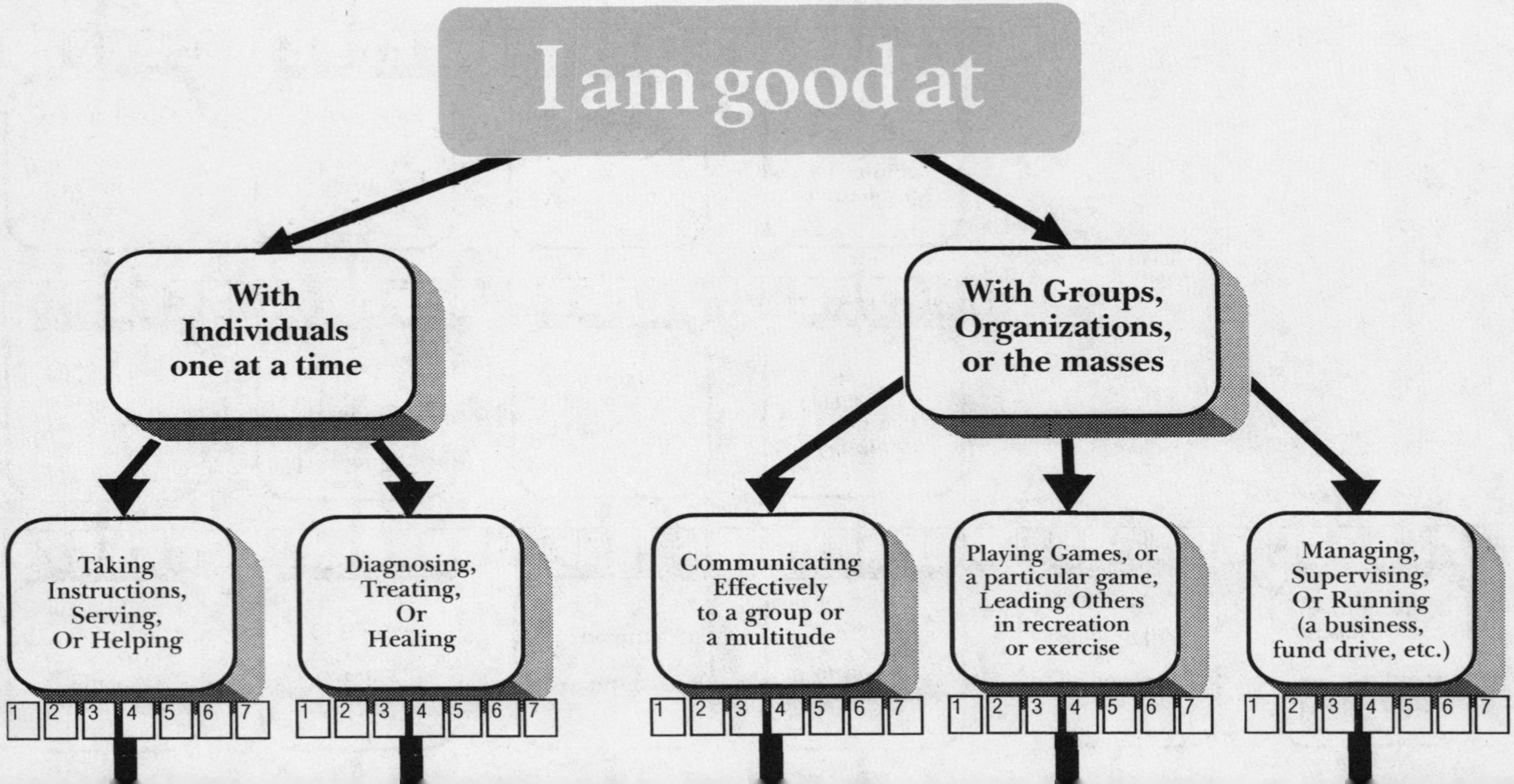

I am good at

With Individuals one at a time

- Taking Instructions, Serving, Or Helping — 1 2 3 4 5 6 7
- Diagnosing, Treating, Or Healing — 1 2 3 4 5 6 7

With Groups, Organizations, or the masses

- Communicating Effectively to a group or a multitude — 1 2 3 4 5 6 7
- Playing Games, or a particular game, Leading Others in recreation or exercise — 1 2 3 4 5 6 7
- Managing, Supervising, Or Running (a business, fund drive, etc.) — 1 2 3 4 5 6 7

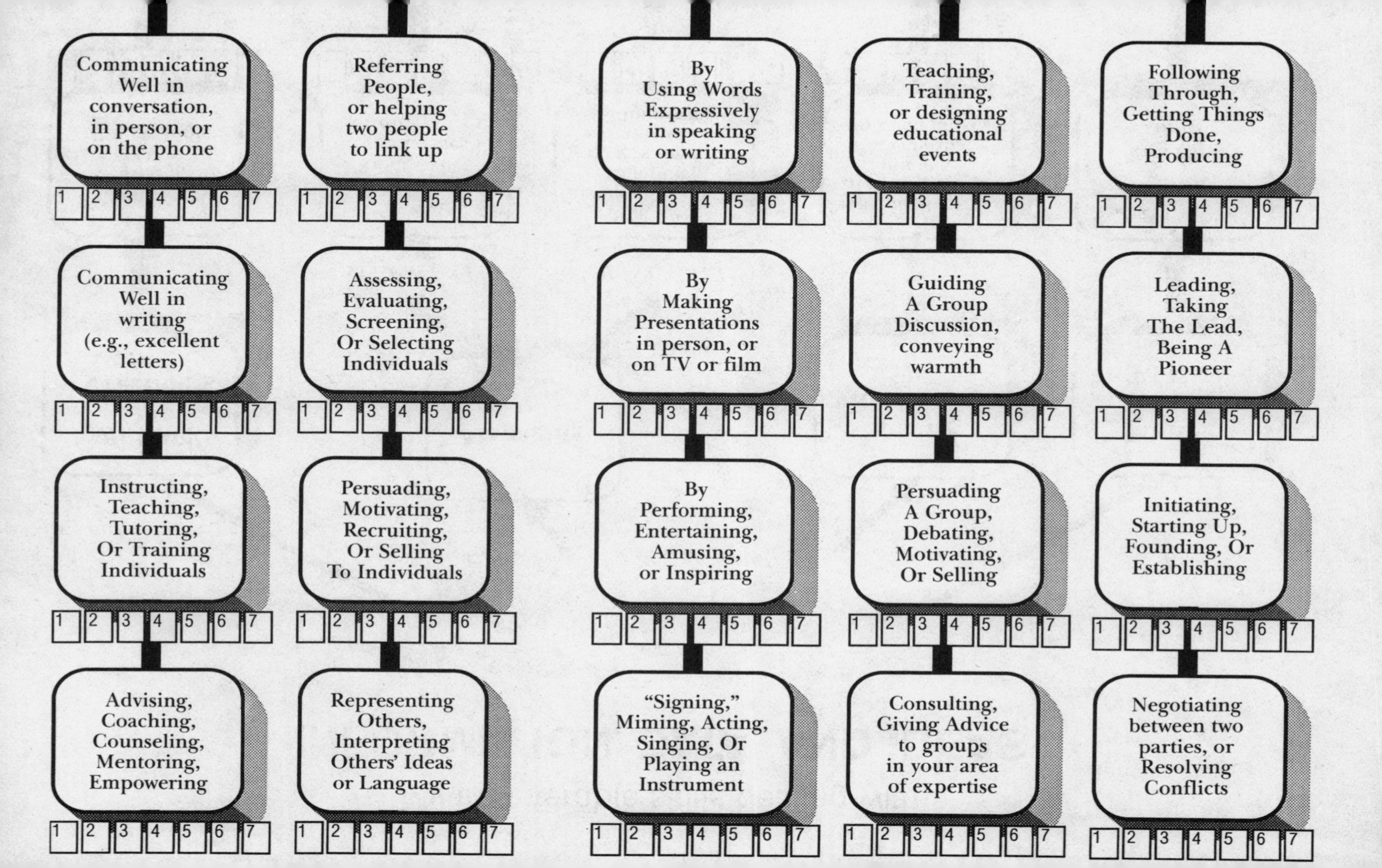

Communicating Well in conversation, in person, or on the phone
1 2 3 4 5 6 7
Communicating Well in writing (e.g., excellent letters)
1 2 3 4 5 6 7
Instructing, Teaching, Tutoring, Or Training Individuals
1 2 3 4 5 6 7
Advising, Coaching, Counseling, Mentoring, Empowering
1 2 3 4 5 6 7
Referring People, or helping two people to link up
1 2 3 4 5 6 7
Assessing, Evaluating, Screening, Or Selecting Individuals
1 2 3 4 5 6 7
Persuading, Motivating, Recruiting, Or Selling To Individuals
1 2 3 4 5 6 7
Representing Others, Interpreting Others' Ideas or Language
1 2 3 4 5 6 7
By Using Words Expressively in speaking or writing
1 2 3 4 5 6 7
By Making Presentations in person, or on TV or film
1 2 3 4 5 6 7
By Performing, Entertaining, Amusing, or Inspiring
1 2 3 4 5 6 7
"Signing," Miming, Acting, Singing, Or Playing an Instrument
1 2 3 4 5 6 7
Teaching, Training, or designing educational events
1 2 3 4 5 6 7
Guiding A Group Discussion, conveying warmth
1 2 3 4 5 6 7
Persuading A Group, Debating, Motivating, Or Selling
1 2 3 4 5 6 7
Consulting, Giving Advice to groups in your area of expertise
1 2 3 4 5 6 7
Following Through, Getting Things Done, Producing
1 2 3 4 5 6 7
Leading, Taking The Lead, Being A Pioneer
1 2 3 4 5 6 7
Initiating, Starting Up, Founding, Or Establishing
1 2 3 4 5 6 7
Negotiating between two parties, or Resolving Conflicts
1 2 3 4 5 6 7

My transferable skills dealing with

INFORMATION, DATA, AND IDEAS

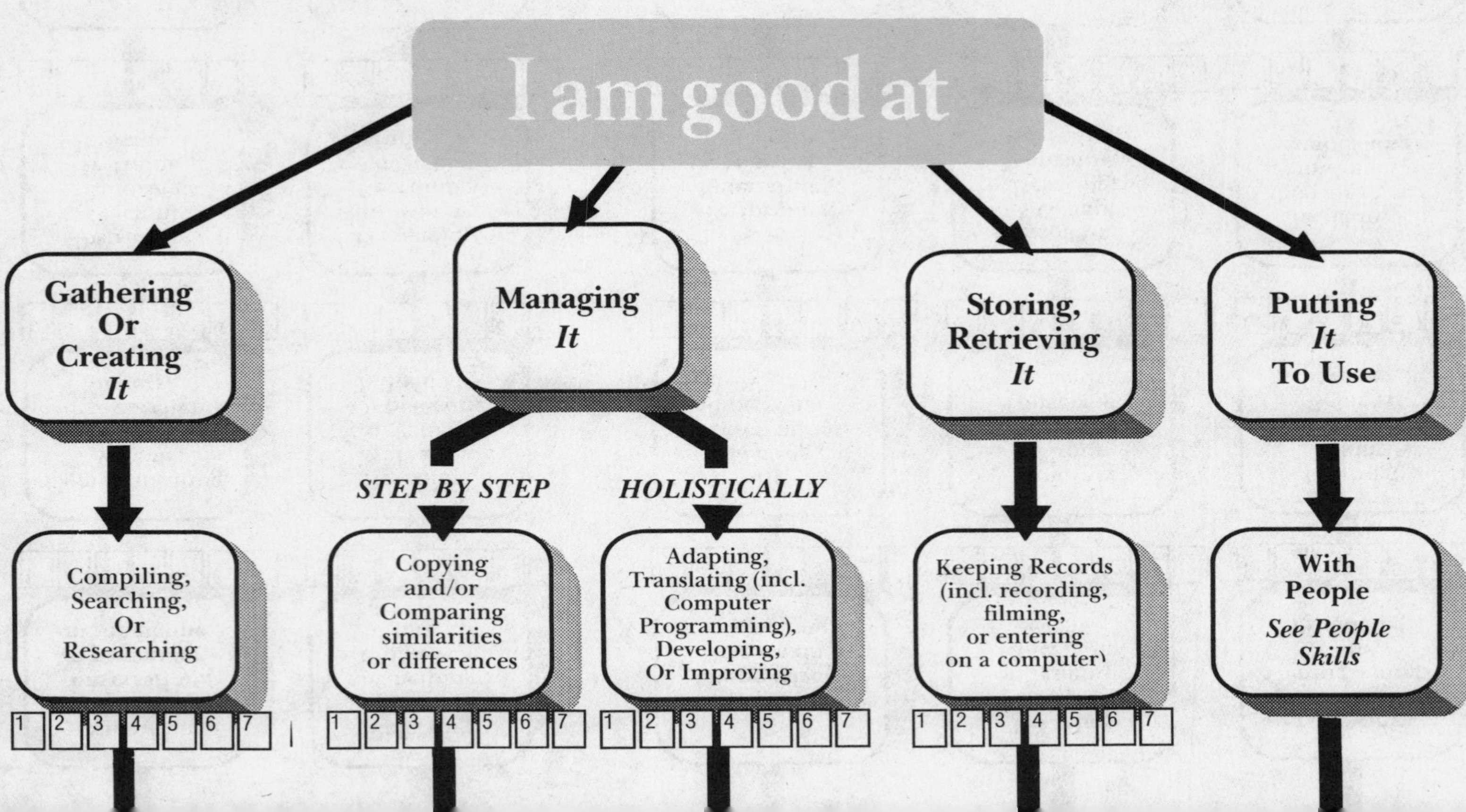

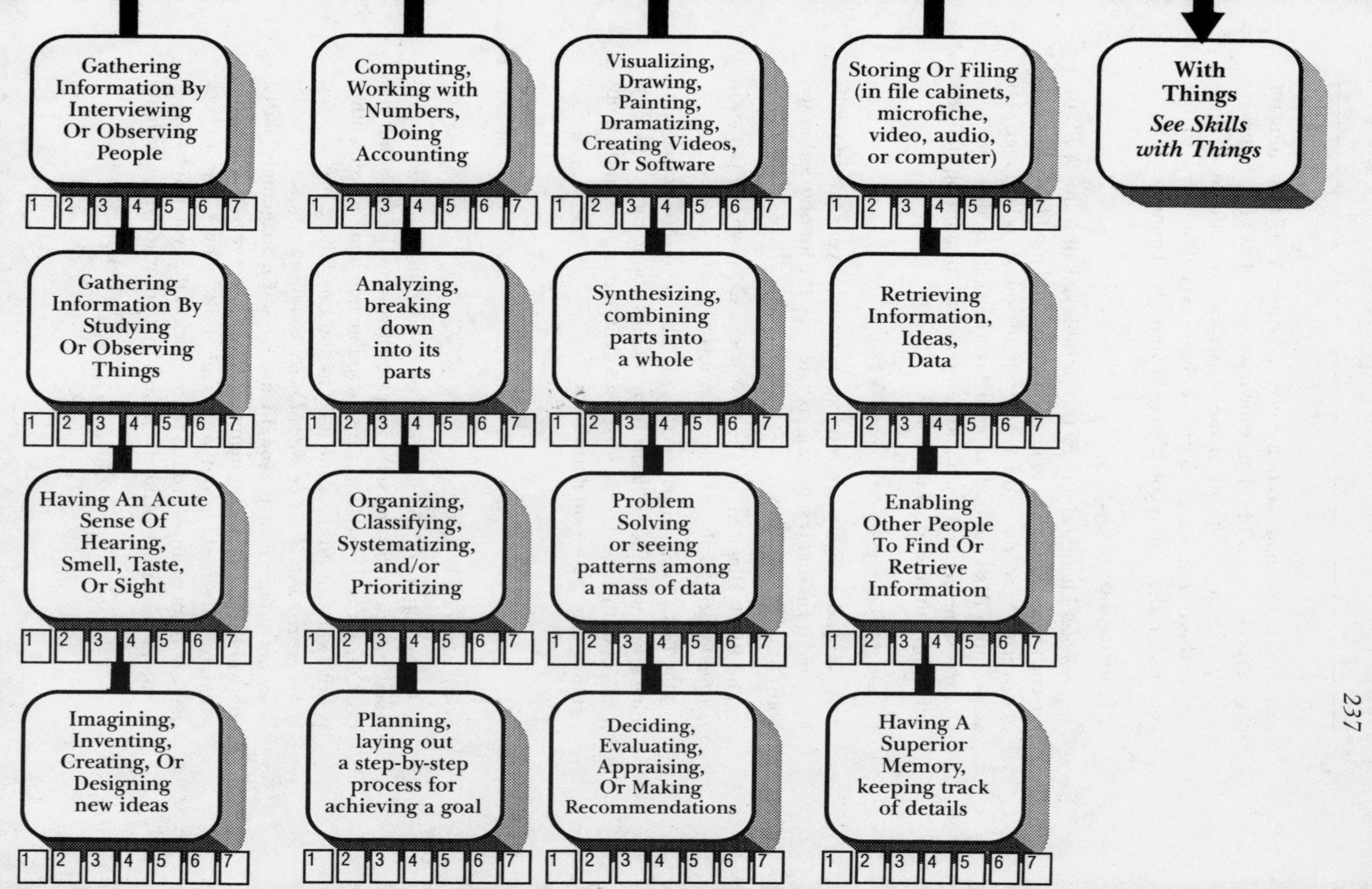

Gathering Information By Interviewing Or Observing People
1 2 3 4 5 6 7
Gathering Information By Studying Or Observing Things
1 2 3 4 5 6 7
Having An Acute Sense Of Hearing, Smell, Taste, Or Sight
1 2 3 4 5 6 7
Imagining, Inventing, Creating, Or Designing new ideas
1 2 3 4 5 6 7
Computing, Working with Numbers, Doing Accounting
1 2 3 4 5 6 7
Analyzing, breaking down into its parts
1 2 3 4 5 6 7
Organizing, Classifying, Systematizing, and/or Prioritizing
1 2 3 4 5 6 7
Planning, laying out a step-by-step process for achieving a goal
1 2 3 4 5 6 7
Visualizing, Drawing, Painting, Dramatizing, Creating Videos, Or Software
1 2 3 4 5 6 7
Synthesizing, combining parts into a whole
1 2 3 4 5 6 7
Problem Solving or seeing patterns among a mass of data
1 2 3 4 5 6 7
Deciding, Evaluating, Appraising, Or Making Recommendations
1 2 3 4 5 6 7
Storing Or Filing (in file cabinets, microfiche, video, audio, or computer)
1 2 3 4 5 6 7
Retrieving Information, Ideas, Data
1 2 3 4 5 6 7
Enabling Other People To Find Or Retrieve Information
1 2 3 4 5 6 7
Having A Superior Memory, keeping track of details
1 2 3 4 5 6 7
With Things *See Skills with Things*

turn to the vocabulary section called "Uniquely You," beginning on page 276. Look up the skills which you picked as your favorites, and see if you prefer any of the words that are offered as alternatives there. You can, of course, rephrase even *these* words, so that your list, in the end, is completely in your own language.

'Fleshing Them Out'

A *complete* identification of a transferable skill of yours *should* (in the end) have three parts to it: verb, object, and modifier (adjective or adverb). Now that you have *the verb* in your own language you *may* want to flesh out each of your favorite skills so that each one also has some general *object* and *modifier*, e.g., "organizing" fleshed out to "organizing ideas logically."

Copying Them onto the Skills Diagram

As we said earlier, when you have your list of your favorite skills in a final form that is satisfying to you, copy the list onto either (or both) of these diagrams:

The Block Diagram, on the next page, allows you to put your *Top Ten* favorite skills, in order of priority.

The Tasks Petal on pages 240–241 allows you to do the same things, but with more 'fleshed-out' details about each skill. You have room for a verb (of course), a modifying phrase, and an object. See page 82 for an illustration.

■ ■ ■

Your *Style* of Working

At the bottom of *The Tasks Petal* on pages 240-241, space is provided for you to list **the style** with which you do the skills that you do. Often it is this style which sets you apart from nineteen other people who can do the same tasks as you can. Therefore, *this part of the exercise should not be skipped over*. Following is a list of styles (they are often called **personal traits** or **self-management skills**; you will further note that many of them can serve as the **modifier** when you are fleshing out your skill verbs, above). Put a check mark in front of any word (or phrase) below that you think applies to you in your work. Add any others that occur to you, which are

(continued on page 242)

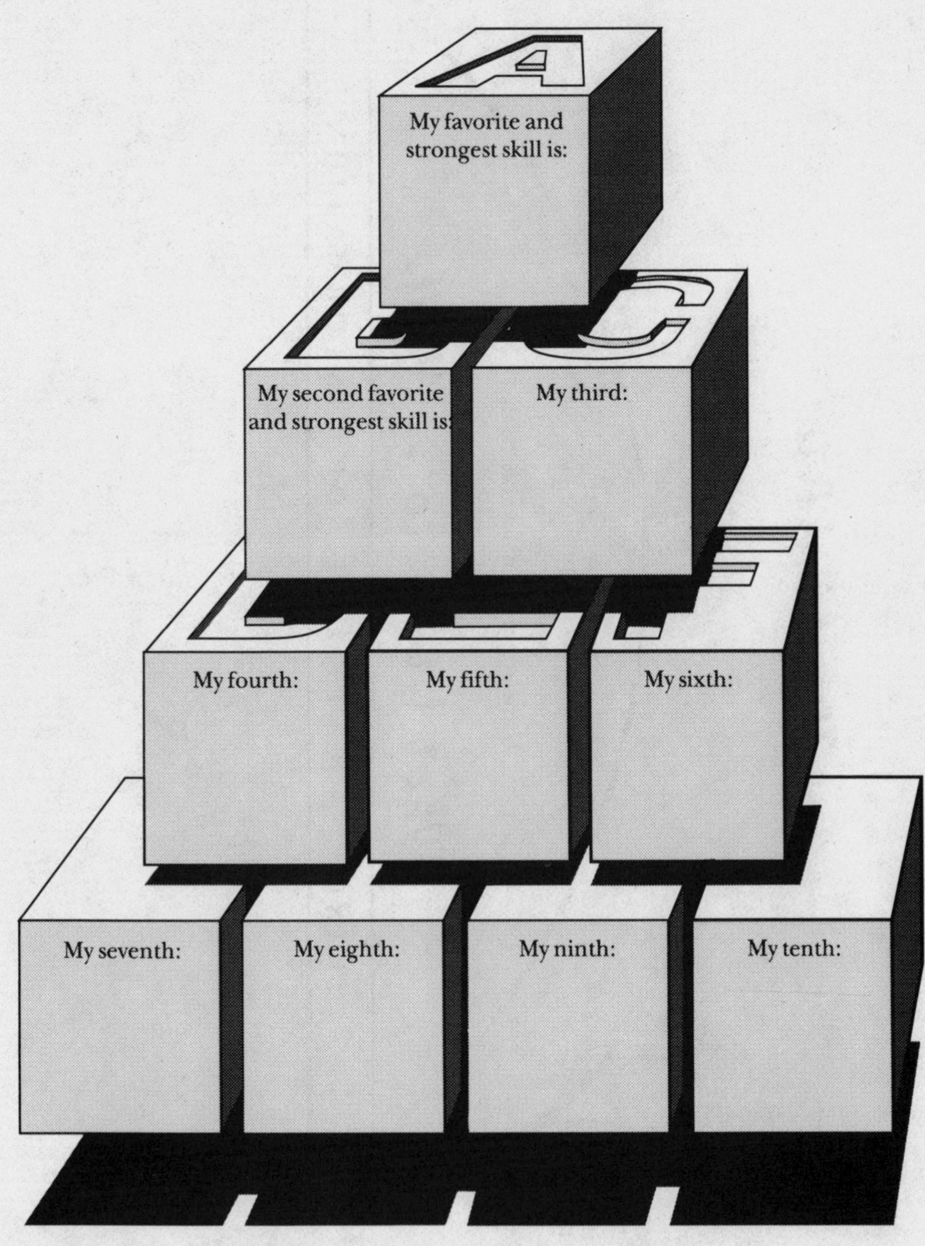
A
My favorite and strongest skill is:
My second favorite and strongest skill is:
C
My third:
My fourth:
My fifth:
My sixth:
My seventh:
My eighth:
My ninth:
My tenth:

The Third Petal

Tasks

In order to do my favorite Tasks,
I need to be using my favorite
Functional/Transferable Skills.
These are:

What I Like to Do With

THINGS OR PEOPLE OR INFORMATION

1.

2.

3.

4.

5.

6.

7.

8.

My Style of Doing Them:

(so-called "traits" or "self-management skills")
e.g., "quickly," "thoroughly," "painstakingly," etc.

not on this list. Then when you are done checking, pick the ten that you think are **most** important, and copy them onto the bottom part of *The Tasks Petal -- in their order of importance to you, if you can.* This matter of *importance* will most often come down to a question of which style you are proudest of, next proudest of, and so forth. Use the Prioritizing Grid if you need to (on page 218).

Style with Which I Do These Skills

• I am VERY:

- ☐ Accurate
- ☐ Achievement-oriented
- ☐ Adaptable
- ☐ Adept
- ☐ Adept at having fun
- ☐ Adventuresome
- ☐ Alert
- ☐ Appreciative
- ☐ Assertive
- ☐ Astute
- ☐ Authoritative
- ☐ Calm
- ☐ Cautious
- ☐ Charismatic
- ☐ Competent
- ☐ Consistent
- ☐ Contagious in my enthusiasm
- ☐ Cooperative
- ☐ Courageous
- ☐ Creative
- ☐ Decisive
- ☐ Deliberate
- ☐ Dependable/have dependability
- ☐ Diligent
- ☐ Diplomatic
- ☐ Discreet
- ☐ Driving
- ☐ Dynamic
- ☐ Extremely economical
- ☐ Effective
- ☐ Energetic
- ☐ Enthusiastic
- ☐ Exceptional
- ☐ Exhaustive
- ☐ Experienced
- ☐ Expert
- ☐ Firm
- ☐ Flexible
- ☐ Humanly oriented
- ☐ Impulsive
- ☐ Independent
- ☐ Innovative
- ☐ Knowledgeable
- ☐ Loyal
- ☐ Methodical
- ☐ Objective
- ☐ Open-minded
- ☐ Outgoing
- ☐ Outstanding
- ☐ Patient
- ☐ Penetrating
- ☐ Perceptive
- ☐ Persevering
- ☐ Persistent
- ☐ Pioneering
- ☐ Practical
- ☐ Professional
- ☐ Protective
- ☐ Punctual
- ☐ Quick/work quickly
- ☐ Rational
- ☐ Realistic
- ☐ Reliable
- ☐ Repeatedly
- ☐ Resourceful
- ☐ Responsible
- ☐ Responsive
- ☐ Safeguarding
- ☐ Self-motivated
- ☐ Self-reliant
- ☐ Sensitive
- ☐ Sophisticated, very sophisticated
- ☐ Strong
- ☐ Supportive
- ☐ Tactful
- ☐ Thorough
- ☐ Unique
- ☐ Unusual
- ☐ Versatile
- ☐ Vigorous

• I am a person who:

With respect to execution of a task, and achievement

- ☐ Takes initiative
- ☐ Is able to handle a great variety of tasks and responsibilities simultaneously and efficiently

- ☐ Takes risks
  - ☐ Takes calculated risks
- ☐ Is expert at getting things done

With respect to time, and achievement

- ☐ Consistently tackles tasks ahead of time
- ☐ Is adept at finding ways to speed up a task
- ☐ Gets the most done in the shortest time
- ☐ Expedites the task at hand
- ☐ Meets deadlines
  - ☐ Delivers on promises on time
  - ☐ Brings projects in on time and within budget

With respect to working conditions

- ☐ Maintains order and neatness in my workspace
- ☐ Is attendant to details
- ☐ Has a high tolerance of repetition and/or monotonous routines
- ☐ Likes planning and directing an entire activity
- ☐ Demonstrates mastery
- ☐ Promotes change
- ☐ Works well under pressure and still improvises
- ☐ Enjoys a challenge
- ☐ Loves working outdoors
- ☐ Loves to travel
- ☐ Has an unusually good grasp of . . .
- ☐ Is good at responding to emergencies
- ☐ Has the courage of his or her convictions

When you are done with this exercise, copy the results at the bottom of the Tasks petal. You are now ready to move on.

The Things You Like to Act Upon

These next three steps, and the next three petals as a matter of fact, are called "**Tools or Means**." Skills *always* require some tool or means. A tool or means is something you love **to handle**, or something you like **to use**, or something you like **to work on**, or **act upon**. It may be *people*, or *information*, or a *thing*.

For example, if you love to hammer things, you need both a hammer and a thing to hammer -- let us say a nail. The hammer and the nail are the tools or means that enable you to use your skill -- of hammering. And, in this case, they are *things*. Of course, you also need some knowledge of *how to hammer*, and that means that some *information* is also used here, as a tool or means.

On the succeeding three petals, and in the succeeding three steps, we will look first at People, and then at Information, and then at Things, to see which of these are your favorites.

Step Four: My Favorite People to Work With

If you checked any skills with People, as your favorites, in Step Three, it is important that you now specify *what kind* of People you prefer to work with. Let us say, for example, that you checked "teaching" as one of your favorite skills. The question now is: *What* people do you most enjoy teaching? All people? Particular age groups? If so, which ones? People with particular problems? If so, which ones? People who are working on particular issues in their life? If so, which ones?

Following is a list of people. Put a check mark in front of any description that describes people you particularly like (or think you would particularly like) to work with -- as clients, customers, students, or whatever, in your work. Add any others that may occur to you, which are not on the list. Then when you are done checking, pick the ten that you think are **most** important, and copy them onto the Petal called *Tools or Means: 1* (found on page 249) -- *in your order of preference. "I would most enjoy working with these people, next with these people, next with these people,"* etc. *Use the Prioritizing Grid if you need to (on page 218).*

Kinds of People I Prefer to Serve Or Try to Help

- ☐ Men
- ☐ Women
- ☐ Individuals
- ☐ Groups of eight or less
- ☐ Groups larger than eight
- ☐ Babies
- ☐ School-age children
- ☐ Adolescents or young people
- ☐ College students
- ☐ Young adults
- ☐ People in their thirties
- ☐ The middle-aged
- ☐ The elderly
- ☐ The retired
- ☐ All people regardless of age
- ☐ Heterosexuals
- ☐ Homosexuals
- ☐ All people regardless of sex
- ☐ People of a particular cultural background
- ☐ People of a particular economic background
- ☐ People of a particular social background
- ☐ People of a particular educational background
- ☐ People of a particular philosophy or religious belief:
- ☐ Certain kinds of workers (blue-collar, white-collar, executives, or whatever):
- ☐ People who are poor:
- ☐ People who are powerless:
- ☐ People who wield power:
- ☐ People who are rich:
- ☐ People who are easy to work with:
- ☐ People who are difficult to work with:
- ☐ People in a particular place (the Armed Forces, prison, etc.)

Kinds of Problems I Like to Try to Help People With:

- ☐ Physical handicaps
- ☐ Overweight
- ☐ Mental retardation
- ☐ Pain
- ☐ Disease in general
  - ☐ Hypertension
  - ☐ Allergies
  - ☐ Self-healing, psychic healing
  - ☐ Terminal illness
  - ☐ Holistic health
- ☐ Life/work planning or adjustment
- ☐ Identifying and finding meaningful work
- ☐ Job-hunting, career change, unemployment, being fired or laid off
- ☐ Illiteracy, educational needs
- ☐ Industry in-house training
- ☐ Performance problems, appraisal
  - ☐ Low energy
  - ☐ Nutritional problems
  - ☐ Physical fitness
  - ☐ Work satisfaction
  - ☐ Discipline problems, self-discipline
  - ☐ Stress
  - ☐ Sleep disorders
- ☐ Relationships
  - ☐ Personal insight, therapy
  - ☐ Loneliness
  - ☐ Boredom
  - ☐ Complaints, grievances
  - ☐ Anger
  - ☐ Anxiety
  - ☐ Fear
  - ☐ Shyness
    - ☐ Meeting people, starting friendships

- ☐ Communications, thoughts, feelings
- ☐ Love
  - ☐ Self-acceptance and acceptance of others
  - ☐ Learning how to love
- ☐ Marriage
  - ☐ Competing needs
- ☐ Sexual education, sexual problems
  - ☐ Sexual dysfunction
- ☐ Pregnancy and childbirth
- ☐ Parenting
- ☐ Physical abuse
- ☐ Rape
- ☐ Divorce
- ☐ Death and grief
- ☐ Addictions
  - ☐ Drug problems
  - ☐ Alcoholism
  - ☐ Smoking
- ☐ Mental illness
  - ☐ Depression
  - ☐ Psychiatric hospitalization
- ☐ Personal economics
  - ☐ Financial planning
  - ☐ Possessions
  - ☐ Budgeting
  - ☐ Debt bankruptcy
- ☐ Values
- ☐ Ethics
- ☐ Philosophy or religion
  - ☐ Worship
  - ☐ Stewardship
  - ☐ Life after death
  - ☐ Psychic phenomena

If while you are checking off these descriptions, you see any which apply to the kind of **co-workers** you would most like to have, copy them onto the bottom part of the same petal. (You may also find clues about your preferred co-workers, in *the Styles list* that you worked on in the previous exercise.) The following list may also help. Check off the descriptions which apply, or add any others which occur to you:

My Preferred Co-workers:

I prefer to work with what kinds of co-workers or colleagues, bosses, or subordinates?

- ☐ Both sexes
  - ☐ Men primarily
  - ☐ Women primarily
- ☐ People of all ages
  - ☐ Adolescents or young people
  - ☐ College students
  - ☐ Young adults
  - ☐ People in their thirties
  - ☐ The middle-aged
  - ☐ The elderly
  - ☐ The retired
- ☐ All people regardless of sexual orientation
  - ☐ Heterosexuals
  - ☐ Homosexuals

- ☐ All people regardless of background
  - ☐ People of a particular background:
    - ☐ People of a particular cultural background:
    - ☐ People of a particular economic background:
    - ☐ People of a particular social background:
    - ☐ People of a particular educational background:
    - ☐ People of a particular philosophy or religious belief:
    - ☐ Certain kinds of workers (blue-collar, white-collar, executives, or whatever):
    - ☐ People in a particular place (the Armed Forces, prison, etc.):
- ☐ People who are easy to work with:
- ☐ People who are difficult to work with:

In the bottom part of this same Petal, on page 249 you will see an outline of a hexagon. This represents the Party Exercise, found on page 224, and is put there to remind you that you *may* want to put down *the descriptions* from your *favorite* corners of the hexagon, as descriptions of what you would like your co-workers to be doing (true, the corners you chose were supposed to be descriptive of *you*, but in identifying co-workers you would like to work with, the ancient truth is that birds of a feather tend to like to flock together -- e.g., artistic types tend to like to work and communicate with other artistic types, not accountants in three-piece suits -- and vice versa). Within the hexagon on that petal, you will see a figure resembling a cross -- to remind you (you are at the center of the figure) to think out what kind of person you want *over* you as boss (top of the figure), *beside* you as co-workers (middle of the figure) and *below* you, as subordinates (bottom of the figure).

When you are all done with this exercise, you will have now finished the fourth petal out of eight; the picture of your ideal job should be starting to get clearer. Also you can begin to see how you are cutting down the size of the job-market that you will need to explore, to a much more manageable territory. On to the next step.

The Fourth Petal

Tools or Means: 1

Kinds of PEOPLE I Like To Use These Skills With

As Clients,
Customers,
Students, or
Other:

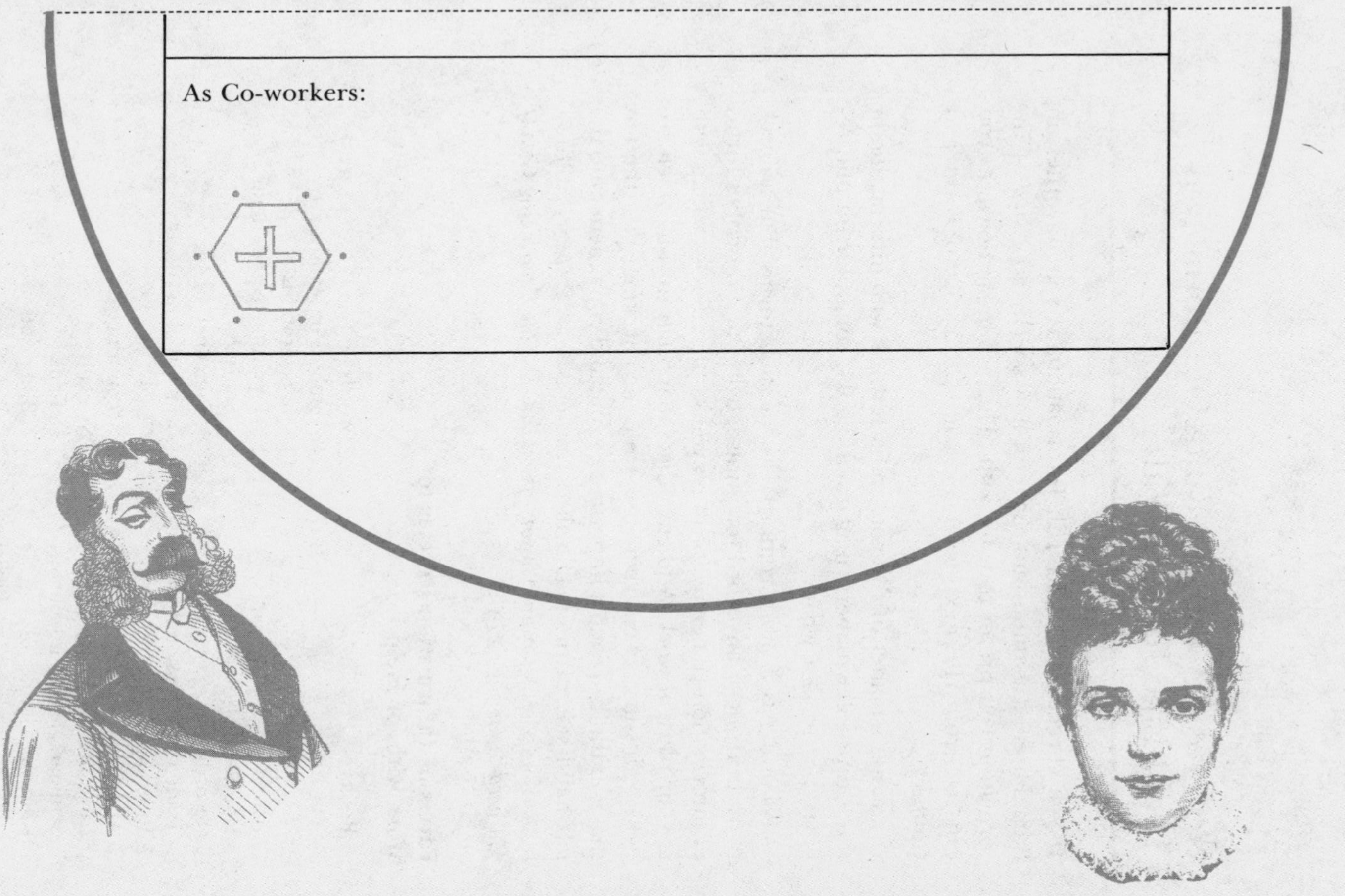
As Co-workers:

Step Five: My Favorite Kinds Of Information That I Like To Work With

If you checked any skills with Information, as your favorites, in Step Three, it is important that you now specify *what kind* of Information you prefer to work with. This will break down, as you can see from the next petal, on pages 252–253 to **Form** and **Content**.

Form is a matter of: Do you prefer to work with information in the form of newspapers, magazines, books, computer output, reports, pictures, or what?

Following is a more complete list of such forms. Put a check mark in front of any word (or phrase) below that describes forms of information you enjoy (or think you would enjoy) working with at your place of work. Add any others that occur to you, which are not on this list. Then when you are done checking, pick the ten that you think are **most** important to you, and copy them onto the left hand side of the petal called *Tools or Means: 2 (pages 252f.) -- in their order of importance to you, if you can. Use the Prioritizing Grid if you need to on page 218.*

Forms of Information I Prefer to Work with, or Help Produce:

- ☐ Books
- ☐ Magazines
- ☐ Newspapers
- ☐ Catalogs
- ☐ Handbooks
- ☐ Records, files
- ☐ Trade or professional literature
- ☐ Videotapes
- ☐ Audiotapes
- ☐ Computer printouts
- ☐ Seminars, learning from trainers
- ☐ Courses, learning from teachers
- ☐ Words
- ☐ Numbers or statistics
  - ☐ Specifications
  - ☐ Precision requirements
  - ☐ Statistical analyses
  - ☐ Data analysis studies
  - ☐ Financial needs
- ☐ Costs
- ☐ Accountings
- ☐ Symbols
- ☐ Designs
  - ☐ Blueprints
  - ☐ Wall-charts

- ☐ Time-charts
- ☐ Schema
- ☐ Facts
- ☐ History
- ☐ Ideas
- ☐ Conceptions
- ☐ Investigations
- ☐ Opinion-collection
- ☐ Points of view
- ☐ Surveys
- ☐ Research projects, research and development projects, project reports
- ☐ Procedures
- ☐ Guidebooks
- ☐ Manuals

I Like to Collect or Deal with Information about Any of the Following:

- ☐ Principles
- ☐ Physical principles
- ☐ Spiritual principles
- ☐ Values
- ☐ Standards
- ☐ Repeating requirements
- ☐ Variables
- ☐ Frameworks
- ☐ Organizational contexts
- ☐ Boundary conditions
- ☐ Parameters
- ☐ Systems
- ☐ Programs
- ☐ Operations
- ☐ Sequences
- ☐ Methods
- ☐ Techniques
- ☐ Procedures
- ☐ Specialized procedures
- ☐ Analyses
- ☐ Data analysis studies
- ☐ Schematic analyses
- ☐ Intuitions

I Like to Help Put Information to Use in Any of the Following Practical Ways:

- ☐ Principles applications
- ☐ Recommendations
- ☐ Policy recommendations
- ☐ Goals
- ☐ Project goals
- ☐ Objectives
- ☐ Solutions
- ☐ New approaches
- ☐ Plans
- ☐ Tactical needs
- ☐ Performance characteristics
- ☐ Proficiencies
- ☐ Deficiencies
- ☐ Reporting systems
- ☐ Controls systems

The Fifth Petal

Tools or Means: 2

Kinds of INFORMATION I Like To Use These Skills With

FORM	CONTENT
e.g., "Do you prefer to work with information in the form of newspapers, magazines, books, computer output, reports, or pictures?" etc.	Among the fields of knowledge which you know something about, which ones are your favorites? And in what order of priority?
1.	1.
2.	2.

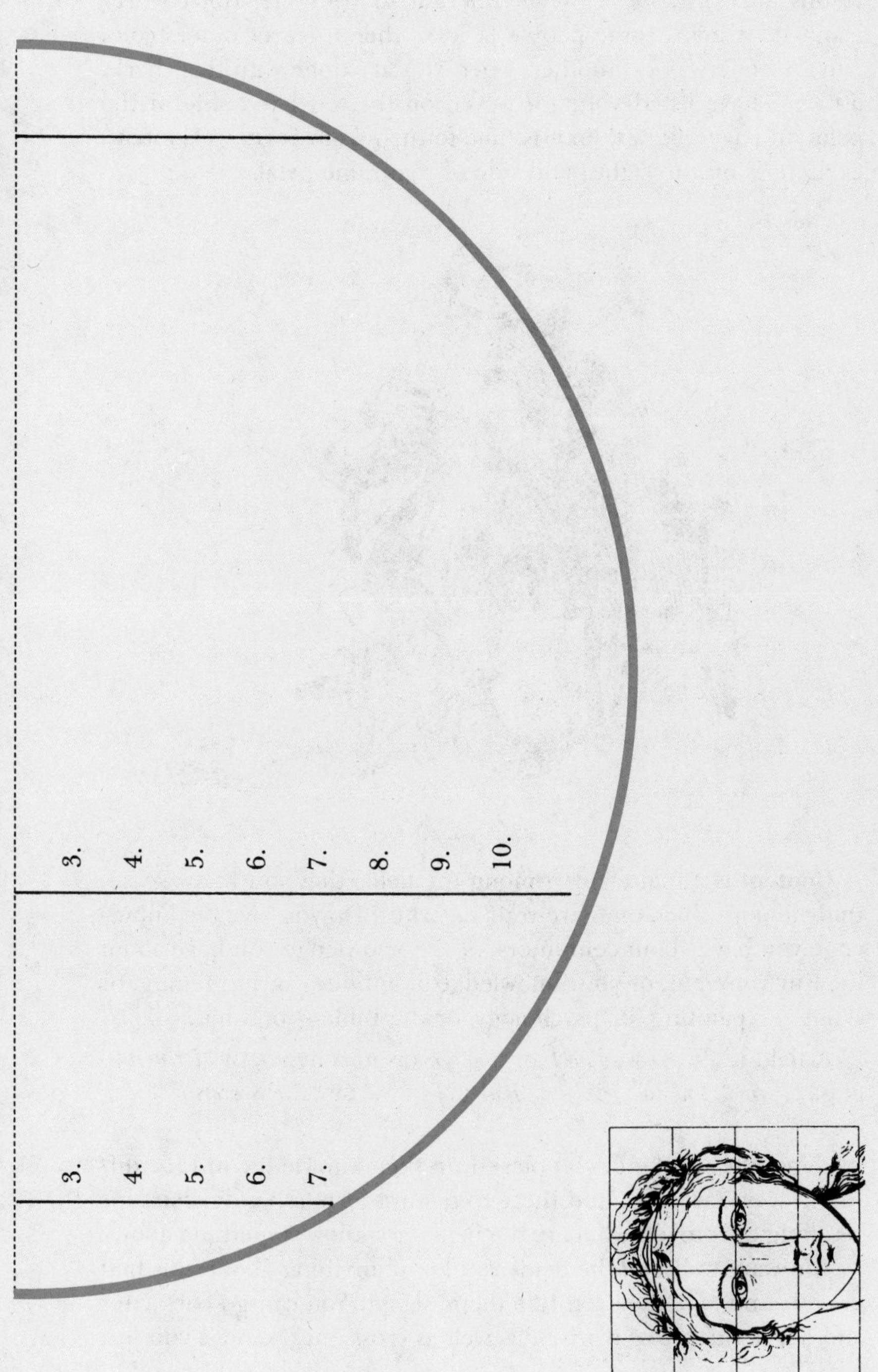
3.
4.
5.
6.
7.
8.
9.
10.
3.
4.
5.
6.
7.

If this checklist doesn't seem relevant to your life, don't worry about it. It helps some people (a lot), while it leaves others cold. Anyway, one way or another, when you are done with this checklist, and have listed your top seven on the left hand side of the petal on page 252f., then it is time to turn from **Form** to **Content**. Content is on the right hand side of that same petal.

Content is a matter of: Among the fields that you know something about, which ones are your favorites? Do you love the knowledge you have about computers, or the knowledge you have about the Environment, or your knowledge of antiques, or gardening, or skiing, or painting, or psychology, or the Bible -- or what?

A field is always a *subject*, or a *major* (as in college), or "*Principles of* . . . ," or "*How to* . . . ," or "*Rules of* . . . ," or "*The Secrets of* . . . ," etc.

Generally speaking, you picked up such knowledge in four different ways (at least), and these four ways form a handy chart for recalling to yourself what are the fields you know something about.

You want to list *all* the fields you know anything about, this first time 'round, whether you **like** them or not. You can go back later and check off your favorites, as well as cross out the ones you just hate.

Fields of Knowledge That You Learned About

In School or College (At Home or Work)	On the Job, or Just by Doing (At Home or Work)	From Seminars or Workshops	By Personal Instruction from People or by Reading a Lot

Here are some *examples* to guide you in filling in the chart:

Fields of Knowledge I Learned About in School or College

e.g., Spanish
Psychology
Biology
Geometry
Accounting
Music appreciation
Typing
Sociology

(continued on next page)

Fields of Knowledge I Learned About on the Job, or Just by Doing (at Home or Work)

e.g., How to operate a computer
How a volunteer organization works
Principles of planning and management

Fields of Knowledge I Learned from Seminars or Workshops

e.g., The way the brain works
Principles of art
Speed reading
Drawing

Fields of Knowledge I Learned About by Personal Instruction from People or by Reading a Lot

e.g., How to sew
How to drive an automobile
How computers work
Principles of comparison shopping
Knowledge of antiques
Principles of outdoor survival

You may want to look back at your Memory Net, pages 226–227, at this point, for help in filling in the preceding chart. *And*, to further aid you, you may want to see a list, or at least a sampler, of other possible fields of knowledge, just to jog your memory. Following is such a list. Put a check mark in front of any word (or phrase) that describes possible fields of knowledge that you already are familiar with, and would enjoy getting a chance to use in your ideal job. Write in any others that occur to you, as you go down this list.

A SAMPLER OF POSSIBLE FIELDS
YOU MAY KNOW ABOUT

Primarily about People

- ☐ Sociology
- ☐ The *how to* of customer relations and service
- ☐ Principles of group dynamics
- ☐ Principles of behavioral modification
- ☐ Instructional principles and techniques
- ☐ Organization planning
- ☐ Manpower requirements analysis and planning
- ☐ Personnel administration
- ☐ Recruiting
- ☐ Performance specifications

Primarily about Things

- ☐ Physics
- ☐ Astronomy
- ☐ Computer programming
- ☐ Knowledge of a particular computer and its applications
- ☐ Design engineering
- ☐ Interior decorating
- ☐ How to run a particular machine
- ☐ Horticulture
- ☐ Car repairs
- ☐ Industrial applications
- ☐ Government contracts
- ☐ Maintenance
- ☐ Financial planning and management
- ☐ Bookkeeping
- ☐ Fiscal analysis, controls, reductions and programming
- ☐ Accounting
- ☐ Taxes
- ☐ R & D program and project management
- ☐ Merchandising
- ☐ Systems analysis
- ☐ Packaging
- ☐ Distribution
- ☐ Marketing/sales

Other Fields (not easily categorized)

- ☐ Principles of art
- ☐ Cinema
- ☐ Principles of recording
- ☐ Knowledge of foreign countries (which ones?)
- ☐ Musical knowledge and taste
- ☐ Graphic arts
- ☐ Photography
- ☐ Broadcasting
- ☐ How to make videos
- ☐ Linguistics or languages
- ☐ Spanish
- ☐ Music
- ☐ Policy development
- ☐ Religion

You will of course want to know if you can put down some field that you are not yet knowledgeable about: what we would call a field of *interest*, which you think you would love to learn about and use in your future ideal job. Well, sure, if you are absolutely, one hundred per cent, planning on studying that field in the near future. Or if you want to find a volunteer job or an apprenticeship where you could pick up knowledge of that field *on the job*. But let's not just talk about what you do not yet have; in addition to these **do** list fields you already know something about.

When you are all done listing or checking off all the fields you already know something about, **then** go back over the list and check your favorites, as well as cross out the ones you just hate. And, from among your favorites, pick the ten that you feel are **most** important to you to be able to use in your future ideal job, (from both the chart *and* this list), and copy these ten onto the right hand side of the petal called *Tools or Means: 2* (page 252f.) *in their order of importance to you, if you can. Use the Prioritizing Grid if you need to (on page 218).*

When you are done, you are now ready to move on to:

Step Six: My Favorite Kinds Of Things That I Like To Work With

If you checked any skills with Things, as your favorites, in Step Three, it is important that you now specify *what kind* of Things you prefer to work with.

Following is such a list of Things. Put a check mark in front of any word that describes *things* you particularly like (or think you would particularly like) to use, or act upon, or help produce in your work. Add any others that may occur to you, which are not on the list. Then when you are done checking, pick the ten that you think are **most** important, and copy them onto the Petal on pages 262–263, in your order of preference. *"I would most enjoy working with this thing in my ideal job; next this thing; next this thing;" etc. Use the Prioritizing Grid if you need to (on page 218).*

Things I Enjoy Working With:

Types of Material

- ☐ Paper
- ☐ Pottery
- ☐ Pewter
- ☐ Paraffin
- ☐ Papier-mâché
- ☐ Wood
- ☐ Other crafts materials
- ☐ Bronze
- ☐ Brass
- ☐ Cast iron, ironworks
- ☐ Steel
- ☐ Aluminum
- ☐ Rubber
- ☐ Plywood
- ☐ Bricks
- ☐ Cement
- ☐ Concrete, cinder-blocks
- ☐ Plastics
- ☐ Textiles
- ☐ Cloth
- ☐ Felt
- ☐ Hides
- ☐ Synthetics
- ☐ Elastic
- ☐ Crops
- ☐ Plants
- ☐ Trees

Types of Manufactured stuff

- ☐ Machines
- ☐ Tools
- ☐ Toys
- ☐ Equipment
- ☐ Controls, gauges
- ☐ Products

☐ **Housing Items**

- ☐ Tents
- ☐ Trailers
- ☐ Apartments
- ☐ Houses
  - ☐ Chimneys
  - ☐ Columns
  - ☐ Domes
  - ☐ Carpenter's tools
  - ☐ Paint
  - ☐ Wallpaper
  - ☐ Heating elements, furnaces
  - ☐ Carpeting
  - ☐ Fire extinguishers, fire alarms, burglar alarms
  - ☐ Household items
    - ☐ Furniture
    - ☐ Beds
    - ☐ Sheets, blankets, electric blankets
    - ☐ Laundry
    - ☐ Washing machines, dryers
    - ☐ Washday products, bleach
    - ☐ Kitchen appliances, refrigerators, microwaves, ovens, dishwashers, compactors
    - ☐ Kitchen tools
    - ☐ Dishes
    - ☐ Pots and pans
    - ☐ Can openers
    - ☐ Bathtubs
    - ☐ Soaps
    - ☐ Cosmetics
    - ☐ Toiletries
    - ☐ Drugs
    - ☐ Towels
    - ☐ Tools, power tools

☐ **Old Equipment**

- ☐ Clocks
- ☐ Telescopes
- ☐ Microscopes

- ☐ **Foods or Food Manufacturing Equipment**
- ☐ Wells, cisterns
- ☐ Meats
- ☐ Breads and other baked goods
- ☐ Health foods
- ☐ Vitamins
- ☐ Dairy equipment
- ☐ Winemaking equipment

- ☐ **Clothing Items**
- ☐ Clothing
- ☐ Raingear, umbrellas
- ☐ Spinning wheels, looms
- ☐ Sewing machines
- ☐ Patterns, safety pins, buttons, zippers
- ☐ Dyes
- ☐ Shoes

- ☐ **Electrical and Electronics**
- ☐ Radios
- ☐ Records
- ☐ Phonographs
- ☐ Stereos
- ☐ Tape recorders
- ☐ Cameras
- ☐ Television cameras
- ☐ Television sets
- ☐ Videotape recorders
- ☐ Movie cameras, film
- ☐ Electronic devices
- ☐ Electronic games
- ☐ Lie detectors
- ☐ Radar equipment

- ☐ **Amusement, recreation**
- ☐ Games
- ☐ Cards
- ☐ Board games, checkers, chess, Monopoly, etc.
- ☐ Kites
- ☐ Gambling devices or machines

- ☐ **Musical Instruments**
- ☐ Specify:

- ☐ **Financial Things**
- ☐ Calculators
- ☐ Adding machines
- ☐ Cash registers
- ☐ Financial records
- ☐ Money

- ☐ **Office Related Things**
- ☐ PBX switchboards
- ☐ Desks, tables
- ☐ Desktop supplies
- ☐ Pens, ink, felt-tip, ballpoint
- ☐ Pencils, black, red or other
- ☐ Typewriter
- ☐ Computers
- ☐ Copying machines, mimeograph machines, printers

- ☐ **Communication Things**
- ☐ Telephones, answering machines
- ☐ Cellular phones
- ☐ Telegraph
- ☐ Fax machines, teleprinters
- ☐ Voice mail machines
- ☐ Ship-to-shore radio, shortwave, walkie-talkies

- ☐ **Printing Materials**
- ☐ Printing presses, type, ink

- ☐ **Art Materials**
- ☐ Woodcuts, engravings, lithographs
- ☐ Paintings, drawings, silk screens

- ☐ **Reading Materials**
- ☐ Books, braille books
- ☐ Newspapers
- ☐ Magazines

☐ **Educational Materials**
☐ Transparencies

☐ **Manufacturing or Warehouse Supplies**
☐ Dollies, handtrucks
☐ Containers
☐ Bottles
☐ Cans
☐ Boxes
☐ Automatic machines
☐ Valves, switches, buttons
☐ Cranks, wheels, gears, levers
☐ Hoists, cranes

☐ **Things that produce Light**
☐ Matches
☐ Candles
☐ Lanterns, oil lamps
☐ Light bulbs, fluorescent lights
☐ Laser beams

☐ **Energy Things**
☐ Fuel cells
☐ Batteries
☐ Transformers, electric motors, dynamos
☐ Engines, gas, diesel
☐ Windmills
☐ Waterwheels
☐ Water turbines
☐ Gas turbines
☐ Steam turbines
☐ Steam engines
☐ Dynamite
☐ Nuclear reactors

☐ **Transportation Things**
☐ Land
☐ Roads
☐ Bicycles
☐ Motorcycles
☐ Mopeds
☐ Automobiles
☐ Parking meters
☐ Traffic lights
☐ Trains
☐ Subways
☐ Air
☐ Gliders
☐ Balloons
☐ Airplanes
☐ Parachutes
☐ Sea
☐ Rivers
☐ Lakes
☐ Streams
☐ Canals
☐ Ocean
☐ Boats
☐ Steamships
☐ Other vehicles

☐ **Medical Materials or Equipment**
☐ Medicines
☐ Vaccines
☐ Anesthetics
☐ Thermometers
☐ Hearing aids
☐ Dental equipment
☐ X-ray machines
☐ False parts of the human body
☐ Spectacles, glasses, contact lenses

☐ **Gym Equipment**

☐ **Sports Equipment**
☐ Fishing rods, fishhooks, bait
☐ Traps, guns

☐ **Gardening or Farm Equipment**
☐ Garden tools
☐ Shovels
☐ Picks
☐ Rakes
☐ Lawnmowers
☐ Ploughs
☐ Threshing machines, reapers, harvesters
☐ Fertilizers
☐ Pesticides
☐ Weed killers

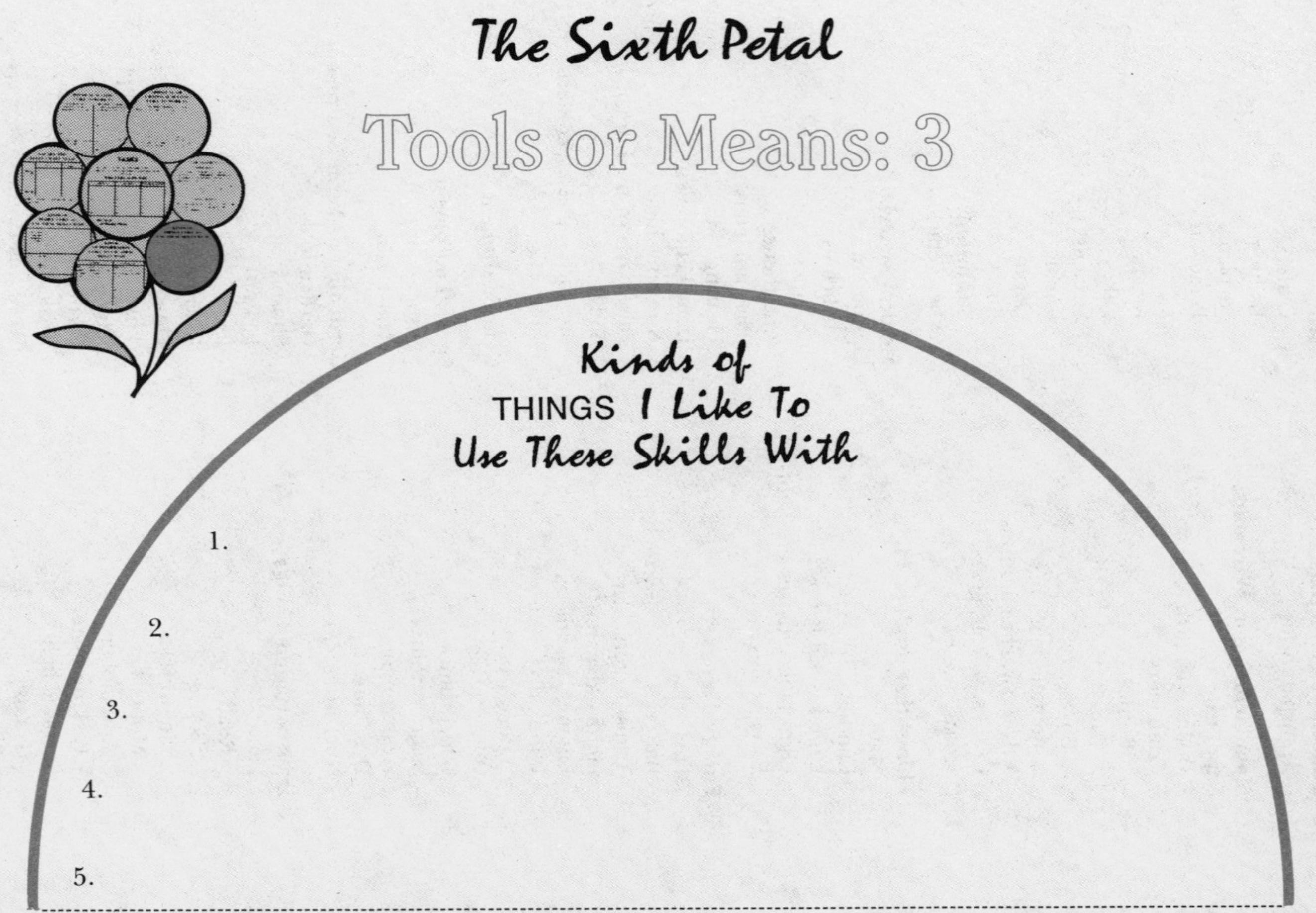
The Sixth Petal
Tools or Means: 3
Kinds of
THINGS I Like To
Use These Skills With
1.
2.
3.
4.
5.

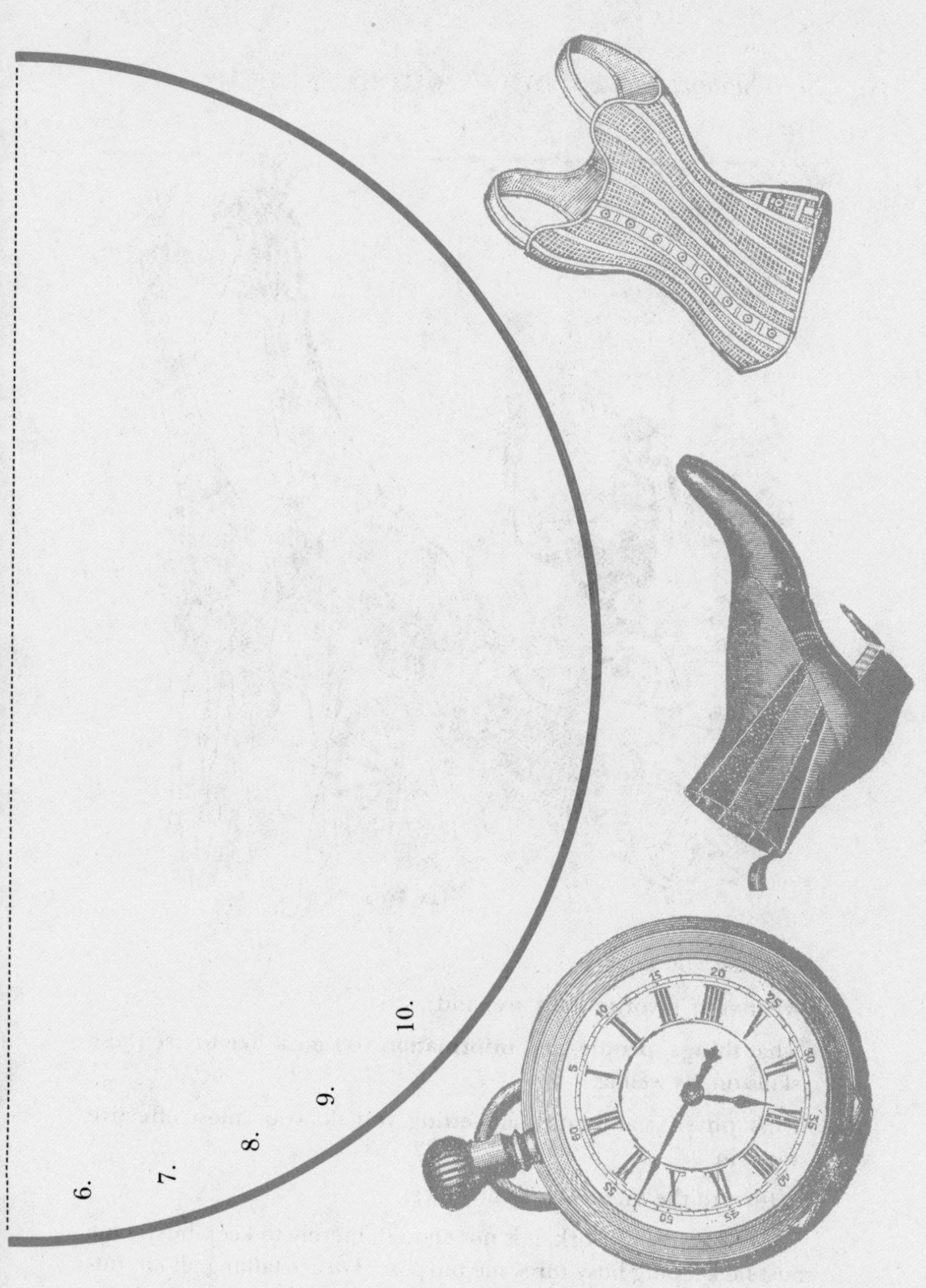
6.
7.
8.
9.
10.

Step Seven: My Favorite Outcomes, Immediate and Long-range

Now that you know:

- what your favorite skills are, and
- what **things**, **people**, and **information** you most like to use these skills on, as well as
- what physical and spiritual **setting** you do your most effective work in,

we turn to the question of outcomes.

In the world of work, it is not enough merely to keep busy. One must be keeping busy for some purpose. We are talking about **outcomes**, or **where does it all lead to?** In the world of work, this is often called "the bottom line." I remember some years ago sending out two of my staff to find some materials for me, and after four hours' fruitless search, one turned to the other and said, "Well let's go back. At least we tried." And the other replied, "Unfortunately, in the world of work you're not usually rewarded for *trying*; you're only rewarded for *succeeding*." So they kept on, until they found what they were looking for. This underlines the point here: generally speaking, when you set about to use your skills in the world of work, you must be aiming at some **result** -- in accordance with some **purpose** or **goal**, defined by either you or the organization (preferably *both*).

So, look at the Petal on the next page. There you will see that *Outcomes* divides into two parts: **Immediate** and **Long-range**.

Immediate Results of Your Work

Immediate results, at your place of work, is a matter of: "At the work I'd most love to do, what result am I aiming at? Do I want to help produce a **product**, or do I want to help offer some **service** to people, or do I want to help gather, manage, or disseminate **information** to people? Or all three? Or two? And in what order of priority? Do I think the world basically needs me to help it have: more information, or more service, or more of some product -- such as food, clothing, or shelter?

Once you've answered that, the next question *of course* is: **what** product, or service, or information?

Well, the *what* is relatively easy to answer (I said *relatively*). If your preferred outcome is some **product** that you'd like to help produce or market, you'll probably find it identified on your *Favorite Things* petal, on page 262f. If your preferred outcome is some **service** to people, you'll probably find it identified on your *Favorite People* petal, on page 248f. And if your preferred outcome is some kind of **information** that you'd like to help gather, manage, or disseminate, you'll probably find it identified on your *Favorite Information* petal, on page 252f.

Another way of looking at this subject of Immediate Outcomes is to study your seven stories, to see what central motivation seems always to be driving you, what one result you seem always to be reaching for -- above all others. Here is how to discover that:

(continued on page 268)

The Seventh Petal

Outcomes

Immediate

At the work I'd most love to do,
do I want to help produce a **product**
or do I want to help offer some **service** to people,
or do I want to help gather, manage or disseminate **information** to
people? Or all three? Or two? And what kind of product, service, or info?

And, what do I see as my central driving motivation in whatever job I take, or in whatever career I pursue?

Long-range

My long-range goals for my life -- the things I want to do, or the goals I'd like to accomplish -- before I die, are:

Outcomes: The Central Motivation -- One Result

Go through your seven stories and underline in purple all your verbs. See which of the verbs below get repeated over and over again. These describe **the one result** *that you are always attempting to reach,* **the one outcome** *that you find to be your chief and most coveted reward, in all you do. You, of course, don't want to be pinned down to just one; you want to be able to choose three, or four, or more. Fine, just prioritize them afterward on a prioritizing grid.*

Acquire / Possess *(Money / Things / Status / People)* Wants to have own . . . baby, toys, possessions, houses, family.

Be in Charge / Command *(of Others / Things / Organization)* Wants to be on top, in authority, in the saddle -- where it can be determined how things will be done . . .

Combat / Prevail *(over Adversaries / Evil / Opposing Philosophies)* Wants to come against the bad guys, entrenched status quo, old technology . . .

Develop / Build *(Structures / Technical Things)* Wants to make something where there was nothing. . . .

Excel / Be the Best *(versus: Others / Conventional Standards)* Wants to be the fastest, first, longest, earliest, or more complicated, better than others . . .

Exploit / Achieve Potential *(of Situations / Markets / Things / People)* Sees a silk purse, a giant talent, a hot product, or a promising market before the fact . . .

Gain Response / Influence Behavior *(from People / Through People)* Wants dogs, cats, people, and groups to react to their touch . . .

Gain Recognition / Attention *(from Peers / Public Authority)* Wants to wave at the cheering crowd, appear in the newspaper, be known, dance in the spotlight . . .

Improve / Make Better *(Oneself / Others / Work / Organizations)* Makes what is marginal, good; what is good, better; what makes a little money, make a lot of money. . . .

Make the Team / Grade *(Established by Others or the System)* Gains access to the varsity, Eagle Scout rank, Silver Circle, Thirty-ninth Masonic Order, the country club, executive dining room . . .

Meet Needs / Fulfill Expectations *(that are Demanded / Needed / or Inherent)* Strives to meet specifications, shipping schedules, what the customer wants, what the boss has expressed . . .

Make Work / Make Effective *(Things / Systems / Operations)* Fixes what is broken, changes what is out-of-date, redesigns what has been poorly conceived. . . .

Master / Perfect *(Some Subject / Skill / Equipment / Objects)* Goes after rough edges, complete domination of a technique, total control over the variables . . .

Organize / Operate *(Business / Team / Product Line)* The entrepreneur, the beginner of new businesses . . .

Overcome / Persevere *(Obstacles / Handicaps / Unknown Odds)* Goes after hungry tigers with a popgun, concave mountains with slippery boots. . . .
Pioneer / Explore *(Technology / Cultures / Ideas)* Presses through established lines, knowledge, boundaries . . .
Serve / Help *(People / Organizations / Causes)* Carries the soup, ministers to the wounded, helps those in need . . .
Shape / Influence *(Material / Policy / People)* Wants to leave a mark, to cause change, to impact . . .

(Adapted by Richard N. Bolles from Miller, Arthur F., and Mattson, Ralph T., The Truth About You: Discover what you should be doing with your life, 1st ed., 1977, pp. 68–69. Not to be reproduced without written permission from Arthur Miller, People Management Inc., 10 Station Street, Simsbury, Conn. 06070.)

The Long-range Results of Your Work

As a result of **all** the work you do here on earth, what results or outcome do you want to achieve by the time that you die? What goals do you want to accomplish, what things do you want to do? Your answer to this should be written out, thoughtfully, on a single piece of scratch paper (no more than one page, please) -- and then the most important points in your statement should be copied onto the bottom part of the petal on page 266f. Go back, also, and look at your philosophy of life, on page 220.

Incidentally, if while you are writing this statement, you find yourself setting down some long-range goals that really have nothing to do with *your work* as such, but have to do more with your overall *life* -- such as, "Before I die, I want to travel all over the world" -- write them down *anyway.* You just never know when a job might be offered to you somewhere down the road that would make it possible for you to achieve some of your **life**-goals, and not just your work or achievement-goals.

And now on to the last step in your putting together a picture of your ideal job:

Step Eight: My Favorite Rewards at Work

If you look at page 272–273, you will see the final petal of your *flower* picture of the ideal job for you. It is entitled "Rewards." Virtually all of us hope for some reward from our job that is different than, and distinguishable from, *the outcomes* which we saw in the previous Step. That is to say, in addition to producing a product, service, or information, we (usually) want our work to put bread on our table, clothes on our back, and a roof over our head -- at a minimum.

The petal speaks of **Level** and **Salary**. It asks you to think out what is the *minimum* salary you would need from your next job or career, and what is the *maximum* salary you would like to have if things were ideal.

Hand in hand with *salary* goes the question of *level.* If you aspire, in matters of salary, to $70,000 a year, but you aspire, in the matter of level, to being an office boy, there is something flawed about your dream. Level and salary usually go hand in hand. Office boys don't make $70,000 a year.

On this petal, salary is relatively easy to figure out. Minimum is what you simply *must* make, or you will starve. It requires a little budget figuring, and that's all. Maximum is what you would *like* to make. It requires a little searching of your daydreams, and that's all.

Level is harder to figure out. To some degree, it's what you find out as you conduct your informational interviewing after you have completed this booklet. For example, let us say that you discover from your flower picture, that your ideal job would involve doing research into how one prolongs human life. As you visit the various places that are involved in such research, you discover that an apprentice researcher makes barely your minimum desired salary. A team member with ten years' experience makes $10,000 more than your minimum salary, while only a senior researcher who is head of a research team makes the maximum salary that you have put on your petal here. It is at this point (and this point only) that you can really fill out the level part of this petal: e.g., apprentice researcher.

But, there are some questions about *level* -- let's call them "some preliminary hunches" that you *can* put down, even now. For example, in your ideal job do you want to work:

- ☐ by yourself and for yourself;
- ☐ by yourself but for another person or organization;
- ☐ in *tandem* with one other person;
- ☐ as a member of a team of equals;
- ☐ as a member of a hierarchy where you carry out directions;
- ☐ as a member of a hierarchy where you are the boss or supervisor or owner;
- ☐ or what?

Jot down, on the petal, as many ideas or hunches as occur to you at the moment. You can always change them later (as indeed, you can change *any* petal) after you have conducted your own research or informational interviewing about your *flower* picture.

At the bottom of this petal, you will see that space has been provided for you to add any other rewards that you would like your ideal job to give you. What do we mean by this? Well, many people hope their job will give them more by way of reward, than just money. *For example* (put a check mark in front of any that apply to you):

- ☐ Social contact
- ☐ A chance to help others
- ☐ A chance to bring others closer to God
- ☐ Intellectual stimulation
- ☐ A chance to use my expertise
- ☐ A chance to make decisions
- ☐ A chance to be creative
- ☐ A chance to exercise leadership
- ☐ A chance to be popular
- ☐ Respect
- ☐ Adventure
- ☐ Challenge
- ☐ Influence
- ☐ Security
- ☐ Independence
- ☐ Wealth
- ☐ Power
- ☐ Fame

Jot down any others that may occur to you, which are not on this list. When you are done, rank them in their order of importance to you (you may use the Prioritizing Grid, on page 216, if you wish), and then copy them in order, on the bottom part of this petal.

The Eighth Petal

Rewards

Salary and Level I Want/Need

	LEVEL	SALARY
MAX		

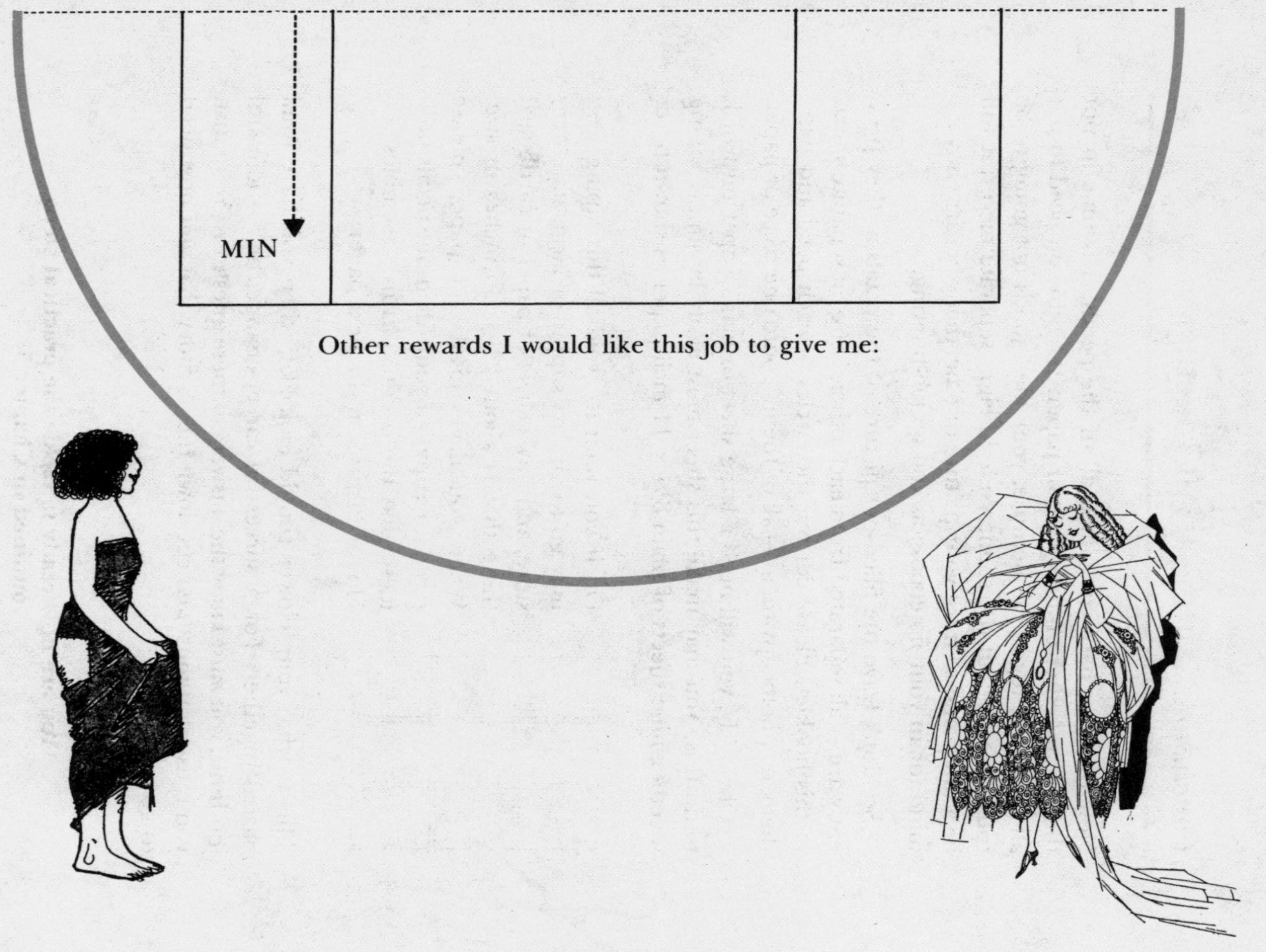
MIN
Other rewards I would like this job to give me:

Conclusion: Putting It All Together

Now that you have completed all of the petals, it is time to put them all together on one piece of paper. Why do you need to put all the petals together? Because, your ideal job is not going to be found lying about the countryside in eight separate pieces; it will be a unity, and so must your picture of it be, that you carry in your mind (or in your notebook) as you go job-hunting.

So, don't leave the filled-out picture of the petals as they presently are -- all separated from each other, lying on separate sheets in this booklet. Please cut out the circles of each petal and paste them, or photocopy them -- all of them -- onto one piece of paper.

Obviously, you will need a large sheet of blank paper on which to do this. You may make this sheet most easily by simply taping together nine sheets of plain 8½ × 11 inch paper as shown here:

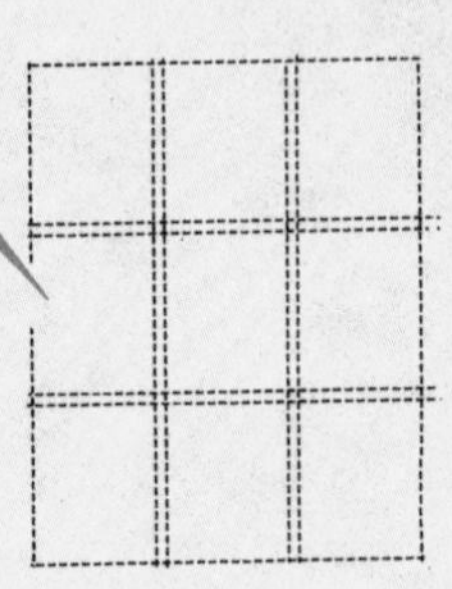

Or, if you want to avoid all this taping, you may go to any art supply or large stationery store, and buy a sheet of paper or cardboard there that is about 24 × 36 inches in size. When you have this larger paper, **please** paste (or copy) all your filled-out petals onto it, so that the overall picture resembles the Flower Picture on the next page:

This is what your Flower should look like, when you have it all pasted together: For a successful career-change, or a successful job-hunt, you ***must*** know the answers to these questions. You must, you must, you must *thus* cut down the territory that you now need to go exploring.

You are now ready to tackle the practical steps outlined in Chapter 5.

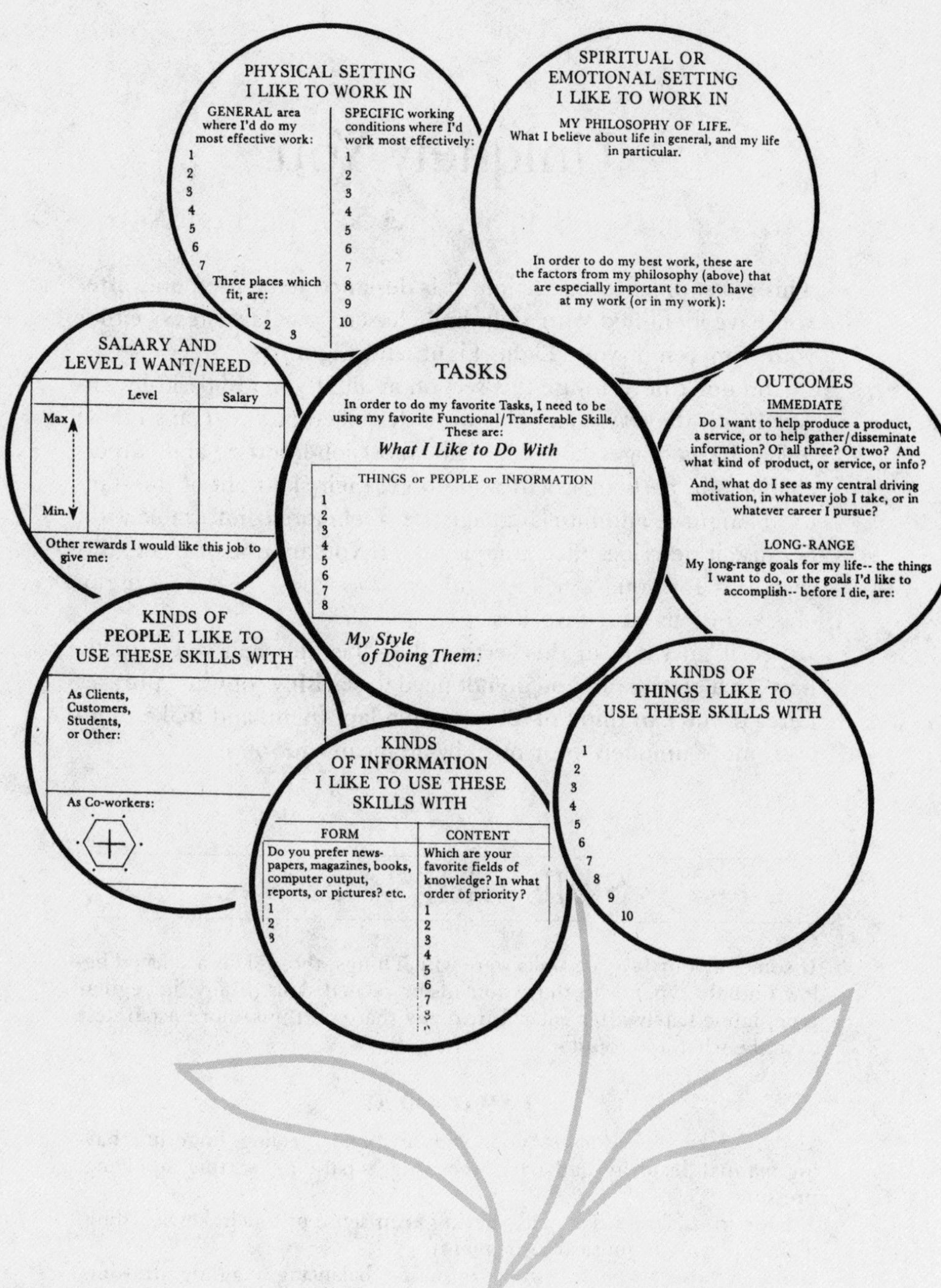
PHYSICAL SETTING
I LIKE TO WORK IN
GENERAL area where I'd do my most effective work:
1
2
3
4
5
6
7
Three places which fit, are:
1
2
3
SPECIFIC working conditions where I'd work most effectively:
1
2
3
4
5
6
7
8
9
10
SPIRITUAL OR
EMOTIONAL SETTING
I LIKE TO WORK IN
MY PHILOSOPHY OF LIFE.
What I believe about life in general, and my life in particular.
In order to do my best work, these are the factors from my philosophy (above) that are especially important to me to have at my work (or in my work):
SALARY AND
LEVEL I WANT/NEED
Level
Salary
Max
Min.
Other rewards I would like this job to give me:
TASKS
In order to do my favorite Tasks, I need to be using my favorite Functional/Transferable Skills. These are:
What I Like to Do With
THINGS or PEOPLE or INFORMATION
1
2
3
4
5
6
7
8
My Style
of Doing Them:
OUTCOMES
IMMEDIATE
Do I want to help produce a product, a service, or to help gather/disseminate information? Or all three? Or two? And what kind of product, or service, or info?
And, what do I see as my central driving motivation, in whatever job I take, or in whatever career I pursue?
LONG-RANGE
My long-range goals for my life-- the things I want to do, or the goals I'd like to accomplish-- before I die, are:
KINDS OF
PEOPLE I LIKE TO
USE THESE SKILLS WITH
As Clients, Customers, Students, or Other:
As Co-workers:
KINDS OF
THINGS I LIKE TO
USE THESE SKILLS WITH
1
2
3
4
5
6
7
8
9
10
KINDS
OF INFORMATION
I LIKE TO USE THESE
SKILLS WITH
FORM
Do you prefer newspapers, magazines, books, computer output, reports, or pictures? etc.
1
2
3
CONTENT
Which are your favorite fields of knowledge? In what order of priority?
1
2
3
4
5
6
7
8

Uniquely You

A Dictionary of Skill Synonyms or Related Words

This is a supplemental section. It is designed to be used only **after** you have identified your skills **and** chosen your favorites -- either your Top Ten or your Eight, Eight, and Eight.

You don't need to use this section at all, if you are basically satisfied with the way your skills were described on the Transferable Skills charts (pages 232–237). But most job-hunters, and career-changers in particular, **will** want to get their skills out of the standard language and into language they feel more comfortable with, because it describes their uniqueness. If you are one of those, this section is for you. You need only look up those skills which you checked off as your favorites.

See if anything in this section describes the skill you actually have, in a better way. You do not need to slavishly copy any phrases here. If you can think of any way to adapt them, and make them even more uniquely your own, by all means do so.

Skills with Things

If some of your favorite skills were with **Things**, those skills are listed below (in **bold** type), with the synonyms or related skills (if any) in regular type, immediately after each. Circle any that you think more accurately describe what it is you do.

I AM GOOD AT

Using my hands or fingers: good with my hands; feeling, fingering, having manual dexterity, gathering, receiving, separating, sorting, applying, pressing

Having great finger dexterity: having keen sense of touch, keyboarding, typing, playing (a musical instrument)

Using my eyes and hands in coordination: balancing, juggling, drawing, painting

Motor/physical coordination with my whole body: possessing fine motor coordination, raising, lifting, carrying, pushing, pulling, moving, unloading, walking, running, backpacking, swimming, hiking, mountaineering, skiing

Having agility, speed, strength or stamina: displaying great physical agility, possessing great strength, demonstrating outstanding endurance, maintaining uncommon physical fitness, acting as bodyguard

Crafting, sewing, weaving, hammering, etc.: knitting, collecting

Cutting, carving or chiseling: logging, mining, drawing samples from the earth

Fashioning, molding, shaping or sculpting: working (materials)

Finishing, painting, refinishing, or restoring: binding, sandblasting, grinding

Precision working with my hands: making miniatures, skilled at working in the micro-universe

Washing, cleaning or preparing:

Handling, or expediting: using particular tools (say which), placing, guiding, receiving, shipping, distributing, delivering

Making, producing, manufacturing (cooking): having great culinary skills

Maintaining, preserving, or repairing, objects, tools, instruments:

Precision working with tools or instruments: precise attainment of set limits, tolerances, or standards; having great dexterity with small instruments (e.g., tweezers); keypunching; drilling; enjoy working within precise limits or standards of accuracy

Setting up or assembling: clearing, laying, installing, displaying

Operating, controlling, or driving: piloting, navigating, guiding, steering, mastering machinery against its will

Tending, minding, feeding, or emptying: monitoring machines or valves, giving continuous attention to, regulating controls of, watching to make sure nothing goes wrong, making a ready response in any emergency, checking, pushing buttons, starting, flipping switches, switching, adjusting controls, turning knobs, making adjustments when machine threatens to malfunction, placing, inserting, stacking, loading, dumping, removing, disposing of

Maintaining, cleaning or repairing equipment, machinery, or vehicles: changing, refilling, tuning, adjusting, fitting, doing preventative maintenance, trouble-shooting, restoring, fixing

Breaking down, disassembling, or salvaging: mopping up, cleaning up, knocking down

Constructing or reconstructing: erecting, putting together

Modeling or remodeling: able to perform magic on a room

Having a green thumb, causing growing things to flourish: helping to grow, farming, digging, plowing, tilling, seeding, planting, nurturing, groundskeeping, landscaping, weeding, harvesting

Having skills with animals, raising, training, or treating, etc: animal training, ranching, sensing, persuading, etc. *With higher animals, the skills used are very similar to people skills (see below).*

Skills with People

If some of your favorite skills were with **People**, those skills are listed below (in **bold** type), with the synonyms or related skills (if any) in regular type, immediately after each. Circle any that you think more accurately describe what it is you do.

WITH INDIVIDUALS,
I AM GOOD AT

Taking instructions, serving, or helping: following detailed instructions, rendering support services, preparing (something for someone), hostessing, waiting on tables, protecting, rendering services to, dealing patiently with difficult people

Communicating well in conversation, in person or on the phone: hearing and answering questions perceptively, adept at two-way dialogue, being sensitive and responsive to the feelings of others, empathizing, showing warmth, good telephoning skills, developing warmth over the telephone, creating an atmosphere of acceptance, keen ability to put self in someone else's shoes, signaling, talking, telling, informing, giving instructions, exchanging information

Communicating well in writing: (see above), also: expressing with clarity, verbalizing cogently, uncommonly warm letter composition

Instructing, teaching, tutoring, or training individuals: guiding, interpreting and expressing facts and ideas

Advising, coaching, counseling, mentoring, empowering: facilitating personal growth and development; helping people identify their problems, needs, and solutions; interpreting others' dreams; raising people's self-esteem

Diagnosing, treating, or healing: prescribing, attending, caring for, nursing, ministering to, caring for the handicapped, having true therapeutic abilities, having healing abilities, powerful in prayer, rehabilitating, curing, raising people's self-esteem

Referring people, or helping two people to link up: recommending, making and using contacts effectively, acting as a resource broker, finding people or other resources, adept at calling in other experts or helpers as needed

Assessing, evaluating, screening, or selecting individuals: having accurate gut reactions, sizing up other people perceptively, quickly assessing what's going on, realistically assessing people's needs, perceptive in identifying and assessing the potential of others, monitoring behavior through watching, critical evaluation, and feedback

Persuading, motivating, recruiting, or selling individuals: influencing, moving, inspiring, displaying charisma, inspiring trust, evoking loyalty, convincing, motivating, developing rapport or trust, recruiting talent or leadership, attracting skilled, competent and creative people, enlisting, demonstrating (a product), selling tangibles or intangibles

Representing others, interpreting others' ideas or language: translating jargon into relevant and meaningful terms, helping others to express their views, speaking a foreign language fluently, serving as an interpreter, clarifying values and goals of others, expert at liaison roles, representing a majority or minority group in a larger meeting or assembly

WITH GROUPS, I AM GOOD AT

Communicating effectively to a group or a multitude, by . . .

Using words expressively in speaking or writing: outstanding writing skills; making oral presentations; exceptional speaking ability; addressing large or small groups confidently; very responsive to audience's moods or ideas; thinking quickly on my feet; speechwriting, playwriting and writing with humor, fun and flair; employing humor in describing my experiences; ability to vividly describe people or scenes so that others can visualize them; very explicit and concise writing; making people think; doing excellent promotional writing; creating imaginative advertising and publicity programs; keeping superior minutes of meetings

Making presentations in person, or on TV or film: using voice tone and rhythm as unusually effective tools of communication, giving radio or TV presentations, giving briefings, making reports

Performing, entertaining, amusing, or inspiring: exhibiting showmanship, having strong theatrical sense, understudying, provoking laughter, making people laugh, distracting, diverting

Signing, miming, acting, singing, or playing an instrument: dramatizing, modeling, dancing, playing music, giving poetry readings, relating seemingly disparate ideas by means of words or actions, exceptionally good at facial expressions or body language to express thoughts or feelings eloquently

Playing games, or a particular game, leading others in recreation or exercise: excellent at sports; excellent at a particular sport (tennis, gymnastics, running, swimming, golf, baseball, football); helping others to get fit; creating, planning, and organizing outdoor activities; leading backpacking, hiking, camping, mountain-climbing expeditions; outdoor survival skills; excellent at traveling

Teaching, training, or designing educational events: lecturing; explaining; instructing; enlightening; demonstrating; showing; detailing; modeling (desired behavior); patient teaching; organizing and administering in-house training events; planning and carrying out well-run seminars, workshops, or meetings; fostering a stimulating learning environment; ability to shape the atmosphere of a place so that it is warm, pleasant, and comfortable; instilling in people a love of the subject being taught; explaining difficult or complex concepts or ideas; putting things in perspective; showing others how to take advantage of a resource; helping others to experience something; making distinctive visual presentations

Guiding a group discussion, conveying warmth: skilled at chairing meetings; group-facilitating; refusing to put people into slots or categories; treating others as equals, without regard to education, authority, or position; discussing; conferring; exchanging information; drawing out people; encouraging people; helping people make their own discoveries; helping people identify their own intelligent self-interest; adept at two-way dialogue; ability to hear and answer questions perceptively

Persuading a group, debating, motivating, or selling: publicizing, promoting, reasoning persuasively, influencing the ideas and attitudes of others, selling a program or course of action to decision-makers, obtaining agreement after the fact, fund-raising, arranging financing, writing a proposal, promoting or bringing about major policy changes, devising a systematic approach to goal setting

Consulting, giving advice to groups in my area of expertise: advising, giving expert advice or recommendations, trouble-shooting, giving professional advice, giving insight concerning

Managing, supervising, or running a business, fund drive, etc.: coordinating, overseeing, heading up, administering, directing, controlling (a project), conducting (an orchestra), directing (a production, or play), planning, organizing, and staging of theatrical productions, adept at planning and staging ceremonies, deft at directing creative talent, interpreting goals, promoting harmonious relations and efficiency, encouraging people, organizing my time expertly, setting up and maintaining on-time work schedules, establishing effective priorities among competing requirements, coordinating operations and details, sizing up situations, anticipating people's needs, deals well with the unexpected or critical event, skilled at allocating scarce financial resources, bringing projects in on time and within budget, able to make hard decisions

Following through, getting things done, producing: executing, carrying out decisions reached, implementing decisions, expediting, building customer loyalty, unusual ability to work self-directedly without supervision, able to handle a variety of tasks and responsibilities simultaneously and efficiently, instinctively gathering resources even before the need for them becomes clear, recognizing obsolescence of ideas or procedures before compelling evidence is yet at hand, anticipating problems or needs before they become problems, decisive in emergencies, continually searching for more responsibility, developing or building markets for ideas or products, completing, attaining objectives, meeting goals, producing results, delivering as promised, increasing productivity, making good use of feedback

Leading, taking the lead, being a pioneer: determining goals, objectives, and procedures, making policy, willing to experiment with new approaches, recognizing and utilizing the skills of others, organizing diverse people into a functioning group, unifying, energizing, team-building, delegating authority, sharing responsibility, taking manageable risks, instinctively understand political realities, acting on new information immediately, seek and seize opportunities

Initiating, starting up, founding, or establishing: originating, instituting, establishing, charting, financing startups

Negotiating between two parties, or resolving conflicts: mediating, arbitrating, bargaining, umpiring, adjudicating, renegotiating, reconciling, resolving, achieving compromise, charting mergers, getting diverse groups to work together, adept at conflict management, accepting of differing opinions, handling prima donnas tactfully and well, collaborating with colleagues skillfully, handling super-difficult individuals in situations, without stress, skilled at arriving at jointly agreed-upon decisions or policy or program or solutions, working well in a hostile environment, confronting others with touchy or difficult personal matters, treating people fairly.

Skills with Information

If some of your favorite skills were with **Information**, those skills are listed below (in **bold** type), with the synonyms or related skills (if any) in regular type, immediately after each. Circle any that you think more accurately describe what it is you do.

I AM GOOD AT

Compiling, searching, or researching: have exceptional intelligence tempered by common sense; like dealing with ideas, information and concepts; exhibit a perpetual curiosity and delight in new knowledge; relentlessly curious; have a love of printed things; reading avidly; reading ceaselessly; committed to continual personal growth, and learning; continually seeking to expose self to new experiences; love to stay current, particularly on the subjects of . . . ; continually gathering information with respect to a particular problem or area of expertise (say *what*); finding and getting things not easy to find; searching databases; discovering; discovering resources, ways, and means; investigating; detecting; surveying; identifying; ascertaining; determining; finding; assembling; compiling; gathering; collecting; surveying organizational needs; doing economic research

Gathering information by interviewing, or observing people: skilled at striking up conversations with strangers, talking easily with all kinds of people, adept at gathering information from people by talking to them, listening intently and accurately, intuiting, inquiring, questioning people gently, highly observant of people, learn from the example of others, study other people's behavior perceptively, accurately assessing public moods

Gathering information by studying, or observing things: paying careful attention to, being very observant, keenly aware of surroundings, examining, concentrating, focusing on minutiae

Having an acute sense of hearing, smell, taste, or sight: ability to distinguish different musical notes, perfect pitch, having uncommonly fine sense of rhythm, possessing color discrimination of a very high order, possessing instinctively excellent taste in design, arrangement, and color

Imagining, inventing, creating, or designing new ideas: devising, generating, innovating, formulating, conceptualizing, having conceptual ability of a high order, hypothesizing, discovering, conceiving new concepts, approaches, interpretations, being an idea man or woman, having "ideaphoria," demonstrating originality, continually conceiving, generating and developing innovative and creative ideas, creative imagining, possessed of great imagination, having imagination and the courage to use it, improvising on the spur of the moment, composing (music), continually conceiving, generating and developing music, continually creating new ideas for systems, methods, and procedures

Copying, and/or comparing similarities or differences: addressing, posting, making comparisons, checking, proofreading, perceiving identities or divergencies, developing a standard or model, estimating (e.g., the speed of a moving object), comparing with previous data

Computing, working with numbers, doing accounting: counting, taking inventory, counting with high accuracy, having arithmetical skills, calculating, performing rapid and accurate manipulation of numbers, in my head or on paper, having very sophisticated mathematical abilities, solving statistical problems, using numbers as a reasoning tool, preparing financial reports, estimating, budgeting, projecting, ordering, purchasing, acquiring, auditing, maintaining fiscal controls

Analyzing, breaking down into its parts: reasoning, dissecting, atomizing, figuring out, finding the basic units, breaking into its basic elements, defining cause-and-effect relationships, doing financial or fiscal analysis, doing effective cost analysis

Organizing, classifying, systematizing, and/or prioritizing: putting things in order, bringing order out of chaos (with ideas, data, or things), putting into working order, perceiving common denominators, giving a definite structure and working order to things, forming into a whole with connected and interdependent parts, formulating, defining, clustering, collating, tabulating, protecting, keeping confidential

Planning, laying out a step-by-step process for achieving a goal: determining the sequence of tasks after reviewing pertinent data or requirements, planning on the basis of learnings from the past, determining the sequence of operations, establishing logical, sequential methods to accomplish stated goals, making arrangements for the functioning of a system, planning for change

Adapting, translating, computer programming, developing, or improving: updating, expanding, improving, upgrading, applying, arranging (e.g., music), redesigning, improvising, adjusting, interpreting, extrapolating, projecting, forecasting, creating a new form of something, taking what others have developed and applying it to new situations, making practical applications of theoretical ideas, deriving applications from other people's ideas, able to see the commercial possibilities in a concept, idea, or product, revising goals, policies, and procedures, translating numbers and words into electronically coded computer data

Visualizing, drawing, painting, dramatizing, creating videos, or software: continually conceiving, generating, and developing pictures, able to visualize shapes, able to visualize in three dimensions, conceiving shapes, colors, or sounds, having form perception, skilled at symbol formation, creating symbols, conceiving symbolic or metaphoric pictures of Reality, designing, designing in wood or other media, fashioning, shaping, making models, designing handicrafts, creating poetic images, thinking in pictures, visualizing concepts, illustrating, sketching, coloring, drafting, graphing, mapping, photographing, doing computer graphics, doing mechanical drawing, able to read blueprints, able to read graphs quickly, using video or other recording equipment to produce imaginative audio/visual presentations, good at set designing

Synthesizing, combining parts into a whole: transforming apparently unrelated things or ideas, by forming them into a new whole, relating, combining, integrating, unifying, producing a clear, coherent unity, seeing 'the big picture,' always seeing things in a larger context

Problem solving, or seeing patterns among a mass of data: diagnosing, intuiting, figuring out, perceiving patterns or structures, recognizing

when more information is needed before a decision can be reached, proving, disproving, validating
Deciding, evaluating, appraising, or making recommendations: love making decisions that require personal judgment, making judgments about people or data or things, keeping confidences, keeping secrets, encrypting, inspecting, studying data to determine compliance with an established norm, checking, testing, weighing, appraising, assessing, determining the fair market value of an object, reviewing, critiquing, discriminating between what is important and what is unimportant, separating the wheat from the chaff, summarizing, editing, reducing the size of a database, judging, selecting, screening, screening out, extracting, reviewing large amounts of material and extracting its essence, writing a precis, conserving, making fiscal reductions, eliminating, simplifying, consolidating
Keeping records, including recording, filming, or entering on a computer: transcribing, reproducing, imitating, keeping accurate financial records, operating a computer competently, word processing, maintaining databases
Storing, or filing, in file cabinets, microfiche, video, audio, or computer: good clerical ability
Retrieving information, ideas, data: extracting, reviewing, restoring, reporting, giving out information patiently and accurately, good at getting materials that are needed
Enabling other people to find or retrieve information: filing in a way to facilitate retrieval, classifying expertly, organizing information according to a prescribed plan, am an excellent 'resource broker'
Having a superior memory, keeping track of details: easily remember facts and figures, having a keen and accurate memory for detail, recalling people and their preferences accurately, retentive memory for rules and procedures, expert at remembering numbers and statistics accurately and for a long period, having exceedingly accurate melody recognition, exhibiting keen tonal memory, accurately reproducing sounds or tones (e.g., a foreign language, spoken without accent), easily remembering faces, accurate spatial memory, having a memory for design, having a photographic memory.

Now, you will want to finish the statement of skills in your own language, by describing **degree**. Here are some possible modifiers you may want to put in front of **the skills you are best at** *(one usually omits the words "I . . ." or "I have . . ." or "I am . . . ," which are understood).*

- Good at . . . ,
- Exceptionally good at . . . ,
- Adept at . . . ,
- Expert at . . . ,
- Deft at . . . ,
- Excel at . . . ,
- Unusually skillful at . . . ,
- Unusual ability to . . . ,
- Skilled at . . . ,
- Demonstrated exceptional ability to . . .

When you are done with this section, before you copy them onto the *Tasks/Transferable Skills* petal on page 240f., flesh out your favorite skills, viz., adding to the verb an object and a modifier as described on page 238. In this fleshing out, the phrases above can be used as modifiers of particular skills, if they are used in their adjective or adverb form, e.g., *"Exceptional," "uncommon," "adeptly," "expertly," "skillfully," "unusually,"* and so forth.

8 DAY
JAVA

My son, be admonished:
of making many books there is no end;
and much study is a weariness of the flesh.

Ecclesiastes

Appendix B

Special Problems in the Job-Hunt

additional readings and comments

BOOKS

Every book has a different voice. That's fortunate. No one book *(including this one)* can reach every reader. If you find *Parachute* didn't give you all that you wanted or needed, here are some other books that may succeed for you. Different voices.

It may also be that while *Parachute* helped you, there are still some *areas of interest* where you need or want more light shed. These books *(and my comments)* may help. Different lights.

An asterisk (*) in front of a listing means it is listed here for the first time, or is newly revised.

IN GENERAL: HIGHLY RECOMMENDED

*Lathrop, Richard, *Who's Hiring Who?* 12th Edition. Ten Speed Press, Box 7123, Berkeley, CA 94707. 1989, 1977, 1976, 1971, 1967, 1966, 1961, 1960, 1959. First-class, highly recommended. Simply excellent resource, best by a long shot on the subject of resumes (or *qualifications briefs*, as Dick calls them). Used more often by our readers than any other book, besides *Parachute*.

*Wegmann, Robert, and Chapman, Robert, *The Right Place at the Right Time: Finding a Job in the 1990s*. Ten Speed Press, Box 7123, Berkeley, CA 94707. 1987, revised and updated, 1990. Highly highly recommended. Bob Wegmann knows more about what is currently going on in the world of work than anyone else I know.

Wegmann, Robert, and Chapman, Robert, and Johnson, Miriam, *Work in the New Economy: Careers and Job Seeking into the 21st Century*. JIST Works, 720 North Park Ave., Indianapolis, IN 46202. 1989. Updated. Also recommended, of course. Bob Wegmann's insights in another form.

Sher, Barbara, *Wishcraft: How to Get What You Really Want*. Ballantine Books, 201 E. 50th St., New York, NY 10022. 1983. A very helpful book; our readers love it.

Jackson, Tom, *Guerrilla Tactics in the Job Market* (revised). Bantam Books, 666 Fifth Ave., New York, NY 10103. 1980. A very popular and useful book. Tom has some great ideas and insights found in no other authors.

Figler, Howard E., *The Complete Job-Search Handbook: All the Skills You Need to Get Any Job and Have a Good Time Doing It*. Henry Holt & Co., Inc., 115 W. 18th St., New York, NY 10011. 1988. Identifies the twenty skills the job-hunter needs in order to pull off a job hunt *successfully*. A very unusual approach to the subject of skills, as well as to the subject of the job-hunt.

Germann, Richard, and Arnold, Peter, *Bernard Haldane Associates' Job*

---

* ***Throughout this Appendix, an asterisk in front of a book's listing is for the benefit of our annual readers who are trying to find what's new in this year's edition. An asterisk indicates a title newly revised, or just added to* Parachute *this year.***

and Career Building. Ten Speed Press, Box 7123, Berkeley, CA 94707. 1981, 1980. A detailed description of how to find a job, once you know what it is you want to do; adapted from the well-known program of Bernard Haldane Associates.

Miller, Arthur F., and Mattson, Ralph T., *The Truth About You: Discover What You Should Be Doing with Your Life*. Ten Speed Press, Box 7123, Berkeley, CA 94707. 1989, 1977. A first-class book, very helpful. I like Arthur a lot. I like this book a lot. I know of no other book that sets out to do what Arthur has here set out to do: look for *overall patterns* in people's choices of jobs -- within the overarching context of *faith*.

Wallach, Ellen J., and Arnold, Peter, *The Job Search Companion: The Organizer for Job Seekers*. The Harvard Common Press, 535 Albany St., Boston, MA 02118. 1984. Primarily a book of very useful "forms" for keeping track of your job-search. Intended as a supplement to other job-hunting books. If I myself were going job hunting tomorrow, I would definitely use the forms in this book to help organize my job hunt.

Haldane, Bernard, and Haldane, Jean, and Martin, Lowell, *Job Power: The Young People's Job Finding Guide*. Acropolis Books Ltd., 2400 17th St. NW, Washington, DC 20009. 1980. Undoubtedly the best book available for high school students.

Haldane, Bernard, *Career Satisfaction and Success: How to Know and Manage Your Strengths*. Now published by Wellness Behavior, 4502 54th Ave., NE, Seattle, WA 98105. 1988.

Irish, Richard K., *Go Hire Yourself an Employer*. Anchor Press, Doubleday, New York, NY. 1987. An old and popular classic, now reissued (in its third edition).

Campbell, David P., *If You Don't Know Where You're Going, You'll Probably End Up Somewhere Else*. Argus Communications, Niles, IL. 1974. Useful for those who need to be convinced of the need for career planning.

OTHER RESOURCES FOR THE JOB-HUNTER OR CAREER-CHANGER BY RICHARD BOLLES

Crystal, John C., and Bolles, Richard N., *Where Do I Go From Here With My Life?* 272 pages. Ten Speed Press, Box 7123, Berkeley, CA 94707. 1974.

Bolles, Richard N., *The Three Boxes of Life, and How To Get Out of Them*. 480 pages. Ten Speed Press, Box 7123, Berkeley, CA 94707. 1978.

*Bolles, Richard N., *How to Create A Picture of Your Ideal Job or Next Career, Advanced Version (revised) of the Quick Job-Hunting (And Career-Changing) Map*. Ten Speed Press, Box 7123, Berkeley, CA 94707. 1989. An 8-1/2 x 11-inch 48 page workbook version of the 1989 edition of Appendix A, in color.

Bolles, Richard N., *The New Quick Job-Hunting Map for Beginners*. Ten Speed Press, Box 7123, Berkeley, CA 94707. 1990. A workbook version of the Map for high school students just entering the labor force, and those other job-hunters who may prefer a simpler alternative to the Map above.

Bolles, Richard N., "How to Choose and Change Careers." A 57-minute *Psychology Today* audio cassette. Available from Education Services Corporation, 1725 K St. NW, #408, Washington, DC 20006. 202-298-8424.

OTHER VERSIONS OF PARACHUTE

German: Bolles, Richard N., *Job-Hunting, Ein Handbuch für Einsteiger und Aufsteiger.* Goldmann Verlag, Neumarkterstrasse 18, 8000 München. 1987.

Spanish: Bolles, Richard, N., *¿De Qué Color Es Su Paracaídas?* Editorial Diana, S.A., Roberto Gayol 1219, Mexico, D.F. 1983.

French: Bolles, Richard N., *Chercheurs d'emploi, n'oubliez pas votre parachute.* Translated by Daniel Porot. Sylvie Messinger, éditrice, 31 rue de l'Abbé-Grégoire, Paris 6e, France. 1983. Also: Bolles, Richard N., *Chercheurs d'emploi, n'oubliez pas votre parachute.* Translated by Daniel Porot. Guy Saint-Jean Editeur Inc. 674 Place Publique, Laval, Quebec H7X 1G1, Canada. 1983.

Dutch: Bolles, Richard N., *Werk zoeken-een vak apart, Een professionele aanpak voor het vinden van een (nieuwe) baan.* Translated by F. J. M. Claessens. Uitgeverij Intermediair, Amsterdam/Brussels. 1983.

Japanese: Bolles, Richard N., *'87 What Color Is Your Parachute?* (In Japanese) Japan UNI Agency, Inc., Ten Speed Press and Writers House, Inc., NY. 1986.

CAREER BOOKS IN OTHER COUNTRIES AND LANGUAGES

French: *Porot, Daniel, *Votre entretien d'embauche: 107 conseils pour le Réussir.* Première édition. Les Editions d'organisation, 26, avenue Emile-Zola, F -- 75015 Paris. Tel: 45-78-61-81. 1990. Highly, highly recommended.

Danish: *Lausten, Torben, *Kan vingerne bære? Håndbog i JOBJAGT og karriereudvikling.* Udgivet af Forlaget Thorsgaard ApS, Frederikssund, Denmark. 1989.

SPECIAL PROBLEMS IN THE JOB-HUNT

Most of you will find that *Parachute* gives you all you need to know, in order to successfully conduct your job-hunt. However, *if* you feel you need additional guidance or information about particular subjects, *listed below*, I have made further commentary, and listed some additional resources, in the following sections of this Appendix:

The Parts of the Flower Diagram (see Appendix A)

After You Get Hired or When You Get Tired of the Job

Alternative Forms of Jobs

Particular Kinds of Jobs

Special Problems

The So-Called Handicapped or People with Disabilities:

If you have a particular interest, and no helpful book is listed in this Appendix *(or any unhelpful ones, either)*, and you are desperate for further information, there are three alternative routes open to you:

One is your friendly **reference librarian** at your local public library, or nearby community college library. If these libraries have such persons, they can often be worth their weight in gold to you. Tell them your problem or interest, and see what they can dig up. They often know of hidden treasures, buried in articles and clippings, as well as books, which could be the answer to your prayers.

The second is **your local bookstores** -- go there, browse, and see what they have.

The third is **mail order**. There are a number of such places which specialize in career books. I have listed *some* of them at the end of this Appendix, on page 327.

The Parts of the Flower Diagram

1. SKILLS IDENTIFICATION

Fine, Sidney A., *Functional Job Analysis Scales: A Desk Aid.* A catalog and hierarchy of the various skills people use with data, people, and things. In 1989, Sidney self-published a vastly updated version of this desk aid, reflecting his latest thinking. Contact him for details: 1229 N. Jackson, #302, Milwaukee, WI 53202.

Figler, Howard E., *The Complete Job-Search Handbook: All the Skills You Need to Get Any Job and Have a Good Time Doing It.* Henry Holt & Co., Inc., 115 W. 18th St., New York, NY 10011. 1988. Identifies twenty skills the job-hunter reveals, and uses, in the actual process of their job-hunt.

Scheele, Adele, *Skills for Success: A Guide to the Top for Men and Women.* Ballantine Books, 201 E. 50th St., New York, NY 10022. 1979. A vastly successful and popular book, for the past ten years.

Myers, Isabel Briggs, and Myers, Peter B., *Gifts Differing.* Consulting Psychologists Press, Inc., 577 College Ave., Palo Alto, CA 94306. 1980. Related to the increasingly popular Myers-Briggs Test.

2. PHYSICAL SETTING: GEOGRAPHY INCLUDING OVERSEAS

The average American, it is claimed, moves eleven times between birth and death. So, geography *is* an important consideration in life/work planning -- believe me. Sometimes you have no choice as to where you are moving; other times, you do. For you, some helps:

Boyer, Richard, and Savageau, David, *Places Rated Almanac: Your Guide to Finding the Best Places to Live in America. All 333 metropolitan areas ranked and compared for living costs, job outlook, crime, health, transportation, education, the arts, recreation, and climate.* Rand McNally & Co., Box 7600, Chicago, IL 60680. 1989. An *immensely* helpful book for *anyone* weighing where to move next. Has numerous helpful diagrams, charts and maps, showing (for example) earthquake risk areas, tornado and hurricane risk areas, the snowiest areas, the stormiest areas, the driest areas, and so on. Don't leave home without it.

Fraser, Jill Andresky, *The Best U.S. Cities for Working Women.* Plume Books, New American Library, 1633 Broadway, New York, NY 10019. 1986.

Regarding overseas work: at least three out of every 100 U.S. workers, are employed by foreign-owned companies, and work here *in this country*. Others actually work overseas. *Sometimes,* of course, working in the U.S. for a foreign-owned company can be the ticket to eventually getting work overseas. But not necessarily. Anyway, you want to work overseas, *right now,* don't you? Herewith a few tips before you plunge in:

Many people assume you find an overseas job by packing a bag, buying a ticket and passing out resumes at your foreign destination. But work permit requirements and high unemployment make finding jobs at foreign destinations difficult or impossible. The wiser approach is to conduct your overseas job search in the U.S. If you're hired in the U.S. by a company who'll send you overseas, they'll take care of the visa and work permit red tape, pick up your travel bill, and provide other helpful benefits.

Every *successful* search for an overseas job starts with (unfortunately) *a resume* and a source of information on "who's hiring now." Major metropolitan newspapers, professional association magazines, and "networking" will provide leads on current employers. Beware of directories advertised in newspapers, etc. as *listing overseas employers.* Many are out of date and tend to report on "who **was** hiring" versus "who is hiring *now.*"

If you choose to do your own research about overseas work, how do you go about it? Well, first of all, talk to everyone you possibly can who has in fact been overseas, most especially to the country or countries that interest you. A nearby large university will probably have such faculty or students (ask). Companies in your city which have overseas branches (your library should be able to tell you which they are) should be able to lead you to people also -- possibly to the names and addresses of personnel who are still "over there" to whom you can write for the information you are seeking. Alternatively, try asking every single person you meet for the next week (at the supermarket checkout, at your work, at home, at church or synagogue, etc.) if they know someone who used to live overseas and now is in your city or town. By doing research with such people, you will learn a great deal.

Talking to the consulate of the country in question (should you live *in* or *near* a major city) may also be very enlightening. Books from your local library or local bookstore *(in the travel section)*, if they are recent, may also tell you much.

As for the general facts about living overseas, both newsletters and books on this subject keep getting regularly published. Some flourish for a season, and then die; others go on for years. Currently the live ones are:

International Employment Hotline, Box 3030, Oakton, VA 22124. Published monthly since 1980, this newsletter provides job-search advice and names and addresses of employers hiring for international work in government, nonprofit organizations, and private companies. They also have other titles on overseas work, which you can ask them about.

The Fischer Report and *Manlink,* Group Fischer, 110 Newport Center Drive, Suite 150, Newport Beach, CA 92660. You can write to them and

ask for their pamphlet "Group Fischer Information Services," which describes their programs and package, whose cost is expensive, from the point of view of a *poor* job-hunter. The *best* sentences in their pamphlet: "If you are looking for a job, you should understand that no one can get you a job except you. You will be hired because you are in the right place, at the right time, with the right skills . . . The ONLY services that anyone can render you in your job search are: 1) Information, 2) Introduction, 3) Advice. No employment agency, employment service, job listing service, membership organization (excluding unions), recruiting or executive search firms, or any publication can do more. How this is done is what makes the difference."

For teachers wishing to work overseas, the Department of Defense publishes a pamphlet, with application, entitled *Overseas Employment Opportunities for Educators*. Write to U.S. Department of Defense Dependent Schools, Recruitment and Assignments Section, Hoffman Bldg. I, 2461 Eisenhower Ave., Alexandria, VA 22331-1100, for the pamphlet/application.

Schuman, Howard, *Making It Abroad -- The International Job Hunting Guide*. John Wiley & Sons, 605 Third Ave., New York, NY 10158-0012. 1988.

Mullett, Joy, and Darley, Lois, *Careers for People Who Love to Travel*. Arco Books, One Gulf+Western Plaza, New York, NY 10023. 1986.

Casewit, Curtis W., *How to Get a Job Overseas*. Arco Publishing, Inc., One Gulf+Western Plaza, New York, NY 10023. 1984.

Griffith, Susan, *Work Your Way Around the World*. Writer's Digest Books/North Light Books, 1507 Dana Ave., Cincinnati, OH 45207. 1989.

Griffith, Susan, and Legg, Sharon, *The Au Pair & Nanny's Guide to Working Abroad*. Writer's Digest Books/North Light Books, 1507 Dana Ave., Cincinnati, OH 45207. 1989.

Green, Mary, and Gillmar, Stanley, *How to Be an Importer and Pay for Your World Travel*. Ten Speed Press, Box 7123, Berkeley, CA 94707.

Your library should also have books such as Angel, Juvenal, *Dictionary of American Firms Operating in Foreign Countries* (World Trade Academy Press).

And to research overseas public companies which sell stock in this country, the Securities Exchange Commission will have their Form 6-K, which they filed in order to be able to sell that stock.

In general, the principles found on page 119 will apply to seeking overseas employment, with equal or greater force.

If you want more books about overseas work (or study), write to WorldWise Books, P.O. Box 3030, Oakton, VA 22124, and/or Writer's Digest Books, 1507 Dana Ave., Cincinnati, OH 45207, and ask for their catalogs.

3. PHYSICAL SETTING: WORKING CONDITIONS

Levering, Robert, *A Great Place to Work*. Random House, Inc., 201 E. 50th St., New York, NY 10022. 1988. A study of what makes some employers so good and most so bad.

Levering, Robert, and Moskowitz, Milton, and Katz, Michael, *The 100 Best Companies to Work for in America*. Addison-Wesley Publishing Co., Route 128, Reading, MA 01876. 1984. The problem is: is there any such animal as "the 100 best companies to work for," or are some companies excellent on the fifth floor, but poor down on the second floor? Nonetheless, this is a fascinating book, as is everything these authors have written.

Peters, Thomas J., and Waterman, Robert H., Jr., *In Search of Excellence: Lessons from America's Best Run Companies*. Harper & Row, 10 E. 53rd St., New York, NY 10022. 1982. An instant classic. The title says it all.

See also section 18, ***Working at Home or at Your Vacation Spot,*** *for those whose preferred working conditions are that they be able to enjoy their home or vacation environment while they are doing their work.*

4. SPIRITUAL OR EMOTIONAL SETTING: VALUES

Gilligan, Carol, and Ward, Janie, and Taylor, Jill, eds., with Bardige, Betty, *Mapping the Moral Domain*. Harvard University Press, Cambridge, MA. 1989. A contribution of women's thinking to psychological theory and education.

Sinetar, Marsha, *Elegant Choices, Healing Choices*. Paulist Press, 997 Macarthur Blvd., Mahwah, NJ 07430. 1988.

Hagberg, Janet, and Leider, Richard, *The Inventurers: Excursions in Life and Career Renewal*. Addison-Wesley Publishing Co., Route 128, Reading, MA 01867. 1988.

Lydenberg, Steven D., with Marlin, Alice Tepper, and Strub, Sean O'Brien, and the Council on Economic Priorities, *Rating America's Corporate Conscience: A Provocative Guide to the Companies Behind the Products You Buy Every Day*. Addison-Wesley, Route 128, Reading, MA 01876. 1986. Has rated major companies on corporate social responsibility, as to which of these large companies are "best" in this moral sense.

Jaffe, Dennis T., and Scott, Cynthia D., *Take This Job and Love It*. Fireside Books, Simon & Schuster Bldg., Rockefeller Center, 1230 Avenue of the Americas, New York, NY 10020. 1988. How to change your work without changing your job.

Long, Charles, *How to Survive Without a Salary*. Summerhill Press, Ltd., Toronto, Ontario, Canada. Distributed by Collier Macmillan Canada, 50

Gervais Dr., Don Mills, Ontario M3C 3K4, Canada. Coping in today's inflationary times by learning how to live the Conserver Life-style.

Edwards, John F., *Starting Fresh.* Prima Publishing & Communications, P.O. Box 1260SF, Rocklin, CA 95677. 1988. How to plan for a simpler, happier, and more fulfilling new life in the country.

Kirkpatrick, Frank, *How to Find and Buy Your Business in the Country.* Storey Communications, Inc., Pownal, VT 05261. 1985. While this would appear to belong to the geography section, what it is talking about is a simpler life-style, away from the hustle and bustle of the city. Therefore it is talking primarily about the emotional setting, not the physical.

See also the books listed in Section 22, and at the end of Appendix E, on page 405.

5. GOALS AND OUTCOMES FOR YOUR WORK

Leider, Richard J., *The Power of Purpose.* Ballantine Books, 201 E. 50th, New York, NY 10022. 1985.

Anderson, Nancy, *Work With Passion: How to Do What You Love for a Living.* A co-publication of Carroll & Graf Publishers, Inc., 260 Fifth Ave., New York, NY 10001, and Whatever Publishing, Inc., Box 137, Mill Valley, CA 94942. 1984. Good on how to establish contact with people.

Sinetar, Marsha, *Do What You Love, The Money Will Follow: Discovering Your Right Livelihood.* Paulist Press, 997 Macarthur Blvd., Mahwah, NJ 07430. 1987.

Caple, John, *The Right Work: Finding It and Making It Right.* Dodd, Mead & Company, Inc., 71 Fifth Ave., New York, NY 10003. 1987.

Cohen, Steve, and de Oliveira, Paulo, *Getting to the Right Job.* Workman Publishing Company, Inc., 1 W. 39th St., New York, NY 10018. 1987.

Snelling, Robert O., Sr., *The Right Job.* Viking Penguin Inc., 40 W. 23rd St., New York, NY 10010. 1987.

Straat, Kent L., with Sabin, Nellie, *What Your Boss Can't Tell You: How to Evaluate Your Company, Your Job, Your Goals and Your Performance.* AMACOM, 135 West 50th St., New York, NY 10020. 1988.

6. RESUMES

Lathrop, Richard, *Who's Hiring Who?* Ten Speed Press, Box 7123, Berkeley, CA 94707. *See the "Highly Recommended" section, at the beginning of this Appendix.*

*Parker, Yana, *The Damn Good Resume Guide. New edition.* Ten Speed Press, Box 7123, Berkeley, CA 94707. 1989, 1986, 1983. Describes how to write a *functional* resume. All new resumes in this new edition. Employers' comments upon resumes which actually got people jobs, are especially helpful. A very popular and useful book.

Parker, Yana, *The Resume Catalog: 200 Damn Good Examples.* Ten Speed Press, Box 7123, Berkeley, CA 94707. 1988. The title says it all. A supplement to the book above.

Jackson, Tom, *The Perfect Resume.* Anchor Press/Doubleday, Garden City, NY 11530. 1981. This is Tom's best-selling book, and with good reason.

*Schmidt, Peggy, *The 90 Minute Resume*. Peterson's Guides, P.O. Box 2123, Princeton, NJ 08543. 1990. Written by the career columnist for *The New York Post*. Contains interesting sections, such as "How to Make an Ordinary Job Sound Important."

*Washington, Tom, *Resume Power: Selling Yourself on Paper*. Mount Vernon Press, 1750 112th N.E. C-247, Bellevue, WA 98004. 1990, 1988, 1985.

Williams, Eugene, *Getting the Job You Want with the Audiovisual Portfolio*. Comptex Associates, Inc., Box 6745, Washington, DC 20020. 1982. Manual for job-seekers and career changers in professions other than teaching, who want to present something audiovisual rather than a written resume.

There are more books on resumes than you can shake a stick at. If the above sampling is not enough for you, see your local bookstore.

7. INTERVIEWING

Yate, Martin John, *Knock 'Em Dead with Great Answers to Tough Interview Questions*. Bob Adams, Inc., 260 Center St., Holbrook, MA 02343. 1988.

*Bowman, David, and Kweskin, Ronald, ***Q:*** *How Do I Find The Right Job?* ***A:*** *Ask The Experts*. John Wiley & Sons, Inc., Professional and Trade Division, 605 Third Ave., New York, NY 10158-0012. 1990.

Zimbardo, Phillip G., *Shyness, What It Is, What to Do About It*. Jove Publications, 757 Third Ave., New York, NY 10017. 1977.

Hellman, Paul, *Ready, Aim, You're Hired!: How to Job-Interview Successfully Anytime, Anywhere with Anyone*. AMACOM, 135 W. 50th St., New York, NY 10020. 1986.

8. SALARY NEGOTIATION

Wright, John W., *The American Almanac of Jobs and Salaries, 1987–1988*. Avon Books, Dept. FP, 1790 Broadway, New York, NY 10019. 1987.

Snelling, Robert O., *Jobs! What They Are . . . Where They Are . . . What They Pay!* Fireside Edition, Simon & Schuster, Inc., Rockefeller Center, 1230 Avenue of the Americas, New York, NY 10020. 1986.

After You Get Hired or When You Get Tired of the Job

9. PROMOTIONS, RAISES, HANGING ON TO YOUR PRESENT JOB

There is not enough said, generally, in job-hunting books about surviving *after* you get the job. The enemies are both within, and without. From within, the now-familiar problem of burnout. From without, various adversaries -- both animate and inanimate.

You will find many useful suggestions in Marilyn Moats Kennedy's very helpful books, listed below. Also, in John Crystal's book, *Where Do I Go From Here With My Life?* (Ten Speed Press, Box 7123, Berkeley, CA 94707, 1974), pages 241–245 ("Understanding the Nature of the World of Work"), and 150–160 ("How to Survive After You Get the Job").

If the place where you are working is a Mom-and-Pop operation, promotion will probably depend upon your staying on their good side, and trying to anticipate what they need to have done before they ask for it. You won't have to worry about whether or not they know all you've done for them; *they'll know*. You may, however, need to *ask* for a raise or promotion, rather than simply assuming that *they* will take care of it automatically.

On the other hand, if the place where you are working is larger than a Mom-and-Pop operation, maybe *much* larger, what you do there may be lost from sight. In such a situation, therefore, your survival and promotion (hence, raises) will *generally speaking* depend on your ability:

1) to get your boss to like you; 2) to figure out how the place *actually* works (not how they *claim* it works); 3) to learn who to trust there, and who not to trust; 4) to pick up the internal gossip at the place *first*, and not last, so that you get *early warning* about what's going to happen next; 5) to pick up challenging assignments; 6) to work across departments or even outside the company, so that you are seen, seen, seen; 7) to be results-oriented, and never offer excuses for why something didn't get done; and, 8) to keep track of your own accomplishments there, in a weekly private diary, which you then summarize annually on a one-page sheet, for your boss's eyes.

For further advice, see:

Kennedy, Marilyn Moats, *Office Politics: Seizing Power, Wielding Clout*. Warner Books, 666 Fifth Ave., New York, NY 10103. 1981.

Kennedy, Marilyn Moats, *Career Knockouts: How to Battle Back*. New Century Publishers, Inc., 275 Old New Brunswick Rd., Piscataway, NJ 08854. 1980.

Mackay, Harvey B., *Swim with the Sharks without Being Eaten Alive*. William Morrow & Co., 105 Madison Ave., New York, NY 10016. 1988. Probably destined to be a classic.

10. QUITTING, GETTING FIRED, GETTING LAID OFF

*Gale, Barry, and Gale, Linda, *Stay or Leave: A Complete System for Deciding Whether to Remain at Your Job or Pack Your Traveling Bag*. Harper & Row, 10 East 53rd Street, New York, NY 10022-5299. 1989.

Levinson, Jay Conrad, *Quit Your Job! Making the Decision, Making the Break, Making It Work*. Dodd, Mead & Co., 71 Fifth Ave., New York, NY 10003. 1987.

Pines, Ayala, and Aronson, Elliot, *Career Burnout: Causes and Cures*. The Free Press, 866 Third Ave., New York, NY 10022. 1988.

Employment Law in the 50 States: A Reference for Employers. CUE/NAM, 1331 Pennsylvania Ave. NW, Suite 1500 - North Lobby, Washington, DC 20004-1703. 1987.

Layard, Richard, *How To Beat Unemployment*. Oxford University Press, Walton St., Oxford, OX2 6DP, U.K. 1986.

11. MID-LIFE, CAREER-CHANGE, AND RETIREMENT

During the 1990s, this country's 76 million 'baby boomers' will enter middle age or mid-life -- a time when, according to popular mythology, many people make the break, and go for a career-change. In actual fact, about one million people a year make this sort of dramatic **mid-life career change**. The following resources deal with this phenomenon:

Robbins, Paula I., *Successful Midlife Career Change: Self-Understanding and Strategies for Action*. AMACOM, 135 W. 50th St., New York, NY 10020. Very thorough, very helpful. The best book dealing with this problem.

Golzen, Godfrey, and Plumbley, Philip, *Changing Your Job After 35*. Kogan Page Ltd., 120 Pentonville Rd., London Nl 9JN. 1988.

Falvey, Jack, *What's Next? Career Strategies After 35*. Williamson Publishing, Charlotte, VT 05445. 1987.

Kanchier, Carole, *Questers: Dare to Change Your Job and Your Life*. R&E Publishers, P.O. Box 2008, Saratoga, CA 95070. 1987.

Now, a word or two about **retirement**: most women now leave the work force before they turn 60, and most men before they turn 63. Not all are happy with this turn of events. According to a recent study (reported in *The New York Times*, 4/22/90) half of the elderly who are out of the work force are satisfied with their situation, one quarter are simply unable to work (presumably because of health), and one quarter are very unhappy with the fact that they aren't working. The numbers (reported in *National Business Employment Weekly*, 2/18/90) are these: 21.5 million Americans are between ages 50 and 64, of whom 13.3 million are working, and 8.3 million are not. Of the latter, 4.7 million don't want to work, 1.6 million are unable to, and almost 2 million would like to be back at work. The situation of the latter is complicated by Social Security requirements: in order to continue to receive full benefits, retirees must not earn more than $6,840 a year if they are under 65, or more than $9,360 if they are 65 to 69. After they reach 70, however, there is no limit.

*Dychtwald, Ken, and Flower, Joe, *Age Wave: The Challenges and Opportunities of an Aging America*. Bantam Books, 666 Fifth Ave., New York, NY 10103. 1990. The most important book out yet on all the implications of aging.

*Bolles, Richard N., "The decade of decisions," in *Modern Maturity* magazine, February-March 1990 issue (see your local library). Discusses the six possibilities you can choose between during the final ten years of your life in the world of work.

Best-Rated Retirement Cities & Towns, Consumer Guide Publications International, Ltd., 7373 N. Cicero Ave., Lincolnwood, IL 60646. 1988. A review of 100 of the most attractive retirement locations across America.

Boyer, Richard, and Savageau, David, *Places Rated Retirement Guide: Finding the Best Places in America for Retirement Living*. Rand McNally and Co., Box 7600, Chicago, IL 60680. 1983.

How to Plan Your Successful Retirement, AARP Book Publication. AARP, 1909 K St., NW, Washington, DC 20049. 1988.

12. GOING BACK TO SCHOOL OR GETTING AN EXTERNAL DEGREE

In that poll reported in *U.S.A. Today* (7/25/89), where people were asked what they would do if they won one million dollars, 20% of them said they would go back to school. Many would go on through college, because they know the difference higher education increasingly makes, in the matter of one's salary. How much difference? Oh, about $28,000 *a year* per couple. Yes, as reported in the *San Francisco Chronicle* (7/26/89) working couples with college degrees together averaged $59,750 in their annual household income *in 1987*, which was $28,000 higher than couples with only high school diplomas.

If *you* want more education, or if you want credit for what you've *already* learned out there in Life, here are some helps:

To get equivalency examinations for the knowledge or experience you've already acquired out of life, write to CLEP (College-Level Examination Program), College Entrance Examination Board, Box 1822, Princeton, NJ 08541, or Box 1025, Berkeley, CA 94701. It is a national standardized examination program for college credit.

Bear, John, *Bear's Guide to Earning Non-Traditional College Degrees*. Ten Speed Press, Box 7123, Berkeley, CA 94707. 1988. John gives you some very useful advice, to keep from getting 'taken.' You might also want to read: Apille, Henry A., and Stewart, David W., *Diploma Mills: Degrees of Fraud*. Macmillan Publishing Co., 866 Third Ave., New York, NY 10022.

Mendelsohn, Pam, *Happier By Degrees: A College Reentry Guide for Women*. Ten Speed Press, Box 7123, Berkeley, CA 94707. 1986.

Schlachter, Gail Ann, with Goldstein, Sandra E., *Directory of Financial Aids for Women 1987–1988*. Reference Service Press, 10 Twin Dolphin Dr., Suite B-308, Redwood City, CA 94065. 1987.

Gross, Ronald, *The Independent Scholar's Handbook: How to Turn Your Interest in Any Subject into Expertise*. Addison-Wesley, General Books Division, Route 128, Reading, MA 01867. 1982.

Alternative Forms of Jobs

13. VOLUNTEERING

Peter Drucker calls volunteerism "the third sector" of the nation's economy, and estimates that 90 million people work as volunteers, in addition to, or instead of, a regular job.

If you are interested in volunteering full-time to work for social justice, primarily with the poor, the elderly, and the handicapped, working either in the U.S. or in the developing countries, you should contact The St. Vincent Pallotti Center for Apostolic Development, Inc., 159 Washington St., Brighton, MA 02135. They act as a resource center for anyone interested in such work. Most volunteer programs are for a summer or for one to two years. However, **some** are as short as a long weekend, and some for as long as five years. A directory, called CONNECTIONS, is free to anyone who requests it. The East Coast office's phone is 617-783-3924; the West Coast office's phone is 415-989-0508. Incidentally, when volunteers complete their term of service, the Center assists them in finding relevant work that pays a living wage, using *Parachute.*

High school graduates, college students, and recent college graduates may be placed as volunteers through the *Learning through Service Program* of the Association of Episcopal Colleges, Episcopal Church Center, 815 Second Ave., New York, NY 10017-4594. 212-986-0989.

For other places, see:

Shenk, Ellen J., ed., *Directory of Volunteer Opportunities.* Career Information Centre, University of Waterloo, Waterloo, Ontario, N2L 3G1 Canada. 1986.

Some people want to travel during their volunteering work. Many unusual opportunities are described in:

*Frommer, Arthur, *New World of Travel 1990: Vacations that Cater to Your Mind, Your Spirit and Your Sense of Thrift.* A Frommer Book, published by Prentice-Hall Trade Division, One Gulf+Western Plaza, New York, NY 10023. 1990.

If you want to catalog what skills you've learned from volunteer work or what skills you have to bring to volunteer work, you will find *this* book immensely useful, written originally for women but equally useful for men:

Ekstrom, Ruth B.; Harris, Abigail M.; and Lockheed, Marlaine E., *How to Get College Credit for What You Have Learned as a Homemaker* ***and Volunteer.*** Project HAVE SKILLS, Education Testing Service, Princeton, NJ 08541. 1977. They also publish the: *HAVE SKILLS Women's Workbook, HAVE SKILLS Counselor's Guide,* and *HAVE SKILLS Employer's Guide.* The lists in this book are based upon the pioneering work, in the assessment of volunteer skills and knowledge, of the Council of National Organizations for Adult Education. Skills are classified under the various role-titles of: administrator/manager, financial manager, personnel manager, trainer, advocate/change agent, public relations/communicator, problem surveyor, researcher, fund raiser, counselor, youth group leader, group leader for a serving organization, museum staff assistant, tutor/teacher's aide, manager of finances, nutritionist, child caretaker, designer and maintainer, clothing and textile specialist, and horticulturist. *Very* helpful book, with accompanying aids.

See also the next section on ***Internships*** *as well as section 22,* ***Jobs Dealing with Social Change****, on page 313.*

14. INTERNSHIPS

**National Directory of Internships*. Published by the National Society for Internships and Experiential Education (NSIEE), 3509 Haworth Drive, Suite 207, Raleigh, NC 27609. Updated regularly. Highly recommended.

Directory of Internships, Work Experience Programs, and On-the-Job Training Opportunities. Ready Reference Press, Box 5169, Santa Monica, CA 90405. Also available -- *The First Supplement to the Directory*.

Jobst, Katherine, *Internships: 38,000 On-the-Job Training Opportunities for College Students and Adults*. Writer's Digest Books, 1507 Dana Ave., Cincinnati, OH 45207. Issued in updated revisions, annually, with the year of the revision appearing in its title.

Community Jobs, 1516 P St. NW, Washington, DC 20005, 202-667-0661. Published monthly by Community Careers Resource Center. Lists jobs and internships in nonprofit, community organizations. Write directly to them for subscription information.

Bard, Ray, and Elliott, Susan K., *The National Directory of Corporate Training Programs*. Bantam Doubleday Dell Publishing Group, Inc., 666 Fifth Ave., New York, NY 10103. 1988.

**Guide to Volunteer and Internship Programs in Public Broadcasting*. Corporation for Public Broadcasting, Human Resources Department, 1111 16th St. N.W., Washington, DC 20035.

*Stanton, Timothy K., and Ali, Kamil, *The Experienced Hand: A Student Manual for Making the Most of an Internship*. Published by the National Society for Internships and Experiential Education (NSIEE), 3509 Haworth Drive, Suite 207, Raleigh, NC 27609. Is actually for all ages.

15. TEMPORARY WORK, TEMPORARY REST

Mayall, Donald, and Nelson, Kristin, *The Temporary Help Supply Service and the Temporary Labor Market*. Olympus Research Corp., 1670 E. 13th South, Salt Lake City, UT 84105. 1982.

Rubin, Bonnie Miller, *Time Out*. W.W. Norton & Co., 500 Fifth Ave., New York, NY 10110. 1987. How to take a year (more or less) off without jeopardizing your job, your family, or your bank account.

See also sections 16 through 20, below.

16. PART-TIME WORK, OR HOLDING SEVERAL SMALL JOBS

One in every 16 workers, currently, holds two or more jobs. This added up to 7.2 million people, as recently as 1989. Almost half of these do it in order to survive economically. So, if you are considering taking a second job, you have lots of company. It can be done impulsively, or creatively. For the creative-minded, some reading:

Levinson, Jay Conrad, *Earning Money Without a Job: The Economics of Freedom*. Holt, Rinehart, Winston, 521 Fifth Ave., New York, NY 10175. 1979. The first part of this book is excellent as Jay sets forth his idea of "modular economics" -- putting together several small jobs, rather than one big one -- and having time left over for leisure.

Employee Benefits for Part-Timers. Association of Part-Time Professionals, Crescent Plaza, Suite 216, 7700 Lessburg Pike, Falls Church, VA 22043. 703-734-7975. Primarily directed at employers of part-time workers. Describes benefit packages put together by various private firms for their part-time employees; intended to serve as models for others.

If the second job you are thinking about, involves starting your own business out of your house, see sections 18, 19 and 20. If you are thinking of part-time work, please see the next section, and particularly the agencies listed therein.

17. JOB-SHARING, AND OTHER ALTERNATIVES TO 9–5

People are discovering there are all kinds of alternatives to the traditional nine-to-five, Monday-thru-Friday job. There is job-sharing with another worker, or flextime, where you decide which hours of the day you want to work; there is the four-day work week; there is holding down three to five small jobs rather than one full-time job (see section above); there is working long and hard two or three days a week, then having the other days to yourself; etc. If such alternatives appeal to you, my advice is to do your informational interviewing with people who have already gone that route, first; and then when you are ready to interview for an actual job, go after smaller employers -- who are often more open than are larger employers, to new patterns of work. Don't omit larger employers, however, from your search -- *some* of them are very open to such alternatives. The places listed below often know who they are.

Olmsted, Barney, and Smith, Suzanne, *Creating a Flexible Workplace: How to Select and Manage Alternative Work Options*. American Management Association. 1989. Order from: New Ways to Work, 149 Ninth St., San Francisco, CA 94103.

Olmsted, Barney, and Smith, Suzanne, *The Job Sharing Handbook*. Ten Speed Press, Box 7123, Berkeley, CA 94707. 1983. How to share a full-time job with another person, if you don't want to work full-time.

A Selected Bibliography on Work Time Options. 1989. Order from: New Ways to Work, 149 Ninth St., San Francisco, CA 94103. A 42 page listing of various books, articles, etc., about new ways to work.

Work Times Newsletter, published by New Ways to Work, 149 Ninth St., San Francisco, CA 94103. An international information exchange on alternative work time; 415-552-1000.

In addition to New Ways to Work, there are other centers that are dedicated to helping people who want to find flexible work-time options, such as job-sharing. These places often have helpful pamphlets and other publications. Ask.

Association of Part-Time Professionals
Crescent Plaza, Suite 216
7700 Leesburg Pike
Falls Church, VA 22043
703-734-7975

Austin Women's Center
1700 S. Lamar, #203
Austin, TX 78704
512-447-9666

Focus
509 Tenth Ave. E.
Seattle, WA 98102
206-329-7918

Harper & Harris
6101 S. Rural Rd., #128
Tempe, AZ 85283
602-839-8284

Job-Sharing Manuals
Human Resources Dept.
City of Lansing
119 N. Washington Sq.
Lansing, MI 48933
517-483-4479
(Ask for a list of their publications, and prices)

San Diego Center for Worktime Options
1200 Third Ave.
Suite 1200
San Diego, CA 92101
619-456-4424

Work Options
1611 N. Mosley
Wichita, KS 67214
316-264-6604

Workshare
311 E. 50 St.
New York, NY 10022
212-832-7061

See also sections 15, 16, 18, 19 and 20.

18. WORKING AT HOME OR AT YOUR VACATION SPOT

Two hundred years ago, nearly everybody worked at home or on their farm. That idea is now finding new life, because of congestion on the highways. According to the F.H.A. (*Federal Highway Commission*), in twenty years congestion on our nation's freeways will be four times as bad as it is today, while congestion on non-freeways will be twice as bad as it is today. *(Zero Population Growth Fact Sheet, June, 1989)*

This fact above all else -- the U.S. moving more and more toward nationwide gridlock, at least in big metropolitan areas -- is making the idea of working at home more and more attractive. Some have, accordingly, called working at home 'the world's fastest commute.' Surveys indicate that currently 26.6 million people (nearly a quarter of the work force) do at least *some* work out of their homes. 6.7 million of these work full-time at home while almost 20 million are part-time, many of them women.

Just under three million of these 26.6 million are genuine '*telecommuters*' -- a term coined by Jack Nilles in 1973 -- people who, technically, are supposed to have offices elsewhere, but are allowed by their employers to work at home at least some of the time (*from two to 4½ days per week*), connected to their offices by computer-network telephone lines. Telecommuting is a mixed bag. Some telecommuters boost their output and productivity by 3–5%, due to lack of interruption from co-workers, and the desire to prove that they aren't goofing off. Others, however, experience a fall-off in productivity, due to childcare demands, and other interruptions. Lack of socialization with other workers, being passed over for promotion, and sometimes having uneven work flow, are other downsides to the practice of telecommuting.

Nonetheless, many people -- particularly professionals, consultants, and crafts-people -- are opting for working at home. Computers, modems, voice/electronic mail, fax machines, cellular telephones, 'call-forwarding' (whereby people call one fixed telephone number, and then get automatically forwarded to wherever you are) all help make it possible for you to work out of your preferred environment, which doesn't even have to be 'at home.' If you are working for yourself, it can be your favorite vacation spot, for example a skiing chalet.

The two major problems of homebased businesses: according to one expert, home-based workers earn only 70% of what their full-time office-based equals do (obviously this is not as true of 'telecommuters.') Also, it's often difficult to separate business and family time, so sometimes the *family* time gets short-changed, while in other cases the demands of family (particularly with small children) may become *so* interruptive, that the *business* gets short-changed. Anyway, if this idea interests you, there are the following guides:

*Schepp, Brad, *THE TELECOMMUTER'S HANDBOOK: How to Work for a Salary -- Without Ever Leaving the House*. Pharos Books: A Scripps Howard Company, 200 Park Ave., New York, NY 10166. 1990. It describes the jobs best suited for telecommuting, names and addresses of more than 100 companies that allow employees to work at home, pros and cons of telecommuting for both employee and employer.

*Brabec, Barbara, *Homemade Money: The Definitive Guide to Success in a Home Business*. 3rd ed. Betterway Publications, Inc., White Hall, VA 22987. 1989, 1986, 1984. A very fine book, with an A to Z business section, and a most helpful summary of which states have laws regulating (or prohibiting) certain home-based businesses; it is updated regularly. *Barbara also publishes a newsletter,* National Home Business Report. *If you wish more information, you can ask for her catalog, by writing to National Home Business Network, P.O. Box 2137, Naperville, IL 60567.*

*Arden, Lynie, *The Work-at-Home Sourcebook*. 3rd ed. Live Oak Publications, P.O. Box 2193, Boulder, CO 80306. 1990.

Edwards, Paul and Sarah, *Working from Home: Everything You Need to Know about Living and Working under the Same Roof*. J. P. Tarcher, Inc., 5858 Wilshire Blvd., Los Angeles, CA 90036. 1985. Now revised and expanded. 436 pages. Has a long section on computerizing your home business, and on telecommunicating.

The Home Office Newsletter. A monthly publication for individuals who run businesses from their homes. Newsletter is also available in electronic database form through Genie and Delphi information services. Subscribe to Compusystems Management, 4734 E. 26th St., Tucson, AZ 85711. 602-790-6333.

Homeworking Mothers, a quarterly newsletter for women who want to start their own businesses and work from their homes. Mother's Home Business Network, Box 423, East Meadow, NY 11554.

Behr, Marion, and Lazar, Wendy, *Women Working Home: The Homebased Business Guide and Directory*. Women Working Home, Inc., 24 Fishel Rd., Edison, NJ 08820. 1983. The authors were co-founders of the National

Alliance of Homebased Businesswomen, a New Jersey-based group, with 1500 members currently.

Hoge, Cecil C., Sr., *Mail Order Moonlighting*. Ten Speed Press, Box 7123, Berkeley, CA 94707. 1988.

See also sections 15, 16, 17, 19, and 20.

19. WORKING FOR YOURSELF (SELF-EMPLOYMENT)

The Chances of Your Succeeding

In that poll reported in *USA Today* (7/25/89), where people were asked what they would do if they won one million dollars, 27% of them said they would start their own business. Thus we see that the self-employment route is exceedingly attractive to those of us who are employed -- so you can imagine how attractive it is to us when we are unemployed, because *in addition to all its other virtues*, it looks like a clever way to avoid the job-hunt altogether. If we are unable to find work, we figure we have nothing to lose.

But of course we do. Our shirt. Or our blouse. In case you haven't heard, the statistics on new businesses are depressing: **65% of all new businesses fail within five years**. That means, for example, that of the 684,109 new businesses incorporated in 1988 (*Inc. Magazine*, 11/89), 444,670 will likely fail. That's the bad news.

The good news, if you're the type who likes to look on the bright side of things, is that -- as David Birch points out in his great book (below) -- only about 25% of new businesses fail *in any given year*; so, year by year, you have a 75% chance of succeeding. Furthermore, there are about 28 old businesses in this country, for every new business that starts up. This keeps the national bankruptcy/failure rate much lower than most people think. Back in 1986, the most recent year for which I have these statistics, out of every 10,000 businesses in this country 120 failed. That means that 9880 out of every 10,000 businesses survived -- right? So, *if* you can make it through the first few *very* difficult years in a new business, you'll probably have a good chance of surviving. If you decide to go into business for yourself guess what your biggest continuing problem is likely to be (this should strike you as ironic): **finding good employees.**

You must not even for a moment think that the self-employment route is a good way to avoid the rigors of the job-hunt. On the contrary, **you'll have to work harder at your research, harder at interviewing people who are already doing what you would like to do, harder at setting up your business, harder at finding customers (should you be offering a service or product) than you ever would in a normal job-hunt** -- if your experience is at all like the self-employed from whom I regularly hear. *You will look back at the regular job-hunt as an elementary school exercise by comparison.*

If you can move *gradually* into self-employment, doing it as a moonlighting activity first of all, while you are still holding down a regular job somewhere else, you would be showing a wisdom far beyond your years. That way, you can test out your enterprise, as you would a floorboard in a very old run-down house, stepping on it cautiously without at first putting your full weight on it, to see whether or not it will support you. But if you're not employed, and you're determined to try the self-employment route, for heaven's sakes have a plan B: "I'm going to try out this self-employment, and my plan B is that if after a certain number of months it doesn't look like it's going to make it, then I'm going to ________ (fill in the blank *carefully*, with an alternative)." And **give some time to the exploration of that *alternative* before you start your self-employment thing -- so that your plan B is "all in place,"** as they say.

If You Decide On An Established Franchise

Many of the would-be self-employed decide to cut the risk down somewhat by going after an already-established business, i.e., **a franchise**. That's why there are more than 600,000 franchised businesses operating in this country, employing more than 5 million people. If this idea interests you, *please* do your research *very* thoroughly. Books on franchising, to help you get started with that research, are listed below. Go talk to everyone you can, who is doing the type of franchised work that you are thinking of doing.

Incidentally, the ten *riskiest* small businesses, according to experts, are local laundries and dry cleaners, used car dealerships, gas stations, local trucking firms, restaurants, infant clothing stores, bakeries, machine shops, grocery or meat stores, and car washes.

Inventing Your Own Business

If you are not buying in on a franchise, but rather *inventing* your own business, think seriously about **offering a service or product *you* would like to have,** or of ***improving* something for which there is already a known market,** *rather than trying to create something brand new that nobody in the world has ever heard of, before.* Examples of improving something, are: making folding-bicycles, or beach towels with weights in the corners. These *principles* apply, whether it is a **service** you are thinking of offering, or you want to act as a **consultant**, or you are thinking about creating some **gadget** or tool.

If you're absolutely baffled about what field to go into that would use your best skills, think out **what *services* people need** and want the most. The one common theme among many successful businesses is that they cater to those families where both husband and wife work, since over 21.5 million mothers are currently in the work force. The theme is **time-saving products and services.** Among ideas worth at least *exploring*: evening delivery services, fast foods with home deliveries, daytime office cleaning services and evening home cleaning services, home repairs, landscaping, care for the elderly in their own homes, pick up and delivery (at the office), automobile care services, short-term business consultants (in various fields). Key to standing out from other similar businesses and holding on to the customers you do get: "the customer is *always* right."

No matter how inventive you are about self-employment, you're probably *not* going to create a job no one has ever heard of; in all likelihood you're only going to create a job that *most* people have never heard of. But someone, somewhere, in this world of endless creativity, has probably already put together the kind of job you're dreaming about. Your task: to go find her, or him, and interview them to death. Why should you have to invent the wheel all over again? They've already stepped on all the landmines for you. They know where all the pitfalls are in this business you're dreaming of starting.

But suppose you can't find such a person? Well, then, figure out who is doing something that is *close* to what you're dreaming of doing, and go interview *that* person. For example, let's suppose your dream is to use computers to monitor the growth of plants at the Arctic. And you can't find anybody who's ever done such a thing. Well, then, break it down into its parts: computers, plants, and Arctic. Try combining *two* parts with each other, and you'll see what your research task is: to find someone who's used computers with plants, or computers at the Arctic, or someone who's worked with plants at the Arctic (yes, I know this is a moderately ridiculous example, but I want to stretch your imagination). My point is a simple one: you can *always* find someone who has done something that at least *approximates* what it is you want to do, and from her or him you can learn a great deal. Better yet, they may lead you to others who have done something even closer to what it is you want to do.

Getting Funded

How do you get funded for a new job no one has ever heard of? Well, if it's a *product* or *service* you are offering, you get funded by convincing people to buy it. (And you ask people already offering a similar product or service how they got people to buy theirs, so you'll know what the general principles are, regarding what works and what doesn't work.)

But admittedly, this *can* be "the pits" if you have to go out and convince people, one by one, to buy your product, services, or whatever. No wonder, then, that a number of (hopefully) soon-to-be self-employed persons find the idea of a foundation grant or government grant tremendously attractive and winsome. How, they ask, can I find such a grant? Well, basically the same way you find a job. Thorough-going research.

If you decide that applying for a grant is the way in which you would like to try to get funded, there are some rules. As Matthew Lesko (*see below*) points out:

1. If it is a government grant you seek, look at state and local governments as well as the Federal.
2. The money may not be where logic would suggest it should be. For example, the Department of Labor funds doctoral dissertations, the Department of Agriculture funds teenage entrepreneurs, and the like.
3. Talk to the people at the agency who are in charge of dispersing the grant funds.
4. When you have located an appropriate agency for what you want to do, ask to see a copy of a successful application (under the Freedom of Information Act).
5. If they make clear that they will not give you a large amount, ask for a small amount for a year; and let them get to know you.

To get you started with funding possibilities, consult your library (or else your banker) for one of the directories of grants (already) given. Such directories as:

Annual Register of Grant Support, published by Marquis Academic Media, 200 E. Ohio St., Rm. 5608, Chicago, IL 60611. The directory or register covers 2,300 current grant programs, and has four helpful indexes.

The Foundation Center, 79 Fifth Ave., New York, NY 10003, is an independent, nonprofit organization offering assistance in locating grants. It publishes *The Foundation Directory*, which lists over 4,400 U.S. foundations, whose grants accounted en toto for 92% of all U.S. dollars awarded in three typical years. There are four reference collections operated by the Center, in New York, Washington, DC, Cleveland, and San Francisco. There are also dozens of cooperating collections nationwide. For information on locations nearest you, call 800-424-9836.

Lesko, Matthew, *Getting Yours: The Complete Guide to Government Money*. Viking Penguin Inc., 40 W. 23rd St., New York, NY 10010. 1987.

Books On All Kinds of Self-Employment

Birch, David, *Job Creation In America*. The Free Press, 866 Third Ave., New York, NY 10022. 1987. Where the new jobs are coming from and how our smallest companies put the most people to work. David is an excellent researcher, and knows more about small businesses than anyone else in the country.

*Stolze, William J., *Startup: An Entrepreneur's Guide to Launching & Managing a New Venture*. Rock Beach Press, 1255 University Ave., Rochester, NY 14607. 1989.

Kamoroff, Bernard, *Small-Time Operator*. Bell Springs Publishing, P.O. Box 640, Laytonville, CA 95454. 1988. How to start your own small business, keep your books, pay your taxes, and stay out of trouble.

Jones, Constance, *The 220 Best Franchises to Buy*. Philip Lief Group, 319 E. 52nd St., New York, NY 10022. 1987. A sourcebook for evaluating the best franchise opportunities.

Silliphant, Leigh and Sureleigh, *Making $70,000+ a Year As a Self-Employed Manufacturer's Representative*. Ten Speed Press, Box 7123, Berkeley, CA 94707. 1988.

Hawken, Paul, *Growing a Business*. Simon & Schuster, Inc., Rockefeller Center, 1230 Avenue of the Americas, New York, NY 10020. 1987. This is the companion volume to the public televison series by the same name.

Nicholas, Ted, *How to Form Your Own Corporation Without a Lawyer for Under $50.00. Complete with Tear-Out Forms, Certificate of Incorporation, Minutes, By-Laws*. Enterprise Publishing Co., Inc., 1000 Oakfield Lane, Wilmington, DE 19810. 1973.

*Cohen, William A., *The Entrepreneur and Small Business Problem Solver: An Encyclopedic Reference and Guide; second ed.* John Wiley & Sons, 605 Third Ave., N.Y., NY 10158-0012. It is, indeed, encyclopedic, covering almost every kind of problem you can think of.

*The CompuMentor Project, Inc., *CompuMentoring: People Helping Computers Help People: A step-by-step guide: How to recruit computerists to aid nonprofits in local communities*. The CompuMentor Project, 385 8th St., 2nd Fl., San Francisco, CA 94103. 415-255-6040. 1989. For those nonprofit organizations who want help in employing computers better at their work.

Levinson, Jay Conrad, *Guerrilla Marketing Attack: New Strategies, Tactics, and Weapons for Winning Big Profits for Your Small Business*. Houghton Mifflin

Co., 2 Park St., Boston, MA 02108. 1989.

Levinson, Jay Conrad, *Guerrilla Marketing: Secrets for Making Big Profits from Your Small Business*. Waldentapes, Box 1084, Stamford, CT 06904. 1985. Listen & Learn Cassettes, ISBN 0-681-30739-0.

Barnett, Frank and Sharan, *Working Together: Entrepreneurial Couples*. Ten Speed Press, P.O. Box 7123, Berkeley, CA 94707. 1989.

Starting a Small Business in Ontario. Ministry of Industry, Trade, and Technology, Small Business Branch, 7th Floor, Hearst Block, 900 Bay Street, Toronto, Ontario M7A 9Z9, Canada.

Golzen, Godfrey, *Working for Yourself*. Kogan Page Ltd., 120 Pentonville Rd., London N1 9JN. 1987. How to start a business, raise capital, etc.

And now, a special word about women and self-employment. There are over 15 million small business enterprises in the U.S. Women own 25% of them but only take in 9% of all small business income. According to experts, that's mostly because they price goods and services too low, are not able to take risks to the same degree as men are, and often get turned

down for financing because of their sex. Of course, this is changing -- but unfortunately it is changing very slowly.

Women who are thinking of starting their own business can get counseling over the phone, from the American Women's Economic Development Corporation (AWED), Monday through Friday, between 9 a.m. and 6 p.m. Eastern time, at a cost of $10 for up to ten minutes. The hotline offers an expert in the area in which the caller needs help. Longer counseling, up to one and a half hours, is also offered, at a cost of $35. If calling from New York City, Alaska or Hawaii, call 212-692-9100. If calling from New York State, call 1-800-442-AWED. If calling from any other area, call 1-800-222-AWED. Both services may be charged to major credit cards.

See also sections 15, 16, 17, 18 and 20.

20. FREE-LANCING, OR CONTRACTING OUT YOUR SERVICES

Writers, copy writers, artists, songwriters, photographers, illustrators, interior designers, video people, film people, consultants, retired people of various backgrounds, are only *some* examples of the type of people who free-lance, these days. Their common denominator? They must *constantly* seek employment. They are, in this sense, **perpetual job-hunters** -- always seeking new clients, which is to say, new employers. It gets easier if, along the way, you start to become better known. But, in any case, it is a difficult way of life. You would do well to *study* the section above on self-employment, because many of the points made there will apply to you as well. In general, if you are just starting out -- or having great difficulty in surviving -- you will want to seek out people who are already doing free-lancing successfully (in the same or related businesses) and ask them **how they got started, and how they are surviving** (two *relatively* non-threatening questions) -- *before* you ever try to go out and do this yourself.

For books to help you with your particular specialty, see such catalogs as that of Writer's Digest Books/North Light Books, 1507 Dana Ave., Cincinnati, OH 45207.

See also sections 15 through 19, above.

Particular Kinds of Jobs

21. GENERAL DIRECTORIES OF OCCUPATIONS

Ninety per cent of the work force of 120 million workers in this country are employed in just 300 job-titles. In fact, half of the work force is employed in just 50 job-titles. These are: automobile mechanics, carpenters, electricians, light- or heavy-truck drivers, construction laborers, welders & cutters, groundskeepers & gardeners, electrical and electronic engineers, freight, stock, and material movers or handlers, guards and police, production occupations supervisors, farmers, commodities sales representatives, laborers, lawyers, farm workers, stockhandlers & baggers, insurance sales, janitors & cleaners, managers & administrators, supervisors & proprietors, machine operators, teachers -- university, college, secondary and elementary school, stock & inventory clerks, accountants & auditors, underwriters and other financial officers, secretaries, receptionists, childcare workers, registered nurses, typists, bookkeepers, textile sewing machine operators, nursing aides, orderlies & attendants, hairdressers & cosmetologists, waiters & waitresses, maids and housemen, cashiers, general office clerks, administrative support occupations, sales workers, computer operators, miscellaneous food preparation occupations, production inspectors, checkers & examiners, cooks, real estate sales, and assemblers.

But you are probably looking here because you want something *different* and *unusual*, right? Below are the directories to expand your mental horizons, so far as your options are concerned:

Dictionary of Occupational Titles (DOT), 4th ed. Supt. of Documents, U.S. Govt. Printing Office, Washington, DC 20402. A catalog of the 12,860 occupations known to exist in the U.S. at present. 1977. *Supplements:* 1982, 1986, 1987. Readers have reported that this is, for them, a hopeless maze when they venture into it. If you want to plumb its depths, I would recommend strongly that you *first* use Holland's Self-Directed Search, and thence *his* Dictionary (described below) to tell you which occupations to go seeking in the DOT. You *will* remember, won't you, that your purpose in browsing the DOT is only to get some *suggestions* of where to *begin* your information interviewing. It will help you with the beginning of your search, not the end. (See Chapter 5.)

U.S. Dept. of Labor, Employment and Training Admin., *Selected Characteristics of Occupations Defined in the Dictionary of Occupational Titles.* Supt. of Documents, U.S. Govt. Printing Office, Washington, DC 20402. 1981.

*Bureau of Labor Statistics, *Occupational Outlook Handbook, Bulletin 2300.* Supt. of Documents, U.S. Govt. Printing Office, Washington, DC 20402. Occupations organized by interest and job title. This has also been published commercially under the title, *America's Top 300 Jobs,* by JIST Works, Inc., 720 N. Park Ave., Indianapolis, IN 46202-3431. 1990. The latter has some helpful indices and supplemental material.

Holland, John L., and Gottfredson, Gary D., *Dictionary of Holland Occupational Codes: A Comprehensive Cross-Index of Holland's RIASEC Codes with 12,000 DOT Occupations.* Psychological Assessment Resources, Inc., Odessa, FL 33556. 1989. 2nd ed., revised and expanded. This immensely helpful book, if you are working with Holland's system, gives a comprehensive list of occupations which your "code" suggests, plus the DOT number for each of 12,860 occupations, thus enabling you to go to the *Dictionary of Occupational Titles* and look up more detailed information on each occupation that looks of interest -- before you go out to do your informational interviewing or research. *It has some 'glitches' in it, where occupations you would expect to find in it are nowhere to be seen. So, don't take it as 'gospel.' Nonetheless, highly recommended.* (Other Holland materials, which I also highly recommend, are to be found on page 355.)

*Petras, Kathryn, and Petras, Ross, *Jobs '90: by Career, by Industry, by Region; Leads on More Than 40 Million Jobs and How to Get Them: The Complete Job Bank for All Job Hunters and Career Changers.* Prentice Hall Press, 15 Columbia Circle, New York, NY 10023. 1990. Well, I think the cover's title, referring to the 40 million jobs, overstates the case -- since the average reader will hear it as "job *openings*," which is not the case; nonetheless, this book has some very interesting information in it. I do want to underline something that the Authors say in their introductory note: "Any recommendations of companies and careers that we do make is our own opinion based on the data available to us -- the reader must do further research on his or her own to determine if a career or a company is the right choice." *Amen, brethren and sistern.*

*Hopke, William E., ed., *Encyclopedia of Careers and Vocational Guidance, 7th ed. 3 volumes.* Garrett Park Press, PO Box 190 W, Garrett Park, MD 20896. 1987.

Sacharov, Al, *Offbeat Careers: The Directory of Unusual Work.* Ten Speed Press, P.O. Box 7123, Berkeley, CA 94707. 1988.

Feldman, Beverly Neuer, *Jobs/Careers Serving Children and Youth* (including Supplement: Appendix C and Index -- inserted into the book, but separate). Till Press, Box 27816, Los Angeles, CA 90027. 1978. Groups the jobs and careers according to how much education the job-hunter has had. For all those who want to work with youth or children.

22. JOBS DEALING WITH SOCIAL CHANGE, INCLUDING NONPROFIT ORGANIZATIONS

Careers in this arena are often called "public service careers." Public service careers include such varied occupations as:

- city planner,
- community services officer at a community college,
- gerontology specialist,
- officials dealing with foster parent programs for mentally retarded persons,
- public health officials,
- recreation education,
- social service technician,
- welfare administration,
- workers in the child welfare program,
- workers with the handicapped.

Potential employers for social or public service occupations include **government** *(Federal, State, or Local)*, **nonprofit organizations**, **agencies** *(independent of state or local government, but often cooperating with them)*, **colleges** *(particularly community colleges)*, **associations, social welfare agencies, public health departments, correctional institutions, government offices, Job Partnership Training offices, hospitals, rest homes, elementary and secondary schools, parks and recreation agencies**, etc.

If you are interested in this general field of social service, you ought to do extensive research, with a heavy emphasis on talking with people actually doing the work you think you would like to do; you will find their names through the national associations in the fields that interest you, also in State departments, and County and City governments (your local reference librarian in your local library can help you locate these associations -- also see the list on page 131).

If you know exactly what it is you want to do, but funding is the problem, thorough research on your part will often reveal ways in which funding can be found for positions not yet created; it all depends on your finding a person who knows something about that.

As for what career to choose within this broad category, there are these helps:

Alternative America: 1990 ed. Alternative America, Box 1067, Harvard Square Stn., Cambridge, MA 02238-1067. 1990. A directory of 13,000+ alternative, progressive, innovative, experimental groups and organizations, with a geographical index, name index, and subject index. Lists such groups as bookstores, communes, ecology groups, film/video groups, human potential movement, alternative radio stations, women's groups, etc. Includes about 1,000 foreign places.

"I'm hoping to find something in a meaningful, humanist, outreach kind of bag, with flexible hours, non-sexist bosses, and fabulous fringes."

*Smith, Devon, ed., and LaVeck, James, asst. ed., *Great Careers: The Fourth of July Guide to Careers, Internships, and Volunteer Opportunities in the Nonprofit Sector.* 2nd ed. Garrett Park Press, P.O. Box 190B, Garrett Park, MD 20896. 1990. *Very* useful book with essays and lists of places; includes arts-related careers, and careers dealing with such issues as hunger, animal rights, the environment, homelessness, international jobs, working with people who are disabled, social action, and peace.

*Cohen, Lilly, and Young, Dennis R., *Careers for Dreamers and Doers: A Guide to Management Careers in the Nonprofit Sector.* The Foundation Center, 79 Fifth Ave., New York, NY 10003. 1989. The authors say that this sector has 900,000 organizations and employs over 8 million people.

Powell, Thomas J., *Self-Help Organizations and Professional Practice.* National Association of Social Workers, Inc., Silver Springs, MD. 1987.

Schmolling, Paul, Jr., with Burger, William R. and Youkeles, Merrill, *Careers in Mental Health: A Guide to Helping Occupations.* Garrett Park Press, Box 190, Garrett Park, MD 20896.

*The CEIP Fund, *The Complete Guide to Environmental Careers: Forestry, Parks & Recreation, Environmental Planning, Air & Water Quality Control, Hazardous Waste Management, Land & Water Conservation, Fishery & Wildlife Management, Solid Waste Management.* Island Press, Washington, D.C. 1989. Order from: The CEIP Fund, Dept. BKS, 68 Harrison Ave., Fifth Fl., Boston, MA 02111-1907.

Hughes, Kathleen, ed., *Good Works: A Guide to Social Change Careers.* Center for Study of Responsive Law, Box 19367, Washington, DC 20036. 1982.

Brand, Stewart, editor emeritus, *The Essential Whole Earth Catalog.* Doubleday & Co., Inc., Garden City, NY. A *wonderful* book.

23. ARTS AND CRAFTS

If your creativity is not out of the left-hemisphere of your brain *(words, words, words),* but out of the right-hemisphere *(pictures, art, crafts, and so forth),* there are some books to help you, many of these issued in annual revisions:

Gibson, James, *Getting Noticed: A Musician's Guide to Publicity & Self-Promotion.* Writer's Digest Books/North Light Books, 1507 Dana Ave., Cincinnati, OH 45207. 1987.

Garvey, Mark, ed., *1991 Songwriter's Market.* Writer's Digest Books/ North Light Books, 1507 Dana Ave., Cincinnati, OH 45207. 1989.

Marshall, Sam, ed., *1991 Photographer's Market.* Writer's Digest Books/ North Light Books, 1507 Dana Ave., Cincinnati, OH 45207. 1989.

Conner, Susan, ed., *1991 Artist's Market.* Writer's Digest Books/North Light Books, 1507 Dana Ave., Cincinnati, OH 45207. 1989.

If it is the visual arts that interest you, you may contact the Alliance of Independent Colleges of Art, 633 E St. NW, Washington, DC 20004. They have a quarterly magazine.

24. WRITING, OR PUBLISHING

I used to live in an apartment-complex, and as I walked through the courtyard each day, I could hear typewriters going incessantly, out of almost every open window. They couldn't **all** be office-workers, operating out of their own home with computer and fax machine. Obviously, there are a lot of budding authors and authoresses in the land. For them, some helps:

Miller, Casey, and Swift, Kate, *The Handbook of Nonsexist Writing,* 2nd Ed. Harper & Row, Inc., 10 E. 53rd St., New York, NY 10022. 1988. Newly revised, and a classic in its field. I use its guidelines in writing *Parachute.*

Appelbaum, Judith, *How to Get Happily Published,* Third Edition. Harper & Row, Inc., 10 E. 53rd St., New York, NY 10022. 1988. A good and helpful book, by an expert.

Neff, Glenda Tennant, ed., *1991 Writer's Market.* Writer's Digest/North Light Books, 1507 Dana Ave., Cincinnati, OH 45207. 1989.

Jerome, Judson, ed., *1991 Poet's Market.* Writer's Digest Books/North Light Books, 1507 Dana Ave., Cincinnati, OH 45207.

Boswell, John, *The Awful Truth about Publishing: Why They Always Reject Your Manuscript -- and What You Can Do about It.* Warner Books, 666 5th Ave., New York, NY 10103. "Why doesn't someone write a book about the behind-the-scenes in publishing?" Well, they have.

For more books in this field, write away for catalogs -- such as that of Writer's Digest Books/North Light Books, 1507 Dana Ave., Cincinnati, OH 45207.

25. TEACHING

Just because you have defined your dream of life for yourself as "teacher" doesn't mean you have even begun to narrow the territory down sufficiently for you to start looking for a job. You still have more research, and information gathering to do, before you have defined exactly *what kind* of teaching, *with what* kind of *groups, in what* kind of *place*. In other words, Chapters 4 through 6 in this book apply to you as much as, or even more than, anyone else.

The range of jobs that are done under the broad umbrella of Education is multitudinous and varied; just for openers, there is: *teaching* (of course), *counseling* (an honorable teaching profession, where it isn't just used by a school system as the repository for teachers who couldn't 'cut it'), *general administration, adult education programs, public relations, ombudsman, training, human resource development*, and the like. If the latter -- i.e., training and development -- is of particular interest to you, you will find there is a very useful description of the particular competencies, skills, and knowledges needed in the training and development fields. You'll find it in *Training and Development Competencies*, Patricia A. McLagan, Volunteer Study Director. Published in 1983, it is available from the American Society for Training and Development. Also see: Stump, Robert W., *Your Career in Human Resource Development: A Guide to Information and Decision Making*. American Society for Training and Development, 1630 Duke St., Box 1443, Alexandria, VA 22313. 31 pages. 1985. There is also Kimeldorf, Martin, *Educator's Job Search: A Guide to Finding Positions in Education*. Ednick Communications, Inc., P.O. Box 3612, Portland, OR 97208. 1988.

Our Canadian friends, namely the Ontario Society for Training and Development, have also put out a helpful guide, entitled *Competency Analysis for Trainers: A Personal Planning Guide*. It is available from O.S.T.D., 111 Queen E., Toronto, Ontario M5C 1S2, Canada, 416-367-5900. It outlines the kinds of skills which people who are entering this field ought to possess, and provides a checklist against which one can compare one's own skills.

If you have been a teacher, and have decided now to look elsewhere than teaching, there are aids for you:

Bastress, Frances, *Teachers in New Careers: Stories of Successful Transitions*. The Carroll Press. 1984. From: Career Development Services, Box 30301, Bethesda, MD 28104.

Beard, Marna L., and McGahey, Michael J., *Alternative Careers for Teachers*. "The complete job-changing handbook for educators." Arco Publishing, Inc., One Gulf+Western Plaza, New York, NY 10023. 1985.

There are also aids for particular teaching specialties; e.g., for history majors there is: *Careers for Students of History*, from the American Historical Association, 400 A St. SE, Washington, DC 20003. 1977. While, for English majors, there is: *Aside from Teaching English, What in the World Can You Do?* by Dorothy K. Bestor, available from: University of Washington Press, Seattle, WA 98105. 1982, revised.

26. WORKING FOR THE GOVERNMENT

As with any other kind of job, you've got to decide **where** it is you want to work, what skills you want to be able to use, and what it is you want to do *(in other words, Chapters 4 and 5 in this book apply to you as much as to non-governmental workers).*

If you are new to the idea of the government as your employer, you will of course suppose that researching them won't do you any good, because you are going to have to take a Civil Service examination of one kind or another. Well, eventually you probably **are** going to have to take that exam. But all the principles in Chapter 6 apply just as much to government managers as they do to other employers. I've talked to a number of government managers, and they too are tired of hiring people ill-suited for the job. Civil service exams don't give these managers any better clues than resumes do for non-governmental employers. So if, in the course of your research, you happen to visit the government person who has the power to hire you, and if he or she takes a real liking to you, you can bet your bottom dollar they will do everything *they can* to guide you through the examination maze, so that you can end up in their office. This is supposed to be a deep dark secret, but honestly, any government manager worth his or her salt knows how to manipulate -- ah, excuse me, creatively use -- the government's standard operating procedures, so that everything works out to their best advantage.

If you want to work for the government, here are some places to start:

Federal Jobs Digest, Billing Dept., P.O. Box 594, Millwood, NY 10546-9989. 800-824-5000. They have a special edition called "Introduction to the Federal Employment Process," which some of our readers have found **very** helpful. The *Digest* is published bi-monthly. It can often be found at your local public library, as can the following:

Federal Research Service, Inc., *Federal Career Opportunities*. Federal Research Service, Inc., 370 Maple Ave. W., Box 1059, Vienna, VA 22180, 703-281-0200. Bi-weekly 64-page magazine. Six issues. Up-to-date listing of available federal jobs plus application instructions.

Federal Yellow Book. An organizational directory of the top-level employees of the Federal departments and agencies. See your library. The publisher (Washington Monitor, Inc., 1301 Pennsylvania Ave., NW, Washington, DC 20004) also publishes *Congressional Yellow Book*, an up-to-date loose-leaf directory of members of Congress, their committees and their key aides.

Lauber, Daniel, *The Compleat Guide to Finding Jobs in Government*. Planning/Communications, 7215 Oak Ave., River Forest, IL 60305-1935. 1989. Where and how to find professional and non-professional positions in local, state, and federal government in the U.S., Canada and overseas.

Guide to Careers in World Affairs, published by the Foreign Policy Association, 729 Seventh Ave., New York, NY 10019, 212-764-4050. Lists more than 250 sources of employment in the world affairs field.

Special Problems

27. IMMIGRANTS TO THE U.S.

*Friedenberg, John E., Ph.D., and Bradley, Curtis H., Ph.D., *Finding a Job in the United States.* VGM Career Books, 4255 W. Touhy Ave., Lincolnwood, IL 60646-1975. 1986. A guide for immigrants, refugees, limited-English-proficient job-seekers, foreign-born professionals -- anyone who is baffled by the process of finding, and keeping, a job in the U.S. It contains job information based on the successful experience of job-seekers, plus advice from the U.S. Department of Labor. Includes information about American job customs and laws related to immigration, as well as a systematic plan for job-hunting.

28. ELEMENTARY SCHOOL STUDENTS, HIGH SCHOOL STUDENTS, AND SUMMER JOBS

The U.S. is developing into a nation of educational *haves* and *have-nots.* The *have-nots* are those who lack adequate skills in **reading, writing, math or typing (as, on a computer keyboard)**; and unfortunately the job-market is increasingly discriminating against them for this deficiency. *For example,* the average young adult in this country is reading at only a 2.6 level of English proficiency, while current jobs require a proficiency, on the average, of 3.0 (*going up to 3.6 by the year 2000, experts say*). Some companies report that even now, fewer than 1 in 10 applicants meet their skills-needs. Needless to say, those 9 educational *have-nots* usually don't get hired in any *decent-paying* job.

If you are still in high-school, **get those skills** in reading, writing, math, and typing, while you still have the chance. If you are *out* of high school, but lack these skills, consider seriously going to night school at your local high school or community college, to make up for lost time.

Here are some books that parents, counselors, and high school students may find helpful:

Otto, Luther B., *How to Help Your Child Choose a Career.* M. Evans & Co., 216 E. 49th St., New York, NY 10017. 1984.

Hummel, Dean L., and McDaniels, Carl, *How to Help Your Child Plan a Career.* Acropolis Books, Ltd., Colortone Bldg., 2400 17th St., NW, Washington, DC 20009. 1979.

*Farr, J. Michael, *A Young Person's Guide to Getting and Keeping a Job.* JIST Works, 720 N. Park Ave., Indianapolis, IN 46202. 1990.

Kennedy, Joyce Lain, and Laramore, Dr. Darryl, *Joyce Lain Kennedy's Career Book.* VGM Career Books, 4255 W. Touhy Ave., Lincolnwood, IL 60646-1975. 1988. Joyce is a very popular and knowledgeable syndicated writer on the subject of careers, while Darryl has written other books on youth and jobs.

The Guide to Basic Skills Jobs, Vol. 1. RPM Press, Inc., Verndale, MN. 1986. A catalog of viable jobs for individuals with only basic work skills.

This volume identifies 5,000 major occupations within the U.S. economy which require no more than an eighth grade level of education, and no more than one year of specific vocational preparation.

Mosenfelder, Donn, *Vocabulary for the World of Work.* Educational Design, Inc., 47 W. 13th St., New York, NY 10014. 1985. The 300 words that people entering the work force most need to know.

Henderson, Douglass, *Get Ready: Job-Hunters Kit* (for high school students). This package includes: *Get Ready, Teachers Manual; Get Ready, Students Manual;* and cassette. Get Ready, Inc., a subsidiary of Educational Motivation, Inc., Box 18865, Philadelphia, PA 19119. 1980.

Kimeldorf, Martin, *Job Search Education.* Educational Design, Inc., 47 W. 13th St., New York, NY 10011. 1985. Worksheets for the young job-hunter. Educational Design puts out a number of different books for elementary and high school students, in addition to the ones listed above, and they do have a catalog of such materials, which you can ask for.

*Kimeldorf, Martin, *Write Into a Job: Resumes and More.* Meridian Education Corporation, 236 E. Front St., Bloomington, IL 61701. 1990. Written particularly for entry-level or high school job-seekers. Teaches them how best to describe their marketable skills, in resumes or in other forms.

As for **summer jobs,** whether for high school or college students, here are the best-known directories. Most of them are annually updated, and the year of their revision often appears in their title:

Schocket, Sandra, *Summer Jobs, Finding Them, Getting Them, Enjoying Them.* Peterson's Guides, Dept. 5602, Princeton, NJ 08540. 1985.

Beusterien, Pat, ed., *Summer Employment Directory of the United States.*

Writer's Digest Books/North Light Books, 1507 Dana Ave., Cincinnati, OH 45207. Issued in annual revisions.

Woodworth, David, ed., *Directory of Overseas Summer Jobs*. Writer's Digest Books/North Light Books, 1507 Dana Ave., Cincinnati, OH 45207. Issued in annual revisions.

Hatchwell, Emily, ed., *Summer Jobs in Britain*. Writer's Digest Books/North Light Books, 1507 Dana Ave., Cincinnati, OH 45207. Issued in annual revisions.

See also Section 14: Internships, on page 302.

29. COLLEGE STUDENTS

Figler, Howard, *Liberal Education and Careers Today*. Garrett Park Press, Box 190, Garrett Park, MD 20896. 1989. Good stuff.

*Shingleton, Jack, *Which Niche?* Bob Adams, Inc., 260 Center St., Holbrook, MA 02343. 1989. Illustrated by Phil Frank. Wonderful cartoons, good advice, a darling little book from an old pro on the college scene.

Phifer, Paul, *College Majors and Careers: A Resource Guide for Effective Life Planning*. Garrett Park Press, Box 190, Garrett Park, MD 20896. 1987.

Ranno, Gigi, ed., *Careers and the MBA, 1989*. Bob Adams, Inc., 260 Center St., Holbrook, MA 02343. 1989.

Moore, Richard W., Ph.D., *Winning the Ph.D. Game: How to Get Into and Out of Graduate School with a Ph.D. and a Job*. Dodd, Mead & Co., 79 Madison Ave., New York, NY 10016. 1985. This seems to me to be an unusually helpful and well-researched book for Ph.D. graduates.

See also Section 14: Internships, on page 302. Books on summer jobs are listed in Section 28, above.

30. WOMEN

When women first started coming into the world of work in droves, in the early 1970s, there was a widespread feeling that they needed special job-hunting techniques -- and career counselors who catered particularly to women job-hunters. Consequently, books for women job-hunters came out by the bushel basket, and counselors catering just to women *thrived*. I think that day is rapidly passing, and now it is being more and more widely recognized that the problems of women in the job-hunt are the same as the problems of *everyone* in the job-hunt. Some problems still re-

main, of course. For example, some employers *still* believe that if they hire a woman, she will be out sick more than a man. It is therefore useful for a woman job-hunter to have some statistics at her fingertips. In this instance, the statistics (from the National Center for Health Statistics) are: women average 5.5 lost work days per year while men miss 4.3 days. In other words, women take one more sick day *per year* than men do. Small potatoes!

But basically the advice for women who go job-hunting is the same as it is for men: *Know your skills. Know what you want. Talk to people who have done it. Do your homework, on yourself and the companies, thoroughly.* There has consequently been a tremendous decline in the number of job-hunting books aimed just at women, though a few do still appear each year.

However, *after* they get the job, women still have very special problems of their own. Salary is a major one. While the wife is out-earning her mate in roughly one out of every five marriages, on average working wives earned $13,250 in 1987 compared to working husbands who averaged $29,150 that year. Part of this inequity is due to the fact that 50% of all working wives only work part-time. Wives working full-time averaged $18,930 in 1987 which is better -- but still far below husbands' average salary.

Another problem is childcare. In 1987, it was found, about one-third of the nation's 18.2 million working mothers had to pay for childcare -- and this cost them between $2,000 and $6,000 annually; the average was $2,305. For the working poor, childcare costs represented one-fifth of their income. Needless to say, these costs reduce the *net* amount of their already-low paycheck, considerably.

The following books may help you in your job-hunt:

Ekstrom, Ruth B., and Harris, Abigail M., and Lockheed, Marlaine E., *How to Get College Credit for What You Have Learned as a Homemaker and Volunteer*. 1977. Project HAVE SKILLS, Education Testing Service, Princeton, NJ 08541. They also publish the: *Have Skills Women's Workbook, Have Skills Counselor's Guide*, and *Have Skills Employer's Guide*. All of these include the famous "I CAN" lists, based upon the pioneering work, in the assessment of volunteer skills and knowledge, of the Council of National Organizations for Adult Education. The preeminent resource for women coming out of the home into the marketplace, who wonder what they can claim about their home experience. It applies to all homemakers returning to the marketplace, regardless of whether or not they wish college credit for what they have learned so far in life. I think it would also be useful to househusbands who want to now return to the marketplace. These workbooks classify the homemaker's skills under the various roles of: administrator/manager, financial manager, personnel manager, trainer, advocate/change agent, public relations/communicator, problem surveyor, researcher, fund-raiser, counselor, youth group leader, group leader for a serving organization, museum staff assistant (docent), tutor/teacher's aide, manager of home finances, home nutritionist, home child caretaker, home designer and maintainer, home clothing and textile specialist, and home horticulturist. *Very* helpful book, with accompanying aids.

Doss, Martha Merrill, *Women's Organizations: A National Directory*. Lists over 2,000 women's organizations nationwide as well as locally, plus much more. Garrett Park Press, Box 190, Garrett Park, MD 20896. 1986.

The New York Daycare Directory (Includes northern New Jersey and southwestern Connecticut). Bob Adams, Inc., 260 Center St., Holbrook, MA 02343. 1989.

The Boston Daycare Directory. Bob Adams, Inc., 260 Center St., Holbrook, MA 02343. 1989.

If you are interested in sales positions, you will want to know about the National Association for Professional Saleswomen, P.O. Box 2606, Novato, CA 94948. They have chapters across the country, and they publish a newsletter, called *Successful Saleswoman.*

31. MINORITIES (BLACK, HISPANIC, NATIVE AMERICANS, OR ASIAN)

One out of every three *new* workers is either Black, Hispanic or Asian, according to the Bureau of Labor Statistics. One out of every five workers, new or experienced, was from one of these minorities in 1986 and one out of every four workers will be, by the year 2000. Yet they face great difficulty in finding meaningful work. Part of the problem is that many live in the inner-cities across our country, while the jobs are increasingly moving to the suburbs.

Nonetheless, the false tribalism which I explain at length in Appendix D is still the major enemy of minorities, when they go looking for a job or career.

Everyone is familiar with the consequences that this tribalism has had for **blacks**: while the number of affluent black households (a yearly income of $50,000 or more) doubled between 1982 and 1987, nonetheless 33% of the nation's 30.2 million blacks still live in poverty; black unemployment in 1988 averaged 11.7%, versus 5.5% for the nation; the median 1987 income of black families was only 56% of that of white families.

Other minorities run into the same tribalism. So, if you're a member of a minority, that's what you're up against. Now, what can you do about it -- what will help you compete more successfully in the job-market? Answer: you need to follow the steps in Chapters 4, 5, and 6 in this book, plus Appendix A, *as though your life depended on it.* Cut no corners, take no shortcuts.

Some support for you in your efforts may be found through the following directories:

Cole, Katherine W., ed., *Minority Organizations: A National Directory.* 3rd ed. Garrett Park Press, Box 190, Garrett Park, MD 20896. 1987. An annotated directory of 7,700 Black, Hispanic, Native American, and Asian American organizations.

The Black Resource Guide. Black Resource Guide, Inc., 501 Oneida Pl., NW, Washington, DC 20111. 1987. A comprehensive list of over 3,000 black resources or organizations in the U.S.

*Aitken, Larry P., and Haller, Edwin W., *Two Cultures Meet: Pathways For American Indians to Medicine.* University of Minnesota -- Duluth. Published and distributed by Garrett Park Press, PO Box 190B, Garrett Park, MD 20896. 1990. A key source of information on medical study for American Indians.

Johnson, Willis L., ed., *Directory of Special Programs for Minority Group Members: Career Information Services, Employment Skills Banks, Financial Aid Sources*, 4th ed. Garrett Park Press, Box 190, Garrett Park, MD 20896. 1986.

There is a *Financial Aid for Minority Students Series*, for which there is a booklet on each of the following subjects: *Financial Aid for Minorities: Awards Open to Students with any Major; in Business and Law, Education, Engineering and Science, Health Fields, Journalism and Mass Communications, Medicine, and Science*. Garrett Park Press, Box 190, Garrett Park, MD 20896. 1987.

Minority Student Enrollments in Higher Education: A Guide to Institutions with Highest Percent of Asian, Black, Hispanic, and Native American Students. Garrett Park Press, Box 190, Garrett Park, MD 20896. 1987.

As for periodicals, or magazines, there are:

US Black Engineer, Hispanic Engineer, and *US Black Engineer/Hispanic Engineer Professional*. These are three different magazines, published for minorities who are interested in jobs within science and technology. If you are interested in them, they are published by: Career Communications Group, Inc., 729 E. Pratt St., Suite 504, Baltimore, MD 21202.

The national periodical for black college students is called *The Black Collegian*. Kuumba Kazi-Ferrouillet is the Managing Editor. It is published four times yearly. If you are interested in it, their address is: The Black Collegian, 1240 South Broad St., New Orleans, LA 70125.

32. EXECUTIVES, THE BUSINESS WORLD AND CORPORATE JOBS

Age, and the amount of salary that is sought, are the biggest determiners of the length of an executive's job-hunt, male or female. One large outplacement firm kept records and discovered that if an executive was 25–34 years of age, the average length of their job-hunt was about 20 weeks, but if over 55 years in age, it took almost 30 weeks. They further discovered that for those seeking an annual salary of $40,000 to $75,000, the average length of their job-hunt was about 25 weeks, while for those seeking more than $100,000, the average length of their job-hunt was almost 30 weeks. (Source: *National Business Employment Weekly*, 8/27/89.) That's what you're up against. Chapters 4, 5, 6 and Appendix A in this book, religiously followed, should help cut the time down. If you want further helps, here they are:

Boll, Carl R., *Executive Jobs Unlimited*. Updated edition. Macmillan Publishing Co., Inc., 866 Third Ave., New York, NY 10022. 1979, 1965. **One of the two classics** in the executive job-hunting field.

Drucker, Peter, *Management: Tasks, Responsibilities, Practices*. Harper & Row, Publishers, 10 E. 53rd St., New York, NY 10022. 1973. **The other classic** in this field. Should be absolutely required reading for anyone contemplating entering, changing to, or becoming a professional within any organization in the business world.

Cole, Kenneth J., *The Head-hunter Strategy*. John Wiley & Sons, Inc., 605 Third Ave., New York, NY 10158. 1985.

Corporate Jobs Outlook, "The Key to America's Top Employers," P.O. Drawer 100, Boerne, Texas 78006, is a newsletter published bi-monthly, with detailed information about current situations at top corporate employers. Your library may have it, and it is also available on-line, for those of you who have a computer and subscribe (or want to subscribe) to **NewsNet** (the telephone number is 800-345-1301, except in Pennsylvania or outside the U.S., where it is 215-527-8030). They emphasize that the seven keys to look for in your research of any corporate employer are: financial stability; growth plans; research and development programs; product development or manufacturing -- emerging products, services, or use of new technologies; marketing and distribution methods; employee benefits; and quality of work factors -- continuing training, health programs, childcare, promote-from-within, performance reviews.

See also the resources listed in Chapter 5, beginning on page 131.

33. 'RECOVERING PEOPLE' (FROM ALCOHOLISM, DRUGS, OTHER CHEMICAL DEPENDENCIES, CO-DEPENDENCIES), AND OTHER '12-STEP PROGRAM PEOPLE'

*Tanenbaum, Nat, and Eric A., *The Career Seekers: A Program for Career Recovery*. The Working Press, a division of The Career Center, Inc., P.O. Box 49631, Atlanta, GA 30359. 1988. This book is for people who are actively practicing any 12-step program, or are in counseling for co-dependency; but its principles apply to all who see themselves as 'recovering people.' Very useful supplement to *Parachute*.

34. EX-MILITARY

Like clergy (below), the military have been living in a sub-culture within our general culture, and this sub-culture is in many respects like the general job-market, except that it has its own unique vocabulary. It is *crucial* that ex-military sit down and inventory the skills they have been using during their time in the military (Appendix A in this book is *mandatory* for them), and that especial care be observed to take these skills and special knowledges out of the military *jargon* and translate them into language that is understood in the general marketplace.

The Retired Officers Association (TROA), 201 North Washington Street, Alexandria, VA 22314-2529, 703-838-8117 has an Officer Placement Service which maintains a comprehensive job search library, computerized placement service, and resume critique. It is, however, open only to members of TROA.

There is a company in Pennsylvania which operates a free computerized resume database for all military personnel. Such databases typically are much more used by job-seekers than they are by employers, but you may want to try it anyway. Write to MILITRAN, 1255 Drummers Lane, Suite 306, Wayne, PA 19087.

As for books, there is:

*Schlachter, Gail Ann, and Weber, R. David, *Financial Aid for Veterans, Military Personnel, and Their Dependents 1990–1991*. Reference Service Press, 1100 Industrial Road, Suite 9, San Carlos, CA 94070. 1990. Outlines over 1,000 programs open to veterans and their dependents.

35. CLERGY AND RELIGIOUS

Like the military (above), clergy have been living in a sub-culture within our general culture, and when they want to go job-hunting out in the secular world it is crucial not only that they know the skills they have been using during their time in the parish (or wherever), but that these skills and fields of knowledge be taken out of clergy *jargon* and expressed in language understood in the general marketplace.

Wild Life, by John Kovalic, © 1989 Shetland Productions. Reprinted with Permission.

In addition to Appendix A in this book, which is *mandatory* for you to do, *thoroughly*, there are places for you to visit. No profession has developed, or had developed for it, so many resources to aid in career assessment as has your profession. Many of these places have broadened their services to include all church members, and not just clergy.

All counselors in these centers are sincere; many are also very skilled. If you run into a clerical counselor who is sincere but inept, you will probably discover that the ineptness consists in an inadequate understanding of the distinction between career **assessment** -- roughly comparable to taking a snapshot of people as they are in one frozen moment of time -- vs. career **development** -- which is roughly comparable to teaching people how to take their own motion pictures of themselves, from here on out.

Having issued this caution, however, I will go on to add that at some of these centers, listed below, are some simply *excellent* counselors who fully understand this distinction, and are well trained in that empowering of the client, which is what career *development* is all about.

THE OFFICIAL INTERDENOMINATIONAL CAREER DEVELOPMENT CENTERS

The Career and Personal
Counseling Service
St. Andrew's Presbyterian College
Laurinburg, NC 28352
919-276-3162
Also at: 4108 Park Rd., Suite 200
Charlotte, NC 28209
704-523-7751
Elbert R. Patton, Director

The Career and Personal
Counseling Center
Eckerd College
St. Petersburg, FL 33733
813-864-8356, Ext. 356
John R. Sims, Director

The Center for Ministry
7804 Capwell Dr.,
Oakland, CA 94621
415-635-4246
Robert Charpentier, Director

Lancaster Career
Development Center
561 College Ave.
Lancaster, PA 17603
717-397-7451
L. Guy Mehl, Director

North Central Career
Development Center
3000 Fifth St. NW
New Brighton, MN 55112
612-636-5120
John Davis, Director

Northeast Career Center
83 Princeton Ave. Suite 2D
Hopewell, NJ 08525
609-466-0774
Roy Lewis, Director

Career Development Center
of the Southeast
531 Kirk Rd.
Decatur, GA 30030
404-371-0336
Robert M. Urie, Director

Midwest Career
Development Service
Box 7249
Westchester, IL 60153
312-343-6268
Ronald Brushwyler, Director

Southwest Career
Development Center
Box 5923
Arlington, TX 76011
817-265-5541
William M. Gould, Jr.,
Director-Counselor

Center for Career
Development and Ministry
70 Chase St.
Newton Center, MA 02159
617-969-7750
Harold D. Moore, Director

The centers listed above are all accredited and coordinated by the Career Development Council, Room 774, 475 Riverside Dr., New York, NY 10115. Some of them accept directors of Christian Education, ministers of music, and others in addition to clergy; some centers are open to all and not merely to church-related clients; some are open to high school students, as well as to adults.

ALSO DOING WORK IN THIS FIELD:

CareerWorks -- a division of Intercristo. 19303 Fremont Ave. N., Seattle, WA 98133, 206-546-7395. Jeff Trautman, Director.

Enablement Information Service, Inc., 14 Beacon St., Rm. 707, Boston, MA 02108, 617-742-1460. James L. Lowery, Jr., Executive Director.

Mid-South Career Development Center, 113 River Dr., McMinnville, TN 37110, 615-473-6984. W. Scott Root, Director.

Career and Personal Counseling Center, 1904 Mt. Vernon St., Waynesboro, VA 22980, 703-943-9997. Lillian Pennell, Director.

Bernard Haldane, Wellness Education Council, 4502 54th NW, Seattle, WA 98105, 206-525-2205. A pioneer in the clergy career management and assessment field, Bernard teaches *(totally independently of the agency which bears his name)* seminars and training of volunteers *(particularly in churches)* to do job-search counseling.

Life/Career Planning Center for Religious, 10526 W. Cermak Rd., Suite 111, Westchester, IL 60153, 312-531-9228. Dolores Linhart, Director. Doing work with Roman Catholics.

Books looking at job-hunting and career-changing from a religious point of view are to be found at the end of Appendix E, on page 405.

36. EX-OFFENDERS

Federal/State Employment Offices can often be of particular assistance to ex-offenders. All offices can provide for bonding of ex-offenders, if needed to obtain employment. They also have information on tax-breaks for employers who hire ex-offenders. The larger offices even have Ex-Offender Specialists.

You can obtain a "Pre-Employment Curriculum" from the American Correctional Association, 4321 Hartwick Rd., College Park, MD 20740.

There is also: *A Survival Source Book for Offenders*, from Contacts, Inc., Box 81826, Lincoln, NE 68501.

Addendum

OTHER CAREER BOOKS

Some mail-order places carry a lot of books related to job-hunting and career-change, that are not listed in this Appendix. Naturally, these places publish catalogs. Below is a *sampling* (only) of such catalogs -- *you were dying, weren't you, to have a few more catalogs in your mail box, in addition to the 400 that you are already receiving?:*

**The Whole Work Catalog: Career Resources 1991.* The New Careers Center, Inc., 1515 23rd Street, P.O. Box 297, Boulder, CO 80306.

**Career Planning and Job Search Catalog.* JIST Works, Inc., 720 North Park Avenue, Indianapolis, IN 46202.

**Career Development Resources Catalog.* Career Research & Testing, 2005 Hamilton Ave., San Jose, CA 95125.

**Job & Career Library.* Consultants Bookstore, Templeton Road, Fitzwilliam, NH 03447.

*Careers Department, Impact Publications, 10655 Big Oak Circle, Manassas, VA 22111-3040.

*VGM *Career Books.* NTC Publishing Group, 4255 West Touhy Ave., Lincolnwood, IL 60646-1975.

Other resources, including periodicals, that are designed particularly for counselors, are listed at the end of Appendix C, beginning on page 351.

Two are better than one;
for if they fall,
the one will lift up his fellow;

but woe to him that is alone when he falleth,
and hath not another to lift him up.

Ecclesiastes

Appendix C

when books are not enough and you want a live person to help you:

Career Counselors and Other Resources

LOOK BEFORE YOU LEAP:

How to Choose a Career Counselor, If You Decide You Need One

Okay, so you've decided you've got to find somebody to help you with your job-hunt or career-change, because:

Either

a) you *tried* doing the exercises in the book, and you just aren't getting anywhere; or

b) you've read the book -- sections of it anyway -- and without even trying the exercises, you know yourself well enough to know you need someone who will explain it all to you, step by step. You're an "ear" person, more than an "eye" person, and you do better when a human being is explaining something to you, than when you're trying to read it for yourself; OR

c) you've not read the book, nor tried any of the exercises, but you **have** counted the number of pages in the book, and other than using it as a doorstop, you've decided to give up on it before you even begin. *Help! HELP!*

You've turned to this section because you figure that back here must be some sort of "authorized list" of names: people who understand this whole job-hunting process thoroughly, know how to do all the exercises in this book, have been through some kind of careful credentialing process, and received the Parachute Seal of Approval.

Ah, dear reader, how I wish it were so. But, unhappily, there is no such list. First of all, while I do train people once a year, I have trained only 3,000 over the years -- a drop in the bucket, compared to the number of career counselors that are *out there*. Moreover, I can't *guarantee* that simply because they've been through my hands, they truly understand. So, publishing a list of their names wouldn't necessarily give you the information you want.

Secondly, there are lots of people "out there" who understand the whole job-hunting process thoroughly and well, even though they've never been trained by me and may not even (necessarily) have read this book. In most cases, of course, I've never met them, and consequently I don't know who they are or where they are. I simply know *that* they are.

What this all adds up to, you've already guessed. **Hunting for a decent person or place to help you is just like hunting for a job. You've got to do your own research, and your own interviewing, in your own area, or you will deserve what you get.**

YOU, ONLY YOU

Getting somebody else's opinion, in effect letting them do your research for you, is job-hunting suicide. First of all, their information is often outdated, and therefore of questionable value to you. Maybe the counselor or place they're telling you about is one they used a year ago. The counselor was excellent, at that time. But since then (unbeknownst to your friend) that counselor has been through a really rough time, personally: divorce, burnout, overwhelming fatigue -- the works. It's affected their counseling, to say the least; they're no longer functioning at the level they were a year ago. Your friend's recommendation is outdated -- at least for now. And, of course, it can be just the other way around. Your friend tells you someone is terrible, as a counselor, because when your friend used them, two or three years ago, it was painfully true. But, that counselor has had dozens and dozens of clients since then, and learned *a lot* (most career counselors are trained by their clients, you know). That counselor is now very good. Your friend's "dis-recommendation" is now undeserved.

Secondly, the three things you absolutely want from anyone you're paying your own good money to, are:

a) a firm grasp of the whole job-hunting process, at its most creative and effective level;
b) the ability on their part to communicate that information lucidly and clearly to you;
c) rapport with you.

This last is the killer. Without that, you can forget the first two. But who can tell you, in the absence of your very own research, that you aren't going to get along with this counselor? Maybe he's a wonderful man, but unhappily he reminds you of your Uncle Harry. You've always **hated** your Uncle Harry. No one knows that, but you.

I repeat: no one can do this research for you. Because the real question is not "Who is best?" but "Who is best **for you**?" Those last two words demand that it be you who does this search.

AN OUTLINE OF THE REST OF THIS APPENDIX

What I want to do for you now is:

1. Give you a brief crash course about this whole field of career counseling.
2. Tell you where to find some names with which **to start** your search for "who is best for you."
3. Give you some questions, that will help you separate the sheep from the goats, and make an intelligent decision.

Okay, here we go:

1. A CRASH COURSE ABOUT THIS WHOLE FIELD OF CAREER COUNSELING

In the whole big field of The Job-Hunt, all professional help divides (I regret to report) into the following three categories, so far as you the job-hunter, or career-changer, are concerned:

1. Professionals who are sincere and skilled.
2. Professionals who are sincere but inept.
3. Professionals who are insincere and inept.

The problem we all face when we decide to seek help with our job-hunt or career-change, is: **which is which?** Or, who is who. You want a career counselor who falls into category No. 1; if he or she falls into either of the other two categories, which of the two they fall into is really irrelevant: ineptness is ineptness, whether it is sincere or not.

The various clues which may at first occur to us, for identifying good career counselors, are upon more serious examination not terribly fruitful. Let us tick some of them off, and see why:

✶ **Clue No. 1: Perhaps we can tell who is sincere and skilled, by the name or job-title that they bear.** Difficulty: job-titles vary greatly from one operation to another, even when the operations are similar. Among the job-titles which some counselors or agencies bear, you will find: executive career counselors, executive career consultants, career management teams, vocational psychologists, executive consulting counselors, career guidance counselors, executive advisors, executive development specialists, executive job counselors, manpower experts, career advisors, employment specialists, executive recruitment consultants, professional career counselors, management consultants, placement specialists, executive search specialists, vocational counselors, life/work planners, etc. If, tomorrow, some legitimate counselor who is sincere and skilled takes on a new job-title, the day after that some counselor who is insincere and inept will copy it directly. What it all comes down to, is this: Wolves need sheep's clothing. Job-titles are sheep's clothing. Trouble is, hidden in there are some genuinely helpful people. We need another clue.

✶ **Clue No. 2: Perhaps we can tell who is sincere and skilled by reading everything that the agency or counselor has written.** Difficulty: both good and bad counselors know the areas where the job-hunter feels exceedingly vulnerable. Consequently, there are "turn on" words which occur in almost *everybody's* advertisements, brochures, and books: *we will give you help,* say they, *with evaluating your career history, in-depth analysis of your background, establishment of your job objective, in-depth analysis of your capabilities, writing an effective resume, names of companies, preparing the covering letter,*

background materials on companies, interviewing techniques, video playback of mock interviews between you and a pretend-employer, salary negotiations, filling out forms, answering ads, aptitude tests, special problems -- unemployment, age, too broad a background, too narrow a background, too many job changes, too few job changes, poor references, etc. We will, they say, *open doors for you, tell you which companies are hiring, and so forth and so on.* Both the counselors who are skilled and those who are inept will never get anyone in their doors if they don't mention the areas that have put the job-hunter in Desperation City. So how they describe their services (real or alleged) doesn't separate the sheep from the goats -- unfortunately. Next clue?

✶ **Clue No. 3: Perhaps we can tell who is sincere and skilled by the fee they charge? I mean, they wouldn't charge a high fee, would they, if they weren't skilled?** Difficulty: as insiders say, low fees may mean well-intentioned but amateurish help. However, the reverse of this is **not** true. As we have already mentioned, the vacuum created by the chaotic condition of our job-hunting process has attracted both competent counselors *and* counselors who are determined to prey upon the acute state of anxiety that job-hunters find themselves in. And when the latter say "Let us prey" they *really* prey. And they *thrive*. They charge anywhere from $2,000 to $10,000 (it's solely dependent on your previous salary) **up front**, before they've given you *any* services or help at all. And if you are later dissatisfied, your chances of getting your money back are remote, indeed -- no matter what the contract said. (They've fashioned every legal loophole in the book, into that contract, so that they can keep your money, once they've got it.) P. T. Barnum knew what he was talking about.[1] Next.

✶ **Clue No. 4: Perhaps we can tell which professionals are both sincere and skilled, by talking to satisfied clients -- or asking our friends to tell us who was helpful to them.** If you stop to think about it, you will realize this most important truth: all that your friends can possibly tell you about, is the particular counselor that they worked with, at that agency, in that particular city. Should **you** go to the same place, and get a different counselor, you might have a very different experience. One bad counselor in an agency that has say, six good ones, can cost you money, time, and self-esteem, if *you* get that bad one as *your* counselor. The six good ones might as well be in Timbuktu, for all the good they'll do you. So should any of your friends recommend a place they went to, be sure to find out the counselor (or counselors) they worked with, there, *by name*, if you decide to investigate or follow their lead, and when you go there to investigate, ask for that counselor by name. Incidentally, if they won't let you see him or her, but confront you with someone who seems very polished and smooth, you're probably face-to-face with an agency that has a sales force. And it is the salesman *(rarely, saleswoman)* you are talking to, not the counselor you would eventually have (maybe) if you decided to sign up. Were I in your shoes, and I discovered I was dealing with a salesman or saleswoman, I would run -- not walk -- right out of that place and never look back.

---

1. "A sucker is born every minute." Or as the post office has updated it: "A sucker is shorn every minute."

Before we abandon this clue, let me also observe that while most professional career counselors can show you letters from satisfied customers, or even (in some cases) give you their names to check out, it is impossible to find out what percentage of their total clientele these satisfied persons represent: 100%? 10? 1? .1? a fluke? You may make what you will out of the fact that the top officers of the largest executive counseling firm, which allegedly did over 50% of the business in the industry here in the U.S. before it declared bankruptcy in the U.S. in the fall of 1974 (*namely*, Frederick Chusid & Co.) gave testimony during a civil suit in a New York Federal district court which indicated that only three or four out of every ten clients had been successful in getting a new job, during a previous six-month period (a 60-70% failure rate, right?). More recently, another prominent executive counseling firm was reported by the Attorney General's Office of New York State to have placed only 38 out of 550 clients (a 93% failure rate).[1] Are these figures average for the industry? Better than average? Worse? Nobody knows. But that should certainly be enough to make you wary. Do you want to bet up to $10,000 (or whatever their fee is), where there is a 60 to 93% chance that you **won't** get anything back, for your money? Go to Las Vegas; even it has better odds.

One thing I will guarantee you: no career counselor or career counseling firm will **ever** show you letters from **dis**satisfied clients. Were you to be given access to such letters (the files of the Better Business Bureaus, the Consumer Fraud division of your state or city Attorney General's office, not to mention the Federal Trade Commission, are loaded with such letters) you would find all the complaints have a painful familiarity: *the career counselor or career counseling firm being complained about,* they all say, *did not do what they **verbally** promised to do, have exclusive lists of job openings they claimed to have, nor the success rate they claimed, nor did they give the amount of time to the client they **verbally** promised in advance (sometimes it turned out to be as few as six hours). 'Job campaigns' for the clients were slow to start, usually not until the full advance fee was paid, promised lists were slow in being provided and often were outdated and full of errors, the friendly 'intake counselor' was actually a salesperson, and is never seen again once the contract is signed, the actual counselor was often difficult (or impossible) to get ahold of after a certain period of time (sometimes coinciding with the final payment by the client of the advance fee), the 'plan' was often no news at all to the client, the promised contact with employers on the client's behalf was not forthcoming, phone calls or letters of complaint were ignored, and the fee was not refunded in whole or in part, when the client was dissatisfied, despite implicit (or explicit) promises to the contrary.* Whew!

Well, that's enough of a crash course on career counseling, and the pitfalls that await the unwary or the innocent.

If you are **dying** to know more, and your local library has back files of magazines and newspapers (on microfiche, or otherwise) there was a period when bad firms and counselors came under heavy fire (1978–1982) and you can look up some of the articles of that period, as well as those articles which have appeared more recently, to wit:

"A Consumer Guide to Retail Job-Hunting Services," Special Report, reprinted

1. "Career Counselors: Will They Lead You Down The Primrose Path?" by Lee Guthrie, in the December 1981 issue of *Savvy Magazine*, pp. 60ff.

from the *National Business Employment Weekly*; available from Dow Jones Reprint Service, P.O. Box 300, Princeton, NJ 08543-0300. A *very* thorough series of articles on the industry, which names *names,* and gives the addresses of Consumer protection agencies in each state, to whom you may complain. **Required reading,** for anyone who wants to avoid getting 'burned.'

"'Employment counselors' costly, target of gripes," *The Arizona Republic,* October 8, 1989.

"Career-Counseling Industry Accused of Misrepresentation," *New York Times,* Sept. 30, 1982, p. C1.

"Consumer Law: Career Counselors and Employment Agencies" by Reed Brody, *New York Law Journal,* Feb. 26, 1982, p. 1. Reed was Assistant Attorney General of the State of New York, and more recently Deputy Chief of the Labor Bureau within that State's Department of Law; in this capacity he became the leading legal expert in the country, on career counseling malpractices, though subsequently he has gone into overseas work.

"Career Counselors: Will They Lead You Down the Primrose Path?" by Lee Guthrie, *Savvy Magazine,* Dec. 1981, pp. 60ff.

"Franklin Career Search Is Accused of Fraud In New York State Suit," *Wall Street Journal,* Jan. 29, 1981, p. 50.

"Job Counseling Firms Under Fire For Promising Much, Giving Little," *Wall Street Journal,* Jan. 27, 1981, p. 33.

A number of these articles refer to Stuart Alan Rado. Mr. Rado is a former victim of one of the career counseling agencies, and ever since has been waging a sort of "one-man crusade" against career counseling firms which take advantage of the job-hunter. **His** advice, as the result of counseling many victims, is: don't go to **any** firm which requires the fee all in advance. If you are reading this too late, did pay some firm's fee all in advance, and feel you were ripped off, send Mr. Rado a self-addressed stamped envelope, and he will send you a one-page sheet of some actions you can take. His address is: 1500 23rd St., Sunset Island #3, Miami Beach, FL 33140. 305-532-2607. He is working to help bring about new state laws, which will make it at least *a little more difficult* for unscrupulous career counseling firms to take advantage of the hapless job-hunter or career-changer. Some states, such as California, have already adopted such laws.

2. SOME NAMES WITH WHICH TO START YOUR SEARCH FOR WHO IS BEST *FOR YOU*

I am printing here a Sampler (only) of some of the kinds of places to be found around the country. This is not a complete directory of anything. It is exactly what its name implies: a sample. Countless good people, agencies, and places exist, which will not be found in this Sampler. *Also, countless bad people, places, and agencies will not be found in this Sampler.* To list all the counselors out there, would require an encyclopedia. Some states, in fact, have *encyclopedic* lists of counselors and businesses, in various books or directories, and where possible I have listed those books -- under the appropriate state.

What this list is not: the listing of an organization, agency or person here is NOT a recommendation or endorsement of that organization, agency or person by me, nor are they allowed to advertise or imply that it is. *(If they do, we reluctantly remove them.)*

What this list is: This list is simply a sampler of the kinds of places that are out there, who claim some expertise in helping readers use *Parachute*

(text continues on page 347)

A Sampler

We contacted all of these listings during 1990, to check for accuracy and currentness. So, as we go to press, it's as accurate as we can make it. *Unfortunately*, however, there is **no way** any Sampler can remain up-to-date and accurate, for more than about two days, and six hours. Their staff changes. Their phone numbers change. Places move, or fold, almost weekly in this field. I apologize for any information or listing that proves to be inaccurate by the time you get to use it. If you find a place that is no longer in existence, or impossible to get ahold of, or is -- in your opinion -- totally unhelpful you could be of great service to our other readers by dropping us a line and telling us so. My dream is to keep this listing as current as possible, filled only with useful resources. (I said *dream*.)

If you have a favorite place that is not listed below, send us the pertinent information. We will then ask them some intelligent questions about their familiarity with this book, and if we find their answers acceptable we will list them in the next edition. *Don't, however, bother to send us college services which are available* only *to the students and alumni or alumnae of that college. After many complaints from readers, it is now our policy that we no longer list places that thus restrict their clientele. If you discover that we have inadvertently included a place that only serves Their Own, please let us know immediately, and we'll gently remove them from the next edition.*

If the listings here aren't helpful for the geographical location where you are, ask everyone you know -- family, friends, and even people you've just met -- if they know any really helpful career counselors in your area.

Try also your telephone book's local Yellow Pages, under the headings (in the index) of *Personnel & Employment*, under *Business and Financial Services*. This index will likely refer you to such entries in the body of the Yellow Pages as: *Aptitude and Employment Testing*, *Career and Vocational Counseling*, *Personnel Consultants* and (if you are a woman) *Women's Organizations and Services*. You will discover, however, that even the Yellow Pages can't keep up with the additional groups that spring up daily, weekly, and monthly -- including job clubs and other group activities. Fortunately, many of these *are* listed in the *National Business Employment Weekly*, on its pages called "Calendar of Career Events." Available on newsstands, $3.50 per issue; or, order an issue directly from: National Business Employment Weekly, 420 Lexington Ave., New York, NY 10170. 212-808-6792, or 800-JOB HUNT. Among all the listings below, as well as those that you turn up on your own, you will have to pick and choose **very carefully**. I repeat: you **must** do your own comparison shopping, and do your own sharp questioning before you ever sign up with **anyone**. If you don't, you will deserve whatever you get (or, more to the point, *don't* get).

The listings below are alphabetical within each state, except that counselors listed by their name are alphabetized by their *last* name. To make this clear, only their last name is in **bold**.

Generally speaking, the places below counsel *anybody*. A few, however, take only women as clients. Ask. If they aren't able to take you, your phone call wasn't wasted, *so long as* you then go on to ask them "who else in the area can you tell me about, and are there any among them that you would particularly recommend?"

ALABAMA

Enterprise State Junior College, Women's Center, Career Development Center, Box 1300, Enterprise, AL 36331, 205-347-2623 or 393-3752.

ARIZONA

College PLUS Career Connections, 4540 S. Rural Rd., #P-8, Tempe, AZ 85282, 602-730-5246. Dr. Warren D. Robb, Director.

Lou Ann S. **Dickson,** Ph.D., 2131 E. Southern Ave., Tempe, AZ 85282, 602-820-1599.

PHR & Associates, 6101 S. Rural Rd., #128, Tempe, AZ 85283, 602-839-8284. Also at 3200 E. Shea, #110, Phoenix, AZ 85028, 602-839-8284. Phyllis Harper Rispoli.

Southwest Institute of Life Management, 11122 E. Gunshot Circle, Tucson, AZ 85749, 602-749-2290. Theodore Donald Risch, Director.

For further listings in Arizona and the rest of the Southwest:

Block, Barbara and Benjamin, Janice, *How to Become Happily Employed in Phoenix.* Career Management Center, 8301 State Line Rd., Suite 202, Kansas City, MO 64114. 1988.

Adams, Robert Lang, ed., *The Southwest Job Bank.* Bob Adams, Inc., 260 Center St., Holbrook, MA 02343. 1983.

ARKANSAS

Donald **McKinney,** Ed.D., Career Counselor, Rt. 1, Box 351-A, DeQueen, AR 71832, 501-642-5628.

CALIFORNIA

Alumnae Resources, 120 Montgomery St., Suite 1080, San Francisco, CA 94104, 415-274-4700.

Judy Kaplan **Baron Associates,** 6046 Cornerstone Ct. W., Suite 208, San Diego, CA 92121, 619-558-7400. Judy Kaplan Baron, Director.

Branham & Associates, 1979 Greengrove St., Orange, CA 92665, 714-637-4694.

Career Action Center, 445 Sherman Ave., Palo Alto, CA 94306, 415-324-1710.

Career Development Institute, 690 Market St., Suite 404, San Francisco, CA 94104, 415-982-2636.

Career Development Life Planning, 3585 Maple St., Suite 237, Ventura, CA 93003, 805-656-6220. Norma Zuber, M.S.C., & Associates.

Career Dimensions, Box 7402, Stockton, CA 95267, 209-473-8255. Fran Abbott.

Careerpath Guidance, 3368 Second Ave., Suite E, San Diego, CA 92103, 619-296-1055. Carla Grindle.

Career Planners Personnel Service, 2667 Camino del Rio South, Suite 258, San Diego, CA 92108, 619-299-0455. Richard H. Peerson, Ph.D.

Career Planning Center/Business Action Center, 1623 S. La Cienega Blvd., Los Angeles, CA 90035, 213-273-6633.

Career Strategy Associates, Koll Center Newport, 5000 Birch St., Suite 3000, Newport Beach, CA 92660, 714-476-3652. Betty Fisher.

Civic Center Volunteers, Marin County Personnel Office, Administration Bldg., Civic Center, San Rafael, CA 94903, 415-499-6104.

Constructive Leisure, Patsy B. Edwards, 511 N. La Cienega Blvd., Los Angeles, CA 90048, 213-652-7389.

Consultants in Career Development, 2017 Palo Verde Ave., Suite 201B, Long Beach, CA 90815, 213-598-6412. Dean Porter, Senior Partner.

Criket Consultants, 502 Natoma St., P.O. Box 6191, Folsom, CA 95630, 916-985-3211.

Cypress College, Career Planning Center, 9200 Valley View St., Cypress, CA 90630, 714-826-2220, ext. 120.

Margaret L. **Eadie,** M.A., A.M.Ed., WHAT NEXT Education and Career Consultant, Box 725, Solana Beach, CA 92075, 619-436-1516.

Experience Unlimited, Mr. Herman L. Leopold, Coordinator, Employment Development Dept., 1225 4th Ave., Oakland, CA 94606, 415-464-1259/464-0659.

Beverly Neuer **Feldman,** Ed.D., President of Career Tech Associates, 2656 Aberdeen Ave., Los Angeles, CA 90027, 213-665-7007.

Mary Alice **Floyd,** M.A., N.C.C.C. and Gerald L. **Floyd,** M.A., N.C.C.C., Career Counselor/Consultant, 3233 Lucinda Lane, Santa Barbara, CA 93105, 805-687-5462.

Judith **Grutter,** M.S., N.C.C.C., Career Development Consultant, 1499 Huntington Dr., #402, South Pasadena, CA 91030, 818-441-1888.

Arthur M. **Hugon,** 9432 Gerald Ave., Sepulveda, CA 91343, 818-893-0098.

Life Career Development, 4035 El Macero Dr., Davis, CA 95616, 916-758-1439. Russell A. Bruch, Director, Career Consultant.

Life's Decisions, 2701 Cottage Way, #1, Sacramento, CA 95825, 916-486-0677. Joan E. Belshin, M.S.

Carol **March Associates,** 2107 Van Ness Ave., Suite 402, San Francisco, CA 94109, 415-775-5588.

Susan W. **Miller,** M.A., 6363 Wilshire Blvd., Suite 210, Los Angeles CA 90048, 213-837-7768/651-5514.

Modern Career Decisions, 1811 Santa Rita Rd., Suite 224, Pleasanton, CA 94566, 415-846-9071. Rod Meyer, CPC, Executive Director.

National University Career Center, 4007 Camino Del Rio S., San Diego, CA 92108, 619-563-7250.

Project J.O.Y. (*Job Opportunities for Youth*), East Oakland Youth Development Center, 8200 E. 14th St., Oakland, CA 94621, 415-569-8088. Al Auletta, Director.

Sacramento Women's Center, Women's Employment Services and Training, 2306 "J" St., Suite 200, Sacramento, CA 95816, 916-441-4207.

Saddleback College, Counseling Services and Special Programs, 28000 Marguerite Pkwy., Mission Viejo, CA 92692, 714-582-4571. Jan Fritsen, Counselor.

San Jose State University, Re-Entry Advisory Program, Adm. 201, San Jose, CA 95192.

Marion Bass **Stevens,** Ph.D., Career & Employment Counseling, The Peninsula Regent, One Baldwin Ave., #208, San Mateo, CA 94401, 415-344-0809.

Stoodley & Associates, 15750 Winchester Blvd., #104, Los Gatos, CA 95030, 408-354-2259. Martha Stoodley, M.S., M.F.C.C., President.

The **Successful Job Search Center,** 1700 N. Broadway, Suite 407, Walnut Creek, CA 94596, 415-283-1776. Marston Watson, President.

Linda Loomis **Teurfs,** 24582 Via Del Oro, Laguna Niguel, CA 92656, 714-831-1006. An associate of the Crystal-Barkley Corp. (see New York).

Transitions, 171 N. Van Ness, Fresno, CA 93701, 209-233-7250. Margot E. Tepperman, L.C.S.W.

Turning Point Career Center, University YWCA, 2600 Bancroft Way, Berkeley, CA 94704, 415-848-6370. Winnie Froehlich, M.S., Director.

UCLA Extension Advisory Service, 10995 Le Conte Ave., Rm. 114, Los Angeles, CA 90024, 213-206-6201.

Caroline **Voorsanger,** Career Counselor for Women, 2000 Broadway, Suite 1108, San Francisco, CA 94115, 415-567-0890.

Patti **Wilson,** 15880 Rose Ave., Los Gatos, CA 95030, 408-354-1964.

Women at Work, 78 N. Marengo Ave., Pasadena, CA 91101, 818-796-6870.

The **Women's Opportunities Center,** University of California Extension, P.O. Box 6050, Irvine, CA 92716-6959.

For further listings in California (well, you *might* need some):

Camden, Thomas M., and Pine, Evelyn Jean, *How to Get a Job in San Francisco.* Surrey Books, 101 E. Erie St., Suite 900, Chicago, IL 60611. 1989.

Beach, Janet L., *How to Get a Job in the San Francisco Bay Area.* Contemporary Books, Inc., 180 North Michigan Ave., Chicago, IL 60601. 1983.

Fien, Lorri, *The Directory of Bay Area Associations, First ed.* Bay Area Resource Exchange, 544 Ygnacio Valley Rd., Suite 150, Walnut Creek, CA 94596-8040.

Block, Barbara, and Benjamin, Janice, with Marks, Linda, *How to Become Happily Employed in San Francisco, 2nd ed.* Career Management Center, 8301 State Line Rd., Suite 202, Kansas City, MO 64114. 1988.

Adams, Robert Lang, ed., *San Francisco Job Bank, 4th ed.* Bob Adams, Inc., 260 Center St., Holbrook, MA 02343.

Adams, Robert Lang, ed., *The Northern California Job Bank.* Bob Adams, Inc., 260 Center St., Holbrook, MA 02343. 1986.

Camden, Thomas, and Polk, Karen Tracy, *How to Get a Job in Los Angeles/San Diego, 1989*. Surrey Books, 101 E. Erie St., #900, Chicago, IL 60611. 1989.

California Connections Publication, Box 90396, Long Beach, CA 90809. A directory of public sector employment opportunities.

COLORADO

Arapahoe Community College, Career Resource Center, 5900 S. Santa Fe Dr., Littleton, CO 80120, 303-794-1550.

CRS (Career Resource Services) Human Resource Innovations, 425 W. Mulberry, Suite 101, Ft. Collins, CO 80521, 303-484-9810. Contact Lorie A. Smith, M.S.

Samuel **Kirk and Associates,** Central Office, 1418 S. Race, Denver, CO 80210, 303-722-0717.

Patricia **O'Keefe,** M.A., 350 Cook St., Denver, CO 80206, 303-393-8747.

Women's Center, Box 6, Red Rocks Community College, 13300 W. 6th Ave., Lakewood, CO 80401-5398, 303-988-6160, ext. 213.

Women's Resource Agency, 1011 N. Weber St., #C, Colorado Springs, CO 80903, 719-471-3170.

For further listings in Colorado:

Adams, Robert Lang, ed., *The Denver Job Bank, 2nd ed.* Bob Adams, Inc., 260 Center St., Holbrook, MA 02343. 1989.

Faaborg, Barbara, and Renault, Susan, *Job Resources for Colorado Women -- Where to Find Good Advice Cheap*. Subar Publications, 2118 Payton Circle, Colorado Springs, CO 80915. 1986.

CONNECTICUT

Accord Consultants, Inc., The Exchange, Suite 305, 270 Farmington Ave., Farmington, CT 06032, 203-674-9654. J. Tod Gerardo, President and Director.

Career Choices, Oak Park, Madison, CT 06443, 203-245-4123.

Career Services, 94 Rambling Rd., Vernon, CT 06066, 203-871-7832. Jim Cohen, Ph.D., President.

Fairfield University, Fairfield Adult Career & Educational Services (FACES), North Benson Rd., Julie Hall, Fairfield, CT 06430, 203-254-4110.

Gillespie Associates, 9 Berkeley St., Norwalk, CT 06850, 203-838-8464. Jonathan B. Horwitz, Ed.D.

Ilise **Gold Associates,** Career and Life Planning Specialists, 164 Kings Highway N., Westport, CT 06880, 203-222-9223.

People Management, Inc. See the listing under Washington State.

Vocational and Academic Counseling for Adults (VOCA), 115 Berrian Rd., Stamford, CT 06905, 203-329-1955.

John H. **Wiedenheft,** M.A., Career Development, 38 Barker St., Hartford, CT 06114, 203-527-5523 or 1-800-654-4320.

DELAWARE

Life/Career Planning, 2413 Brickton Rd., Wilmington, DE 19803, 302-478-7186. Minh-Nhat Tran, Consultant.

The **Women's Center,** YWCA of New Castle County, 233 King St., Wilmington, DE 19801, 302-658-7161. Mona B. Bayard, Program Coordinator.

DISTRICT OF COLUMBIA

Community Vocational Counseling Service, The George Washington University Counseling Center, 718 21st St. NW, Washington, DC 20052, 202-994-4860. Robert J. Wilson, M.S., Coordinator.

Comptex Associates, Inc., P.O. Box 6745, Washington, DC 20020, 301-599-9222. Mary H. Johnson, President, and Eugene Williams, Sr., Executive Vice President.

George Washington University, Continuing Education for Women, 801 22nd St. NW, Suite T409, Washington, DC 20052, 202-994-5762, or -8164, or -8165.

For further listings in Washington:

Adams, Robert Lang, ed., *The Metropolitan Washington Job Bank, 3rd ed.* Bob Adams, Inc., 260 Center St., Holbrook, MA 02343.

FLORIDA

The **Career and Personal Counseling Center,** Eckerd College, Box 12560, St. Petersburg, FL 33733, 813-864-8356. John R. Sims.

Center for Career Decisions, 980 N. Federal Hwy., Suite 203, Boca Raton, FL 33432, 407-394-3399. Linda Friedman, M.A., Director.

Center for Continuing Education for Women, Valencia Community College, Winter Park Center, 1010 N. Orlando Ave., Winter Park, FL 32789, 407-628-1976.

Centre for Women, 305 S. Hyde Park Ave., Tampa, FL 33606, 813-251-8437. Beth Ficquette, Executive Director.

Chabon & Associates, 2090 Palm Beach Lakes Blvd., Suite 1000, West Palm Beach, FL 33409, 407-640-8443. Toby G. Chabon, M.Ed., N.C.C.C., President.

Challenge: The Displaced Homemaker, Florida Community College at Jacksonville, 101 W. State St., Jacksonville, FL 32202, 904-633-8316. Joan Putnam, Project Coordinator.

Crossroads, Palm Beach Community College, 4200 Congress Ave., Lake Worth, FL 33461, 407-433-5995. Pat Jablonski, Program Manager.

FACE Learning Center, Inc., 12945 Seminole Blvd., Bldg. II, Suite 8, Largo, FL 34648, 813-585-8155 or 586-1110.

Ellen O. **Jonassen,** Ph.D., Harbor Oak Medical Center, 1106 Druid Rd. S., Suite 201, Clearwater FL 34616, 813-442-6007

Life Designs, Inc., 7860 SW 55th Ave. #A, South Miami, FL 33143, 305-665-3212 or 665-9393. Dulce Muccio and Deborah Tyson, co-founders.

Stetson University Counseling Center, Campus Box 8365, North Woodland Blvd., De Land, FL 32720, 904-734-4121, ext. 215.

For further listings in Florida:

Adams, Robert Lang, ed., *The Florida Job Bank.* Bob Adams, Inc., 260 Center St., Holbrook, MA 02343.

Fencl, George Jr., and Pritchett, Janie, *The Central Florida Career Guide.* Edge Publishing, P.O. Box 3621, Longwood, FL 32779. 1987.

GEORGIA

Career and Education Information Center, Lenox Square Professional Concourse, Suite 103, 3393 Peachtree Rd. NE, Atlanta, GA 30326, 404-233-7497. Barbara Buchanan, Executive Director.

Career Planning Center of Grace United Methodist Church. Mark Canfield, Director, 458 Ponce de Leon Ave., Atlanta, GA 30308, 404-876-2678.

Career Pursuit, 2971 Flowers Rd. S., Suite 101, Atlanta, GA 30341, 404-457-9636. Estelle Ford-Williamson, M.A., Career and Management Development Specialist.

Charles W. **Cates,** Ph.D., 1485 N. Decatur Rd., Atlanta, GA 30306, 404-373-0336.

St. Jude's Job Network Club, St. Jude's Catholic Church, 7171 Glenridge Dr., Sandy Springs, GA 30328.

Mark **Satterfield,** 5262 Walker Rd., Stone Mountain, GA 30088, 404-469-3462.

For further listings in Georgia:

Adams, Robert Lang, ed., *The Atlanta Job Bank, 2nd ed.* Bob Adams, Inc., 260 Center St., Holbrook, MA 02343.

ILLINOIS

Abbot Services, 6057 W. Eddy St., Chicago, IL 60634, 312-545-5892. Richard Gans, Career Counselor.

Applied Potential, Box 585, Highland Park, IL 60035, 708-234-2130.

Career Directions, Inc., 5005 Newport Dr., Suite 404, Rolling Meadows, IL 60008, 312-870-1290. Peggy Simonsen, Director. Also at 25 E. Washington St., #1500, Chicago, IL 60602.

Career Path, 3033 Ogden Ave., Suite 203, Lisle, IL 60532, 312-369-3390. Donna Sandberg, M.A., Owner/Counselor.

Career Resources, Inc., and **Chicago Career Groups,** 1426 Grant Rd., Northbrook, IL 60062, 708-272-1079. Barbara Hill, President.

Career Workshops, 5431 W. Roscoe St., Chicago, IL 60641, 312-282-6859. Patricia Dietze.

Jean **Davis,** Career Counseling, 1405 Elmwood Ave., Evanston, IL 60201, 312-492-1002.

Harper College Community Counseling Center, Palatine, IL 60067, 708-397-3000, ext. 2577.

David P. **Helfand,** Ed.D., N.C.C.C., 250 Ridge, Evanston, IL 60202, 708-328-2787.

Illinois Vocational Student Services Network, 145 Fisk St., Dekalb, IL 60115, 815-758-8597. Olive Poliks, Career Guidance Consultant. The Network also has offices in Springfield, Addison, Macomb, Rantoul, Grayslake, Belleville, and Olney.

Lansky Career Consultants, 233 E. Erie #611, Chicago, IL 60611, 312-642-5738.

McFadden & Associates, 135 Columbus Ave., Galesburg, IL 61401, 309-343-7714.

Midwest Women's Center, 53 W. Jackson Blvd., Suite 1015, Chicago, IL 60604, 312-922-8530.

Moraine Valley Community College, Job Placement Center, 10900 S. 88th Ave., Palos Hills, IL 60465, 708-974-5737.

The **Professional Career Counselors & Consultants Network (PCCN),** 307 N. Michigan #2001, Chicago, IL 60601, 312-332-4516. For $5, PCCN will send you a directory of their members who offer consulting to the public. Jack Chapman, President.

Jane **Shuman,** Career Management Consultant, 122 Circle Dr., Springfield, IL 62703, 217-529-7220.

University of Illinois Urbana-Champaign, Office for Women's Resources and Services, Room 2, Student Services, 610 E. John St., Champaign, IL 61820, 217-333-3137.

For further listings in Illinois:

Camden, Thomas M., and Schwartz, Susan, *How to Get a Job in Chicago: The Insiders' Guide*. Surrey Books, 101 E. Erie St., Suite 900, Chicago, IL 60611. 1989.

Adams, Robert Lang, ed., *The Greater Chicago Job Bank,* 5th edition. Bob Adams, Inc., 260 Center St., Holbrook, MA 02343.

INDIANA

Ball State University, Career Services, Muncie, IN 47306, 317-285-5634 or 285-1522.

Career Consultants, 107 N. Pennsylvania St., Suite 404, Indianapolis, IN 46204, 317-639-5601. Mike Kenney, Senior Partner.

Indiana University, Continuing Education for Women, Owen Hall 201, Bloomington, IN 47405, 812-855-0225.

John D. **King & Associates,** Career Counseling and Consulting, 205 N. College, Suite 614, Bloomington, IN 47404, 812-332-3888.

William R. **Lesch,** M.S., Career & Life Planning, Health Associates, 9240 N. Meridian St., Suite 292, Indianapolis, IN 46260, 317-844-7489.

YWCA of St. Joseph County, 802 N. Lafayette Blvd., South Bend, IN 46601, 219-233-9491.

IOWA

Adult Career Change Center, Drake University, 26th and University, Des Moines, IA 50311, 515-271-2916.

University of Iowa, Business and Liberal Arts Placement/Career Information Services, IMU, Iowa City, IA 52242, 319-335-3201.

KANSAS

KENTUCKY

Ronniger Associates, Inc., First Trust Centre, 200 S. 5th St., Louisville, KY 40202, 502-583-4115.

LOUISIANA

Career Planning and Assessment Center, Metropolitan College, University of New Orleans, New Orleans, LA 70148, 504-286-7100.

Career Strategies, Inc., Two Lakeway Center, 3850 N. Causeway Blvd., Suite 210, Metairie, LA 70002, 504-836-7538. William M. O'Toole, Career Consultant.

MARYLAND

Careerscope, Inc., Suite 219, Harper's Choice Village Center, 5485 Harper's Farm Rd., Columbia, MD 21044, 301-992-5042/596-1866. Ann Sim, Executive Director.

Career Transition Services, 3126 Berkshire Rd., Baltimore MD 21214, 301-444-5857. Michael Bryant, Founder and Director.

College of Notre Dame of Maryland, Continuing Education Center, 4701 N. Charles St., Baltimore, MD 21210, 301-532-5303.

Goucher College, Goucher Center for Continuing Studies, Towson, Baltimore, MD 21204, 301-337-6200.

Maryland New Directions, Inc., 2517 N. Charles St., Baltimore, MD 21218, 301-235-8800. Rose Marie Coughlin, Director.

Prince George's Community College, Career Assessment and Planning Center, 301 Largo Rd., Largo, MD 20772, 301-322-0886. David C. Borchard, Director.

MASSACHUSETTS

Alewife Counseling Associates, 18 Palmer St., Arlington, MA 02174, 617-643-2988. Jane Hynes.

Career Directions Inc., 10 Kearney Rd., Needham, MA 02194, 617-449-3336. David Eysmann, Director.

Career Management Consultants, Thirty Park Ave., Worcester, MA 01605, 617-853-8669. Patricia M. Stepanski, President.

Career Resource Center, Worcester YWCA, 1 Salem Square, Worcester, MA 01608, 617-791-3181.

Center for Career Development & Ministry, 70 Chase St., Newton Center, MA 02159. Violet Grennan, O.S.F., Associate Director.

Center for Careers, Jewish Vocational Service, 105 Chauncy St., 6th Fl., Boston, MA 02111, 617-451-8147.

Changes, 134 Cornell St., Newton, MA 02162, 617-244-7172. Carl Schneider.

David J. **Giber,** Ph.D., 80 Waverley St., Arlington, MA 02174, 617-648-5732.

Jewish Vocational Service, Mature Worker Programs, 333 Nahanton St., Newton, MA 02159.

Wynne W. **Miller,** 785 Centre St., Newton, MA 02158-2599, 617-527-4848.

Murray Associates, 555 Washington St., Wellesley, MA 02181, 617-235-8896. Robert Murray, Ed.D., Licensed Psychologist.

Neville Associates, Inc., 6 New England Executive Park, Suite 400, Burlington, MA 01803, 617-272-8519. Dr. Joseph Neville, Career Development Consultant.

New Beginnings Career Center, Assabet Center for Continuing Education, Fitchburg St., Marlborough, MA 01752.

Radcliffe Career Services, 77 Brattle St., Cambridge MA 02138.

Suit Yourself, Inc., 115 Shade St., Lexington, MA 02173, 617-862-6006 or 508-358-4567. Debra Spencer.

Women's Educational & Industrial Union, Career Services, 356 Boylston St., Boston, MA 02116, 617-536-5657.

For further listings in Massachusetts:

Boyd, Kathleen, and Ramsauer, Constance Arnold, and Senft, Ruth, *Career Connections: A Guide to Career Planning Services in Massachusetts.* Bob Adams, Inc., 260 Center St., Holbrook, MA 02343. 1983.

Adams, Robert Lang, ed., *The Boston Job Bank.* Bob Adams, Inc., 260 Center St., Holbrook, MA 02343. 1989.

MICHIGAN

Career Options, The 511 Bldg., 511 Monroe, Kalamazoo, MI 49007, 616-382-3993.

Ellman & Associates, Suite 220-B, 7001 Orchard Lake Rd., West Bloomfield, MI 48322, 313-737-7252. Barbara Kabcenell Ellman, M.A., N.C.C.C., and Lou Ellman, Career Management Professionals.

Every Woman's Place, 1706 Peck St., Muskegon, MI 49442, 616-726-4493.

Macomb Community College, Professional and Continuing Education, 14500 Twelve Mile Rd., K-332, Warren, MI 48093, 313-445-7417.

Michigan Technological University, Educational Opportunities, Youth Programs, Rm. 119, Academic Offices Bldg., Houghton, MI 49931, 906-487-2219.

C.S. Mott Community College, Guidance Services and Counseling, 1401 E. Court St., Flint, MI 48503, 313-762-0356.

Oakland University, Continuum Center for Adult Counseling and Leadership Training, Rochester, MI 48063, 313-370-3033.

Thibaudeaux Personnel of Grand Rapids, 820 Commerce Bldg., Grand Rapids, MI 49503, 616-459-8396. Donald D. Fink, Ed.D., Director of Career Counseling.

University of Michigan, Center for the Education of Women, 330 East Liberty, Ann Arbor, MI 48104, 313-998-7080.

Women's Resource Center, 252 State St. SE, Grand Rapids, MI 49503.

For further listings in Michigan:

Adams, Robert Lang, ed., *The Detroit Job Bank.* Bob Adams, Inc., 260 Center St., Holbrook, MA 02343.

MINNESOTA

Career Dynamics, Inc., 8300 Norman Center Dr., #240, Bloomington, MN 55437, 612-921-2378. Joan Strewler, Psychologist.

Chart/WEDCO, 2324 University Ave., Suite 200, St. Paul, MN 55114, 612-332-1942.

Leider, Inc., 7101 York Ave. S., Minneapolis, MN 55435, 612-921-3334. Richard J. Leider, Executive & Professional Career Consultant.

Minnesota Women's Center, University of Minnesota, 5 Eddy Hall, Minneapolis, MN 55455, 612-625-2874.

Working Opportunities for Women, 2700 University Ave., #120, St. Paul, MN 55114, 612-647-9961.

For further listings in Minnesota:
Adams, Robert Lang, ed., *The Minneapolis Job Bank.* Bob Adams, Inc., 260 Center St., Holbrook, MA 02343.

MISSISSIPPI

Mississippi State University, Career Services Center, P.O. Box P, Mississippi State, MS 39762, 601-325-3344. Gloria H. Reeves, Director.

MISSOURI

Career Planning and Placement Center, Adult Evening Program, 110 Noyes Hall, University of Missouri, Columbia, MO 65211, 314-882-6803.

The Women's Center, University of Missouri, Kansas City, 104 Scofield Hall, 5100 Rockhill Rd., Kansas City, MO 64110, 816-276-1638.

For further listings in Missouri:

Adams, Robert Lang, ed., *The St. Louis Job Bank.* Bob Adams, Inc., 260 Center St., Holbrook, MA 02343.

MONTANA

Women's Employment Network, Missoula YWCA, 1130 W. Broadway, Missoula, MT 59802, 406-543-6768.

Women's Resource Center, 15 Hamilton Hall, Montana State University, Bozeman, MT 59717, 406-994-3836.

NEBRASKA

Career Planning Center, Central Community College, Hastings Campus, Hastings, NE 68901, 402-461-2456.

Clemm C. **Kessler** III, Kessler & Associates, Executive Plaza, 6818 Grover St., Omaha, NE 68106, 402-397-9558.

NEW JERSEY

Adult Advisory Services, Kean College of New Jersey, Administration Bldg., Union, NJ 07083, 201-527-2210.

Adult Resource Center, 100 Horseneck Road, Montville, NJ 07045, 201-335-6910.

Arista Concepts Career Development Service, P.O. Box 2436, Princeton, NJ 08540, 609-921-0308. Kera Greene, M.Ed.

Bergen Community College, Division of Community Services, 400 Paramus Rd., Paramus, NJ 07652, 201-447-7150.

Caldwell College, Career Development Center, Caldwell, NJ 07006, 201-228-4424, ext. 307.

Career Options Center, YWCA Tribute to Women and Industry (TWIN) Program, 232 E. Front St., Plainfield, NJ 07060, 201-756-3836.

Loree **Collins,** 3 Beechwood Rd., Summit, NJ 07901, 201-273-9219.

Douglass College, Douglass Advisory Services for Women, Rutgers Women's Center, 132 George St., New Brunswick, NJ 08903, 201-932-9603.

Fairleigh Dickinson University, Career Planning & Placement, 285 Madison Ave., Madison, NJ 07940, 201-593-8945. Monday-Friday, 9 am–5 pm.

Sandra **Grundfest,** Ed.D., Princeton Professional Park, 601 Ewing St., Suite C-1, Princeton, NJ 08540, 609-921-8401.

Jersey City State College, The Women's Center, 2039 Kennedy Blvd., Jersey City, NJ 07305, 201-547-3189.

Middlesex County College, Community Advisement and Resource Center, 155 Mill Rd., Edison, NJ 08818, 201-906-2550.

Minsuk, Macklin, Stein & Associates, 14 Washington Rd., Princeton Junction, NJ 08550-1028, 609-275-5800. Also: 115 Rt. 46, Bldg. F, Mountain Lakes, NJ 07045. 201-402-4294.

Montclair State College, Women's Center, Student Center, Rm. 420-422, Upper Montclair, NJ 07043, 201-893-5114/or -7130.

W. L. **Nikel & Associates,** Career Development and Outplacement, 28 Harper Terrace, Cedar Grove, NJ 07009, 201-575-5700. William L. Nikel, M.B.A., Founder.

The **Professional Roster,** 171 Broadmead, Princeton, NJ 08540, 609-921-9561.

Women's Center, Princeton University, 201 Aaron Burr Hall, Princeton, NJ 08544, 609-452-5565.

NEW MEXICO

Young Women's Christian Association, YWCA Career Services Center, 7201 Oasei Del Norte NE, Albuquerque, NM 87113, 505-822-9922.

NEW YORK

Academic Advisory Center for Adults, Turf Ave., Rye, NY 10580, 914-967-1653.

The **Career Center,** 1525 Western Ave., Albany, NY 12203, 518-869-1311. Thomas J. McKenna, Director.

Career Development Services, 14 Franklin St., Temple Bldg., Suite 1200, Rochester, NY 14604, 716-325-2274.

Career Services Center, Long Island University, C.W. Post Campus, Brookville, NY 11548, 516-299-2251. Mince Kohler, Director.

The John C. **Crystal Center,** 111 E. 31st St., New York, NY 10016, 212-889-8500. Nella G. Barkley, President. *(John died in 1988; Nella was his business partner, for many years preceding his death.)*

Susan **Hadley,** Career and Life/Work Planning Consultant, 59 Jefferson St., Nyack, NY 10960, 914-353-0579.

Hofstra University, Counseling Center, 240 Student Center, Hempstead, NY 11550, 516-560-6788.

Kingsborough Community College, Office of Career Counseling and Placement, 2001 Oriental Blvd., Rm. C102, Brooklyn, NY 11235, 212-934-5115.

Janice **La Rouche Assoc.,** Workshops for Women, 333 Central Park W., New York, NY 10025, 212-663-0970.

Miriam J. **Mennin,** M.A., N.C.C.C., 33 Andrea Lane, Scarsdale, NY 10583, 914-725-5501.

Network Career Resumes, 60 E. 42nd St., Suite 2901, New York, NY 10165, 212-687-2411. John Aigner, Counselor.

New Options, 960 Park Ave., New York, NY 10028, 212-535-1444.

Orange County Community College, Office of Community Services, 115 South St., Middletown, NY 10940, 914-341-4890.

Celia **Paul Associates,** 200 Madison Ave., New York, NY 10016, 212-873-3588.

Personnel Sciences Center, 41 E. 42nd St., New York, NY 10017, 212-661-1870.

Regional Learning Service of Central New York, 405 Oak St., Syracuse, NY 13203, 315-425-5252.

Ruth **Shapiro Associates,** 200 E. 30th St., New York, NY 10016, 212-889-4284, 212-679-9858.

SUNY at Buffalo, Career Planning Office, 252 Capen Hall, Buffalo, NY 14260, 716-636-2231.

WIN Workshops (Women in Networking), Emily Koltnow, 730 Fifth Ave., New York, NY 10019, 212-333-8788.

Women's Center for Continuing Education, Syracuse University College, 610 E. Fayette St., Syracuse, NY 13244, 315-423-4116. Phyllis R. Chase, Director.

Women's Network of the YWCA, 515 North St., White Plains, NY 10605, 914-949-6227.

For further listings in New York:

Camden, Thomas M., and Fleming-Holland, Susan, *How to Get A Job In New York: The Insiders' Guide. 2nd ed.* Surrey Books, 500 N. Michigan Ave., Suite 1940, Chicago, IL 60611. 1990.

Adams, Robert Lang, ed., *The Metropolitan New York Job Bank, 5th ed.* Bob Adams, Inc., 260 Center St., Holbrook, MA 02343.

NORTH CAROLINA

Thomas S. **Baldwin,** Ph.D., Licensed Practicing Psychologist, 87 S. Elliott Rd., Suite 200, Chapel Hill, NC 27514, 919-929-0496.

Career, Educational, Psychological Evaluations, 6725-C Fairview Rd., Charlotte, NC 28210, 704-362-1942. Nancy Cook.

Career Management Center, 3203 Woman's Club Drive, Suite 217, Raleigh, NC 27612, 919-787-1222. Temple G. Porter, Director.

Sally **Kochendofer,** Ph.D., 20109K Henderson Rd., Davidson, NC 28036, 704-892-4975.

Joyce **Richman & Associates, Ltd.,** 2911 Shady Lawn Dr., Greensboro, NC 27408, 919-288-1799.

Women's Center of Raleigh, 315 E. Jones St., Raleigh, NC 27601, 919-755-6840. Anne D. Britt, Career Services Coordinator.

OHIO

Adult Resource Center, The University of Akron, Akron, OH 44325, 216-972-7448.

Career Resources, Society Bank Bldg., 32 N. Main St., Suite 1245, Dayton, OH 45402, 513-223-8000.

Cuyahoga County Public Library Info-PLACE Service, Career, Education & Community Information Service, 5225 Library Lane, Maple Heights, OH 44137-1291, 216-475-2225.

J & K Associates, 607 Otterbein, Dayton, OH 45406-4507, 513-274-3630. Pat Kenney, Ph.D., President.

Kahnweiler Associates, 455 Delta Ave., Suite 205, Cincinnati, OH 45226, 513-533-5800. Jennifer B. Kahnweiler, Owner.

New Career, 328 Race St., Dover, OH 44622, 216-364-5557. Marshall Karp, M.A., N.C.C., L.P.C., Owner.

Pyramid Career Services, Inc., 1642 Cleveland Ave., NW, Canton, OH 44703, 216-453-3767. Zandra Bloom, Director.

For further listings in Ohio:

Adams, Robert Lang, ed., *The Ohio Job Bank, 2nd ed.* Bob Adams, Inc., 260 Center St., Holbrook, MA 02343.

OKLAHOMA

Career Development Services, 4823 S. Sheridan, Suite 304, Tulsa, OK 74145, 918-665-1161/1162. William D. Young, Ed.D., L.P.C.

OREGON

CareerMakers, 1336 SW Bertha, Portland, OR 97219, 503-244-1055. Pam Gross, Executive Director.

Joseph A. **Dubay,** 2153 S.W. Main Street, Portland, OR 97205, 503-224-3600.

PENNSYLVANIA

Career Management Consultants, Inc., 3207 N. Front St., Harrisburg, PA 17110, 717-233-2272. Louis F. Persico, Career Consultant.

Cedar Crest College, Women's Center, Allentown, PA 18104, 215-437-4471.

Center for Adults in Transition, Bucks County Community College, Newtown, PA 18940, 215-968-8188. Patricia Sharer, Assistant Director.

Job Advisory Service, Center for Professional Development, Chatham College, Woodland Rd., Pittsburgh, PA 15232, 412-365-1142.

Options, Inc., 215 S. Broad St., Philadelphia, PA 19107, 215-735-2202. Marcia P. Kleiman, Director.

Priority Two, Rm. 208, Pittsburgh National Bank Bldg., Beaver & Blackburn Rds., Sewickley, PA 15143, 412-741-8368. Five locations in the Pittsburgh area.

Resources for Excellence, P.O. Box 8989, 726 South Ave., Pittsburgh, PA 15221, 412-242-3001. David R. Johnson, Director.

David C. **Rich,** Director, United Ministries in Higher Education, Pennsylvania Commission, 13 Victoria Way, Camp Hill, PA 17011.

Villa Maria College of Gannon University, Counseling Services for Women, 2551 West Eighth St., Erie, PA 16505, 814-838-1966.

For further listings in Pennsylvania:

Adams, Robert Lang, ed., *The Philadelphia Job Bank*. Bob Adams, Inc., 260 Center St., Holbrook, MA 02343.

Connelly, Betty, *Find A Good Job In Pittsburgh*. Job Advisory Service, Center for Professional Development, Chatham College, Woodland Rd., Pittsburgh, PA 15232. 1989.

RHODE ISLAND

Options, Inc., 245 Waterman St., Providence, RI 02906, 401-331-1727. Dr. Rollin Karnehm, President.

SOUTH CAROLINA

Converse College, Office of Career Services, Spartanburg, SC 29302-0006, 803-596-9027.

Greenville Technical College, Career Advancement Center, Greenville, SC 29606, 803-250-8281. Larry A. Hudson, Counselor.

SOUTH DAKOTA

Career Concepts, Centennial Square, 2100 S. 7th St., Suite 255, Rapid City, SD 57701, 605-394-5783. Melvin M. Tuggle, Jr., President.

Sioux Falls College, The Center for Women, Clidden Hall, Sioux Falls, SD 57105, 605-331-6697.

TENNESSEE

Career Resources, 2323 Hillsboro Rd., Suite 300, Nashville, TN 37212, 615-297-0404. Jane C. Hardy, President.

Mid-South Career Development Center, 113 River Dr., McMinnville, TN 37110, 615-473-6984. W. Scott Root, President/Counselor.

Secretarial Office Services, 314 N. White St., Athens, TN 37303, 615-745-4513. Adelia Wyner, Consultant.

TEXAS

Austin Women's Center, 1700 S. Lamar Blvd., Suite 203, Austin, TX 78704, 512-447-9666.

Career Action Associates, First Interstate Bank Plaza, Suite 512, 12655 N. Central Expressway, Dallas, TX 75243, 214-392-7337. Rebecca Hayes, Licensed Professional Counselor.

Career Decisions Job Finder's Club, 2103 S. Clear Creek Rd., Killeen, TX 76542. 817-634-2142.

Catalyst Career Consultants, 2520 Longview, Suite 112, Austin, TX 78705, 512-474-7773. Joia Jitahidi, Senior Consultant.

Richard S. **Citrin,** Ph.D., Psychologist, Iatreia Institute, 1152 Country Club Ln., Ft. Worth, TX 76112, 817-654-9600.

Creative Careers, 9030 Wurzbach Rd., San Antonio, TX 78240-1040, 512-735-7287. Jon Patrick Bourg.

Employment/Career Information Resource Center, Corpus Christi Public Library, 805 Comanche, Corpus Christi, TX 78401, 512-880-7004. Lynda F. Whitton, Career Information Specialist.

Executive Recruiter Connection (ERC), 5025 Arapaho, Suite 400, Dallas TX 75248.

Life/Work Design, c/o The Listening Tree, 3906 N. Lamar, Suite 202, Austin, TX 78756, 512-458-2844 or 926-7662.

Ministry of Counseling and Enrichment, 1333 N. 2nd St., Abilene, TX 79601, 915-675-8131. Mary Stedham, Director.

New Life Institute, Box 1666, Austin, TX 78767, 512-469-9447. Bob Breihan, Director.

San Antonio Psychological Services, 6800 Park Ten Blvd., Suite 208 North, San Antonio, TX 78213, 512-737-2039.

Vocational Guidance Service, Inc., 2525 San Jacinto, Houston, TX 77002, 713-659-1800.

Women's Counseling Service, 1950 W. Gray, Suite 1, Houston, TX 77019, 713-521-9391.

Women's Resource Center, YWCA, 4621 Ross Ave., Dallas, TX 75204, 214-821-9595.

For further listings in Texas:

Adams, Robert Lang, ed., *The Dallas Job Bank*. Bob Adams, Inc., 260 Center St., Holbrook, MA 02343.

Adams, Robert Lang, ed., *The Houston Job Bank*. Bob Adams, Inc., 260 Center St., Holbrook, MA 02343.

Camden, Thomas M., and Bishop, Nancy, *How to Get a Job in Dallas/Ft. Worth: The Insiders' Guide*. 3rd ed. Surrey Books, Inc., 500 N. Michigan Ave., Suite 1940, Chicago, IL 60611. 1990.

Jitahidi, Joia, *Making Austin Work*. "Tips to the hidden job market and a guide to Austin's employment resources." Catalyst Publications, Box 15785, Austin, TX 78761.

UTAH

The **Phoenix Institute,** 1800 S. West Temple, Suite 211, Salt Lake City, UT 84115, 801-484-2882.

University of Utah, Center for Adult Transitions, 1195 Annex Bldg., Salt Lake City, UT 84112, 801-581-3228.

VIRGINIA

Career Development Center for Women, 5501 Backlick Rd., #110, Springfield, VA 22151, 703-750-0633.

Educational Opportunity Center, 7010-M Auburn Ave., Norfolk, VA 23513, 804-855-7468.

Hollins College, Career Counseling Center, Roanoke, VA 24020, 703-362-6364. Peggy Ann Neumann, Director.

Life Management Services, Inc., 6849 Old Dominion Drive, Suite 219, McLean, VA 22101, 703-356-2630. Hal and Marilyn Shook, President and Vice President.

Mary Baldwin College, Rosemarie Sena Center for Career and Life Planning, Staunton, VA 24401, 703-887-7221.

Old Dominion University, Women's Center, 1521 W. 49th St., Norfolk, VA 23529-0536, 804-440-4109.

Psychological Consultants, Inc., 6724 Patterson Ave., Richmond, VA 23226, 804-288-4125.

Swenholt Associates, Inc., 6308 Crosswoods Circle, Falls Church, VA 22044, 703-256-2383. Frankie P. Swenholt, President.

University of Richmond, Women's Resource Center, Richmond, VA 23173, 804-289-8020.

Virginia Commonwealth University, University Advising Center, Box 2523, 827 W. Franklin St., Rm. 101, Richmond, VA 23284-2523, 804-257-0200. Marcia F. Zwicker, Director.

The **Women's Center,** 133 Park St., NE, Vienna, VA 22180, 703-281-2657. Virginia C. Marshall, Director of Program Development.

Woman's Resource Center of Central VA, Inc., Norfolk House, 155 Norfolk Ave., Randolph-Macon Woman's College, Lynchburg, VA 24503, 804-847-0258. Sarah C. Snead, Executive Director.

WASHINGTON

Career Management Institute, 8404 27th St. West, Tacoma, WA 98466, 206-565-8818. Ruthann Reim, M.A., N.C.C.C., President.

The **Individual Development Center, Inc. (I.D. Center),** 1020 E. John, Seattle, WA 98102, 206-329-0600. Mary Lou Hunt, N.C.C.C., President.

People Management Group International, P.O. Box 33608, Seattle, WA 98133, 206-443-1107. Arthur F. Miller, Jr., Chairman. Dick Staub, President.

University of Washington, University Extension GH-21, Career/Life Planning, Seattle, WA 98195, 206-543-2300.

For further listings in Washington State: Adams, Robert Lang, ed., *The Seattle Job Bank.* Bob Adams, Inc., 260 Center St., Holbrook, MA 02343. 1989.

WISCONSIN

Career Connections Center, Career Counseling for Career Changers, Alverno College, 3401 S. 39th St., Milwaukee, WI 53215, 414-382-6010.

Mind's Eye Institute, 16445 Audrey Lane, Brookfield, WI 53005, 414-786-1120. Kathy Kouzmanoff, M.S.

David Swanson, Career Seminars and Workshops, 1033 N. Mayfair Rd., Suite 200, Milwaukee, WI 53226, 414-259-0265.

WYOMING

Lifetime Career Consultants, P.O. Box 912, Jackson, WY 83001, 307-733-6544. Barbara Gray.

National Education Service Center, P.O. Box 1279, Riverton, WY 82501-1279, 307-856-0170.

University of Wyoming, University Counseling Center, PO Box 3708, Laramie, WY 82071, 307-766-2187. Dr. Pat McGinley.

U.S.A. -- NATIONWIDE

Forty Plus Clubs. A nationwide network of voluntary, autonomous nonprofit clubs, manned by its unemployed members, paying no salaries, supported by initiation fees and monthly dues. At this writing, there are clubs in the following cities: Buffalo, Chicago, Columbus, Colorado Springs, Dallas, Denver, Fort Collins, Honolulu, Houston, Los Angeles, New York, Oakland (California), Philadelphia, Salt Lake City, Toronto, and Washington, D. C. If you live in one of these cities, you can check the white pages of your Phone Book; also you can call Forty Plus of New York, 15 Park Row, New York, NY 10038, 212-233-6086 to get current information about any of the nationwide locations -- to see if the club is still there, and what their current address and phone number are.

For further nationwide information:

Bastress, Frances, *The Relocating Spouse's Guide to Employment: Options and Strategies in the U.S. and Abroad.* Woodley Publications, 4620 Derussey Parkway, Chevy Chase, MD 20815.

Adams, Bob, ed., *The 1989 National Job Bank (4th Edition).* Bob Adams, Inc., 260 Center St., Holbrook, MA 02343. 1988. Information on 10,000 of the nation's largest companies. *Very expensive; see if your local library has it.*

CANADA

Robin T. **Hazell** & Associates, 60 St. Clair Ave., E., Toronto, Ontario M4T 1N5, 416-961-3700.

Peat Marwick Stevenson & Kellogg, 90 Sparks St., 10th Fl., Ottawa, Ontario K1P 5T8, 613-238-6512.

YMCA Career Planning & Development, 15 Breadalbane St., Toronto, Canada M4Y 2V5, 416-324-4123.

FOREIGN

Cabinet Daniel Porot, Rue des Vollandes 40, 1207 Geneve, Switzerland, 0114122 7 35 00 14. Daniel Porot, Founder.

Castle Consultants Corporation, 15 White House, Vicarage Crescent, London SW11 3LJ. Walt Hopkins, Founder and Director.

Kessler-Laufbahnberatung, Dorfstr. 55, CH 8715, Bollingen, Switzerland, 055 28 22 80. Peter Kessler, Owner.

Raadgevend Bureau Claessens, B.V., Head Office Zeist, Hoog Beek & Royen, Driebergseweg l, 3708 JA Zeist, Netherlands. Franz Claessens, Founder and Director. This organization has many branch offices throughout W. Germany, Belgium and the Netherlands. Write to the head office for the additional locations.

*Robert J. **Bisdee & Associates,** 22 Allenby Ave., Malvern E., Victoria, Australia 3145, 613-885-4716. Dr. Bob Bisdee, Director.

Centre for WorkLife Counselling, P.O. Box 407, Spit Junction, Australia 2088, 02-969-4548. Paul Stevens, Director.

All the foreign counselors listed immediately above, except Paul Stevens, have attended my two-week workshop.

(Text continued from page 335)

in their job-hunt or career-change; most of these places listed here are here at their own request. We, of course, ask them some detailed questions, before listing them, but obviously at this distance we are in no position to make any final judgement as to their expertise. So, it may be that some unhelpful places got included, even as many good places got left out. To be sure, we never **knowingly** continue to list a place that three or more of our readers have found very unhelpful. *So, if you had a bad experience with any of them, you will help other readers by letting us know (our address is in the rear of this book, on the UPDATE form).*

But even with this pruning, the fact remains: you **must** do your own research, comparison shopping, and sharp questioning before you ever sign up with **anyone**. If you don't comparison shop, you will deserve whatever you get (or don't get). Often you could easily have discovered whether a particular counselor is competent or not, before you ever gave them any of your money, simply by asking the right questions during your preliminary research. The just response to many a sad tale (which we often hear) is, "I'm sorry indeed to hear that you 'got taken'; that is an unfortunate experience, and I've been through it myself. But -- as the Scots would say -- "Ya dinna do your homework."

3. SOME QUESTIONS, BY MEANS OF WHICH YOU MAY BE ABLE TO SEPARATE THE SHEEP FROM THE GOATS

Choose, from the Sampler above, from your friends' recommendations, or from the phone book, **at least three places or counselors. VISIT IN PERSON EACH OF THE THREE PLACES YOU HAVE CHOSEN.** These are exploratory visits only. Leave your wallet and your checkbook home, please! You are only comparison shopping at this point, not decision reaching!!

Make this unmistakably clear, when you are setting up the appointment for the interview.

You will need a notebook. In this notebook, *before* you go to see each career counselor (or firm), you will need to write out the following questions. And, as you ask the questions at each place, take time to write down some notes, (or direct quotes) of their answers, please! *Don't* trust your memory.

You may prefer to make four columns across your notebook, so that it will be easier to compare the places, after you have visited all three:

At each place, with each counselor, ask every one of these questions -- omitting none.

- *What is their program?* When all gimmicks are set aside (and some have great ones, like rehearsing for interviews on closed circuit TV, or using videotape or cassettes to record your skills or your resume, etc.) what are they offering: is it basically "the numbers game" **or** is it some variation of the creative minority's prescription?

- *Who will be doing it?* Do you get the feeling that you must do most of it, with their basically assuming the role of coach? (if so, three cheers); or do you get the feeling that everything (including decision making about what you do, where you do it, etc.) will be done for you (if so, three warning bells should go off in your head)?

- *What guarantee is there that it will work?* If they make it clear that they have had a good success rate, but if you fail to work hard at the whole process, then there is no guarantee you are going to find a job, give them three stars. On the other hand, if they practically guarantee you a job, and say they have never had a client that failed to find a job, no matter what, **watch out.** Pulmotor job-counseling is very suspect; lifeless bodies make poor employees.

- *Are you face-to-face, and talking, with the actual persons who will be working with you, should you decide to become a client?* As we said earlier, you should be aware that some job-hunting or career counseling firms have professional salespeople who introduce you to the company, convince you of their 100% integrity and charm, secure your decision, get you to sign the contract, and then you never see them again. You work with someone entirely different (or a whole team). *Ask the person you are talking to, if they are the one (and the only one) you will be working with, should you eventually decide to become a client.* If they say No, ask to meet those who would actually be

MY SEARCH FOR A GOOD CAREER COUNSELOR

Questions	Answer from Counselor #1	Answer from Counselor #2	Answer from Counselor #3
1. What is their program?			
2. Who will be doing it?			
3. Guarantee?			
4. Who is the actual counselor?			

working with you -- even if it's a whole battery of people. When you actually meet them, there are three considerations you should weigh:

(1) *Do you like the counselor?* Bad vibes can cause great difficulties, even if this person is extremely competent. Don't dismiss this factor!

(2) *How long has the counselor been doing this?* Ask them! And what training did they have for it? (Legitimate questions; if they get huffy, politely thank them for their time, and take your leave gently *but firmly.*) Some agencies hire former clients as new staff. Such new staff are sometimes given only "on-the-job training." Since you're paying (you hope) for Expertise already acquired, you have a *right* to ask about this before making up your mind. Incidentally, beware of double phrases such as "I've had eighteen years' experience in the business and career counseling world." What that may mean is: seventeen and a half years as a fertilizer salesman, and one half year doing career counseling. Persist. "How long have you been doing **formal career counseling**, as you are here?"

(3) *How much time will they give you?* As a minimum? As a maximum? (There's got to be a maximum, no matter what they may at first claim. Every career counselor runs into extremely dependent types as clients,

who would be there all day every day if the counselor or the firm didn't have some policy about time limits. **Press** to find out what it is, just so you'll know.) Over how long a period can you use their services? And, **will they put this in writing?** *That's* the question that separates the men from the boys, and the women from the girls.

• *What is the cost of their services? Is it paid hourly, as you go along, or must it all be paid "up front" before you even start?* You will discover that there are some career counselors that charge you an hourly rate, just as a therapist might. The fee normally ranges between $50 and $85 an hour. Each time you keep an appointment, you pay them at the end of that hour (or hours) for their help. There is no written contract. You signed nothing. You can stop seeing them at any time, if you feel you are not getting the help you wish. Obviously, this sort of arrangement is very much **to the advantage of the job-hunter**. However, you will also discover that there are some career counselors or agencies that, by contrast, have a policy of requiring you to pay for the entire "program" before you start -- or shortly after you start. There is **always** a written contract. You **must** sign it. (If you are married, your spouse will usually be invited to come in, before the contract is signed; you may suspect this is to help "sell" them on the idea of the contract, so they then can sell you. You may be right.) The fee normally ranges between $600 and $10,000.

The contract sometimes allows it to be paid in installments, but you **are** obligated to pay it, one way or the other. You are sometimes **verbally** told that you can get your money back, or a portion of it, at any time, should you be dissatisfied with the career counselor's services. This is often **not** in the written contract. Verbal promises, without witnesses, are difficult if not impossible to enforce. The written contract takes precedence. Sometimes the written contract will provide for a partial refund, up to a certain cut-off point in the program. There is **always** a cut-off point; and many times it is calculated by the counselor or agency in a manner other than the way **you** are calculating it. Consequently you are beyond the cut-off point, and the possibility of any refund, before you know it. Or, you reach the cut-off point and allow it to pass because you are, up to that point, satisfied with their services, and you have been led to believe there is much more to come. Only, there isn't. Once the cut-off point is passed, the career counselor becomes harder and harder to get ahold of.

Clearly this second financial arrangement (as opposed to the hourly) is **to the advantage of the career counselor or agency,** more than it is to the advantage of the job-hunter. There's nothing inherently meritorious about paying someone a whole lot of money before he or she has performed any of the services they say they are going to perform. If you should become increasingly dissatisfied with the counseling or "program" as it progresses, you may be "out" a lot of dough. With no legal recourse.

And so, the moral of this tale:

Don't pay any fee that you can't afford to lose.

While you are still doing your information gathering on the three places, find out which of these two financial arrangements the counselor or agency requires. If a contract will be involved, ask for a copy of it, take it home, and show it to a good lawyer.

Having gotten the information *you* want, and therefore having accomplished *your* purpose for this particular visit, you politely thank them for their time and trouble, and depart. You then go on to two other places, and ask the very same questions, please! There ought to be no charges involved for such comparison shopping visits as this, and if they subsequently bill you, inquire politely whether or not a mistake has been made by their accounting department (good thinking). If they persist in billing you, pay a visit to your local friendly Better Business Bureau, and lodge a nice unfriendly complaint against the firm in question. You'd be surprised at how many firms experience **instant repentance** when the Better Business Bureau phones them. *(They don't want a complaint on their BBB record.)*

BACK HOME NOW, after visiting the three places you chose for your comparison shopping, you have to decide: a) whether you want none of the three, or b) one of the three and if so, which one.

Look over your notes on all three places. Compare those places. Time for thought, maybe using some others as a sounding board: marriage partner, business friend, consultant friend, placement center, buddy, *primary other* or anyone whose judgement you trust.

Remember, you DON'T have to choose **any** of the three counselors, if you didn't really care for any of them. Listen to your intuition. If that is the case, then choose three new counselors, dust off the notebook, and go out again.

It may take a few more hours to find what you want. But remember: the wallet, the purse, the job-hunt, the life, that you save will be your own.

Addendum: IF YOU ARE A CAREER COUNSELOR, OR WANT TO BE ONE

If you liked the subject matter of this book a lot (and, even more, another book of mine called *The Three Boxes of Life and How to Get Out of Them*), you will of course be thinking about the possibility of becoming a career counselor yourself. Those just getting started in the field of career counseling (inside or outside academia) will, of course, want to read this current edition of *Parachute* from cover to cover, and then **do** all the exercises within it, before they inflict them on their helpless students or clients. *Teaching is Sharing, and Sharing should only follow Experiencing.*

Among the following listings, you will find a number of aids designed to help you with that Sharing.

Periodicals or Newsletters:

Career Planning & Adult Development Newsletter, published monthly by the Career Planning and Adult Development Network, 4965 Sierra Rd., San Jose, CA 95132. Richard L. Knowdell, Editor.

CNews: Career Opportunities News, Garrett Park Press, Box 190, Garrett Park, MD 20896. Useful news for counselors (and job-hunters) about employment fields, fellowships, new books, etc.

Career Waves, published four times a year, with Dr. Howard Figler and other contributors. Publishes such articles as "What is Career Counseling, Really?," "Good Work Can Be Found Anywhere," etc. Career Research Publications, P.O. Box 28799, Santa Ana, CA 92799-8799.

**The Journal of Employment Counseling*, a professional journal concerned with research, theory, and new and improved job counseling techniques and tools. The official publication of the National Employment Counselors Association, a division of the American Association for Counseling and Development, 5999 Stevenson Ave., Alexandria, VA 22304.

All the above periodicals or newsletters have a subscription fee. We recommend that you write to them for information and a sample issue, before subscribing.

Books:

*Brown, Duane, Brooks, Linda, and Associates, *Career Choice and Development*. Second Edition. Jossey-Bass Inc., Publishers, 350 Sansome St., San Francisco, CA 94104. 1990. Describes various approaches to career development.

*Hall, Douglas T., and Associates, *Career Development in Organizations*. Jossey-Bass Inc., Publishers, 350 Sansome St., San Francisco, CA 94104. 1986.

Azrin, Nathan H., and Besalel, Victoria A., *Job Club Counselor's Manual: A Behavioral Approach to Vocational Counseling*. Pro-Ed, 8700 Shoal Creek Blvd., Austin, TX 78758, 512-451-3246. For any counselor interested in working with job-hunters more than one at a time, this work is *mandatory* reading. Nathan invented the job club idea, and when followed *faithfully* it has a very high success rate (over 90%). Problem is: every technique described in Nathan's book was designed to eliminate some difficulty or obstacle to your client's job-hunt, and each time you try to take shortcuts with his program and cut out *this* technique or *that* (as counselors are *very* wont to do), you *re-introduce* into your client's job-hunt the problem that the technique was designed to eliminate. Therefore, if you're going to use this manual, use it *faithfully*.

Gysbers, Norman C., with Moore, Earl J., *Career Counseling: Skills and Techniques for Practitioners*. Prentice-Hall, Englewood Cliffs, NJ 07632. 1987.

The Guide to Basic Skills Jobs, Vol. 1. RPM Press, Inc., Verndale, MN 56481. 1986. A catalog of viable jobs for individuals with only basic work skills. This volume identifies 5,000 major occupations within the U.S. economy which require no more than an eighth grade level of education, and no more than one year of specific vocational preparation. Immensely useful book if you counsel that kind of job-hunter.

Career & Job Search Instruction Made Easy, JIST Works, Inc., The Job Search People, 720 North Park Ave., Indianapolis, IN 46202. 1-800-648-JIST.

Job Information and Seeking Training Program Instructor's Guide and Job Seekers Workbook. 1980. JIST Works, Inc., 720 North Park Ave., Indianapolis, IN 46202. 1-800-648-JIST.

Kimeldorf, Martin, *Job Search Education*. Educational Design, Inc., 47 W. 13 St., New York, NY 10011. 1985.

Johnson, Miriam, *The State of the Art in Job Search Training*, Olympus

Publishing Co., Box 9362, Salt Lake City, UT 84109. 1982. "The state of the art" at least as it was in '82.

Baxter, Neale, *Opportunities in Counseling and Development.* VGM Career Horizons, 4255 W. Touhy Ave., Lincolnwood, IL 60646-1975. 1986.

Feingold, S. Norman, and Atwater, Maxine H., *New Emerging Careers: Today, Tomorrow, and in the 21st Century.* Garrett Park Press, Box 190B, Garrett Park, MD 20896. 1988.

Edwards, Patsy B., *Leisure Counseling Techniques.* Constructive Leisure, 511 N. La Cienega Blvd., Los Angeles, CA 90048.

Porot, Daniel, *Comment Trouver Une Situation.* Les Editions d'Organisations, 5, rue Rousselet, F-75007 Paris. 1985. If you read French, this is Daniel's approach to the job-hunt. Since he is *the* expert in Europe, this is well worth reading.

Raelin, Joseph A., *Building a Career: The Effect of Initial Job Experiences and Related Work Attitudes on Later Employment.* W.E. Upjohn Institute for Employment Research, 300 S. Westnedge Ave., Kalamazoo, MI 49007. 1980.

Lathrop, Richard, *The Job Market.* The National Center for Job-Market Studies, Box 3651, Washington, DC 20007. *What would happen if we decreased the length of the job-hunt in America,* and other iconoclastic ideas which are also eminently sensible.

U.S. Dept. of Labor, Bureau of Labor Statistics, *Handbook of Labor Statistics.* Supt. of Documents, U.S. Govt. Printing Office, Washington, DC 20402.

Feingold, S. Norman, and Hansard-Winkler, Glenda Ann, *900,000 Plus Jobs Annually: Published Sources of Employment Listings.* Garrett Park Press, Box 190, Garrett Park, MD 20896.

See also the bibliography in Appendix B, for information on books that are related to particular client populations that you desire to counsel. For example, if you wish to counsel people with limited education, see Section 28 there; if you wish to counsel college students, see Section 29. For books written particularly for counselors, see the AACD Catalog, American Association for Counseling and Development, 5999 Stevenson Ave., Alexandria, VA 22304.

Perspectives:

The essence of the job-hunt is **information** (about oneself, and about the job-market), and the brain is the repository of that information. Working with job-hunters or career-changers, you will find that it is *immensely* helpful to know something about how the brain works.

As we have all read in learned journals (*like, airline magazines*), the human brain has two sides to it. And while it is tempting to build out of this a complete dichotomy between left and right sides of the brain, the truth is that each brain function or skill (*like* spatial visualization) involves *both* left and right sides, in varying proportions. (*In the case of spatial visualization, it is something like a 2 to 1 ratio, in favor of the right side.*) One can, of course, speak of *right* **vs.** *left,* as long as one is clear that this is allegorical or symbolic *representation,* rather than literal physical fact.

Books that can give you a broad overview of the subject, include the following:

*Edwards, Betty, *Drawing on the Right Side of the Brain: A Course in Enhancing Creativity and Artistic Confidence*. Revised ed. J. P. Tarcher, Inc., 5858 Wilshire Blvd., Los Angeles, CA 90036. 1989. Absolutely top-notch -- a book that's fun to look at, and fun to read. In this greatly revised edition, Betty emphasizes that being able to draw depends on five *perceptual* skills: the perception of *edges*, the perception of *spaces*, the perception of *relationships*, the perception of *lights and shadows*, and the perception of *the whole*, or *gestalt*. In this book she teaches those skills. The experienced **career counselor** will understand immediately the parallels to these five skills that exist in job-hunting. The experienced **life/work planner** will understand immediately the parallels to these five that exist in mastering life. A monumentally important book.

Herrmann, Ned, *The Creative Brain*. Brain Books, 2075 Buffalo Creek Rd., Lake Lure, NC 28746. 1988. New and wonderful, if expensive. Ned is probably *the* expert in the country who does seminars about the brain. If you're interested in this subject, you need to know *everything* he has put in print thus far. He is particularly good on the subject of what brain-profiles characterize *particular* occupations.

Segalowitz, Sid J., *Two Sides of the Brain: Brain Lateralization Explored*. Prentice-Hall, Sylvan Way, Englewood Cliffs, NJ 07632. 1983. One of the best on explaining the two sides of the brain to the neophyte.

Springer, Sally P., and Deutsch, Georg, *Left Brain, Right Brain*. Revised. W.H. Freeman and Co., 660 Market St., San Francisco, CA 94104. Another fine book on the same subject.

Ornstein, Robert, *Multimind: A New Way of Looking at Human Behavior*. Houghton Mifflin Co., 2 Park St., Boston, MA 02108. 1986.

Books must, in the very nature of things, lag somewhat behind the fast-moving discoveries about the brain's functioning. Hence, the need for periodicals in this field. The two I like best:

Brain/Mind Bulletin. Marilyn Ferguson, ed. Interface Press, Box 42211, 4717 N. Figueroa St., Los Angeles, CA 90042.

The International Brain Dominance Review, published by Ned & Margie Herrmann, 2075 Buffalo Creek Rd., Lake Lure, NC 28746.

Instruments:

This, of course, is a wide-world. There are a *million* instruments out there: the Strong-Campbell Interest Inventory, the Myers-Briggs, and a host of others -- including my own *Quick Job-Hunting (and Career-Changing) Map: How to Create A Picture of Your Ideal Job or Next Career* -- found in Appendix A here. Aside from that *Map*, my favorites are:

"The Herrmann Brain Dominance Instrument." For those of you who want to find out more about how "left-brained," "right-brained," or "double-dominant" you are, Ned Herrmann has produced this very interesting measure of same. You can contact him at the above address for details as to how to get your hands on it.

"The Self-Directed Search." This is a self-marking test created by John L. Holland, which you can use to discover your "Holland code" and what occupations you might **start** your research with. You can order an SDS Specimen Set for less than $5, which includes the SDS, a brief *Occupations Finder* and a booklet "You and Your Career," from the publisher, Psychological Assessment Resources, Inc., Box 998, Odessa, FL 33556.

To further help you understand and/or use this instrument there is:

Holland, John L., Ph.D., *The Alphabetized Occupations Finder.* This puts the little *Occupations Finder,* mentioned above, into alphabetical order. For use with the Self-Directed Search. Psychological Assessment Resources, Inc., Box 998, Odessa, FL 33556. 1-800-331-TEST. In Florida 1-813-968-3003. 1986.

The background theory for all of this is carefully explained in:

Holland, John L., *Making Vocational Choices. A Theory of Vocational Personalities and Work Environments,* 2nd ed., Prentice-Hall, Inc., Sylvan Avenue, Englewood Cliffs, NJ 07632. 1985. John Holland is one of my favorite people, and this is one of my favorite books. I think it is a **must** for counselors, and very **helpful** to any job-hunter who is looking for a system by which to understand all jobs. Unfortunately, Prentice-Hall has raised its price until it is now over $20 -- *for a 150-page **paperback.*** (I have a policy of not mentioning prices in this book -- because they change so constantly -- but this one is **worth** mentioning.) Also since I have never seen this book in a bookstore, except a college bookstore where it was one of the required texts for some course, if you cannot find it in your local library or you want a permanent copy for your very own, you will **have** to order it directly from the publisher, address above. Phone: 800-223-1360, or 201-767-5937. In so doing, mention the title code number 547596, and the fact that you want the paperback copy.

Once you have found your "Holland code" from the SDS (Self-Directed Search) instrument, I recommend you use the *Dictionary of Holland Occupational Codes* (see section 21, in Appendix B), instead of the more limited *Occupations Finder.*

> *For other instruments available to you, see:* Kapes, Jerome T., and Mastie, Marjorie Moran, eds., *A Counselor's Guide to Career Assessment Instruments.* 2nd ed. Published by the National Career Development Association, a division of AACD, 5999 Stevenson Ave., Alexandria, VA 22304.

Film, Audiotape, Videotape:

Wallach, Ellen J., with Fulford, Nancy, *Career Management: When Preparation Meets Opportunity. Leader's Guide.* AMA Film/Video, 85 Main St., Watertown, MA 02172. An excellent manual, designed to go with the film of the same title, in order to help you to use the film to serve a number of purposes: if you (as counselor) are trying to sell decision makers on the benefits of career management to their organization; or if you want to inform managers about the benefits of career management as part of an overall human resource system; or if you are working with HR professionals to assess organizational career management needs and/or to design a systems approach to career management; or if you want to give individual employees, their managers, or HR professionals an overview of career management; or if you are training personnel who are charged with career guidance responsibilities; or if you want to conduct a career management workshop; or if you are approached by an employee or manager seeking individual career counseling.

Sladey, Pat, *Find the job you want . . . and get it!* A four-**audiocassette** program, on the subjects: Find the Hidden Job Market; Sell Yourself in the Interview; Prepare Winning Resumes & Letters; and Stay Motivated During the Search. Available from: Pat Sladey & Associates, P.O. Box 440352, Aurora, CO 80044. *There is also a **videotape** version of the program, on four videocassettes.*

1991 Catalog. Wintergreen Software, Inc., P.O. Box 1229, Madison, WI 53701. Lists other videos on the subject of the job-hunt.

Computer Software:

The computer is a wonderful tool. I use one all day long, every day that I work (*for the curious, a Macintosh IIx with color screen, or a Macintosh Plus with Radius screen, or a Macintosh Portable*). Nonetheless, my personal opinion is that computer software *for career counselors or job-hunters* is mostly still in the Dark Ages. What help computer software does give with choosing careers is *simplistic*; what help it gives with the actual job-hunt is *elementary* -- except perhaps in the area of resumes.

However, for those who wish to explore this arena further, I list here one journal series of articles, three directories and some *examples* of what is 'out there,' most of which costs less than $150 -- on down to $40. ***Their listing here is not, however, to be construed as a recommendation, in any sense of the word. Reread the previous paragraph*.**

Journal

*"Computers in Career Planning," Summer 1987 issue of *Career Planning: An Adult Development Journal.* To order call 408-559-4946.

Directories

*Walz, Garry R., and Bleuer, Jeanne C., and Maze, Marilyn, *Counseling Software Guide: A Resource for the Guidance and Human Development Professions.* AACD (American Association for Counseling and Development), 5999 Stevenson Ave., Alexandria, VA 22304. 1989. Has 48 pages of reviews of career counseling software, most of which software is targeted at high-school populations, and has to do with elementary career choice, rather than job-search.

**The Personnel Software Census.* Advanced Personnel Systems, P.O. Box 1438, Roseville, CA 95661. Has sections on 'Career Management' and 'Job Search/Resume Writing.' Lists about 20 programs in those two categories. An even more up-to-date listing is available on disk.

**1991 Catalog*. Wintergreen Software, Inc., P.O. Box 1229, Madison, WI 53701. Lists software not found in any other catalog; also videotapes.

Examples of Programs

**Life and Career Planning*. Thoughtware, Inc., P.O. Box 011151, Miami, FL 33101-1151. Self-assessment of life and career, leading to an identification of individual training needs. For IBM computers and compatibles.

*Gonyea, James C., *The Perfect Career*. Mindscape, 3444 Dundee Road, Northbrook, IL 60062. Has a database of 615 occupations. For IBM computers and compatibles.

**Eureka Skills Inventory: Micro Skills I.* Wintergreen Software, Inc., P.O. Box 1229, Madison, WI 53701. For high school students on up to adults. Helps identify transferable skills from past experiences, then summarize them, match them to Holland Codes and compare to a database of 390 occupations. For IBM computers and compatibles; also Apple II+, IIc, IIe. Most expensive program listed here.

**The Computerized D.O.T.: Dictionary of Occupational Titles, 1977 Edition and 1986 Supplement.* Wintergreen Software, Inc., P.O. Box 1229, Madison, WI 53701. The complete D.O.T., computerized. You can ask for an occupation by number, part of a number, title, or part of a title, or G.O.E. number. For IBM computers and compatibles. 15 floppy disks. (It is recommended you have a hard disk.)

**Career Navigator.* Drake Beam Morin, Inc., 100 Park Ave., New York, NY 10017. Computer-based training and guidance during one's job-search. For IBM computers and compatibles.

*Studner, Peter K., *The Super-Search™ System.* Jamenair Ltd., P.O. Box 241957, Los Angeles, CA 90024. A book plus software. The software has the book's resumes on disk, plus databases of contacts, and computerizes one's job-hunt journey. For IBM computers and compatibles.

*Jackson, Tom, *The Perfect Resume Computer Kit.* Permax Systems Inc., P.O. Box 6455, Madison, WI 53716-0455. Assists in preparing resumes, based on Tom's very popular book. Enables the user to prepare customized, target resumes. There is both a Personal Version and a Counselor's Version. For IBM computers and compatibles.

**Resume Writer.* Schonberg Associates, Inc., 2368 Victory Pkwy., Cincinnati, OH 45206. A book plus software. Comes in business or student editions. For IBM computers and compatibles.

Training:

There are countless training opportunities for career counselors in the U.S. and abroad. *Career Planning & Adult Development Newsletter,* mentioned earlier (published monthly by the Career Planning and Adult Development Network, 4965 Sierra Rd., San Jose, CA 95132) maintains a very good calendar of these events, and anyone interested in further training would be well advised to be receiving this *Newsletter.*

Whenever the subject of training comes up, I am asked (endlessly) whether or not *I* do any teaching. We receive hundreds of letters each year asking this. Since I would like to cut down on the mail and also save *you* some trouble, I will give you the desired information, right here.

The only real teaching I do is in *one* annual event, held every August, where I teach nonstop for fifteen days, along with my esteemed colleague from Europe, Daniel Porot, whose insights you have seen frequently referred to, in the main body of this book. We call it:

Fifteen Days of
LIFE/Work Planning
with Vacation
at the Inn of the Seventh Mountain

This is not, as its name would suggest, held in the Orient. The Inn of the Seventh Mountain is a beautiful and popular resort on the outskirts of **Bend, Oregon,** which -- as everyone knows -- is in the center of the United States (Honolulu is 3,000 miles to the West, New York City is 3,000 miles to the East).

The workshop is now fifteen days in length. It is always in August, always the first Friday through the third Saturday. In 1991, the dates are August 2–17. Since fifteen days is a long time, and people who attend usually do so in lieu of their regular summer vacation, we have deliberately put this workshop at a first-class vacation resort, which past participants have absolutely delighted in -- as they can 'have their cake and eat it, too.' *Or, to be more exact, they can have their vacation and still learn a lot.* The Inn has two swimming pools, waterslide, hot baths/saunas, hiking trails, tennis, whitewater rafting, horseback riding, moped rental, bicycle rental, roller-skating, ski-lifts to the top of Mount Bachelor, and other vacation amenities, outdoor eating -- with *wonderful* food -- all in a lovely pine-forest setting near the foot of a large mountain topped with snow even in the summertime. So, you may think of these whole fifteen days as: *Vocation mit Vacation.*

The workshop is led, from beginning to end, by Daniel and myself; we teach as a team. Daniel's expertise is really quite dazzling. And since we want this to be the finest training that career counselors can find anywhere, other distinguished leaders in the career development field sometimes lecture in the evenings. In the past these guest lecturers have included the late John Crystal, Sidney Fine, Arthur Miller, and Bob Wegmann. The total training at this workshop exceeds 100 hours. Normally between 40 and 70 people enroll, each year. In the past they have come from the U.S. (of course), Canada, Central America, England, France, Holland, Belgium, Switzerland, New Zealand, Australia, Singapore and Indonesia. They have embraced ages 17–74, and all ethnic groups.

We have been told by the hundreds of counselors who have attended since 1974 that they find this to be the most thoroughgoing training in the art of career counseling and life/work planning that is available anywhere in the world today. Maybe it is, and maybe it isn't. But one thing it is, for sure. **It is fun.** Year after year people say that this was close to the most enjoyable fifteen days of their entire life. *Be sure to bring your playful self.*

The cost of the entire workshop -- the tuition -- is $1,200 for these fifteen days. This includes all materials and sessions.

The cost of what we choose to call the vacation part -- the room and board at the Inn, with all its facilities -- is additional, and will run you (*or your institution*) around $90 a day *for your room, breakfast, lunch, dinner, and three refreshment breaks each day* -- though this sum can vary, depending on the type of accommodations you want.

If you wish more information about the workshop, and/or a registration blank, you should write to:

Erica Chambré, Registrar
Two-Week Workshop
What Color Is Your Parachute?
P.O. Box 379
Walnut Creek, CA 94597

Phone No.: 1-415-935-1865 (10 a.m.–4:30 p.m. Monday thru Friday, Pacific Coast Time) **After October 6, 1991**, this number will be 1-510-935-1865.
Fax No.: 1-415-932-4864 **After October 6, 1991**, this number will be 1-510-932-4864

If you are interested in attending in a particular year, you are required to register by June 1st of that year, since the Inn releases all its rooms to the general public at that time. We *have* squeezed people in as late as July 15th *if the rooms at the Inn weren't fully booked by then (they often are -- as it is a* **very** *popular resort).*

I should mention that this workshop is open to **people who are not career counselors;** and each year many 'non-counselors' attend -- job-hunters of all ages, career-changers, homemakers, union organizers, CEOs, teachers, people facing a move, people facing retirement, the recently divorced, college students, clergy and so forth. It is also attended by people from all over the world. Our methodology at this workshop is to have you master the principle of life/work planning by rigorously applying them to *your own life* during the two weeks, rather than discussing the problems of clients or their case histories, etc., as is often the fashion these days. Because of this methodology, **the workshop is useful to anyone.**

Every disabled person has the choice
of either 'crying the blues' about their
disability every day of their life, or realistically
acknowledging what they have to do in
order to have a successful, productive life.

The Disability Rag

Appendix D

Job-Hunting Tips For the So-called 'Handicapped' Or People Who Have Disabilities

A Brief Foreword,
Being a Short Course on Disabilities
For those of us who do not (yet) have a disability.

A disability is traditionally defined as *any impairment of some major life activity, that lasts six months or longer.* Typically, it is a permanent impairment. There are, by the the most recently published government census (August, 1989), 13.4 million working-age people in this country who have such an impairment of a major life activity. When to these are added those *under* age 16 or *over* age 64 who have disabilities, the total population of persons with disabilities is commonly estimated to be between 43 and 50 million -- though no one knows how to get an exact count.

Vocabulary is very important to people with disabilities. Generalizations are difficult to make, because vocabulary is hotly debated even within the disabled community. But, *as a general rule,* they prefer to be called "people . . ." or "a person with a disability," thus making them **a person primarily**, and one with a disability secondarily. "Disabled" is second on their list of preferred terms. "Handicapped" has come into great disfavor, although of course it remains up, in many public signs. (Also, managers in various companies often use the term "handicapped" to characterize those already disabled before they begin working at that company, while they reserve the term "disabled" for those who were not disabled when they were hired but became disabled *on the job.*)

Those *in* a wheelchair now generally prefer to be called "those who *use* a chair," since 75% of those who use a chair can get up and move out of it. The former "mentally retarded" now prefer to be called "cognitively disabled." The former "mentally ill" now prefer to be called "emotionally disabled" or "psychiatrically disabled" or "the stabilized mentally ill." The former "physically handicapped" now generally prefer to be called "functionally disabled." "The blind" generally prefer to be called "people who are blind," though some who are not totally blind prefer "visually impaired," "partially sighted," or "print impaired." The deaf generally prefer to be called "people who are deaf," though some who are not totally deaf prefer "a person with a hearing impairment."

About 36% of men with disabilities who are of working age (16–64) are **in the labor force** or *actively seeking work*; for disabled women that figure is 28%. This means 64% of disabled men and 72% of disabled women are *not* in the labor force. These latter percentages are often quoted as the unemployment rate among people with disabilities, though technically one is unemployed only if one *wants* to work, but cannot *find* employment. Nonetheless, even with some allowance for this fact, people with disabilities remain **the group with by far the highest unemployment rate in the U.S. today**. One in five adults with a work disability falls below the poverty line. Experts say that with the necessary support, *at least* 5 million more people with disabilities between the ages of 16 and 64 could be working and want to work. This, of course, represents an untapped labor pool which employers will *have* to pay attention to, along with minorities and the elderly, *if* the labor shortage that has long been predicted, does in fact materialize during the 1990s.

Before this untapped **labor pool** of people with disabilities can be utilized, employers will have to discard many of the myths they believe without thinking -- such as: "People who are retarded can only do single-step repetitious tasks, and they don't mind." Or: "The kind of work people who are deaf should do is work in noisy rooms." Or: "The only place people who are blind can really flourish is in darkrooms."

It is instructive to consider the kinds of jobs people with disabilities actually hold. Let us take people who are blind as an example. The kind of full-time jobs they hold down, include: artists, auto mechanics, ballerinas, beekeepers, bicycle repair people, boat builders, carpenters, chiropractors, college professors, counselors (drug/alcohol/youth/marriage), court reporters, dispatchers for 911 or for transportation companies, fingerpainters, fish-cleaners, food service management, inventors, lawyers, licensed practical nurses, machinists, managers of snack stands and cafeterias in federal and other government buildings, marketing specialists, massage therapists, medical and legal transcribers, models (on runways as well as for magazines), musicians, packagers/assemblers in all kinds of manufacturing, painters, peanut vendors in stands at basketball or football games, professional story tellers, psychiatrists, public relations people, sculptors, strippers, teachers, word processing and data entry people, writers -- and various kinds of self-employment. And this is only a sampling.

What kinds of salaries do people with disabilities make? Well, male workers with disabilities who are working full-time *averaged* $24,200 in annual salary during 1987, while female workers in the same category averaged $15,796. *These figures equalled 81% and 84% respectively, of what their nondisabled counterparts earned, on average, in 1987. (These ratios were a drop from the 91% and 88% ratios attained as recently as 1980.) This disparity (between wages offered a person without a disability and a person with a disability) is shown most dramatically by how a person with a* new *disability is treated, once they become disabled. For example, a roofer earning $40,000 from their employer before a disabling accident, may be offered as little as $12,000* after *the accident.*

While the *average salary earned* seems respectable, it must be set over against the economic **disincentives** for *ever* going to work, once one has a disability and is receiving some sort of disability payments from one's former employer, the State or the Federal government. These disincentives include: **the cost of transportation to work**, especially for severely disabled individuals -- *which incidentally is not tax-deductible*; **the loss of sizeable medical insurance** which one may have been receiving from disability insurance or State/Federal programs (e.g., SSDI -- Social Security Disability Insurance, or SSI -- Supplemental Security Income); **the inability to get similar**

insurance from one's new employer, since private insurance companies will *never* cover 'pre-existing conditions'; **the fact that even if one finds a job, one faces a mandatory time gap of two years** between the time one may lose the job (*due to 'downsizing,' 'hostile takeovers,' or being fired*) and the time that one's old State/Federal medical insurance can be reinstated; and to these economic disincentives we may add: **the lack of physical access in many workplaces that are *otherwise* attractive places for employment;** and **lack of public transportation for the severely disabled** (especially for those who use wheelchairs and have no van or car).

What all this adds up to is that a person with a disability may receive less total income (including medical payments) if they go to work, than if they stayed home. Nonetheless, people with disabilities *still* elect to seek work, even when it is economically disadvantageous to them to do so -- even as people from 'the private sector' may go into government service, despite a similar loss of income. When people with disabilities do so, at such personal cost, it is usually because of the driving need they feel to put their God-given abilities into the service of mankind. And, secondarily, because of their need to maintain or increase their own sense of self-worth, as well as prevent their skills from deteriorating simply through disuse.

It is certainly to our nation's advantage to have every person with a disability in the work force, for the costs to the nation of their *not* working are these: the loss of the **taxes** they would otherwise pay; the loss of the money they would otherwise put into the economy, through their **purchases** of life's necessities; the loss of the **family income and taxes**, where family members are forced to take part-time work or give up work altogether; and the cost of **government funds** to support the unemployed person who has a disability.

While throughout this Appendix, I have spoken of "people with disabilities" as though they were one "tribe," there is in actual fact no such thing as a *typical* disabled person. As experts point out, every disability is a mix of three things: **An Event** (the disability), **The Individual** (his or her attitude, resources, etc.), and **The Environment** (how friendly or barring it is to that disability, how much support it offers that Individual). The outcome of that mix will vary widely from one disabled person to another. The following chart, however, shows *something* of the immense varieties of disability.

Not mentioned in this chart are the varying *causes* of any particular disability. For example, if we see someone using a wheelchair, their "impairment of motion" may be due to: amputation after an auto accident, arthritis, cerebral palsy, epilepsy, muscular dystrophy, polio, spina bifida, spinal cord injuries, etc.

What do these varying causes signify? They signify that disability is not like race, or stature, or your birthplace. Where you were born, will always be so. Your race and your stature also will not change. But whether or not you are one of "the so-called handicapped or disabled," can change during the next twenty-four hours. Five out of every six people with disabilities were NOT born with that disability, but acquired it later in life. *New* causes of disability are

No Two Disabled Persons Are Alike –

Each One is a PERSON who has a disability
that has one of the characteristics on each line below:*

HIDDEN i.e., not immediately apparent to others	VISIBLE i.e., immediately or quickly apparent to others

MILD	MODERATE	SEVERE	PROFOUND

CONGENITAL i.e., it occurred either at birth or before they were 5	ADVENTITIOUS i.e., it came (*advent*) into their life after they were 5

Their impairment only limits their ability to:

SEE	HEAR	SPEAK	MOVE	THINK or LEARN	FEEL or BEHAVE	OTHER	More than one of the previous

With respect to their abilities in other areas:

They are NORMALLY GIFTED in other areas	They are EXTRAORDINARILY GIFTED in one or more other areas

Their attitude toward their disability is:

THEY SEE IT AS A DISASTER which has overwhelmed them	THEY SEE IT AS A CHALLENGE for them to overcome

Their driving motive in life (*besides survival*) is their desire for:

AFFILIATION or the need to relate to people	ACHIEVEMENT or the need to outdo their own record	EXCELLING or the need to outdo others

In dealing with their disability they are:

SOCIALLY ISOLATED hence, dealing with it essentially on their own	SOCIALLY SUPPORTED hence, dealing with it with help from others

In dealing with their **abilities** they are:

UNAWARE of what they can do, and do well, and enjoy	WELL AWARE of what they can do, and do well, and enjoy

**N.B. The categories on one line are NOT necessarily related to the categories immediately below it.*

constantly appearing; among those in the news during the past five years or so: AIDS (of course), Lyme disease, repetitive strain injury, carpal tunnel syndrome and chronic fatigue syndrome (CFS).

All of us, therefore, are only one incident away from joining this group of "people with disabilities." You can become permanently disabled with one accident at home, one falling -- on an icy step, on a slippery sidewalk, on a newly waxed floor, down a flight of stairs, off a ladder, off a roof, on a ski slope, on an amateur playing field -- one unexpected crippling illness (arthritis, heart disease, among others), one auto accident, one encounter with the wrong insect, or virus, or chemical agent. And this Appendix which you read today out of curiosity or compassion for others, may tomorrow become words you need for your very own life.

R.N.B.

Unless you are going to create your own job, looking for work is essentially a matter of finding out about a job, and then **competing** for it. That's true for *anybody*. If you are a person who happens to have a disability, what is different is that you face *tougher* competition. The rules that apply to all job-hunters therefore apply to you in double measure.

You will need *every bit* of the advice in Chapters 4, 5, and 6, and you will need to take *extra care* in doing Appendix A -- because, all of this will dramatically increase your ability to win -- over the competition. On the other hand, trying to use the advice back here in this Appendix, without taking the rest of this book seriously, is a wonderful way to sabotage your job-hunt, before you even start. If, because of your disability, or for some other reason, you can't make your own way through the crucial Appendix A -- then go seek help from family, friends, or a rehab counselor. But, one way or another, you *must* arm yourself as best you can for the competition you will face. There are hurdles or obstacles you must overcome, both 'out there' and inside yourself.

Your main obstacles 'out there' are (of course) the ignorance, fear, anxiety, prejudice, and discrimination that you will run into with employers or your future co-workers. Much of this is based on ignorance which *you* will have to dispel yourself. **As a disabled job-hunter, part of your task in job-hunting is that you will *often* have to educate would-be employers, as you go.**

The main obstacle 'inside yourself' will be the temptation to feel hopelessness. This is based, obviously, on what you already know about the nature of the world of work. Or, rather, on *what you think you know.* The sad truth is, that many of us with disabilities do ourselves believe the damaging myths that 'the world' out there believes, and uses to justify not hiring us.

And what are those myths? Their nature is evident if you just examine *the dark thoughts* that those of us with disabilities often have, when first we set out job-hunting. We compare ourselves, of course, with those who *don't* have any observable disabilities, and it comes out sounding like this:

I am disabled, they are not; *I am probably unemployable*, they are not; *I am filled with a sense of what I cannot do*, while they are filled with a sense of what they can do; *I am set apart from the rest of mankind*, they are not; *I have nothing in common with an employer*, while they do; *I have to ask the employer to redesign the job to accommodate my limitations*, while they do not.

All of these thoughts are common, all of these thoughts are understandable, but *all of these thoughts are untrue*. Moreover, treating them as though they *were* true, will inevitably cause the hopelessness you are trying to avoid.

If you examine **the true nature of the job-hunt,** you will discover that there are four reasons for you to be hopeful. Don't assume that these are commonly understood 'out there.' Mind you, these are *the very four things* that you will probably have to educate employers and others about, as you go. So, get them *very* clear in *your* mind before you go out job-hunting:

FOUR REASONS FOR HOPE

That Are Important to Those of Us with Disabilities (as well as to our Would-be Employers, Counselors, Friends, and Family)

1. Everyone is disabled. And, everyone is employable.

Let us suppose the human race had a Skills Bank, in which there was a total of 13,000 skills, and each one of us at birth had to go to that bank and choose 700 skills that we would use for the rest of our life here on earth. You and I, of course, would not choose the same 700. *You* might choose to be good at *analyzing things*, while *I* might choose to be good at *drawing*. And so forth. The varying skills we chose would make us different from one another, even unique.

But, how would you describe yourself, afterward? Would you point to the 700 things you can do, and do well? If so, you would be emphasizing **your abilities**. Or would you point to the 12,300 things that you still can't do -- even if some *other* members of the human race can? If so, you would be emphasizing **your disabilities**.

The point of this little exercise is: *everyone* has abilities, or things we *can* do. And *everyone* has disabilities, or things we *can't* do. *(The numbers 700 and 13,000 were only chosen for the sake of illustration. No one actually knows how many skills the human race has, or how many a typical individual has.)* The numbers are unimportant. The *principle* is what is important:

Everyone is **enabled**, and everyone is also **disabled.**

Everyone is **free**, and everyone is also **handicapped.** That's the nature of the life that is given to us.

If you speak of yourself only as free, enabled, and as a person with abilities, you are denying *the other side* of your nature. Or if you speak of yourself only as handicapped, disabled, and as a person with disabilities, you are denying the first side of your nature. Each and every human being is both sides.

In interpreting yourself to an employer, it is crucial for you to know this and emphasize this during an interview. You can put it quite simply, "*It's true I have a disability; all of us do. Everyone of us has things he or she cannot do well. But I am here because there are many things I can do, and do well. This is what they are . . . .*" It is these abilities of yours that make you *eminently employable*. Of course, to be able to say what they are, you *must* have done your homework on yourself (Appendix A, of course), and know *what* it is you can do and do well.

If you want the employer to think of you as both enabled and disabled -- just like every other human being -- *you must think of yourself that way too*. And be able to spell it out, in detail. Therein lies your hope.

2. Everyone is a member of many "tribes," and as a general rule employers like to hire those whom they perceive to be members of their own "tribe."

Since disability is a characteristic of us all, it follows from this that your disability ought never to stand in the way of your finding employment. Unfortunately -- as we all know too well -- it sometimes does, and those of us who happen to have obvious disabilities need to know why.

The "why" seems obvious. We run into an obstacle, which is normally called "prejudice" or "discrimination." Trouble is, while this description is true, as far as it goes, it doesn't go anywhere near far enough. Thus it ends up being a woefully inadequate description of our enemy. And when you don't know your enemy, it is almost impossible to win.

The truest description of the enemy we face in the job-hunt (and elsewhere) is **tribalism**. So, understanding tribalism is crucial to the success of your job-hunt. I am not here speaking of "tribes" as understood by Native Americans; I am speaking in a more universal sense.

A "tribe" is any group that gives individuals a feeling of "**we**," as opposed to all *the others* out there, who are "**them**." From way back in our history, we who are human have always tended to organize ourselves into "tribes," both in our thinking and in actuality.

"*Them,*" "*the others,*" may be variously defined as those who belong to a different race, a different religious group, a different nationality, a different social status, or a different economic status, than we do.

Each of us usually belongs to *several* "tribes." Our commitment to one "tribe" may be merely that of sympathy for others who are "like us" -- in this way or that; while our commitment to another "tribe" may be one of fierce loyalty and action unto the death, as in a clan or in a terrorist group.

"Tribes" come in all sizes and shapes. They may be as local as a neighborhood, or as worldwide as a religion. They may be as small as a group of "buddies," or as large as a nation, flaunting fierce patriotism. We see them in clubs, we see them at sporting events, we see them at rallies, we see them at conventions, we see them in political parties, we see them in issues like abortion, we see them when families gather at holidays, and we see them in drug gangs.

While "tribes" *can* perform truly nobly -- they will sometimes give their own members sacrificial devotion and kindness -- on the whole, tribalism has created the darkest pages of mankind's history. Ethics which normally govern daily conduct are tossed out the window when dealing with other "tribes." *One "tribe" is often singled out for particular contempt*, disdain, epithets, hatred and even physical violence. Consider what we see in Ireland, Beirut, Iran, China, Africa, Palestine, and *of course* throughout our own country, with its racism, ageism, prejudice and discrimination.

Even when "tribes" are rather benign in their conduct, they are rarely accused of showing any *sensitivity* to the needs or feelings of those who are not members of that "tribe."

Tribalism not only devastates human relations, it alters the landscape. In any particular geographic area, we see the dominant "tribe" shaping the landscape and the environment to its own liking and its own needs, without much consideration for the other "tribes" who may be living off the same land. We call this insensitive dominance one of "handicapping" the other "tribe" or "tribes." Forcing the other "tribes" to live in a harsh landscape *so far as the needs of those "tribes" are concerned*, the dominant "tribe" usually then thinks of, or calls, the other "tribes" *the handicapped.*

In our country, of course, the dominant "tribe" in charge of human relations, the landscape, and the environment, are the people who have no real impairment of 'any major life activity' -- in other words, *people without disabilities*. This "tribe" treats *the others* with great insensitivity, disdain, fear, and sometimes contempt and animosity. Naturally, this "tribe" has designed its roads, its transportation, its buildings, its doorways, its stairways, its workplaces, its amusement centers, and its bathrooms to suit itself. Needless to say, those who do not belong to this "tribe," those who do have some impairment of 'a major life activity,' *the others, "them,"* often find it difficult to get around or to work, in that inimical environment.

"Tribes," in addition to undermining human relations, and altering the landscape, usually create their own distinctive language. And so it is that the dominant "tribe" in this country, referred to above, has a language which describes themselves as: *we*, "people with abilities," "normal," or "the able-bodied"; while they call all the other "tribes" who *have* some impairment to 'a major life activity': *the others, them*, "people with disabilities," "the disabled" or "the handicapped." It would of course be more accurate if they called us: "those whom we have handicapped by the way we have shaped our environment."

Here endeth our brief course on tribalism. Now, what does all this have to do with our job-hunt? Simply this: when those of us who happen to have disabilities go out job-hunting, we are unconsciously perceived as one "tribe" trying to find employment from another "tribe." And the more *visible* our disability is -- that is, the *more* we are perceived as looking *different* from the dominant "tribe" (people without disabilities) -- the more *some* employers will feel the force of this. And since as a general rule **employers like to hire those whom they perceive to be members of their own "tribe,"** this is not good news. But it can be turned into good news, if you put your thinking cap on. Used rightly, tribalism can become the key to your getting hired.

As I said earlier, everyone is a member of **many** "tribes." Therefore, the key to your having a successful job interview is to ignore "tribes" defined by ability or disability, and **find instead some other "tribe"** in which both you and your would-be employer are members.

Did you both grow up in the same town? -- then you are members of *that* same "tribe." Did you both go to the same school? -- then you are members of *that* same "tribe." Do you both have the same hobbies? -- then you are members of *that* same "tribe." Have you both traveled to the same places? -- then you are members of *that* same "tribe." Or do you both share the same interest? -- then you are members of *that* same "tribe."

It is remarkable how many people know instinctively how important it is to establish this kinship in the same "tribe." Recently the roof of our vacation cottage in Oregon needed repairing, and when the doorbell rang, this is how the roofer began the conversation with my wife: "Carol? How are you? I'm Bill, from the roofing people. Hey, I hear you folks are from Walnut Creek. Is that true? Well, you know, I was born in the very next town, and I grew up there all my boyhood. You know where Monument Boulevard is in Pleasant Hill? Well, that's where I grew up. . . ." In approaching an employer, your job is to make this same kind of connection.

This will be easier if you do enough research on that employer *before you go in* (as described in Chapter 5), so that you have discovered some commonality between you. If you can't discover any such, *before* the interview, then *that discovery* must be your goal *during* the interview.

Once that employer feels that you are both members of *some* "tribe," in common -- despite your disability -- you will have secured that most important of all qualities in a job-interview: **rapport between you and the employer.** And this rapport is **the key** to your getting hired. Because, as I said, employers like to hire those whom they perceive to be somehow members of their own "tribe."

3. Employers never hire a stranger.

Almost every job-hunter who happens to have a disability wants to find some magical way of avoiding going face-to-face with employers. (So do most job-hunters who don't have a disability, incidentally.) Of course we know that job-hunters *have* to go face-to-face. But we hope that maybe we can plead our disability as a reason to be let off the hook, on this one. Especially if our disability is one of limited mobility. Perhaps *we* will be allowed to just communicate with the would-be employer by letter or by telephone?

No such luck! You may do some *preliminary* explorations by letter or telephone, if you wish; but in the end you will *have* to go face-to-face. And risk rejection. Just like every other job-hunter. You too, in a series of job-interviews, may hear the unnerving refrain -- you remember the formula, if you've read the body of this book (you *did*, didn't you?) -- NO NO NO NO NO NO NO NO NO NO NO YES YES. It applies to those of us who happen to have disabilities, just as much as it does to those of us who don't happen to have disabilities (yet).

The reason why you *have* to go face-to-face with a would-be employer, in spite of the possibility of rejection, is that *employers never hire a stranger.* Nathan Azrin was the first to emphasize this (*see the bibliography at the end of this Appendix*). What it means is, that in order to decide to hire you, employers have to:

a) see you,
b) like you,
c) be convinced that there is something you can do for them,
d) and then feel that because of that, they've *got* to have you.

Notice the importance of c) and d). *Some* of us with disabilities think it only takes a) and b). "*Did you get the job?*" "Yes, I did." "*Why did you get hired?*" "Because she liked me." Or: "*Did you get turned down for the job?*"

"Yes, I did." "*Why did you get turned down?*" "Because he didn't like me."

Actually, the employer may have liked you a great deal. But if you couldn't tell him (or her) what you could do for them, then *that* is why you got turned down. Few if any employers are ever going to take the time to do this homework for you. That is not their responsibility.

It's important to recall just what a job *is*. In the beginning, some man or woman decides to go into business for themselves. They want to sell a product, or information, or a service to others. To make this business succeed, they initially do *everything* themselves: making the product, or offering the service, or gathering the information all by their lonesome. In time, the business prospers, and it gets to be too much for one person to do. Our hero or heroine needs help.

What kind of help? Well, first of all they need someone to come and offer them **their time.** But they don't just need time. They need someone who, in that time, can **do the things they need to have done.** Maybe they have no time or skills, themselves, to keep their accounting books. So they need someone to come and help them who knows how to do accounting, and has the time. In exchange for that time and those accounting skills, our hero or heroine is willing to give something in return: **money.** In other words, some of their profits. This exchange turns them into an employer, and the other person into their employee. And so, a job is born.

But: employers never hire a stranger. You must go face-to-face. And, you must help them to know you, *at least a little*, in the interview -- before they will be willing to offer you a job. How can you help them to know you? By telling them **who you are**: that is, what your abilities or skills are, and thus, what you have to offer them that would persuade them to part with some of their money.

Oops, you haven't thought about that? You were only focussed on your **disability**, trying to think of how to get them to ignore it? *Tilt.* No job. You were too focussed on *who you are not*, rather than on who you are; too focussed on what you can't do, rather than on what you can do.

A bit of advice: go home, and before you visit any other employer, be sure you do *you-know-what* (Appendix A) in thorough detail. If you can't do it by yourself, for one reason or another, get a mate, a friend, a counselor, to help you. Then, next time you go for an interview, you will be ready to tell your would-be employer *who you are*, in terms of your abilities, or skills. *Good.* Because, as I said, employers never hire a stranger.

4. Everyone redesigns or modifies their job so as to highlight their abilities and get around their limitations.

It is common for those of us who have disabilities to think that when we go job-hunting, we are going to have to request something unheard of in the world of work: namely, that the job be redesigned, to accommodate our special limitations. *Wrong.*

As Sidney Fine has emphasized, *everyone* redesigns or modifies their job -- in minor ways or major. The reason for this is that no job exactly fits anyone, when they are first hired. Their new job is like an ill-fitting suit. Inevitably, it *has* to be taken in, a tuck here, a tuck there; or it has to be let out, where it is pinching or hugging too tight -- before the person is able to do their best in that job. All of us have to alter, adjust, amend, revise, fine tune, adapt, or shape each new job, in minor ways or major.

For example, let us say that a nondisabled person gets a job on an assembly line, where he is supposed to continually pick up a carton from a whole stack of them that stands to his right. But he is left-handed. So, he redesigns his work space, and moves the stack of cartons over to the left side, in order that he may pick them up more handily. *He has redesigned or modified his job so as to highlight his abilities, and get around his limitations -- but no one thinks anything of it.*

Or, again, let us say a nondisabled person is an executive. Her predecessor always called her subordinates into her office, and listened to their verbal summary of what they needed her decisions on. But *this* executive is more of *an eye person* than *an ear person.* She doesn't absorb their verbal summaries very well, when she is only able to hear them. So she redesigns their encounters, and asks them in addition to their verbal reports to her, to give her a one-page written summary of what they want her decisions on, and wait until she has had a chance to read them. *She has redesigned or modified her job so as to highlight her abilities, and get around her limitations -- but no one thinks anything of it.*

Not just employees but employers also have gotten into this business of redesigning jobs -- to get around the limitations of their employees. And often new technology has to be brought into play. For example, when employers realized that many of the employees they would have to hire couldn't add or subtract, they redesigned cash registers so that these told the employee what change to give back to the customer, once they had keyed in the amount handed over, by the customer. When employers in fast-food places realized that many of the employees they would have to hire couldn't read, they redesigned cash registers with pictures of the food, instead of words. When employers realized many of the employees they would have to hire couldn't remember instructions, they designed cash registers with screens over them that displayed the proper instructions, such as "Close drawer." (I saw this at Macy's recently.) Yet again, when employers discovered that people on assembly lines couldn't read blueprints, they fashioned 'exploded drawings.'

And so we see that redesigning jobs, in order to accommodate the limitations of the person holding down that job, goes on *all the time* in the world of work. It goes on without anyone even batting an eye, or thinking about it -- until, of course, we *who happen to have some obvious disability* walk in, asking for a job there. Then, when it becomes obvious that the price of hiring us is that the job will have to be partially redesigned or modified so as to highlight our abilities and get around our limitations -- perhaps with some new technology, as above -- the employer often acts as though we were asking for something no other job-hunter asks for.

You have to tell him (or her). Tell them gently. Tell them nicely. But *tell* them: "*Employers and employees* continually redesign or modify jobs, so as to highlight employees' abilities and get around their limitations." Same goes for you; *no big deal.*

You will be way ahead of the competition if, in addition to this general assurance, you can indicate more particularly **which tasks** you and the employer will need to redesign. *This will be relatively easy if* before you approach the employer for an interview, you first conduct conversations elsewhere with workers who actually do the work you would like to do. How you find such people is described fully in Chapter 5 on pages 123ff.

One way of approaching such fellow workers is to say, "I need to come in and talk to somebody with your expertise, who can tell me if a person with my abilities, and my disability, can work in this particular field or industry." Your goal during such conversations is to find out the various tasks that make up that job, *and* what skills it takes to do those tasks. Then you can isolate the **problem tasks** (for you). These will be the areas where you need to figure out some job redesigning. Your friends (or counselor) should be able to brainstorm this with you *before* you ever go in to see prospective employers for the particular kind of job that you are interested in.

If you *aren't* able to do this ahead of time, you might say to the employer, "Could you please give me an idea of how you have designed this job in your organization, and what tasks it requires to be done." Then you may break down the job into which tasks you are perfectly able to do, and which tasks you and they would need to redesign.

Well, there are the four principles that are the ground of hope for you, in your job-hunt. If you feel more hopeful, now that these are clear in your mind, that empowers you. And you do want to feel empowered, strengthened, encouraged, or self-actualized, when you go about the job-hunt. For, the basic principle of all job-hunting is: **if you want something to happen, it is you who must make it happen -- with God's help.** That's as true for those of us with disabilities as it is for the nondisabled job-hunter.

This brings us then to our next question:

WHAT DO YOU NEED TO DO, AFTER FINDING HOPE?

You know what I'm going to say, but I'll say it anyway: you need to **read** this whole book. And then you need to **do** the exercises in Appendix A. Then, set about the information-gathering process described in Chapter 5. All of this should help you identify a job (or jobs) you truly can do -- where **your particular disability is no barrier** to doing *that* job well. If you're having trouble, ask yourself, "What is it that I most want to do with my life?" If you're still having trouble, ask yourself, "What is it that no one else in my area wants to do, sell, offer, or make, that I would love to do, sell, offer, or make?"

Once you've identified such a job that you might like to do, go talk to someone with a disability who is doing it. In fact, talk to several people with disabilities who are doing it. Pick their brains for everything you can.

Some agencies maintain lists of such people. For example, the American Foundation for the Blind maintains *The Job Index*, a list of actual jobs held by persons who are blind; if you also are blind or have a sight impairment, the Index people can link you to someone who is doing the job you think you might like to do. *(Their address is Job Index, American Foundation for the Blind, 15 West 16th St., New York, NY 10011, 212-620-2055.)*

You may decide, after talking to such workers, that you want to do this thing on your own. But if you want to work for someone else, this is where you set out to identify employers who have such jobs, again following the process described in Chapter 5. In your information search, pay particular attention to employers with twenty or less employees, as that is where two-thirds of all new jobs are created.

During this information gathering, you may stumble across employers who give special advantage to people with disabilities. San Jose, California, for example, has at this writing a temporary agency, PROJECT HIRE, that sends people with disabilities out to jobs. Again, many states give an exemption to people with severe disabilities who want to work for the federal or state government, so that they do not have to go through civil service lists.

When you find employers that interest you, you will need to approach them. (As we said previously, employers never hire strangers.) During the interview, you need to be quietly assertive and persistent about what you want.

The main thing to remember during your interview with *any* employer, is that **every employer has fears,** and much of your task during the job-interview is to try to put these fears to rest. An employer's *general* fears are outlined in Chapter 6. Read that section several times, to get a good grasp of what they are, *and how to calm them.* But *you*, of course, want to know what *particular* fears the employer is likely to have about *you* just because *you* have a disability. So, let's open that Pandora's box.

THE FEARS AN EMPLOYER HAS
WHEN INTERVIEWING PEOPLE WITH DISABILITIES

If only you could read the employers' thoughts, this is what you might hear:

"I don't exactly understand what this person's disability is, and I'm afraid to ask." *You have to figure out how to disarm this fear.* You will not help matters if you merely stand and deliver the title of your disability. The employer may still be as mystified as before, and *still* afraid to ask. Instead, before you ever go into an interview, you should practice writing down or dictating into an audiocassette the answers to these four questions, until you know them by heart:

1. "What is it that I can do, and do well?"
2. "What is it that I can't do?"
3. "What can I tell them about the ways or strategies I have developed for getting around my limitations?" *For example, if you are a person who is deaf, telling them that you always carry a notepad and pencil around with you.*

4. "What is it that I have learned *through* my disability?" *e.g., if you've trained attendants, you have experience in training people.*

Then when you are face-to-face with an employer, simply find an opportune time in the interview to recite these four things, in exactly that order, and this should put *that* fear to rest, forever. Next fear?

"Will my insurance go up, if I hire this person?" *You have to figure out how to disarm this fear.* This is probably the most common fear among employers, and also the one that is *least* based on facts. Knowledgeable people who work with disabilities do not know of one single insurance company or workperson's compensation program in this country that will raise its premiums if an insured employer hires someone with a disability. Next?

"What if I would like to hire this disabled person, but there is some problem about adapting this particular job to their limitations, and neither they nor I know how to solve that problem?" *You have to figure out how to disarm this fear.* To an employer who says, "I'd hire you, BUT. . . . ." you can say, "Could you please give me some idea of how you have designed this job in your organization? I feel quite confident that I could do the job in general. As for the particular tasks that might give me a problem, I'm usually able to figure out a way to get them accomplished. Just give me a few days to work on it."

There are helps for you in this, such as the Job Accommodation Network (JAN) funded by the President's Committee on Employment of People with Disabilities, and headquartered at the University of West Virginia, 809 Allen Hall, Morgantown, WV 26506. Their phone number is 800-526-7234. They also serve Canada, and the Canadian number is 1-800-526-2262. JAN is essentially a computerized database of job accommodation information (at *their* disposal, not yours). Anyone can call them: job-hunters, employers, or counselors. A job-hunter with a disability, such as yourself, might tell them, "I want to be hired as a ________, and I found a prospective employer, but they said the reason they won't hire me for that position is ________. Is there any gadget or tool or other strategy that would give me a solution to this problem?" JAN will ask you to describe:

The nature of your disability,

What the job is, and what tasks it requires you to perform,

What equipment they give you to perform the job with, and

What **problem** task remains, that you are asking JAN to help you figure some way around (some *functional accommodation*, to use the proper jargon).

JAN will search their database, and formulate strategies for dealing with the problem. Within 24 hours (usually) they will call you back or send you a summary which suggests devices, procedures or other ways of dealing with the problem you described to them. They will also send you information about the manufacturers of any devices they may suggest, and in some cases they may refer you to employers who have successfully dealt with this problem. There is no fee for this service.

Similar, though somewhat more specialized, assistance is provided by the IBM National Support Center for Persons with Disabilities, 800-IBM-2133, and the AT&T Special Needs Center, 800-233-1222, and the National Center on Employment of the Deaf, 716-475-6219.

If special equipment *is* needed in order for you to do that job, the Department or Bureau of Rehabilitation (*Voc Rehab*) has enough funds in some States to purchase such equipment; in other States, it does not. Some States also have Worker Assistance Programs, funded by Private Industry Councils. Furthermore, if the employer decides to purchase the equipment, he or she is usually able to deduct such disability-related expenses from their taxes. The employer may also take money off his or her Federal taxes, just for hiring you, under the Federal Targeted Jobs Tax Credits provision. *You* may have to tell your would-be employer all of this.

You may also need to tell them that in a recent survey *(done by Lou Harris in 1987 for ICD -- the International Center for the Disabled, in New York City)*, in companies which had hired disabled employees, three-fourths of all managers said that the average cost of employing a person with disabilities was about the same as the cost of employing someone without disabilities.

You can further tell them that eight out of ten line managers said disabled employees were no harder to support or supervise than were employees with no obvious disabilities. *(For further information on the Lou Harris survey, see the ICD book mentioned in the bibliography at the end of this Appendix.)* Next?

"Just exactly how would this person get to work, here?" *You have to figure out how to disarm this fear.* It will help a lot if you've thought out some imaginative strategies *ahead of time*. For example, if you find a place that's willing to hire you but there is no public transportation to that part of the city, and you don't have a car, consider alternatives such as carpools, getting a ride with other employees at that firm, asking if there is a company bus, etc.

"What if I hire this disabled person, and they don't work out? What if they quit? What if I have to fire them? I'll be accused of firing them because they are disabled, with maybe a lawsuit in the offing. I can't take that kind of heat." *You have to figure out how to disarm this fear.* It is based on the fact that disabled employees *do* perform their work well. In the Lou Harris Survey alluded to previously, department heads and line managers *(in companies which had hired employees with disabilities)* gave their disabled employees a *good* performance rating 64% of the time, and an *excellent* performance rating 27% of the time, with only 3% rating their job performance as fair, and none evaluating it as poor. The survey concluded "nearly all disabled employees do their jobs as well as or better than other employees in similar jobs. They work as hard or harder than nondisabled employees, and are as reliable and punctual or more so." So, what can you do? Well, generally speaking, you should *anticipate* the fear even before the employer mentions it, with some such words as these: "My injury (or disability) has been a blessing in disguise, because it's forced me to think out a career that I can do well and stay in permanently. If you're willing to take a chance on me, I'll give it my very best shot. But, if things don't work out to our mutual satisfaction, I'd want you to tell me *that* straight out; and I'll pick up my tent peaceably, and move on." Next fear?

"How is this disabled person going to get along with the other workers? What if my other employees are jealous of this new employee just because he or she does a superb job, and they feel that casts some as-

persion on *them*? What if I just *have* to promote him or her over the heads of other workers, on merit alone? I'm afraid that those who were passed over might attribute the promotion solely to my feeling sorry about this person's disability, rather than to their ability; and, if they're angry about it, may bring dissension into my workplace." This is a well grounded fear, since the Lou Harris survey revealed that at least 39% of all line managers *(in companies with disabled employees)* rated them as better than employees with no disabilities, in the areas of willingness to work hard, reliability, attendance and punctuality. *Still, you have to figure out how to disarm this fear.* Again, you may want to defuse this fear before it is even brought up, by saying something *like,* "Wherever I work, I tend to develop a natural rapport with my fellow-workers, so that they're rootin' for me as much as I'm rootin' for them."

"How is this disabled person going to communicate with others at work? I'm afraid that's going to be a serious difficulty." *You have to figure out how to disarm this fear.* It will help if you practice your answers ahead of time. For example, if you are a person who is deaf, you might say, "In the past, it hasn't been a problem. With friends and fellow-workers, I sometimes lip read, I sometimes write, and I also teach some simple sign language to them. It's worked out just fine."

"How will this disabled person avoid accidents on the job? I'm afraid he or she will be a safety hazard." *You have to figure out how to disarm this fear.* It is a significant one. Of those managers who had *not* hired any persons with disabilities during the past three years, 19% cited as the reason "disabled people being a safety risk to themselves and others." So, you *have* to figure out how to disarm this fear. Volunteering your own safety record, in the past, is of course one way to put this fear to rest. Also, you can point out that not only are you not a safety hazard, but you can actually contribute to better safety among the other employees. For example, if you are a person with a back injury who has had to learn proper lifting techniques, you can point out to the employer that you would be able to offer in-service training to the other employees about safe lifting techniques. And now, to the last fear.

"How will this disabled person handle emergencies, such as a fire in the building? I'm afraid they could get burned or killed, and I don't want that responsibility on my shoulders." *You have to figure out how to disarm this fear.* If you use a wheelchair, you can ask the employer to identify three nearby workers who could form a 'buddy' system with you, and help get you down the stairs in such an emergency.

And there you have it: the major fears employers have about hiring someone with a disability. Whatever words you come up with, to lay these fears at rest, be sure to use language that feels *natural* to you. Brainstorming with your family, or friends, or counselor, about this should help immeasurably.

And now, a brief word about **volunteering**. If you are interviewing at a place that interests you greatly, but it doesn't look like they are going to hire you, there is a plan B: *volunteer* your services, without pay, for a set time period at that place (two weeks to two months). *If* they take you up on this offer (they may not), this gives the employer a chance to look at your work *without any risk or cost.* There's *no* guarantee this will eventually get you a job there; but it is a strategy that *has* paid off many times for job-hunters. So it's certainly worth a shot, *if you can afford to do it.*

Volunteering may also be a winning strategy for you if you need to gain **experience** in the job-market, when you don't have any. *(In the Lou Harris survey, line managers said that a lack of past experience is* **the** *factor that hurts disabled applicants the most.)* In this case, you should try to volunteer for some internship or other on-the-job training program *(see Appendix B, page 302).* Volunteering is also an attractive option if you are dying to work, but with your present benefit package you cannot really *afford* to take a job, lest you lose those benefits and medical coverage. By volunteering your services, you get a chance to keep your benefits, and still use your God-given talents or abilities, toward making this world a better place.

WHEN YOU GO FOR AN INTERVIEW, BUT YOU DON'T GET THE JOB

You may have to do *many* interviews, in order to find a job. We're talking about twenty or thirty different places. Giving up after just six interviews and six turndowns is tossing in the towel *much too soon.*

When things aren't going well, you will of course want to blame it on something. *Who don't?* The first tempting target, when you have a disability, is to think that *that* is the reason you are getting turned down. And that may well be so, in this tribal world we live in -- as we saw earlier. Three-quarters of all managers feel that people with disabilities *do* encounter discrimination from employers, according to the Lou Harris survey. On the other hand, most employers (the survey found) *are* willing to employ more people with disabilities *if they are qualified.*

Convincing the employer that you are qualified is *your* job, during the interview. **If you are somehow failing to do this, then it is clear that other things besides your disability are causing you to get turned down.** Facing up to this possibility shows a lot of guts. You are saying, in effect, **"*I* am responsible."** In our society, it is infinitely more popular to blame any failure *(including the failure of our job-hunt)* on **someone else.** The possibilities are endless, just so it's someone *out there* rather than yourself. It could

From the John Callahan cartoon collection, "Do Not Disturb Any Further," William Morrow & Co. Used by permission. To be reproduced by permission of the author only.

be employers, or society, or the government, or the employment service, or the welfare system, or your counselor, or your unsympathetic family.

Of course, there's one small problem with this temptation to always blame our failures on something or someone *out there*. If *something out there* made your job-hunt fail, then you have no power to change that, whatsoever. On the other hand, if it is something *you* are doing, that is making your job-hunt not work, then there is hope -- because, changing that *is* within your power and is within your grasp.

Well, okay, so **how** might you be botching up the interviews with employers? And **why** might you be botching them up? Well, *simple inexperience* in this business of interviewing for a job is one very obvious reason. Also, you may have no desire at all to go back to work (if you became disabled, for example, at a job you hated) -- but you need to go through *the appearances* of job-hunting, in order to mollify your friends and family -- who may be working very hard to support you, with the expectation that *this is all temporary.*

OUR FEARS

Those are the kinds of reasons we may be conscious of. And then there is that vast realm of things we may be unconscious of. We are no different from employers, in that we have our own fears. **Those fears may unconsciously cause us to self-sabotage our own job-hunt.** How? Well, there are several deliciously inventive ways of doing this. The easiest is to just play *into* the employer's fears, instead of reassuring him or her:

Fearful Employer: "If I offer you this job, how are you going to deal with this difficulty that your disability poses?"

Self-sabotaging Job-Hunter: "I'm very glad you asked me that, because personally I think it's going to be a big problem for me."

Another form of self-sabotage is to define what we are looking for in totally unrealistic terms:

Fearful Employer: "If I offer you this receptionist's job, you'll have to be able to type, and work on machines."

Self-sabotaging Job-Hunter: "Oh no, the only thing I want to do is answer the phone, take messages, and greet people."

Or, again:

Fearful Employer: "This is a Mom-and-Pop operation, and we need a bicycle repairman like yourself; but you'd have to be able to run the whole business occasionally, when I need to get away."

Self-sabotaging Job-Hunter: "Oh no, the only thing I want to do is the actual repair work on the bikes. I hate dealing with people."

Sometimes we sabotage ourselves by aiming *too high*, usually because of our identification with someone we admired. He was a policeman. So naturally, we want to be a policeperson. Twenty-twenty vision is *mandated.* We persist even though we have a serious visual impairment which will inevitably get us disqualified. Self-sabotage, again.

Well, you get the picture. If you *are* sabotaging your own job-hunt, you will have to do your best to figure out just exactly what it is that is keeping you from getting hired -- *besides your disability*. As we said earlier, employers will hardly ever help you out, here. You will *never* hear them say, "Something's wrong with you besides your disability," and then spell it out (e.g., "You're too cocky and arrogant during the interview"). You will always be left completely in the dark as to why you aren't getting hired. *Of course, that's true of job-hunters without disabilities too. Employers rarely give* anyone *any feedback.*

One way around this deadly silence, of course, is to *ask* for helpful feedback. This sometimes works, *so long as* you make the inquiry *real general*. For example, after you've gotten turned down at a place, you might say, "You know, I've been on thirteen interviews now, where I've gotten turned down. Is there something about me, besides my disability, that in your view is causing me not to get hired? If so, I'd really appreciate your giving me some pointers."

Most of the time you *still* won't get a frank answer. You'll just get blithering generalities or else a killing silence. This is because of employers' fear of lawsuits and such -- and also because **the world in general is perishing for a lack of those who love us enough to tell us the truth.** It's not just how they deal with you; it's how they deal with everybody.

But occasionally you will run into a loving soul, an employer, who is willing to risk giving you the truth. No matter how painful it is to hear it, thank her or him, from the bottom of your heart. Their advice, seriously heeded, can bring about just the changes in your interviewing strategy that you most need. Bless them, bless them.

In the absence of any help from employers, you're on your own to figure out what you may be doing wrong. So, let's look at some of the possibilities. They all stem from one kind of fear or another, as I said. So, the real question is, **what kinds of fears make us self-sabotage our own job-hunt?**

For starters, some of us have fallen into the bad habit at home of *using* our disability to get what we want: time, attention, and love, based on the age-old principle of "the louder you sniffle, the more you get." We often get a great deal of sympathy for our helplessness, and we fear that going to work will mean the end of this whole way of life -- which we aren't sure we *want* to give up. We are afraid that maybe at work, people will treat us just like any other person. *Well, what can I tell you? We have to learn to overcome that fear.*

Another fear: sometimes we have learned, through the long process of qualifying for disability benefits, that any information we volunteer may be used against us. Hence, in the job-interview, we are afraid to volunteer very much about ourselves. Thus we come across as trying to hide something. *Well, what can I tell you? We have to learn to overcome that fear.*

Again, sometimes we have an irrational fear of the nondisabled and don't particularly want to be around them, as we would have to be if we went to work. *We have to learn to overcome that fear.*

Next: if we've never held a job before, we often know very little about the nature of the world of work, how it performs, and what it's like; and we often have a minimum number of nondisabled friends who could tell us. Since we don't know appropriate social or work behaviors, we are afraid to go into such a strange and uncharted world. *We have to learn to overcome that fear.*

Sometimes we are afraid that if we get a job, we won't be able to 'cut it.' *We have to learn to overcome that fear.*

And then sometimes we are afraid to face our limitations, as putting ourselves to the test at a job would force us to do. *We have to learn to overcome that fear.*

I know, I know. All of that is easy to say. But how exactly *do* we overcome our fears? Well, **the PIE method** described in Chapter 5, *faithfully followed*, helps a lot. So does **practicing** overcoming our fears. You do this by taking one situation a day where your normal behavior is avoidance, based on fear, and you take a risk that day, by acting differently than you normally would. One risk a day. With daily practice, you will get stronger and stronger. It's just like exercising your muscles.

Also, don't overlook the possibility of seeking help from your spiritual life and prayer (see Appendix E). That has helped some job-hunters *immeasurably*, in overcoming their fears. They learn that every experience becomes an adventure for Two: God's Spirit, and You. Together, You can overcome all fear.

BIBLIOGRAPHY

If you want information about what resources exist to help you in your job-hunt, there is the **Clearinghouse on Disability Information**, U.S. Department of Education, Room 3132, Switzer Bldg., Washington, DC 20202-2524, 202-732-1241. It publishes an INFOPAC on *Employment of Individuals with Disabilities*, which you may ask for, that lists all kinds of groups, agencies, and programs throughout the country that exist to assist people with disabilities in finding employment or training for employment. They also publish a list of *Selected Federal Publications Relating to Disability*. January 1989.

They also distribute *Summary of Existing Legislation Affecting Persons with Disabilities*, Publication No. E-88-22014, August 1988, that summarizes in some detail all the federal laws that protect you, serve you, or offer you help. The Clearinghouse has a simpler version of the above publication, called the *Pocket Guide to Federal Help for Individuals with Disabilities*, which you can buy from the Superintendent of Documents, U.S. Government Printing Office, Washington, DC 20402.

If the above information doesn't tell you what you want to know, the Clearinghouse also has a *Directory of National Information Sources on Handicapping Conditions and Related Services*, published May 1986, by the National Institute of Disability and Rehabilitation Research, 330 C St. SW, Room 330C, Washington, DC 20202. This directory has an addendum of address changes, etc. that have occurred up through 6/27/89. The directory and addendum are available from the Clearinghouse on Disability Information, address above. However, since this is an expensive book, see if your local library, or rehabilitation office has a copy -- should you wish to browse it.

You will also want to know about Project LINK, if you live (or want to live) in or near Dallas, Texas, or Washington, D.C. It is a centralized placement service for job-ready persons with disabilities, providing job development and placement to about 400 disabled individuals per year. These placements have a retention rate of about 90%. If you are interested in exploring this service, you may contact them, at either: Project LINK, Mainstream, Inc., 1030 15th St., NW, Suite 1010, Washington, DC 20005, or Project LINK, Mainstream, Inc., 717 North Harwood, Suite 890, Dallas, TX 75201.

For those desiring some information about the 300 or so independent living centers or programs in this country, there is the *Directory of Independent Living Programs*, published by Research and Training Center on Independent Living, 3400 Bissonnet, Suite 101, Houston, TX 77005. Contact Laurel Richards, 713-666-6244.

Azrin, Nathan H., and Besalel, Victoria A., *Job Club Counselor's Manual: A Behavioral Approach to Vocational Counseling*. Pro-Ed, 8700 Shoal Creek Blvd., Austin, TX 78758, 512-451-3246. 1980. This is not a directory, but a detailed description of a particular method of job-hunting, called "the job club." Nathan invented the job club in 1970, in order to find a more structured way in which to help persons with disabilities, as they went about their job-hunt. This manual explains in great detail how to set up such a club. Furthermore, chapter 14 has a section on "Evaluation of the Job Club with Job-Handicapped Persons," which reports the success of this method with those who are disabled: 95% of those people with disabilities who were in the Job Club found jobs within 6 months, compared to 28% in a non-job-club control group. The job club's participants got salaries which were 22% higher than those in the control group who found jobs. Nathan has written another manual for those disabled job-hunters who cannot find a job club near them, spelling out how to follow the job club techniques all by yourself. That book is: Azrin, Nathan H., and Besalel, Victoria A., *Finding A Job*. Ten Speed Press, P.O. Box 7123, Berkeley, CA 94707. 1982.

Another group approach to helping people with disabilities in their job-search is: Ryan, Colleen, *Job Search Workshop for Disabled, Dislocated and Discouraged Workers*. Adult Life Resource Center, Division of Continuing Education, The University of Kansas. 1985.

*Rabby, Rami, and Croft, Diane, *Take Charge: A Strategic Guide for Blind Job Seekers*. National Braille Press Inc., 88 St. Stephen St., Boston, MA 02115. 1989. Orders must be prepaid (NBP does not invoice). Print edition: $23.95; Braille edition: $19.95. Cassette edition: $19.95. IBM disk edition (5¼″ or 3½″ disks): $19.95.

The ICD Survey II: Employing Disabled Americans, conducted by Louis Harris and Associates, Inc., for the International Center for the Disabled, 340 E. 24th St., New York, NY 10010. 1987.

For people with disabilities who have never been in the job-market before, and have only a limited education, there is a very useful *Guide to Basic*

Skills Jobs, Vol. 1. RPM Press, Inc., Verndale, MN 56481. 1986. A catalog of viable jobs for individuals with only basic work skills. This volume identifies 5,000 major occupations within the U.S. economy which require no more than an eighth grade level of education, and no more than one year of specific vocational preparation. Immensely useful book.

McBurney Resource Center, 905 University Ave., Madison, WI 53706. Access to Independence, Inc., 1954 E. Washington Ave., Madison, WI 53704. Lists resources that help with the psychological aspects of job-hunting.

Kimeldorf, Martin, and Edwards, Jean, *Numbers That Spell Success: Transitions to Work and Leisure Roles for Mildly Handicapped Youth*. Ednick Communications, Box 3612, Portland, OR 97208. 1988.

Bowe, Frank, *Handicapping America: Barriers to Disabled People*. Harper & Row, 10 E. 53rd St., New York, NY 10022. 1978.

Klein, Karen, with Hope, Carla Derrick, *Bouncing Back From Injury: How to Take Charge of Your Recuperation*. Prima Publishing & Communications, P.O. Box 1260BB, Rocklin, CA 95677. 1988.

Freedman, Jacqueline, and Gersten, Susan, *Traveling .... Like Everybody Else: A Practical Guide for Disabled Travelers*. Adama Books, 306 W. 38 St., New York, NY 10018. 1987.

Callahan, John, *Don't Worry, He Won't Get Far on Foot: The Autobiography of a Dangerous Man*. William Morrow & Co., Inc. 1989. John became a quadriplegic at the age of 21, due to an automobile accident. However, he has a wicked sense of humor, and so has become a famous cartoonist whose cartoons regard no subject as off-limits: disabilities, sex, religion, government programs, you name it. His cartoons, and this book, are not for those whose sensibilities are easily offended. This book is John's autobiography, and it is graphic, funny and touching. Arnold Beisser (below) wrote a most relevant passage in *his* book, apropos of such 'disabled humor' as John's: "The able-bodied person is likely to be appalled by 'disabled humor' and find nothing funny at all about it. But . . . tragedy and comedy are but two aspects of what is real, and whether we see the tragic or the humorous is a matter of perspective." John's perspective is clearly that he prefers to see the *humorous* amid the tragedy.

Beisser, Arnold R., *Flying Without Wings: Personal Reflections on Being Disabled*. Doubleday, 666 Fifth Ave., New York, NY 10103. 1989. This is *such* an important book, dealing as it does with one's *attitude* toward disability. As one wise man said about his disability in *The Disability Rag* (below): *"Every disabled person has the choice of either 'crying the blues' about their disability every day of their life, or realistically acknowledging what they have to do in order to have a successful, productive life."* Beisser has ultimately opted for the latter, though it was not an easy battle, as this book reveals. His wisdom and compassion are classified under such chapter headings as: *Time*; *Space*; *Relationships*; *The Choice*; and *Humor and Enlightenment*. This should be mandatory reading for *everyone*, but most especially for persons with disabilities who are having a hard time wrestling with their attitude toward their disability.

Journals or Periodicals:

Careers and the Handicapped, 44 Broadway, Greenlawn, NY 11740, James Schneider, ed., 516-261-8899. Published twice yearly.

The Disability Rag, Box 145, Louisville, KY 40201. An avant-garde journal dealing with all the different feelings -- amid a wide range of vocabulary -- that are going on within people who happen to have disabilities. Nothing is off limits. Frank and often graphic, especially in its language. Not for everyone, but has some very informative articles and debates in it.

For persons who are "print handicapped" or for other reasons can't read books or journals:

The National Library Service for the Blind and Physically Handicapped, Library of Congress, 1291 Taylor St. NW, Washington, DC 20542 has put many books on career planning and job-hunting (such as *Parachute*) on tape, which they will send, with special playback equipment, to your home and back, free, if you are able to prove a "print handicap."

Recording for the Blind, Inc., 20 Roszel Rd., Princeton, NJ 08540, likewise has translated job-hunting books for the print handicapped and visually impaired.

Also every state has library services of recorded books, usually lodged in the state library or the state agency for the blind. Any counselor, social worker, or blind person in your state should know where this is.

If there's something you're looking for, and you just can't find it locally, try the Library of Congress in Washington, D.C.

IF YOU ARE NEWLY DISABLED

If you are a newly disabled or injured worker, and you have no idea what benefits there are for you in general, nor what aids exist to help you with your job-hunt, here are some suggestions as to **how you find out** what's available to you:

Talk to other people with disabilities: if you have one who is a friend, or even if you meet one on the street, go up to them and say: "I'm newly disabled: do you know of anyone who could teach me the ropes?"

Visit or call the Disabled Students program of your local community college, college, or university. They will tell you what helps there are for you.

Visit or call one of the 300 Independent Living Centers in the U.S., if there is one near you. They will know.

Visit or call the United Way. They usually maintain an information and referral directory, which includes services for the Disabled.

Visit or call your local public library, particularly its librarian or reference librarian. Say to them, "I just became disabled; could you help me find out who I can go to, that could help me with counseling and the like?" If you're on your own there in the library, look up "handicapped" or "disabled" in the card catalog and see what information or referral directories you can turn up for your local town or city.

Also, local churches or synagogues often will know about resources to help you, since frequently they have people with disabilities in their congregations.

RESOURCES TO HELP YOU

You will find out that among the resources available to help you, there are the following:

Local Resources to help you if you have a disability:

The local offices of the State Rehabilitation Bureau
Independent Living Centers
Catholic Charities
Jewish Vocational Services
Lutheran Family Services
Organizations funded by the United Way (ask)
Private rehab firms and counselors and nurses. These can be *immensely* helpful, but as with career counselors in general (see Appendix C), you will have to choose *very* carefully. The marks of a poor (or burnt-out) rehab counselor are: they have lost the ability to listen; they tend therefore to stereotype you rather than focussing on your uniqueness (you can just hear them thinking, "I've heard this one before"); they only pay lip service to the idea that you can be independent, because in their heart of hearts they really believe the disabled need to be taken care of; they know the anatomy of disabilities, but not the anatomy of abilities. Their basic need is to take care of people, and they set this personal need of theirs ahead of your best interests.

On the other hand, the marks of a **good** rehab counselor are: they have excellent rapport with their clients; they have high expectations of their clients; they feel it is in the client's best interest that the client should make the decisions concerning his or her life; their clients accomplish a great deal. They familiarize themselves with your file, if you have seen other counselors previously, but they do not accept other people's judgements about you, unless or until they see that behavior for themselves. If they have a personality conflict with a client, they refer them immediately to someone more helpful in that situation. Furthermore, they research thoroughly what the disability is, rather than accepting cliches about it. Their basic need is **to act as a facilitator** for you, and their major contribution to your job-hunt is that they are skilled at helping you identify your abilities and then identifying a job which asks for just those abilities, so that when it comes time for you to fill out an application form at some company or organization, and you come to the question, "Do you have any disability that would keep you from performing *this* job?" you can truthfully answer "No."

If you have a counselor already, but after reading this paragraph feel you've unwittingly fallen into the wrong hands, see if you can 'redeem them' (for example, if they keep limiting what you can do with such statements as "Don't do that, you'll lose this benefit or that," ask them for *written facts*, that you can take home and study). If you can't redeem them, make your exit firmly and finally; and seek another.

State Resources to help you if you have a disability. *For example,*

The State Department of Rehabilitation or Rehabilitation Bureau in your state (probably headquartered in the city that is the State Capital). They can be important if you are trying to get hired by a small company, since *sometimes* the State Department or Bureau is in a position to help buy equipment needed to help you function in that particular job.

The Employment Development Department or Job Service in your state. Some offices have job centers for persons with disabilities, and/or veteran's assistance centers.

The state or national committee for your particular disability. For example,
United Cerebral Palsy
Strokes
Epilepsy
Association for Retarded Citizens

Regional centers for the Developmentally Disabled (usually defined as those who were disabled before the age of 18 years or so, though the definition varies from place to place).

Protection and Advocacy groups in major cities which function as ombudsman or legal advocacy persons, on behalf of former mental patients and others.

Federal or National Resources to help you if you have a disability:

Your congressperson. They usually have a social worker on their staff, who is often able to help you if you're running into some kind of a dead-end locally. What you can tell them, for example, is: "I'm a person with *this* disability, and I'm trying to find *this* kind of job, so I've located prospective employers, but this is the problem I'm running into . . . ." Sometimes there's nothing they can do, but other times they can be small miracle workers.

The President's Committee on Employment of Persons with Disabilities, 1111 20th St. NW, Washington, DC 20202.

The Office of Special Education and Rehabilitative Services, U.S. Dept. of Education, Rm. 3225 Switzer Bldg., 330 C St. SW, Washington, DC 20202.

The U.S. Department of Education, Office of Special Education & Rehabilitative Services

The Job Training Partnership Act (JTPA)

For *further* information on resources that may be able to help you, see the resources available from the Clearinghouse on Disability Information, referred to earlier.

A P.S. to Employers: *Do use employees with disabilities to the fullest of their abilities; don't put them in a repetitious, safe, dead-end job, just so that you won't have to spend any time on them. If you hire someone with a disability, be prepared especially to give them some time and attention during the training period. Since* *many employers are prone to take shortcuts in this area with* **all** *their employees, hiring someone with a disability can have a salutary effect on your whole organization, as you have impressed upon you anew the importance of training for all.*

If any of your employees with disabilities aren't working out, tell them so, early on. If problems arise with their performance, don't wait too long to intervene. There are problems that can be solved, if they are tackled early enough, and tackled jointly.

If the person you hire screws up on the job, don't blame it on their disability. Blame it, as you would with any other employee, on human nature. If you have to let them go, again don't blame it on the disability or start gossip with other employers you know, along the lines of, "Well I hired a disabled person, but it just didn't work." One poor employee who has a disability doesn't say anything about other employees with disabilities. It's better to stop such gossip before it starts.

If a nondisabled person at your company becomes *disabled, do go and visit them. A visit from you is important. Say, "We miss you, and we want you back." If you are in a position to offer some economic help toward getting them back on their feet, do it. Your organization will realize cost savings by getting this trained and devoted employee back on the job, even in modified or alternative work.*

The following people helped me in one way or another with this Appendix, and their assistance and generosity is *gratefully* acknowledged -- though, needless to say, they are not responsible for any of the opinions contained herein, nor for any errors that may be found:

Ed Roberts, President and Co-founder of the World Institute on Disability (WID) Berkeley, California; **Judy Heumann**, Vice-president and Co-founder of WID; **Maud Steyaert**, Administrative Asst., WID; **Chuck Young**, Administrator, Oregon Commission for the Blind, Portland, Oregon; **Pam Maxon**, Employment Specialist, Oregon Commission for the Blind; **Linda Blake**, Executive Director, Independent Living Resource, Pleasant Hill, California; **Betty Zarn**, Resource Specialist, ILR, Pleasant Hill; **John Wingate**, Executive Director, International Center for the Disabled, New York, N.Y.; **Marshall Karp**, Director, New Career, Dover, Ohio; **Sidney Fine**, 'father' of the Dictionary of Occupational Titles, Milwaukee, Wisconsin; **Nathan Azrin**, 'father' of Job Clubs, Nova University, Fort Lauderdale, Florida; **Barbara Mitchell**, Job Club Coordinator, Dept. of Rehabilitation, San Rafael (California) Office; **Ms. Terry Stimpson**, Rehabilitation Counselor, Stimpson Associates, Mountain View, California; **Judy Gelwicks**, Judith Gelwicks & Co., Gilroy, California; **James Jackson**, Veterans Representative, EDD Pleasant Hill (California) Office; **Zack Blake**, Office Director, Deaf Counseling, Advocacy, and Referral Agency (DCARA), EDD Pleasant Hill (California) Office; **Martha Server**, Job Placement Specialist, Mirfak Associates, Inc., Oakland, California.

Introduction

As I started writing this section on "Religion and Job-Hunting," I toyed at first with the idea of following what might be described as "an all-paths approach" to religion. But, after much thought, I decided not to try that. This, because I have read many other writers who tried, and I felt the approach failed miserably. An "all-paths" approach to religion ends up being a "no-paths" approach, even as a woman or man who tries to please everyone ends up pleasing no one. It is the old story of the "universal" vs. the "particular."

Those of us who do career counseling could predict, ahead of time, that trying to stay universal is not likely to be helpful, in writing about religion. We know well from our own field that truly helpful career counseling depends upon defining the **particularity** or uniqueness of each person we try to help. No employer wants to know only what you have in common with everyone else. He or she wants to know what makes you unique and individual. As I have argued throughout this book, the identification and inventory of your uniqueness or *particularity* is crucial if you are ever to find meaningful work.

This particularity invades and carries over to *everything* a person does; it is not suddenly "jettisonable" when he or she turns to religion. Therefore, when I or anyone else writes about religion I believe we **must** write out of our own particularity -- which *starts,* in my case, with the fact that I write, and think, and breathe as a Christian. So, this article speaks from a Christian perspective. I want you to be forewarned.

I have always been acutely aware, however, that this is a pluralistic society in which we live, and that I owe a great deal of sensitivity to the readers of my books who may have convictions very different from my own. I rub up against these different convictions, daily. By accident and not design it has turned out that the people who work or have worked here in my office with me, over the years, have been predominantly Jewish, along with some non-religious and a smattering of Christians. Furthermore, **Parachute's** more than 4 million readers have included Christians, Jews, members of the Baha'i faith, Seventh-Day Adventists, Mormons, Hindus, Buddhists, Islamics, and believers in 'new age' religions, as well as (of course) secularists, humanists, agnostics, atheists, and many others. Consequently, I have tried to be very courteous toward the feelings of all my readers who come from other persuasions or convictions than my own, *while at the same time* counting on them to translate my Christian thought forms into their own thought forms -- since this ability to thus translate is the indispensable *sine qua non* of anyone who aspires to communicate helpfully with others.

In the Judeo-Christian tradition from which I come, one of the indignant Biblical questions is, "Has God forgotten to be gracious?" The answer was a clear No. I think it is important *for all of us* also to seek the same goal. I have therefore labored to make this section gracious as well as helpful.

R. N. B.

Appendix E

Religion and Job-Hunting:

How to Find Your Mission in Life

How I Came To Write This

Recently, a woman asked me how you go about finding out what your Mission in life is. She assumed I would know what she was talking about, because of a diagram which appears a number of times in one of my other books, The Three Boxes of Life:

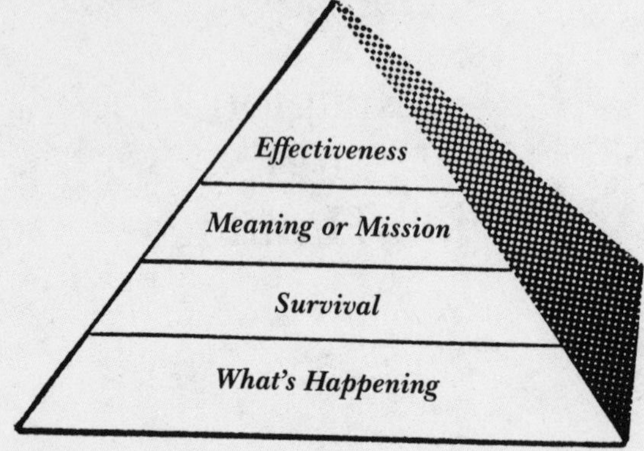

The Issues of the Job-Hunt

As this diagram asserts, the question of one's Mission in life arises naturally as a part of many people's job-hunt.

She told me that what she was looking for was not some careful, dispassionate, philosophical answer, where every statement is hedged about with cautions and caveats -- "It may be . . ." or "It seems to me . . ." Nor did she want to know why *I thought what I did, or* how *I learned it, or what Scriptures* support *it. "I want you to just speak with passion and conviction," she said, "out of what you most truly feel and believe. For it is some vision that I want. I am hungry for a vision of what I can be. So, just speak to me of what you most truly feel and believe about our mission in life. I will know how to translate your vision into my own thought forms for my own life, when I reflect afterwards upon what you have said. But I want you to talk about this now with passion and conviction -- please."*

And so, I did. And I will now tell you what I said to her.

The Motive for Finding A Sense of Mission in Life

We begin with the fact that, according to fifty years of opinion polls conducted by the Gallup Organization, 94% of us believe in God, 90% of us pray, 88% of us believe God loves us, and 33% of us report we have had a life-changing religious experience (*The People's Religion: American Faith in the 90s. Macmillan & Co. 1989*).

It is hardly surprising therefore, that so many of us are searching these days for some sense of mission. Career counselors are often afraid to give help or guidance here, for fear they will be perceived as trying to talk people into religious belief. It is a groundless fear. Clearly, the overwhelming majority of U.S. job-hunters and career-changers already have their religious beliefs well in place.

But, we want some guidance and help in this area, because we want to *marry* our religious **beliefs** with our **work**, rather than leaving the two -- our religion and our work -- compartmentalized, as two areas of our life which never talk to each other. We *want* them to talk to each other and uplift each other.

This marriage takes the particular form of a search for a Sense of Mission because of our conviction that God has made each of us unique, even as our fingerprints attest. We feel that we are not just another grain of sand lying on the beach called humanity, unnumbered and lost in the 5 billion mass, but that God caused us to be born and put here for some unique reason: so that we might contribute to Life on earth something no one else can contribute in quite the same way. At its very minimum, then, when we search for a sense of Mission we are searching for reassurance that the world is at least a little bit richer for our being here; and a little bit poorer after our going.

Every keen observer of human nature will know what I mean when I say that those who have found some sense of Mission have a very special joy, "which no one can take from them." It is wonderful to feel that beyond eating, sleeping, working, having pleasure and *it may be* marrying, having children, and growing older, you were set here on Earth for some special purpose, *and* that you can gain some idea of what that purpose is.

So, how does one go about this search?

I would emphasize, at the outset, two cautions. First of all, though I will explain the steps that seem to me to be involved in finding one's Mission -- based on the learnings I have accumulated over some sixty years, I want to caution you that these steps are not the only Way -- by any means. Many people have discovered their Mission by taking other paths. And you may, too. But hopefully what I have to say may shed some light upon whatever path you take.

My second caution is simply this: you would be wise not to try to approach this problem of "your Mission in life" as primarily an **intellectual** puzzle -- for the mind, and the mind alone, to solve. To paraphrase Kahlil Gibran, Faith is an oasis in the heart that is not reached merely by the journey of the mind. It is your will and your heart that must be involved in the search as well as your mind. To put it quite simply, it takes the total person to learn one's total Mission.

It also takes the total disciplines of the ages -- not only modern knowledge but also ancient thought, including the wisdom of religion, faith, and the spiritual matters. For, to put it quite bluntly, the question of Mission inevitably leads us to God.

The Main Obstacle in Finding Your Mission in Life: Job-Hunting Compartmentalized from Our Religion or Faith

Mission challenges us to see our job-hunt in relationship to our faith in God, because *Mission* is a religious concept, from beginning to end. It is defined by Webster's as "a continuing task or responsibility that one is destined or fitted to do or specially called upon to undertake," and historically has had two major synonyms: *Calling* and *Vocation*. These, of course, are the same word in two different languages, English and Latin. Regardless of which word is used, it is obvious upon reflection, that a Vocation or Calling implies *Someone who calls,* and that a destiny implies *Someone who determined the destination for us.* Thus, unless one opts for a military or governmental view of the matter, the concept of Mission with relationship to our whole life lands us inevitably in the lap of God, before we have even begun.

There is always the temptation to try to speak of this subject of *Mission* in a secular fashion, without reference to God, as though it might be simply "a purpose you choose for your own life, by identifying your enthusiasms, and then using the clues you find from that exercise to get some purpose you can choose for your life." The language of this temptation is ironic because the substitute word used for "Mission" -- *Enthusiasm* -- is derived from the Greek, '*en theos,*' and literally means "God in us."

It is no accident that so many of the leaders in the job-hunting field over the years -- the late John Crystal, Arthur Miller, Ralph Mattson, Tom and Ellie Jackson, Bernard Haldane, Arthur and Marie Kirn, the Pilders -- have also been people of faith. If you would figure out your Mission in life, you must also be willing to think about God in connection with your job-hunt.

The Secret of Finding Your Mission in Life: Taking It in Stages

The puzzle of figuring out what your Mission in life is, will likely take some time. It is not a *problem* to be solved in a day and a night. It is a *learning process* which has steps to it, much like the process by which we all learned to eat. As a baby we did not tackle adult food right off. As we all recall, there were three stages: first there had to be the mother's milk or bottle, then strained baby foods, and finally -- after teeth and time -- the stuff that grown-ups chew. Three stages -- and the two earlier stages were not to be disparaged. It was all Eating, just different forms of Eating -- appropriate to our development at the time. But each stage had to be mastered, in turn, before the next could be approached.

The Three Stages of Mission: What We Need to Learn

By coincidence, there are usually three stages also to learning what your Mission in life is, and the two earlier stages are likewise not to be disparaged. It is all "Mission" -- just different forms of Mission, appropriate to your development at the time. But each stage has to be mastered, in turn, before the next can be approached. And so, you may say either of two things: You may say that you have *Three Missions in Life*. Or you may say that you have *One Mission in Life, with three parts to it.* But there is a sense in which you must discover what those three parts are, each in turn, before you can fully answer the question, "What is my Mission in life?" Of course, there is another sense in which you never master any of these stages, but are always growing in understanding and mastery of them, throughout your whole life here on Earth.

As it has been impressed on me by observing many people over the years (admittedly through *Christian spectacles*), it appears that the three parts to your Mission here on Earth can be defined generally as follows:

(1) *Your first Mission here on Earth* is one which you share with the rest of the human race, but it is no less your individual Mission for the fact that it is shared: and it is, **to seek to stand hour by hour in the conscious presence of God, the One from whom your Mission is derived.** *The Missioner before the Mission,* is the rule. In religious language, your Mission here is: *to know God, and enjoy Him forever, and to see His hand in all His works.*

(2) Secondly, once you have begun doing that in an earnest way, *your second Mission here on Earth* is also one which you share with the rest of the human race, but it is no less your individual mission for the fact that it is shared: and that is, **to do what you can, moment by moment, day by day, step by step, to make this world a better place, following the leading and guidance of God's Spirit within you and around you.**

(3) Thirdly, once you have begun doing that in a serious way, *your third Mission here on Earth* is one which is uniquely yours, and that is:

a) **to exercise that Talent which you particularly came to Earth to use -- your greatest gift, which you most delight to use,**
b) **in the place(s) or setting(s) which God has caused to appeal to you the most,**
c) **and for those purposes which God most needs to have done in the world.**

When fleshed out, and spelled out, I think you will find that there you have the definition of your Mission in life. Or, to put it another way, these are the three Missions which you have in life.

The Two Rhythms of the Dance of Mission: Unlearning, Learning, Unlearning, Learning

The distinctive characteristic of these three stages is that in each we are forced to *let go* of some fundamental assumptions which the world has *falsely* taught us, about the nature of our Mission. In other words, throughout this quest and at each stage we find ourselves engaged not merely in a process of *Learning*. We are also engaged in a process of *Un*-learning. Thus, we can restate the above three Learnings, in terms of what we also need to *un*learn at each stage:

• We need in the first Stage to *un*learn the idea that our Mission is primarily to keep busy *doing* something (here on Earth), and learn instead that our Mission is first of all to keep busy being something (here on Earth). In Christian language (and others as well), we might say that we were sent here to learn how *to be* sons of God, and daughters of God, before anything else. *"Our Father, who art in heaven . . ."*

• In the second stage, "Being" issues into "Doing." At this stage, we need to *un*learn the idea that everything about our Mission must be *unique* to us, and learn instead that some parts of our Mission here on Earth are *shared* by all human beings: e.g., we were all sent here to bring more gratitude, more kindness, more forgiveness, and more love, into the world. We share this Mission because the task is too large to be accomplished by just one individual.

• We need in the third stage to *un*learn the idea that that part of our Mission which is truly unique, and most truly ours, is something Our Creator just *orders* us to do, without any agreement from our spirit, mind, and heart. (On the other hand, neither is it something that each of us chooses and then merely asks God to bless.) We need to learn that God so honors our free will, that He has ordained our unique Mission be something which we have some part in choosing.

• In this third stage we need also to *un*learn the idea that our unique Mission must consist of some achievement which all the world will see, -- and learn instead that as the stone does not always know what ripples it has caused in the pond whose surface it impacts, so neither we nor those who watch our life will always know *what we have achieved* by our life and by our Mission. *It may be* that by the grace of God we helped bring about a profound change for the better in the lives of other souls around us, but it also may be that this takes place beyond our sight, or after we have gone on. And we may never know what we have accomplished, until we see Him face-to-face after this life is past.

• Most finally, we need to *un*learn the idea that what we have accomplished is our doing, and ours alone. It is God's Spirit breathing in us and through us which helps us to do whatever we do, and so the singular first person pronoun is never appropriate, but only the plural. Not "*I* accomplished this" but "*We* accomplished this, God and I, working together . . ."

That should give you a general overview. But I would like to add some random comments on my part about each of these three Missions of ours here on Earth.

Some Random Comments About Your First Mission in Life

Your first Mission here on Earth is one which you share with the rest of the human race, but it is no less your individual Mission for the fact that it is shared: and that is, **to seek to stand hour by hour in the conscious presence of God, the One from whom your Mission is derived.** The Missioner before the Mission, is the rule. In religious language, your Mission is: to know God, and enjoy Him for ever, and to see His hand in all His works.

Comment 1: How We Might Think of God

Each of us has to go about this primary Mission according to the tenets of his or her own particular religion. But I will speak what I know out of the context of my own particular faith, and you may perhaps translate and apply it to yours. I will speak as a Christian, who believes (passionately) that Christ is the Way and the Truth and the Life. But I also believe, with St. Peter, "that God shows no partiality, but in every nation any one who fears him and does what is right is acceptable to him." (Acts 10:34-35)

Now, Jesus claimed many unique things about Himself and His Mission; but He also spoke of Himself as the great prototype for us all. He called himself "the Son of Man," and He said, "I assure you that the man who believes in me will do the same things that I have done, yes, and he will do even greater things than these . . ." (John 14:12)

Emboldened by His identification of us with His life and His Mission, we might want to remember how He spoke about His Life here on Earth. He put it in this context: **"I came from the Father and have come into the world; again, I am leaving the world and going to the Father."** (John 16:28)

If there is a sense in which this is, in even the faintest way, true also of our lives (and I shall say in a moment in what sense I think it is true), then instead of calling our great Creator "God" or "Father" right off, we might begin our approach to the subject of religion by referring to the One Who gave us our Mission and sent us to this planet not as "God" or "Father" but -- *just to help our thinking* -- as: **"The One From Whom We Came and The One To Whom We Shall Return,"** when this life is done.

If our life here on Earth be at all like Christ's, then this is a true way to think about the One who gave us our Mission. We are not some kind of eternal, pre-existent *being*. We are **creatures,** who once did not exist, and then came into Being, and continue to have our Being, only at the will of our great Creator. But as creatures we are both body and soul; and although we know our body was created in our mother's womb, our soul's origin is a great mystery. Where it came from, at what moment the Lord created it, is something we cannot know. It is not unreasonable to suppose, however, that the great God created our *soul* before it entered our body, and in that sense we did indeed stand before God before we were born; and He is indeed **"The One From Whom We Came and The One To Whom We Shall Return."**

Therefore, before we go searching for "what work was I sent here to do?" we need to establish or in a truer sense *reestablish* -- contact with this **"One From Whom We Came and The One To Whom We Shall Return."** Without this reaching out of the creature to the great Creator, without this reaching out of *the creature with a Mission* to *the One Who Gave Us That Mission,* the question ***what** is my Mission in life?* is void and null. The *what* is rooted in the *Who*; absent the Personal, one cannot meaningfully discuss The Thing. It is like the adult who cries, "I want to get married," without giving any consideration to *who* it is they want to marry.

Comment 2: How We Might Think of Religion or Faith

In light of this larger view of our creatureliness, we can see that *religion* or *faith* is not a question of whether or not we choose to (*as it is so commonly put*) "have a relationship with God." Looking at our life in a larger context than just our life here on Earth, it becomes apparent that some sort of relationship with God is a given for us, about which we have absolutely no choice. God and we **were and are** related, during the time of our soul's existence before our birth and in the time of our soul's continued existence after our death. The only choice we have is what to do about **The Time In Between,** i.e., what we want the nature of our relationship with God to be during our time here on Earth and how that will affect the *nature* of the relationship, then, after death.

One of the corollaries of all this is that by the very act of being born into a human body, it is an inevitable that we undergo a kind of *amnesia* -- an amnesia which typically embraces not only our nine months in the womb, our baby years, and almost one third of each day (sleeping), but more importantly any memory of our origin or our destiny. We wander on Earth as an amnesia victim. To seek after Faith, therefore, is to seek to climb back out of that amnesia. Religion or faith is **the hard reclaiming of knowledge we once knew as a certainty.**

Comment 3: The First Obstacle to Executing This Mission

This first Mission of ours here on Earth is not the easiest of Missions, simply because it is the first. Indeed, in many ways, it is the most difficult. All can see that our life here on Earth is a very physical life. We eat, we drink, we sleep, we long to be held, and to hold. We inherit a physical body, with very physical appetites, we walk on the physical earth, and we acquire physical possessions. It is the most alluring of temptations, *in our amnesia,* to come up with just a *Physical* interpretation of this life: to think that the Universe is merely interested in the survival of species. Given this interpretation, the story of our individual life could be simply told: we are born, grow up, procreate, and die.

But we are ever recalled to do what we came here to do: that without rejecting the joy of the Physicalness of this life, such as the love of the blue sky and the green grass, we are to reach out beyond all this to **recall** and recover a *Spiritual* interpretation of our life. *Beyond* the physical and *within* the physicalness of this life, to detect a Spirit and a Person from beyond this Earth who is with us and in us -- the very real and loving and awesome Presence of the great Creator from whom we came -- and the One to whom we once again shall go.

Comment 4: The Second Obstacle to Executing This Mission

It is one of the conditions of our earthly amnesia and our creatureliness that, sadly enough, some very *human* and very *rebellious* part of us *likes* the idea of living in a world where we can be our own god -- and therefore loves the purely Physical interpretation of life, and finds it *anguish* to relinquish it. Traditional Christian vocabulary calls this **"sin"** and has a lot to say about the difficulty it poses for this first part of our Mission. All who live a thoughtful life know that it is true: our greatest enemy in carrying out this first Mission of ours is indeed *our own* heart and our own rebellion.

Comment 5: Further Thoughts About What Makes Us Special and Unique

As I said earlier, many of us come to this issue of our Mission in life, because we want to feel that we are unique. And what we mean by that, is that we hope to discover some "specialness" intrinsic to us, which is our birthright, and which no one can take from us. What we, however, discover from a thorough exploration of this topic, is that we are indeed special -- but only because God thinks us so. Our specialness and uniqueness reside in Him, and His love, rather than in anything intrinsic to our own *being*. The proper appreciation of this distinction causes our feet to carry us in the end not to the City called Pride, but to the Temple called Gratitude.

> What is religion? Religion is the service of God out of grateful love for what God has done for us. The Christian religion, more particularly, is the service of God out of grateful love for what God has done for us in Christ.
>
> Phillips Brooks

Comment 6: The Unconscious Doing of The Work We Came To Do

You may have *already* wrestled with this first part of your Mission here on Earth. You may not have called it that. You may have called it simply "learning to believe in God." But if you ask what your Mission is in life, this one was and is the precondition of all else that you came here to do.

Absent this Mission, and it is folly to talk about the rest. So, if you have been seeking faith, or seeking to strengthen your faith, you have -- willy nilly -- already been about *the doing of the Mission you were given.* Born into **This Time In Between,** you have found His hand again, and reclasped it. You are therefore ready to go on with His Spirit to tackle together what you came here to do -- the other parts of your Mission.

Some Random Comments About Your Second Mission in Life

Your second Mission here on Earth is also one which you share with the rest of the human race, but it is no less your individual mission for the fact that it is shared: and that is, **to do what you can moment by moment, day by day, step by step, to make this world a better place -- following the leading and guidance of God's Spirit within you and around you.**

Comment 1: The Uncomfortableness of One Step at a Time

Imagine yourself out walking in your neighborhood one night, and suddenly you find yourself surrounded by such a dense fog, that you have lost your bearings and cannot find your way. Suddenly, a friend appears out of the fog, and asks you to put your hand in theirs, and they will lead you home. And you, not being able to tell where you are going, trustingly follow them, even though you can only see one step at a time. Eventually you arrive safely home, filled with gratitude. But as you reflect upon the experience the next day, you realize how unsettling it was to have to keep walking when you could see only one step at a time, even though you had guidance in which you knew you could trust.

Now I have asked you to imagine all of this, because this is the essence of the second Mission to which *you* are called -- and *I* am called -- in this life. It is all very different than we had imagined. When the question, *"What is your Mission in life?"* is first broached, and we have put our hand in God's, as it were, we imagine that we will be taken up to *some mountaintop,* from which we can see far into the distance. And that we will hear a voice in our ear, saying, "Look, look, see that distant city? That is the goal of your Mission; that is where everything is leading, every step of your way."

But instead of the mountaintop, we find ourself in *the valley* -- wandering often in a fog. And the voice in our ear says something quite different from what we thought we would hear. It says, **"Your Mission is to**

take one step at a time, even when you don't yet see where it all is leading, or what the Grand Plan is, or what your overall Mission in life is. Trust Me; I will lead you."

Comment 2: The Nature of This Step-by-Step Mission

As I said, in every situation you find yourself, you have been sent here to do whatever you can -- moment by moment -- that will bring more gratitude, more kindness, more forgiveness, more honesty, and more love into this world.

There are dozens of such moments every day. Moments when you stand -- as it were -- at a spiritual crossroads, with two ways lying before you. Such moments are typically called **"moments of decision."** It does not matter what the frame or content of each particular decision is. It all devolves, in the end, into just two roads before you, *every time.* **The one** will lead to *less* gratitude, *less* kindness, *less* forgiveness, *less* honesty, or *less* love in the world. **The other** will lead to *more* gratitude, *more* kindness, *more* forgiveness, *more* honesty, or *more* love in the world. Your Mission, each moment, is to seek to choose the latter spiritual road, rather than the former, *every time.*

Comment 3: Some Examples of This Step-by-Step Mission

I will give a few examples, so that the nature of this part of your Mission may be unmistakably clear.

You are out on the freeway, in your car. Someone has gotten into the wrong lane, to the right of *your* lane, and needs to move over into the lane you are in. You *see* their need to cut in, ahead of you. **Decision time.** In your mind's eye you see two spiritual roads lying before you: the one leading to less kindness in the world (you speed up, to shut this driver out, and don't let them move over), the other leading to more kindness in the world (you let the driver cut in). **Since you know this is part of your Mission, part of the reason why you came to Earth, your calling is clear. You know which road to take, which decision to make.**

You are hard at work at your desk, when suddenly an interruption comes. The phone rings, or someone is at the door. They need something from you, a question of some of your time and attention. **Decision time.** In your mind's eye you see two spiritual roads lying before you: the one leading to less love in the world (you tell them you're just too busy to be bothered), the other leading to more love in the world (you put aside your work, decide that God may have sent this person to you, and say, "Yes, what can I do to help you?"). **Since you know this is part of your Mission, part of the reason why you came to Earth, your calling is clear. You know which road to take, which decision to make.**

Your mate does something that hurts your feelings. **Decision time.** In your mind's eye you see two spiritual roads lying before you: the one leading to less forgiveness in the world (you institute an icy silence between the two of you, and think of how you can punish them or otherwise get

even), the other leading to more forgiveness in the world (you go over and take them in your arms, speak the truth about your hurt feelings, and assure them of your love). **Since you know this is part of your Mission, part of the reason why you came to Earth, your calling is clear. You know which road to take, which decision to make.**

You have not behaved at your most noble, recently. And now you are face-to-face with someone who asks you a question about what happened. **Decision time.** In your mind's eye you see two spiritual roads lying before you: the one leading to less honesty in the world (you lie about what happened, or what you were feeling, because you fear losing their respect or their love), the other leading to more honesty in the world (you tell the truth, together with how you feel about it, in retrospect). **Since you know this is part of your Mission, part of the reason why you came to Earth, your calling is clear. You know which road to take, which decision to make.**

Comment 4: The Spectacle Which Makes the Angels Laugh

It is necessary to explain this part of our Mission in some detail, because so many times you will see people wringing their hands, and saying, *"I want to know what my Mission in life is,"* all the while they are cutting people off on the highway, refusing to give time to people, punishing their mate for having hurt their feelings, and lying about what they did. And it will seem to you that the angels must laugh to see this spectacle. *For these people wringing their hands,* their Mission was right there, on the freeway, in the interruption, in the hurt, and at the confrontation.

Comment 5: The Valley vs. The Mountaintop

At some point in your life your Mission may involve some grand *mountaintop experience,* where you say to yourself, "This, this, is why I came into the world. I know it. I know it." *But until then,* your Mission is here in *the valley,* and the fog, and the little callings moment by moment, day by day. More to the point, it is likely you cannot ever get to your mountaintop Mission unless you have first exercised your stewardship faithfully in the valley.

It is an ancient principle, to which Jesus alluded often, that if you don't use the information the Universe has already given you, you cannot expect it will give you any more. If you aren't being faithful in small things, how can you expect to be given charge over larger things? (Luke 16:10,11,12; 19:11–24) If you aren't trying to bring more gratitude, kindness, forgiveness, honesty, and love into the world each day, you can hardly expect that you will be entrusted with the Mission to help bring peace into the world or anything else large and important. If we do not live out our day-by-day Mission in the valley, we cannot expect we are yet ready for a larger *mountaintop* Mission.

Comment 6: The Importance of Not Thinking of This Mission As 'Just A Training Camp'

The valley is not just a kind of "training camp." There is in your imagination even now an invisible *spiritual* mountaintop to which you may go, if you wish to see where all this is leading. And what will you see there, in the imagination of your heart, but the goal toward which all this is pointed: **that Earth might be more like heaven. That human's life might be more like God's.** That is the large achievement toward which all our day by day Missions *in the valley* are moving. This is a *large* order, but it is accomplished by faithful attention to the doing of our great Creator's **will** in little things as well as in large. It is much like the building of the pyramids in Egypt, which was accomplished by the dragging of a lot of individual pieces of stone by a lot of individual men.

The valley, the fog, the going step-by-step, is no mere training camp. The goal is real, however large. **"Thy Kingdom come, Thy will be done, on Earth, as it is in heaven."**

Some Random Comments About Your Third Mission in Life

Your third Mission here on Earth is one which is uniquely yours, and that is:

a) **to exercise that Talent which you particularly came to Earth to use -- your greatest gift which you most delight to use**
b) **in those place(s) or setting(s) which God has caused to appeal to you the most,**
c) **and for those purposes which God most needs to have done in the world.**

Comment 1: Our Mission Is Already Written, "in Our Members"

It is customary in trying to identify this part of our Mission, to advise that we should ask God, in prayer, to speak to us -- and **tell us** plainly what our Mission is. We look for a voice in the air, a thought in our head, a dream in the night, a sign in the events of the day, to reveal this thing which is otherwise *(it is said)* completely hidden. Sometimes, from just such answered prayer, people do indeed discover what their Mission is, beyond all doubt and uncertainty.

But having to wait for the voice of God to reveal what our Mission is, is not the truest picture of our situation. St. Paul, in Romans, speaks of a law "written in our members," -- and this phrase has a telling application to the question of **how** God reveals to each of us our unique Mission in life. Read again the definition of our third Mission (above) and you will see: the clear implication of the definition is that God has **already** revealed His will to us concerning our vocation and Mission, by causing it to be **"written in our members."** We are to begin deciphering our unique Mission by studying our talents and skills, and more particularly which ones (or One) we most rejoice to use.

God actually has written His will *twice* in our members: *first in the talents* which He lodged there, and secondly *in His guidance of our heart,* as to which talent gives us the greatest pleasure from its exercise **(it is usually the one which, when we use it, causes us to lose all sense of time)**.

Even as the anthropologist can examine ancient inscriptions, and divine from them the daily life of a long lost people, so we by examining **our talents** and **our heart** can *more often than we dream* divine the Will of the Living God. For true it is, our Mission is not something He **will** reveal; it is something He **has already** revealed. It is not to be found written in the sky; it is to be found written in our members.

Comment 2: Career Counseling: We Need You

Arguably, our first two Missions in life could be learned from religion alone -- without any reference whatsoever to career counseling, the subject of this book. Why then should career counseling claim that this question about our Mission in life is its proper concern, *in any way?*

It is when we come to this third Mission, which hinges so crucially on the question of our Talents, skills, and gifts, that we see the answer. If you've read the body of this book, before turning to this appendix, you know without my even saying it, how much the identification of Talents, gifts, or skills is the province of career counseling. Its expertise, indeed its *raison d'être,* lies precisely in the identification, classification, and (forgive me) "prioritization" of Talents, skills, and gifts. To put the matter quite simply, career counseling knows how to do this better than any other discipline -- **including** traditional religion. This is not a defect of religion, but the fulfillment of something Jesus promised: "When the Spirit of truth comes, He will guide you into all truth." (John 16:12) Career counseling is part (we may hope) of that promised late-coming truth. It can therefore be of inestimable help to the pilgrim who is trying to figure out what their greatest, and most enjoyable, talent is, as a step toward identifying their unique Mission in life.

If career counseling needs religion as its helpmate in the first two stages of identifying our Mission in life, religion repays the compliment by clearly needing career counseling as **its** helpmate here in the third stage.

And this place where you are in your life right now -- facing the job-hunt and all its anxiety -- is the perfect time to seek the union within your own mind and heart of both career counseling (as in the pages of this book) and your faith in God.

Comment 3: How Our Mission Got Chosen: A Scenario for the Romantic

It is a mystery which we cannot fathom, in this life at least, as to why one of us has this talent, and the other one has that; why God chose to give one gift -- and Mission -- to one person, and a different gift -- and Mission -- to another. Since we do not know, and in some degree cannot know, we are certainly left free to speculate, and imagine.

We may imagine that before we came to Earth, our souls, *our Breath, our Light,* stood before the great Creator and volunteered for this Mission. And God and we, together, chose what that Mission would be and what particular gifts would be needed, which He then agreed to give us, after our birth. Thus, our Mission was not a command given peremptorily by an unloving Creator to a reluctant slave without a vote, but was a task jointly designed by us both, in which as fast as the great Creator said, **"I wish"** our hearts responded, **"Oh, yes."** As mentioned in an earlier Comment, it may be helpful to think of the condition of our becoming human as that we became amnesiac about any consciousness our soul had before birth -- and therefore amnesiac about the nature or manner in which our Mission was designed.

Our searching for our Mission now is therefore a searching to recover the memory of something we ourselves had a part in designing.

I am admittedly a hopeless romantic, so of course I like this picture. If you also are a hopeless romantic, you may like it too. There's also the chance that it just may be true. We will not know until we see Him face-to-face.

Comment 4: Mission As Intersection

There are all different kinds of voices calling you to all different kinds of work, and the problem is to find out which is the voice of God rather than that of society, say, or the superego, or self-interest. By and large a good rule for finding out is this: the kind of work God usually calls you to is the kind of work (a) that you need most to do and (b) the world most needs to have done. If you really get a kick out of your work, you've presumably met requirement (a), but if your work is writing TV deodorant commercials, the chances are you've missed requirement (b). On the other hand, if your work is being a doctor in a leper colony, you have probably met (b), but if most of the time you're bored and depressed by it, the chances are you haven't only bypassed (a) but probably aren't helping your patients much either. Neither the hair shirt nor the soft birth will do. **The place God calls you to is the place where your deep gladness and the world's deep hunger meet.**

Frederick Buechner
Wishful Thinking -- A Theological ABC

Comment 5: Examples of Mission As Intersection

Your unique and individual mission will most likely turn out to be a mission of Love, acted out in one or all of three arenas: either in the Kingdom of the Mind, whose goal is to bring more Truth into the world; or in the Kingdom of the Heart, whose goal is to bring more beauty into the world; or in the Kingdom of the Will, whose goal is to bring more Perfection into the world, through Service.

Here are some examples:

"My mission is, out of the rich reservoir of love which God seems to have given me, to nurture and show love to others -- most particularly to those who are suffering from incurable diseases."

"My mission is to draw maps for people to show them how to get to God."

"My mission is to create the purest foods I can, to help people's bodies not get in the way of their spiritual growth."

"My mission is to make the finest harps I can so that people can hear the voice of God in the wind."

"My mission is to make people laugh, so that the travail of this earthly life doesn't seem quite so hard to them."

"My mission is to help people know the truth, in love, about what is happening out in the world, so that there will be more honesty in the world."

"My mission is to weep with those who weep, so that in my arms they may feel themselves in the arms of that Eternal Love which sent me and which created them."

"My mission is to create beautiful gardens, so that in the lilies of the field people may behold the Beauty of God and be reminded of the Beauty of Holiness."

Comment 6: Life As Long As Your Mission Requires

Knowing that you came to Earth for a reason, and knowing what that Mission is, throws an entirely different light upon your life from now on. You are, generally speaking, delivered from any further fear about how long you have to live. You may settle it in your heart that you are here until God chooses to think that you have accomplished your Mission, or until God has a greater Mission for you in another Realm. You need to be a good steward of what He has given you, while you are here; but you do not need to be an anxious steward or stewardess.

You need to attend to your health, *but you do not need to constantly worry about it.* You need to meditate on your death, *but you do not need to be constantly preoccupied with it.* To paraphrase the glorious words of G. K. Chesterton: **"We now have a strong desire for living combined with a strange carelessness about dying. We desire life like water and yet are ready to drink death like wine."** We know that we are here to do what we came to do, and we need not worry about anything else.

Final Comment: A Job-Hunt Done Well

If you approach your job-hunt as an opportunity to work on this issue as well as the issue of how you will keep body and soul together, then hopefully your job-hunt will end with your being able to say: "Life has deep meaning to me, now. I have discovered more than my ideal job; I have found my Mission, and the reason why I am here on Earth."

•

For Further Reading

The following resources are written primarily from a Christian orientation, but they should be suggestive and helpful for people of any faith, as you mentally translate these texts into your own thought-forms and the concepts of your own faith:

Mattson, Ralph, and Miller, Arthur, *Finding a Job You Can Love*. Thomas Nelson Publishers, Nelson Place at Elm Hill Pike, Nashville, TN 37214.

1982. The most useful, I think, of all the books in this section.

Stephan, Naomi, *Finding Your Life Mission.* Stephan/Moore Associates, 425 Marine St., Suite 2, Santa Monica, CA 90405. 1988.

Moran, Pamela J., *The Christian Job Hunter.* Servant Publications, 840 Airport Blvd., Box 8617, Ann Arbor, MI 48107. 1984.

Edwards, Lloyd, *Discerning Your Spiritual Gifts.* Cowley Publications, 980 Memorial Drive, Cambridge, MA 02138. 1988.

Moore, Christopher Chamberlin, *What I* Really *Want To Do . . . : How to Discover The Right Job.* CBP Press, Box 179, St. Louis, MO 63166. 1989.

Staub, Dick; Trautman, Jeff; and Cutshall, Mark, eds., *Intercristo's CAREER KIT: A Christian's Guide to Career Building.* Intercristo, 19303 Fremont Ave. N., Seattle, WA 98133. 1985. Booklets (6) and cassette tapes (3) enclosed in binder.

Wehrheim, Carol, and Cole-Turner, Ronald S., *Vocation and Calling. Introduction/Hearing God's Call/Sharing Gifts: An Intergenerational Study Guide.* United Church Press, 475 Riverside Dr., 10th fl, New York, NY 10115. 1985.

Rinker, Richard N., and Eisentrout, Virginia, *Called to Be Gifted and Giving: An Adult Resource for Vocation and Calling.* United Church Press, 475 Riverside Dr., 10th fl., New York, NY 10115. 1985.

See also the books listed in Appendix B, Section 4, on page 295.

Index

D

E

F

K

L

M

T

Y